CW01332595

PEARL HARBOR'S REVENGE

Also by Rod Macdonald
Dive Scapa Flow
Dive Scotland's Greatest Wrecks
Dive England's Greatest Wrecks
Great British Shipwrecks – A Personal Adventure
Force Z Shipwrecks of the South China Sea – HMS Prince of Wales *and HMS* Repulse
Dive Truk Lagoon – The Japanese WWII Pacific Shipwrecks
Dive Palau – The Shipwrecks
Shipwrecks of Truk Lagoon

The Diving Trilogy
Vol. I, *Into the Abyss – Diving to Adventure in the Liquid World*
Vol. II, *The Darkness Below*
Vol. III, *Deeper into the Darkness*

Military History
Task Force 58: The US Navy's Fast Carrier Strike Force that Won the War in the Pacific
HMS Hampshire 100 Survey Report 2016, with Ben Wade, Emily Turton, Paul Haynes, David Crofts and Professor Chris Rowland
HMS K-4 & K-17 Survey Report, 2023

PEARL HARBOR'S REVENGE

How the Devastated U.S. Battleships Returned to War

ROD MACDONALD

FRONTLINE BOOKS

PEARL HARBOR'S REVENGE

First published in Great Britain in 2023 by

Frontline Books
An imprint of
Pen & Sword Books Ltd
Yorkshire – Philadelphia

Copyright © Rod Macdonald, 2023

ISBN 978 1 39901 329 1

The right of Rod Macdonald to be identified as
Author of this work has been asserted by him in accordance
with the Copyright, Designs and Patents Act 1988.

A CIP catalogue record for this book is
available from the British Library

All rights reserved. No part of this book may be reproduced or
transmitted in any form or by any means, electronic or mechanical
including photocopying, recording or by any information storage and
retrieval system, without permission from the Publisher in writing.

Typeset in 10.5/13 pt Palatino
by SJmagic DESIGN SERVICES, India.

Printed and bound in the UK by CPI Group (UK) Ltd.

Pen & Sword Books Ltd incorporates the imprints of Pen & Sword
Archaeology, Atlas, Aviation, Battleground, Discovery, Family History,
History, Maritime, Military, Naval, Politics, Social History, Transport,
True Crime, Claymore Press, Frontline Books, Praetorian Press,
Seaforth Publishing and White Owl

For a complete list of Pen & Sword titles please contact

PEN & SWORD BOOKS LTD
47 Church Street, Barnsley, South Yorkshire, S70 2AS, England
E-mail: enquiries@pen-and-sword.co.uk
Website: www.pen-and-sword.co.uk

Or

PEN AND SWORD BOOKS
1950 Lawrence Rd, Havertown, PA 19083, USA
E-mail: Uspen-and-sword@casematepublishers.com
Website: www.penandswordbooks.com

Contents

Explanatory Notes xi
Introduction xiv

PART I: WAR IN THE PACIFIC

Chapter 1 *Kidō Butai* 3

Chapter 2 7 December 1941 – 'A Date which Will Live in Infamy' 13
      (I) 0749: The First-Wave Planes Attack   20
      (II) 0800–0815: Battleship Row, Pearl Harbor
           Naval Base   23
      (III) 0845: The Second-Wave Planes Attack   36
      (IV) 0930: The Second-Wave Attack Ends   39
      (V) Aftermath   46

Chapter 3 Salvage – Pearl Harbor 51

Chapter 4 The US Standard-Type Battleship 69
      (I) Deck Armour   73
      (II) Transverse Armour Bulkheads   75
      (III) Conning Tower   76
      (IV) Underwater Side-Protection System   76
      (V) Armament   77
          (A) Main Battery   77
             Gunnery 77
             (a) Rangefinding 78
                 (i) Finding the *True Range* 78
                 (ii) Finding the *Gun Range* 79
             (b) Local Control and Director Fire 79

			(c) Elevation Telegraph	81
			(d) Range Clock	81
			(e) Gunhouse	82
			(f) Barbette	83
			(g) Ammunition Hoists, Shell-Handling Flats and Powder-Handling Room	84
			(h) Shells, Propellant and Firing	84
			(a) Shells	84
			(b) Propellant	85
	(B)	Secondary Battery		85
		(a) 5in/51-cal.		86
		(b) 5in/38-cal.		86
	(C)	21in Beam Submerged Torpedo Tubes		86
	(D)	Keel		87
	(E)	Machinery		87
	(F)	Interwar Modernisation		88
	(G)	Speed		89

PART II: BATTLESHIP REVENGE

Chapter 5	USS *California* (BB-44)	95
	(a) Armament	97
	(b) Armour	98
	(c) Propulsion	99
	(d) Topsides	100
	Pearl Harbor, 7 December 1941	101
	Salvage	106
	Battleship Revenge	115
	Return to Service – 1944	115
	(I) The Mariana and Palau Islands Campaign	115
	Battle of Saipan, 15 June–9 July 1944	115
	Battle of Guam, 21 July–10 August 1944	121
	Battle of Tinian, 24 July–1 August 1944	122
	Espiritu Santo Naval Base – Dry Dock, 19 August–17 September 1944	124
	(II) The Philippines Campaign	124
	Battle of Leyte, 17 October– 26 December 1944	124

        The Battle of Leyte Gulf, 23–26 October 1944 134
        (a)   Initial Submarine Action in the Palawan
               Passage, 23 October 1944   136
        (b)   Battle of the Sibuyan Sea, 24 October 1944   138
        (c)   Battle of the Surigao Strait,
               24–25 October 1944   148
        (d)   Battle off Samar, 25 October 1944   154
        (e)   Battle off Cape Engaño, 25 October 1944   158
   (III) 1945 – The Philippines Campaign Continues   166
        The Invasion of Lingayen Gulf,
        3–13 January 1945   166
  (IV) Battle of Okinawa – Operation ICEBERG,
        1 April–22 June 1945   169
   (V) The Invasion of Japan – Operation DOWNFALL 170
  (VI) Occupation of Japan   172

Chapter 6   USS *Maryland* (BB-46)..174
                (a) Armament 177
                (b) Armour 178
                (c) Propulsion 178

                Pearl Harbor, 7 December 1941 180

                Battleship Revenge...182
                Battle of Midway, 4–7 June 1942 183
         (I) The Gilbert and Marshall Islands Campaign,
             November 1943–February 1944   185
             Battle of Tarawa – Operation GALVANIC,
             20–23 November 1943..187
             Battle of Kwajalein and Invasion of Majuro –
             Operation FLINTLOCK, 31 January–
             3 February 1944 192
       (II) The Mariana and Palau Islands Campaign –
             Operation FORAGER, June–November 1944   197
             Battle of Saipan, 15 June–9 July 1944...........................197
             Battle of Peleliu – Operation STALEMATE II,
             15 September–27 November 1944 200
     (III) The Philippines Campaign, 20 October 1944–
             15 August 1945   203
             Battle of Leyte, 17 October–26 December 1944 203
             Battle of the Surigao Strait, 25 October 1944 205

  (IV) 1945   208
   Battle of Okinawa – Operation ICEBERG,
   1 April–22 June 1945 208

Chapter 7   USS *Nevada* (BB-36)..212
  (a) Underwater Protection   216
  (b) Armament   216
  (c) Armour   218
  (d) Propulsion   218

  Modernisation, 1927–9   219

  Pearl Harbor, 7 December 1941   220
  Salvage   226

  Battleship Revenge   230
  Return to Service, 1943   230
   (I) The Aleutian Islands Campaign, 11–30 May 1943   230
   (II) Atlantic Convoy Duty, Mid-1943   230
   (III) Normandy Invasion, June 1944   231
   (IV) Battle of Iwo Jima, 19 February–26 March 1945   236
   (V) Battle of Okinawa – Operation ICEBERG,
    1 April 1945–22 June 1945   238
   (VI) Post-War   239

Chapter 8   USS *Pennsylvania* (BB-38).......................................242
  (a) Armament   244
  (b) Armour   246
  (c) Propulsion   248
  Service Modifications: 1929–31   248

  Pearl Harbor, 7 December 1941   249

  Battleship Revenge   252
   (I) The Aleutian Islands Campaign, 11–30 May 1943   252
   (II) The Gilbert and Marshall Islands Campaign   255
    Battle of Makin – Operation GALVANIC,
    20–24 November 1943 255
    Battle of Kwajalein – Operation FLINTLOCK,
    31 January–3 February 1944..256
    Battle of Eniwetok – Operation CATCHPOLE,
    17–23 February 1944..258
   (III) The Mariana and Palau Islands Campaign –
    Operation FORAGER   259

    Battle of Saipan, 15 June–9 July 1944 261
    Battle of Guam – Operation STEVEDORE,
    21 July–10 August 1944 261
    Battle of Peleliu – Operation STALEMATE II,
    15 September–27 November 1944 262
  (IV) The Philippines Campaign 263
    Battle of Leyte Gulf – Operation KING II,
    23–26 October 1944 263
    Battle of Surigao Strait, 25 October 1944 266
    The Invasion of Lingayen Gulf – Operation MIKE I,
    3–13 January 1945 267
  (V) Task Force 95 – the 2nd East China Sea
    Antishipping Sweep 268
  (VI) The 1946 Bikini Atoll Atomic Tests – Operation
    CROSSROADS 270

Chapter 9 USS *Tennessee* (BB-43) 271

  Pearl Harbor, 7 December 1941 273
  (a) Repair and Modernisation of AA Suite,
    29 December 1941–Late February 1942 276
  (b) Reconstruction and Modernisation,
    September 1942–7 May 1943 277

  Battleship Revenge 279
  (I) The Aleutian Islands Campaign,
    11 May–15 August 1943 279
  (II) The Gilbert and Marshall Islands Campaign 281
    Battle of Tarawa – Operation GALVANIC,
    20–23 November 1943 281
    Battle of Kwajalein – Operation FLINTLOCK,
    31 January–3 February 1944 282
    Battle of Eniwetok – Operation CATCHPOLE,
    17–23 February 1944 283
  (III) The New Guinea Campaign – Operation
    CARTWHEEL 284
    Emirau Island Landing, Bismarck
    Archipelago, 20 March 1944 284
  (IV) The Mariana and Palau Islands Campaign –
    Operation FORAGER 286
    Battle of Saipan, 15 June–9 July 1944 286
    Battle of Guam – Operation STEVEDORE,
    21 July–10 August 1944 288

	Battles of Peleliu and Angaur – Operation STALEMATE II, 17 September–22 October 1944......289	
(V)	The Philippines Campaign	290
	Battle of Leyte Gulf, 23–26 October 1944..................290	
	Battle of Surigao Strait, 25 October 1944..................291	
(VI)	Battle of Iwo Jima – Operation DETACHMENT, 19 February–26 March 1945	292
(VII)	Battle of Okinawa – Operation ICEBERG, 1 April–22 June 1945	294
(VIII)	Post-War	297

Chapter 10 USS *West Virginia* (BB-48) 298

Pearl Harbor, 7 December 1941 301
Salvage 304
Reconstruction and Modernisation,
September 1942–September 1944 308

Battleship Revenge..310
Return to Service – September 1944...................................310
   (I)   The Philippines Campaign   310
         Battle of Leyte Gulf, 23–26 October 1944..................310
         Battle of Surigao Strait, 25 October 1944..................311
         Post-Leyte Operations...312
         The Invasion of Lingayen Gulf 3–13 January 1945...314
   (II)   Battle of Iwo Jima – Operation DETACHMENT, 19 February–26 March 1945   316
   (III)   Battle of Okinawa – Operation ICEBERG, 1 April–22 June 1945   317
   (IV)   Occupation of Japan   319

Notes 321
Select Bibliography 327
Index 332

Explanatory Notes

All weights are given in long tons, where 1 long ton = 2,240 lb.

US Plane General Designations

B-17	US Army Air Force (USAAF) four-engine bomber, the Boeing Flying Fortress
B-24	USAAF four-engine bomber, Consolidated or Ford Liberator
B-25	USAAF two-engine bomber, the North American Mitchell
B-29	USAAF four-engine bomber, the Boeing Super-Fortress
F4U	Navy single-engine fighter, the Chance-Vought Corsair
F6F	Navy single-engine fighter, the Grumman Hellcat
PBY	Navy two-engine long-range maritime reconnaissance flying boat, the Consolidated Catalina
PB4Y	Navy-Marine four-engine bomber, the Consolidated or Ford Liberator
SBD	Navy single-engine Scout Bomber Douglas, the Douglas Dauntless
SB2C	Navy single-engine scout dive bomber, the Curtiss Helldiver
TBD	Navy single-engine torpedo bomber, the Douglas Devastator
TBF	Navy single-engine torpedo bomber, the Grumman Avenger
TBM	Navy single-engine torpedo bomber, the General Motors Avenger

Allied Reporting Code Names of Japanese Aircraft and Designations

BETTY	Mitsubishi G4M/G4M3 Navy Type 1 Attack Bomber
EMILY	Kawanishi H8K Navy Type 2 Flying Boat
JAKE	Aichi E13A Navy Type O Reconnaissance Seaplane

JILL	Nakajima B6N Navy Carrier Attack Bomber
JUDY	Yokosuka D4Y Navy Carrier Bomber Suisei
VAL	Aichi D3A Navy Type 99 Carrier Bomber
ZEKE	Mitsubishi A6M Navy Type O Carrier Fighter Reisen (Zero)

US Naval Squadron/Unit Designations

BatDiv	Battleship Division
CarDiv	Carrier Division
CruDiv	Cruiser Division
DesDiv	Destroyer Division
DesRon	Destroyer Squadron
ServRon	Service Squadron
TF	Task Force
TG	Task Group; a subunit of a Task Force

US Ship Type Designations and Acronyms List

AGC	Amphibious Command Ship
AK	Cargo Ship
AM	Minesweeper
AP	Transport
AO	Fuel Oil Tanker
BB	Battleship
CA	Heavy Cruiser
CL	Light Cruiser
CV	Aircraft Carrier
CVE	Aircraft Carrier Escort
CVL	Light Aircraft Carrier
DD	Destroyer
DUKW	Amphibious trucks ('Ducks')
LCT	Landing Craft, Tank
LCVP	Landing Craft, Vehicle, Personnel – the Higgins boat
LST	Landing Ship, Tank
LVT	Landing Vehicle, Tracked
SS	Submarine
TB	Torpedo Boat

Miscellaneous

AA	Anti-Aircraft
AP	Armour Piercing

EXPLANATORY NOTES

CAP	Combat Air Patrol
CIC	Combat Information Centre, the nerve centre of the ship where information from radars and sounding was plotted and sent to the bridge
CINC	Commander-in-Chief
CINCLANTFLT	Commander-in-Chief, US Atlantic Fleet
CINCPAC	Commander-in-Chief, Pacific Fleet
CINCPACFLT	Commander-in-Chief, US Pacific Fleet
CINCUS	Commander-in-Chief, US Fleet
CINPOA	Commander-in-Chief, Pacific Ocean Areas
COMINCH	Commander-in-Chief, United States Fleet
CNO	Chief of Naval Operations
DP	Dual Purpose
GP	General Purpose
IJA	Imperial Japanese Army
IJN	Imperial Japanese Navy
LCVP	Higgins boat
Nm	Nautical mile
RDF	Radio Direction Finder
SAP	Semi-Armour Piercing
TBS	High-frequency short-range radio used for tactical manoeuvring
UDT	Underwater Demolition Team

Introduction

Most people know that the Japanese surprise six-carrier air raid on Pearl Harbor on 7 December 1941 sunk or damaged the eight US Navy battleships present. Fewer perhaps know that by that time the battleships in the US Navy had morphed into two distinct classes. The eight battleships sunk or disabled at Pearl Harbor were older slower battleships built during or just after the First World War, which although modernised to varying extents, all had a standard top design speed of 21 knots. The newer classes of modern fast battleships that were beginning to be launched after a pause in US battleship construction of some twenty years could make 28 knots.

The eight Pearl Harbor casualties of 7 December 1941 were part of a series of twelve Standard-Type dreadnought-era battleships ordered between 1911 and 1916 – they were the nuclear weapons of the day when they were constructed.

The Washington Naval Treaty of 1922 subsequently limited the number and size of a nation's battleships – bringing battleship building to an abrupt halt. No more US battleships would then be built as the early decades of the twentieth century wore on. When the Japanese threat in the Pacific became increasingly apparent, a second phase of US battleship building began in 1937 with the laying down of the two North Carolina-class fast battleships, *North Carolina* (BB-55) and *Washington* (BB-56). At 728ft long, and 108ft in the beam, these modern battleships were significantly larger than the Standard-Type battleships, they carried nine powerful 16in main-battery guns in three three-gun turrets and could make 28 knots. Only they could accompany the modern 33-knot fast carriers, which were by now the main striking force of the US Navy.

The older Standard-Type battleships may have been slow, but their main and secondary battery guns were still powerful, devastating

INTRODUCTION

weapons when brought to bear. But hampered by the original design speed of 21 knots and unable to keep up with the modern fast battleships or fast carriers, the US battleships had effectively been split into two types, the old 21-knot battleships and the new 28-knot fast battleships. Whereas battleships were given the designation BB and a number, the Standard-Type battleships came to be collectively known in the navy as the old battleships and were referred to as OBBS.

Although the usefulness of the OBBS was at first questioned in the US Navy, after six of the eight OBBS sunk or damaged at Pearl were repaired and brought back to the war, they would go on to play a vital role in the Second World War, when their guns would carry out devastating pre-invasion bombardments of enemy targets ashore. Heavily armoured, they were ideal to provide inshore support for courageous Underwater Demolition Teams of swimmers, sent in in advance of amphibious assaults, to reconnoitre landing beaches, remove underwater obstructions and blast channels through reefs – often under direct enemy observation and fire. The approaches to the landing beaches also had to be swept clear of mines before the landings began – and the heavily armoured OBBS were again ideally suited to operate close in and protect the minesweepers.

Once amphibious troops had made their landings, the OBBS would provide close support ahead of advancing troops, breaking up enemy concentrations, destroying enemy gun emplacements and fortified positions as they moved from target to target and island to island.

When the Allied invasion of the Philippines began in late 1944, the OBBS were tasked to support the Allied landings at Leyte Gulf. The Japanese responded to the landings by sending four powerful naval forces to strike Allied forces ashore and afloat at Leyte Gulf. The OBBS formed line of battle and 'crossed the T' of a Japanese battleship force in the Battle of the Surigao Strait on 25 October 1944 – a battle now famous for being the last battleship versus battleship clash in history. One of the OBBS partially sunk at Pearl, USS *Nevada*, would be refloated and repaired – and would cross the Atlantic to bombard UTAH Beach ahead of the Normandy landings on D-Day, 6 June 1944.

By this time, near the end of the war as the Allies closed on Japan, the great armoured titans had moved from being the most important, or capital, ship in a navy to being bombardment ships and a floating AA platform, their battleship armour, originally designed to take hits from armour-piercing shells, being perfectly designed to protect Allied shipping against kamikaze attack.

But by the time the war ended however, the era of the battleship had passed.

PEARL HARBOR'S REVENGE

I seem to have spent a large portion of my life diving on battleship wrecks from both world wars, I suspect I have seen more battleships than most folk. At Scapa Flow in the Orkney Islands in northern Scotland I have explored the three German König-class dreadnought battleships scuttled in 1919, *König*, *Markgraf* and *Kronprinz Wilhelm* – and the British battleship HMS *Vanguard* destroyed in a cataclysmic magazine explosion in 1917. I have also been privileged to take part in an expedition to survey HMS *Royal Oak*, sunk in Scapa Flow in 1939, the first British battleship to be lost in the Second World War. Further afield, I have dived HMS *Audacious*, sunk by a mine off Northern Ireland in 1914 and the first British battleship to be sunk in the First World War. I have dived many times on the now illegally salved wreck of HMS *Prince of Wales*, sunk with the battlecruiser HMS *Repulse* by almost ninety Japanese aircraft some 200 miles north of Singapore in the South China Sea in December 1941, just days after the Pearl Harbor raid. The loss of the modern battleship *Prince of Wales* to air attack is seen as defining the end of the era of the battleship.

Even with that appreciation of battleships and their history, as the events of the Second World War now pass from living memory, it became clear to me that although much has been written about the Pearl Harbor raid itself, far less has been written about what the US battleships went on to do after the Day of Infamy. It is time that the full story of these amazing Standard-Type battleships is brought together and recorded – so here it is, my take on the Pearl Harbor raid and the the Second World War aftermath of the big guns of the old battleships.

Curiously, had it not been for the raid on Pearl Harbor, and Japan's brutal expansion across the Pacific, I likely would not be here today – and you would likely not be reading these words right now. For in 1941, my father was living with my grandmother and grandfather in Singapore. My dad was only 10 at the time – whilst my grandfather, a First World War Seaforth Highlander veteran, was now serving as a prison officer at Changi Gaol. After Japanese troops landed in northern Malaya and Thailand – the same day as the Pearl Harbor raid – the Japanese fought their way down the Malayan peninsula until they arrived off Singapore Island. Singapore would fall to the Japanese on 14 February 1942, and in the days before the Fall, European expats were rounded up in half-tracks and taken down to the docks where they boarded ships to be evacuated. My dad remembers boarding his ship, which had been bombed and damaged on the way into Singapore a few days earlier with Australian troops.

INTRODUCTION

Although my dad, with his brother and my grandmother, was getting out on one of the last ships out of Singapore before the Fall, my grandfather stayed behind as part of the civilian administration to help preserve order as the Japanese took over. That didn't work out very well, as he and thousands of other Europeans were quickly rounded up and force marched with Allied POWs to Changi Gaol where he was imprisoned for the duration. During his incarceration, being old-school British Army, he refused to bow to the Japanese troops and was beaten several times. He was finally released three-and-a-half years later in a terribly poor condition – after Japan surrendered. The Japanese had not allowed the Red Cross *Service de Prisonniers de Guerre* notification cards to be sent out during his incarceration and my family when they reached refuge in Scotland had no idea between 1942 and 1945 if he was alive or dead. As it was, he had been so poorly treated in internment that it took a full year for him to recuperate in hospital in Singapore before he was able to make the long sea passage back to Scotland.

My dad then grew up in Scotland, before going on to meet my mother at Aberdeen University. They subsequently married – and I was the eventual result. So, in a quirk of history, had Japan not invaded and seized Singapore, my 10-year-old dad would not have been evacuated to Scotland from Singapore – he would have grown up in Singapore and wouldn't have gone to Aberdeen University, and wouldn't have met my mother there – so I wouldn't exist, and you wouldn't be reading these words right now. It's funny how directly connected we all are to the deeds of the past.

Anyway, I digress – back to US battleships!

Fair winds and following seas
Rod Macdonald

Part I
War in the Pacific

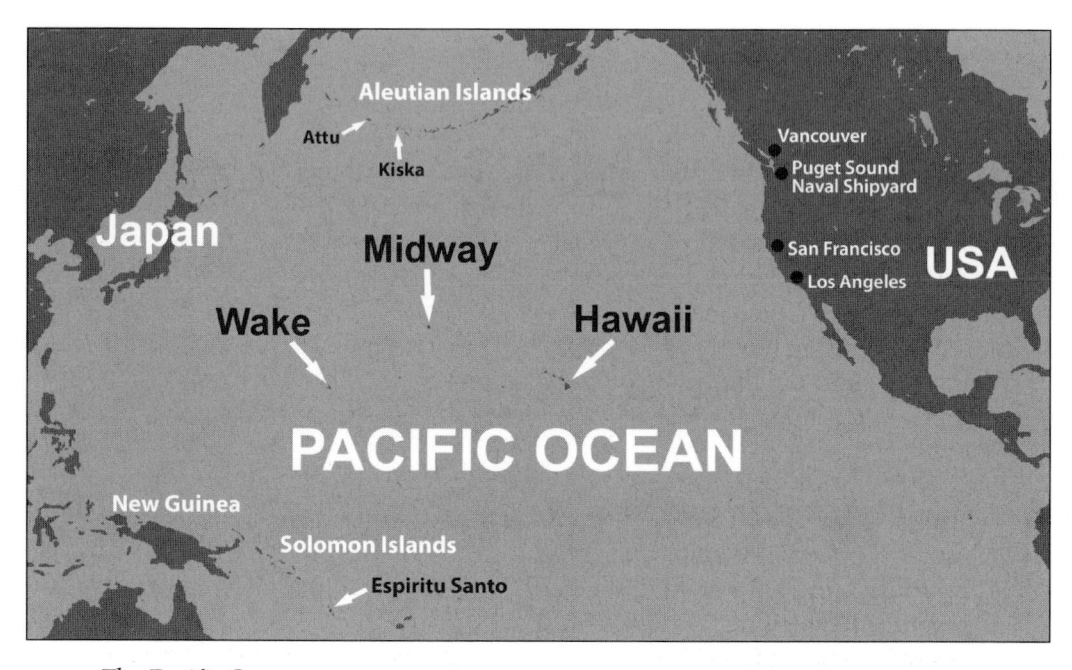

The Pacific Ocean.

Chapter 1

Kidō Butai

The Japanese 1st Air Fleet carrier battle group, known as the *Kidō Butai* (the Mobile Force), was formed on 10 April 1941 and comprised most of Japan's available aircraft carriers and carrier air groups. By the time the new aircraft carrier *Zuikaku* was commissioned on 25 September 1941, 1st Air Fleet included 6 fleet carriers, which along with light carriers could deploy 474 aircraft. The concentration of the six fleet carriers *Akagi*, *Kaga*, *Sōryū*, *Hiryū*, *Shōkaku* and *Zuikaku* into a single tactical formation was something that no Western power had yet done. This revolutionary move would lay the basis for the true carrier task force, a battle group that could range over vast distances and bring overwhelming air power to bear.

Faced with crippling oil and materials embargoes by the Allies, and intent on seizing the resource-rich territories of Southeast Asia, Japan had finalised plans for a knockout blow to their main potential opponent, the US Pacific Fleet in their forward base at Pearl Harbor, Hawaii. By striking powerfully and destroying the battleships and aircraft carriers of the US Pacific Fleet, combined with a rapid expansion and seizure of other Pacific territories, Japan's war planners aimed to quickly build an empire so large that the Western powers would not be able to countenance the cost of retaking it. Japan hoped that in Europe, her Axis partners Germany and Italy would prevail over the Soviets and Britain – and that thereafter Japan might negotiate peace with an isolated USA. Admiral Isoroku Yamamoto, Commander-in-Chief of the Imperial Japanese Navy (IJN) Combined Fleet, however was under no illusions as to the final outcome. He wrote to Prime Minister Konoye – before the raid was finally authorised: 'In the first six to twelve months of a war with the United States and Great Britain, I will run wild and win victory upon victory. But then, if the war continues after that, I have no expectation of success.'

A Japanese model of Pearl Harbor, showing ships located as they were during the 7 December 1941 attack. This model was constructed after the attack for use in a motion picture. The original photo was brought back to the US from Japan at the end of the Second World War by Rear Admiral John Shafroth, USN. Collection of Fleet Admiral Chester W. Nimitz. (*NH 62534 courtesy of the US Naval History & Heritage Command*)

Yamamoto knew Japan only had a limited chance of winning a prolonged war with the USA, but with the forward deployment of the US Fleet to Hawaii the year before, Japan had been offered the opportunity to destroy the main US offensive weapon, its Pacific Fleet, in one blow. *Kidō Butai* was therefore specifically created for a pre-emptive strike on the US Pacific Fleet warships – and was commanded by Vice Admiral Chūichi Nagumo. If an attack on Pearl Harbor could successfully knock out the battleships and aircraft carriers of the US fleet, the eleven IJN battleships, along with the many IJN carriers, cruisers, destroyers and submarines, should be more than a match for any remaining Allied naval forces in the Pacific. The Japanese battleships and aircraft carriers could then be relied upon to shield the army's invasion convoys as they sailed for Southeast Asia. Destroying the US fleet at Pearl Harbor might buy enough time for Japan to forge a viable Pacific Empire.

The standard Japanese aerial torpedo was the Type 91, which could be released by an aircraft at a cruising speed of 180 knots, and also in a power-glide torpedo bombing run at the maximum speed of the Nakajima B5N torpedo bomber of 204 knots. The Nakajima B5N torpedo bomber had been assigned the Allied reporting codename KATE – and the version of the Type 91 torpedo at this time carried a 452lb warhead. The Type 91 Modification 2 carried to Pearl Harbor was developed due to the shallow 45ft depth of the water, which was at first a problem for the Type 91, which went down about 150ft when it entered the water. It took until November 1941 before the torpedo problem was finally solved by the use of a softwood breakaway nose cone and wooden aerodynamic stabilisers attached to the tail fins, that made sure the torpedo was in the correct attitude before entry into the water – when they were shed. A clever advanced angular acceleration control system controlled rolling movements.[1] Later versions carried more powerful warheads.

On 22 November 1941, Vice Admiral Nagumo's naval force for Operation Z, the Hawaiian operation, gathered at Hitokappu Bay on Etorofu Island, in the southern part of the Kuril Arch of fifty-six islands that stretch northeast from Hokkaido in Japan to the Kamchatka peninsula in Russia. At this time (still two weeks until the proposed date for the strike at Pearl Harbor) no definite date for the assault had yet been set – and no one knew if Japan was actually going to go to war with the USA – and whether the strike was indeed on.[2] But the raid had been meticulously planned – the *Kidō Butai* carrier striking force was ready.

The 4,000 nautical miles insertion route from the Kuril Islands of Japan to Hawaii had been specifically chosen to cross a wild area of the North Pacific that was navigated by very few vessels – and had earned the US nickname of the 'Vacant Sea'.[3] The route had been reconnoitred by IJN officers posing as crew aboard the ocean-going liner *Taiyo Maru*, which had sailed from Japan to Honolulu in Hawaii earlier that month. No other ships had been encountered and the liner had not been spotted by US aircraft near Hawaii. One of IJN officers was a midget submarine pilot tasked to scout the entrance to the Pearl Harbor Naval Base.

In support of the operation, on 11 November 1941, six large Kaidai Type 6A 1st-class submarines had departed Saeki (beside Hiroshima towards the south of the Japanese home islands) – initially bound for the advance Japanese base at Kwajalein in the Marshall Islands, some 2,500 miles distant from Hawaii. The six submarines arrived at Kwajalein on 20 November 1941, where they were refuelled and reprovisioned before departing for Hawaii on 23 November 1941, the day after Nagumo's naval force began to gather in the Kuriles. The submarines were tasked to reconnoitre the Lahaina Roads anchorage before taking station off the Hawaiian Islands in advance of the carrier strike taking place. The Lahaina Roads is a sheltered channel and anchorage encompassed by the Hawaiian Islands of Maui, Lanai and smaller islands, and was used by the US Pacific Fleet as an alternative anchorage to Pearl Harbor.

The three Japanese submarines *I-68*, *I-69* and *I-70* were assigned to patrol between 25 and 50 miles south of Oahu. *I-71* would reconnoitre the Alalakeiki Channel between Maui and Kahoolawe whilst *I-72* was to reconnoitre the Kalohi Channel between Molokai and Lanai and then head to the Lahaina Roads on about 5 December. *I-73* would reconnoitre the Kealaikahiki Channel between Maui, Kahoolawe and Lanai before moving on to the Lahaina Anchorage after sundown on 6 December.

The six Kaidai-Type 6A submarines were big: 336ft 7in long at the waterline, they displaced 1,400 tons (S) surfaced and 2,440 tons

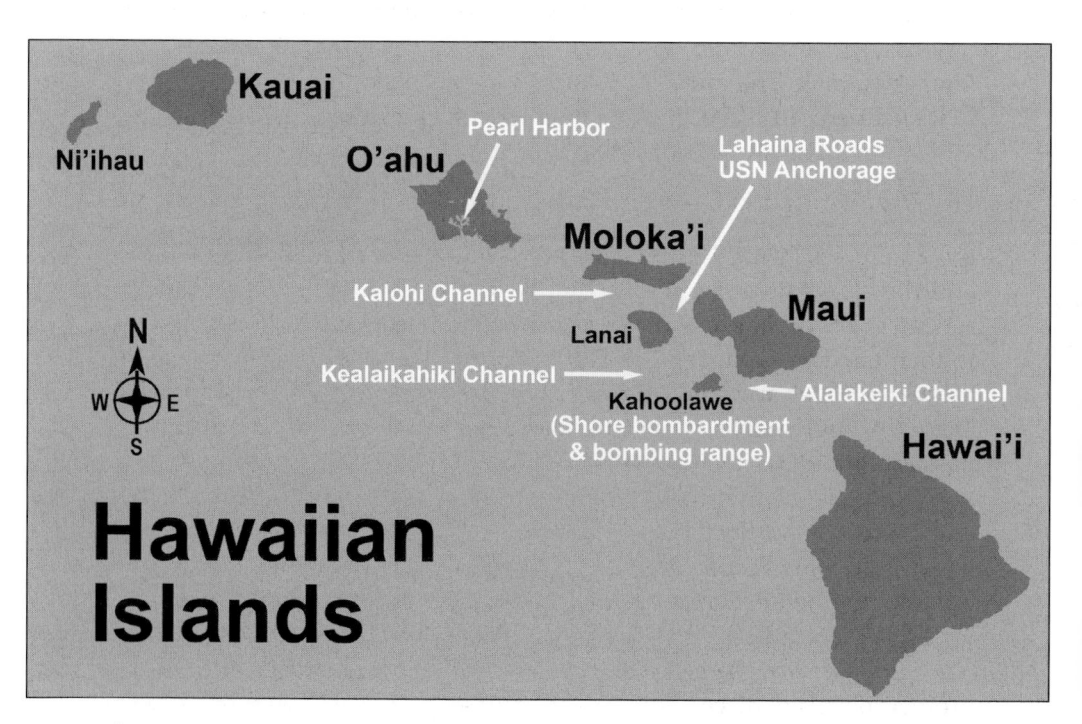

The Hawaiian Islands, showing Pearl Harbor and the Lahaina Roads anchorage used by the US Navy.

submerged. They carried a 10cm (3.9in) high-angle (HA) deck gun mounted in front of the conning tower – the class name *Kaidai* translates as *Kai* meaning 'gun' and *Dai* meaning 'large'.

Five Special Attack Unit Type C-1 mother submarines had been converted the month before in October 1941, to carry a two-man, 46-ton Type A midget submarine aft on deck. On 18 November 1941, each of the five Special Attack Unit Type C-1 submarines embarked a single Type A midget submarine in the Hiroshima Prefecture. The next day, 19 November 1941, all five Special Attack Unit submarines departed for the Hawaiian Islands, using a direct route that passed south of Midway. During the night before the attack, the Type C-1 mother submarines would surface a few miles off Hawaii and launch their Type A midget submarines, which would then attempt to penetrate the Pearl Harbor defences and sink US warships. The Type A midget submarine was 78.5ft long with a height of only 3m and could dive to 30m. It carried two 450mm (17.7in) torpedoes and one 300lb scuttling charge and could make 23 knots surfaced and 19 knots submerged with a range of about 100nm at 3 knots and 80nm at 6 knots. The Type C-1 mother submarines would remain off Hawaii to rescue any downed carrier air crews and any midget submarine crews who might escape from the Naval Base after the attack. The mother submarines would also attack any US ships that steamed out of Pearl Harbor as the attack began.

26 November 1941 – The *Kidō Butai* Sorties

By 26 November 1941, negotiations in Washington between Japan and the USA faltered when the US response to Japan's latest proposal repeated US demands for Japan to withdraw from China and French Indochina. The Japanese Prime Minister General Tōjō Hideki viewed this proposal as an ultimatum and an insult. Meanwhile, the six Kaidai-Type 6A submarines were already three days into their clandestine passage from Kwajalein to Hawaii.

In advance of the final decision being made to strike Pearl Harbor and go to war, at 0600 on 26 November 1941, the 6 *Kidō Butai* carriers began to depart Hitokappu Bay in the Kuril Islands with their escorts. For the planned 2 waves of the attack, the 6 carriers carried a total of 360 strike aircraft of 3 types: fighters, level/torpedo bombers and dive bombers. A further 48 aircraft would provide combat air patrol (CAP) to protect the strike force itself. The 2 battleships *Hiei* and *Kirishima* sailed with the carriers – along with the 2 heavy cruisers *Chikuma* and *Tone*, the light cruiser *Abukuma*, 9 destroyers and ancillary craft. In all there

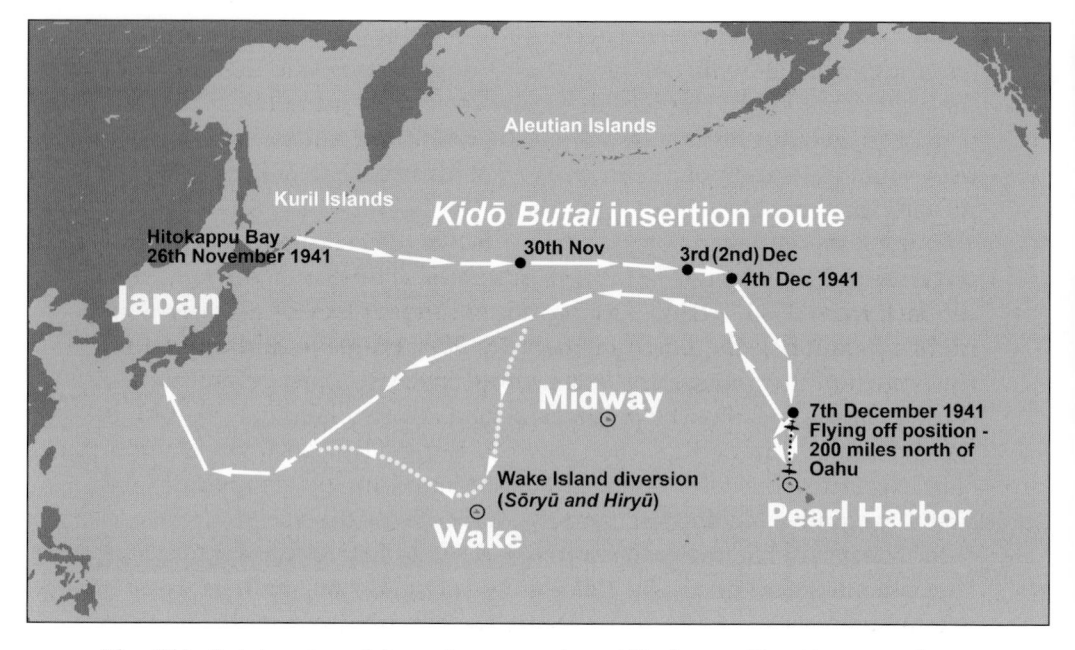

Map: Kidō Butai insertion route — showing Hitokappu Bay (26th November 1941), Kuril Islands, Aleutian Islands, 30th Nov, 3rd (2nd) Dec, 4th Dec 1941, 7th December 1941 Flying off position - 200 miles north of Oahu, Pearl Harbor, Midway, Wake Island diversion (Sōryū and Hiryū), Wake, Japan.

The *Kidō Butai* eastward insertion route from Hitokappu Bay, Japan to flying off position 200nm north of Hawaii for the Pearl Harbor strike. The more southerly western extraction route after the attack is shown – with the dotted line highlighting the detachment of two carriers to assist in the invasion of Wake Atoll.

were 23 warships – and the operation would be supported by 7 oilers, 30 submarines and 5 midget submarines – a total of some 57 vessels.[4]

The 6 carriers sailed in 2 parallel columns of 3 flattops, followed by the oilers. On the outside, the 2 battleships and 2 heavy cruisers took position whilst the whole group was encircled by a screen of the light cruiser and destroyers. The carriers and warships of the *Kidō Butai* refuelled en route from the 7 oilers – and would rendezvous with the oilers to refuel again after the raid had taken place, for the return passage to Japan.

Three submarines were assigned to patrol ahead of Nagumo's *Kidō Butai* – but they remained in close proximity as a result of communication difficulties.

The Japanese attack would be carried out on a Sunday, the day when the US ships would be at their least degree of readiness. The North Pacific in January and February is beset by storms that would make any approach to the Hawaiian Islands impractical during the winter months. With the need for a full moon for navigational purposes, this all pointed to the attack going ahead on Sunday, 7 December 1941 – and this date had been provisionally selected as far back as the first week of October.

The *Kidō Butai* had been allocated thirteen days to make the passage from Japan to Hawaii and reach its flying off position 200 miles to the north of Oahu. The lengthy two-week long advance to Hawaii was required due to the frequency of refuelling and a low average fleet cruising speed of 14 knots, which dropped to 9 knots during refuelling.

During the advance across the North Pacific, a number of changes were made to the original plan of attack. The time of the attack was set back from 0630 to 0800 – as a result of aircrew lack of experience in night operations. The postponement by 90 minutes would mean that the launch of the first strike planes would take place just before sunrise during the half-light of the period known as nautical dawn – and not in darkness. The planned gap between the first and second waves of the strike was closed – to deny the US defenders time to regroup after the first wave and ready themselves for a second wave.

Japanese intelligence had assessed that some 550 US aircraft and seaplanes were stationed on Oahu and that US air reconnaissance was adequate to the west and better to the south – but poor to the north of the Hawaiian Islands. This assessment would prove to be correct – the *Kidō Butai* would not be detected as it approached from the north.

The voyage across the North Pacific proved to be a difficult passage as the *Kidō Butai* encountered snowstorms off the Kuriles – and subsequent frequent storms, calms and fog – before it finally reached the sub-tropical waters north of the Hawaiian archipelago.

1 December 1941

The belligerent Army Minster General Tōjō Hideki had been appointed Prime Minster on 18 October 1941. The army had become dictator to Japan – and Tōjō, the army representative, was now Prime Minister. With the *Kidō Butai* en route crossing the vast expanse of the empty North Pacific, at a Japanese Imperial Conference on 1 December 1941, with no end to the embargos agreed, Tōjō advised that war was necessary to preserve the Japanese Empire – and war was finally sanctioned against the 'United States, England and Holland'.[5]

In the North Pacific, the famous Wabun Code signal '*Niitakayama nobore* (Climb Mount Niitaka) *1208*' was received on 2 December 1941 aboard Nagumo's flagship, the carrier *Akagi*, from Admiral Isoroku Yamamoto, Commander-in-Chief of the IJN Combined Fleet. (Mount Niitaka, located in modern-day Taiwan, was then the highest peak in the Japanese empire.)

On receiving the coded signal, at a position more than 900 nautical miles (nm) to the north of Midway, Vice Admiral Nagumo opened a set of top-secret documents given to him before the *Kidō Butai* sortied from Japan. These confirmed that Japan would be going to war with the USA, Britain and Holland – and gave the date for the opening of hostilities as 8 December 1941, Japan time (7 December 1941 in the USA). The order was duly transmitted to the other vessels in the *Kidō Butai* and Nagumo ordered the carrier task force to increase speed and prepare for battle.

Japan planned to open the war on 7 December 1941 (east of the International Date Line) with five separate simultaneous operations against key strategic targets vital to the Japanese campaign:

1. The six fast carriers of the *Kidō Butai*, after crossing almost 4,000nm of the North Pacific, would strike Pearl Harbor and Hawaiian airfields.
2. Strikes would launch against the American Clark and Iba airfields in the Philippines, a precursor to a full invasion of the Philippines.
3. The strategically important islands of Guam (at the south of the Marianas chain of islands) and Wake, 1,501 miles east of Guam in Micronesia, would be seized along with Tarawa and Makin in the Gilbert Islands. The US airbase at Midway Atoll, between Hawaii and Japan, would be attacked. These operations would allow the establishment of airfields and a defensive perimeter through the Marshalls and Gilberts to New Guinea and the Solomons.
4. Hong Kong would be assaulted – along with attacks on British and US warships at Shanghai. Operations against British positions in Burma and Borneo would soon begin.
5. Landings in Siam (modern-day Thailand) and Malaya would be followed by a thrust south toward the great British naval base of Singapore. From Singapore, the IJN Combined Fleet could operate to meet any threat to the perimeter – allied to the Japanese bases already established at their island bases mandated to them after the First World War, such as Palau, Truk, Kwajalein and the major base of Rabaul in the Bismarck archipelago.

In advance of the deadline for Japanese military operations to commence, as the *Kidō Butai* closed on Hawaii, Japanese forces moved out in total secrecy towards their assigned targets. Japanese troop transports left ports in modern-day Vietnam bound for selected Thai and northern Malayan invasion beaches. There were 26,640 soldiers crammed into

19 troop transports of the first wave of ships deployed from Hainan Island, off China for the invasion of Malaya. These troop transports would sail south close to the coast of Indochina to avoid detection on their four-day journey south towards Singora – relying on the bad weather of the breaking monsoon to shield the convoys from British reconnaissance aircraft.

5 December 1941

The *Kidō Butai* refuelled from the three 2nd Supply Group oilers *Toho Maru*, *Toei Maru* and *Nippon Maru*. Once refuelling was completed the three oilers and a destroyer escort moved off to take station at the designated rendezvous point to meet the *Kidō Butai* carrier group on its return from the Hawaii strike.

6 December 1941

The four oilers of the 1st Supply Group refuelled all remaining units of the *Kidō Butai* before departing with their escorts for the rendezvous point for the return of the *Kidō Butai*.

Once the oilers and escorts had detached, the fast carriers increased speed to 24 knots for the final approach to the flying off position, 200nm north of Oahu. The flag signal, which the Commander-in-Chief of the IJN Combined Fleet Admiral Tōgō Heihachirō had hoisted prior to the Battle of Tsushima in 1905, was raised on *Akagi*: 'The Empire's fate depends upon the result of this battle. Let every man do his utmost duty'.[6]

At 24 knots, the *Kidō Butai* continued its clandestine advance across the North Pacific towards Pearl Harbor – still completely undetected – and as the darkness of the night of 6 December 1941 descended, the carrier force was approaching its flying off position, north of Oahu. It was clear to everyone afloat on the *Kidō Butai* that surprise had been achieved. No other vessels had been seen, no aircraft had spotted the task force and the local Hawaii radio station stayed on air.

The six Kaidai-Type 6A reconnaissance submarines meanwhile reported that no aircraft carriers were present in Pearl Harbor – and that no naval vessels were present in the Lahaina Roads anchorage, or off Niihau.

Early on the morning of 7 December, the *Kidō Butai* reached its flying off position, approximately 200nm north of Oahu.

The scene was set for one of the most famous raids in all of history.

Ford Island, Honolulu, June 1941. Three battleships and an oiler are moored to the interrupted quays of Battleship Row in the middle of the image. (*NH 117884 courtesy of the US Naval History & Heritage Command*)

Chapter 2

7 December 1941 – 'A Date which Will Live in Infamy'

Pearl Harbor is a natural lagoon harbour on the south side of the island of Oahu, west of Honolulu. The shallow harbour is entered through a narrow entrance and accommodated the largest US ships with extensive shore facilities and dry docks.

In June 1940, on President Franklin D. Roosevelt's direction, the US Pacific Fleet had moved its main base from the West Coast in California to Pearl Harbor as a demonstration of US naval power in the Pacific – and as a deterrent to Japanese aggression against US, British and Dutch colonial possessions in East Asia.

Some 18 months later, by 7 December 1941, the great natural harbour was home to 82 warships of all kinds and 16 auxiliaries. The 8 battleships *Arizona*, *California*, *Maryland*, *Nevada*, *Oklahoma*, *Pennsylvania* (in dry dock), *Tennessee* and *West Virginia* were all present – along with 2 heavy cruisers, 6 light cruisers, 30 destroyers, a gunboat, 5 submarines, 5 minelayers, 13 minesweepers, 12 HQ ships and tenders.

However, as the *Kidō Butai* completed its undetected approach across the North Pacific, about one-third of the fighting naval units of the US Pacific Fleet were absent from Pearl Harbor. The heavy cruisers *Indianapolis*, *Minneapolis*, *Pensacola* and *Louisville* were all at sea whilst the battleship *Colorado*, 2 light cruisers, 9 destroyers and 15 submarines were far to the east on the West Coast of the USA. Of the remaining US submarines, 2 were stationed off Wake whilst 2 more were stationed off Midway on picket duty and another was stationed south of Oahu. As a result, a total of 44 of the 82 US Pacific Fleet units were absent from Pearl.

Perhaps most importantly however, all the US Pacific Fleet carriers were also absent. For as tensions had heightened between Japan and the

USA, uppermost in US commanders' minds was reinforcement of the two important forward airbases at Midway Atoll and Wake Atoll – and the protection of US aircraft stationed on Hawaii against sabotage.

The US Navy had a total of six heavy carriers at this time with *Lexington* (CV-2), *Saratoga* (CV-3) and *Enterprise* (CV-6) deployed in the Pacific along with the USA's first carrier, the old, slow and small *Langley* (CV-1), a converted ex-collier. The other three heavy carriers, *Yorktown* (CV-5), *Wasp* (CV-7) and the newly commissioned *Hornet* (CV-8), were deployed in the Atlantic. The smaller *Ranger* (CV-4) was returning to Norfolk, Virginia on the east coast from an ocean patrol to Trinidad and Tobago.

Of the three fleet carriers deployed to the Pacific, eleven months earlier on 6 January 1941, *Saratoga* had entered the Bremerton Navy Yard on the West Coast of the USA to begin a long-deferred modernisation and refit. The refit would be completed late in November 1941 – but she would not be at Pearl Harbor by 7 December.

Enterprise had departed Pearl Harbor on 28 November 1941, with an escort of three heavy cruisers and nine destroyers, to deliver Marine Fighter Squadron 211 planes to Wake Island, nearly 2,500nm due west. On 4 December, once she was within ferry range of Wake, those planes launched from her deck and flew into Wake – allowing *Enterprise* to come about and head back towards Pearl Harbor. She was however still at sea, some 215nm southwest of Oahu, at dawn on 7 December when the *Kidō Butai* began launching their strike planes 200nm north of Oahu. *Enterprise* would enter Pearl Harbor the following evening on 8 December 1941 – to a scene of devastation.

On 5 December 1941, just two days before the raid, *Lexington* had been despatched from Pearl Harbor with an escort of three heavy cruisers and five destroyers, carrying Marine Corps dive bombers destined to reinforce the Midway Atoll airbase. Meanwhile, the elderly *Langley* was off Cavite in the Philippines.

Land-based air defence of Hawaii was provided from a number of airfields spread across Hawaii. Some 223 United States Army Air Corps planes were distributed around the Hickam Airbase, the Wheeler Army Airfield, Bellows Field and Haleiwa Fighter Strip all on Oahu. The US Marine Corp had 74 planes spread around its Marine Corp Air Station Ewa on Oahu - and the Naval Air Stations (NAS) on Midway Island and on Wake Island. The US Naval Base Defence Air Force also had planes spread around the Naval Station Pearl Harbor at Ford Island NAS, the Puunene (Lahaina Roads) NAS and the Kaneohe NAS. The planes were a mixture of fighters such as the Brewster F2A-3 Buffalo and Grumman

7 DECEMBER 1941 – 'A DATE WHICH WILL LIVE IN INFAMY'

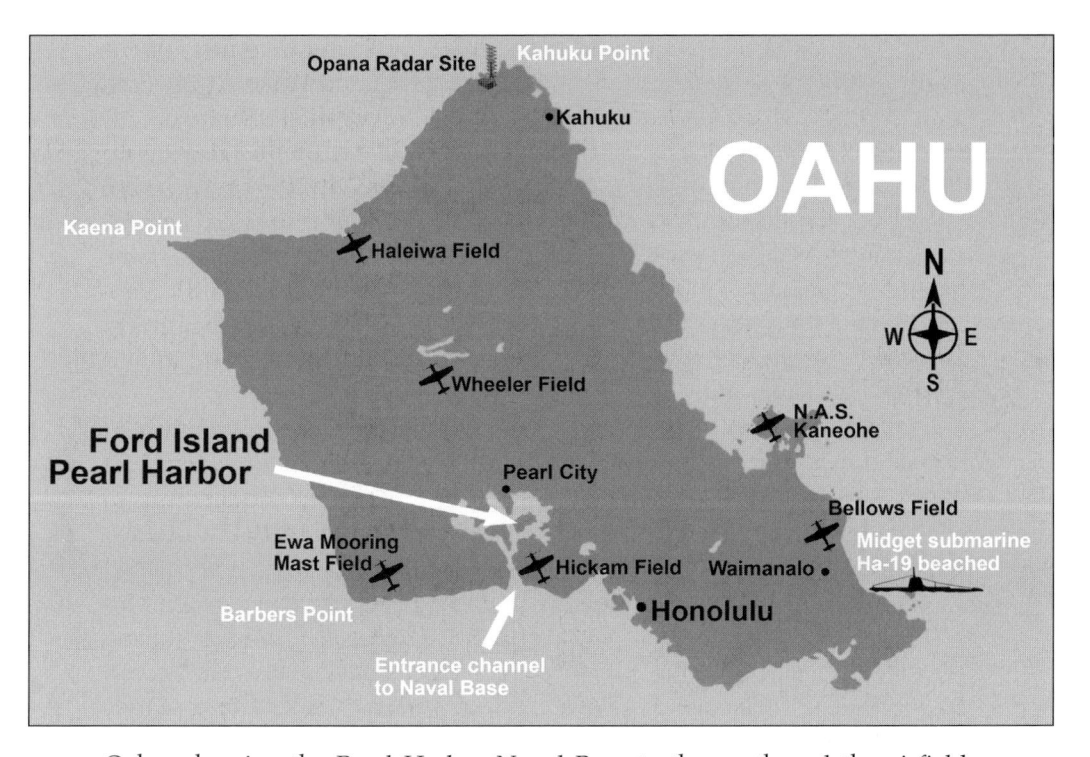

Oahu, showing the Pearl Harbor Naval Base to the south and the airfields attacked by the Japanese during the raid on 7 December 1941. Also shown to the north is the Opana Radar Site, which detected the inbound strike planes – and the location to the southeast where the midget submarine *Ha-19* washed ashore the day after the attack.

F4F-3 Wildcat together with scout/dive bombers such as the Douglas SBD-2 Dauntless and Vought SB2U-3 Vindicator. There were many Consolidated PBY-3 and PBY-5 Catalina scout bomber flying boats and amphibian floatplanes such as the Vought OS2U Kingfisher and Grumman floatplanes.

7 December 1941 – Off Pearl Harbor

Just after midnight, the first midget submarine *Ha-16* launched in pitch darkness at 0042 from the deck of the mother submarine *I-16*, roughly 7nm SSW from the entrance to Pearl Harbor Naval Base. Shortly afterwards at 0116, *I-22* launched *Ha-15* about 9nm from the harbour entrance. At 0215, *I-18* launched *Ha-17* about 13nm off the harbour entrance. At 0257, *I-20* launched *Ha-18*, 5.3nm off the harbour entrance. At 0333, *I-24* launched *Ha-19*, 10.5nm WSW of the harbour entrance.

Once deployed to the water, the midget submarines made their way towards the boom gate and submerged steel nets at the entrance to Pearl Harbor – with instructions to enter the base and attack in the lull between the two waves of air strikes. They would then withdraw and rendezvous 7nm ESE of Lanai Island on 8 December. The submarines *I-68* and *I-69* were ordered to lay off the entrance to Pearl Harbor and rescue any midget submarine crews who exited from Pearl Harbor after the attack.

That night, the wooden hulled ex-trawler minesweeper USS *Condor* (AMc-14) and the YMS-1-class minesweeper USS *Crosshill* (AMS-45) were on patrol south of the gate in the Pearl Harbor entrance channel. At 0342, crew on watch aboard *Condor* spotted a periscope.

The sighting was reported at 0357 to the duty destroyer *Ward* (DD-139), which closed the reported sighting area but was unable to make contact with any submarine herself. *Ward* was stood down at 0435 – and at 0458, *Condor* and *Crosshill* were admitted to the Pearl Harbor Naval Base after the gate was opened. The gate appears not to have been closed after they passed – and was open until 0840. Neither *Ward*, nor the local radio station at Bishop's Point, which had monitored the radio traffic between *Condor* and *Ward* reported the incident up the chain of command. This was possibly a consequence of the many false alarms of recent months – and the fact that *Ward* had not been able to confirm *Condor*'s sighting.

0550 – 200nm North of Oahu
The six *Kidō Butai* carriers and their escorts turned into the easterly 30-knot wind and spent 15 minutes increasing speed to 24 knots to give sufficient wind speed over the flight decks to let the heavily laden Nakajima B5N Kate torpedo bombers take off. The Kates were the standard carrier-based IJN torpedo bomber, with a crew of three. Each Kate could carry a single Type 91 Mod 2 aerial torpedo or a single 1,760lb bomb – or two 550lb bombs or six 132lb bombs. They had a maximum speed of 235mph and a range of about 600nm.

The launching of the Kates was precarious – as the flight decks of the carriers were rising and falling about 40ft in poor sea conditions, with waves breaking over the flight deck as the bows dipped. If this was an exercise, and not a combat strike, the launch would have been aborted.

The first wave of the strike comprised a planned 185 planes – with these planes carrying most of the weapons designed to attack capital ships. Many of the Kates carried specially adapted Type 91 aerial torpedoes whilst others carried Type 99 #80 Mk 5 1,760lb armour-piercing (AP)

7 DECEMBER 1941 – 'A DATE WHICH WILL LIVE IN INFAMY'

bombs (which were essentially large naval shells in an aerodynamic casing), whilst others carried more rudimentary 15in shells to which stabilising fins had been welded to give the characteristics of a spiralling bomb.*

The first wave also included Aichi D3A dive bombers – Allied reporting name VAL – tasked to attack ground targets. This two-crew plane had a top speed of about 270mph and could carry one 550lb bomb under the fuselage and two 130lb bombs under the wings.

Mitsubishi A6M Zero fighters – Allied reporting name ZEKE – would provide fighter escort and establish local air superiority. The Zekes would strafe and destroy as many parked US aircraft as possible to ensure they could not get airborne and attack the slower bombers.

0610

The first wave planes began to roar off the carrier flight decks into the wind. A6M Zero fighters were first off – followed by the B5N Kate torpedo bombers and then the D3A Val dive bombers. In 15 minutes, a total of 183 planes had been launched – there had been 2 operational losses, with 1 A6M Zero fighter crashing and another developing engine trouble.

As they took off, the planes of the port column of Japanese warships, which included the carriers *Sōryū*, *Hiryū* and *Shōkaku*, circled counter clockwise, whilst the planes from the starboard column, which included *Akagi*, *Kaga* and *Zuikaku*, circled clockwise.

The planes from the lead carriers of the two columns, *Akagi* and *Sōryū*, climbed and began to circle at the highest altitude of 1,100ft whilst the planes from the two carriers at the end of the two columns, *Zuikaku* and *Shōkaku*, circled at 550ft. As planes launched, they climbed to their designated altitude and manoeuvred into formation.

0620

With all 183 planes of the first wave now aloft and in formation, Commander Mitsuo Fuchida of the *Akagi*, supreme air commander of the Pearl Harbor Attack Air Groups and flying in one of the Kates, gave the signal for the formation to set course for Pearl.

As they turned to head for Pearl Harbor, the strike aircraft began to climb to their cruising altitudes. Those Kates armed with heavy

---

* Unexploded bombs discovered in the wreck of the *Arizona* after the attack by divers were found to bear the US imprint stamped on the base of the shell and were old US coastal gun shells, long obsolete, that had been sold to Japan as scrap iron years before and repurposed. Commander E.C. Raymer, *Descent into Darkness*, p. 76.

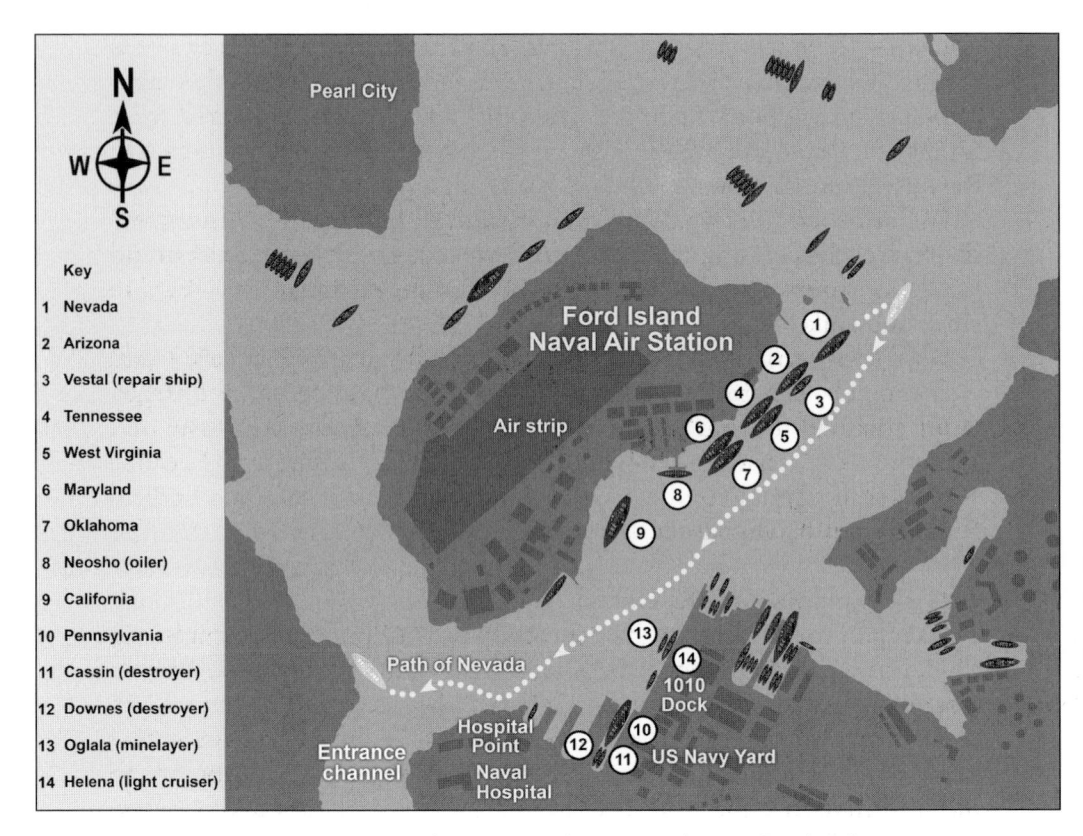

Pearl Harbor Naval Base, with entrance channel to the south. The ships present on Battleship Row on 7 December 1941 are shown. USS *Pennsylvania* is in drydock with the two destroyers *Cassin* and *Downes* in the same dock ahead of her. The light cruiser *Helena* is shown in *Pennsylvania*'s normal 1010 berth with the minelayer *Oglala* moored outboard.

Type 91 torpedoes were allocated an altitude of 9,200ft, whilst those Kates tasked to operate as level bombers were allocated a slightly higher altitude of 9,800ft. The Val dive bombers were allocated a higher altitude of 11,100ft whilst the nimble A6M Zero fighters were deployed above the formation at an altitude of 14,100ft, well above the bombers – from where they could swoop down from height if the lower planes were attacked.

0630 – Off the Entrance to Pearl Harbor

The inbound US stores ship *Antares* (AG-10) was lingering 3–4 miles offshore Oahu, awaiting the arrival of a pilot to guide her into the entrance to Pearl Harbor. Vigilant lookouts aboard *Antares* sighted what

7 DECEMBER 1941 – 'A DATE WHICH WILL LIVE IN INFAMY'

appeared to be the conning tower of a submarine at a range of about 1 mile. The destroyer *Ward* (DD-139) was alerted – and at 0637, her crew also spotted the periscope of an enemy submarine that appeared to be tailing the *Antares* in an effort to enter the harbour through the gate in the anti-submarine nets.

Ward opened fire with her 4in main battery, hitting the submarine at the base of the conning tower near the waterline with the second round from No. 3 gun. The submarine appeared to those aboard the *Ward* to slow, and sink.

Ward then carried out a full pattern depth-charge attack at 0653 – and was joined by a patrolling Catalina flying boat that bombed the target. *Ward* obtained a sonar contact at 0703 with a submerged vessel and dropped a pattern of depth charges. Some 3 minutes later an oil bubble was sighted about 300yd astern. A Contact Report was made back to Pearl Harbor Naval Base at about 0720.*

0645 – Opana Radar Site, Oahu
The Opana Radar Site, at the top of Opana Hill at the northmost tip of Oahu, was scheduled to be switched off at 0700. At 0702, Private Joseph L. Lockard and Private George Elliot detected a large flight of approaching aircraft at a range of 132 miles to the north whilst practising with the radar equipment. They reported the contact to the Information Center at Fort Shafter, the conversation taking about 8 minutes. The Opana Radar Site personnel were told not to worry as there were six scheduled B-17 Flying Fortress bombers en route from California – and the radar contact was from roughly the right direction. There was no coordinated system of US aerial reconnaissance in place at this time. The radar operatives continued to track the incoming flight until 0739 when the contact was lost at a distance of about 20 miles.

0705 – 200nm North of Oahu
About an hour after the first wave planes had launched, the six *Kidō Butai* carriers once again turned into the wind and at about 0715, 170 planes of the second wave launched under the command of Lieutenant Commander Shigekazu Shimazaki of the *Zuikaku* Air Group. During launching, a dive bomber from the *Hiryū* developed engine problems whilst two Vals and a Zeke also experienced difficulties and had to turn

---

* The wreck of the midget submarine was located in the contact area in August 2022 by the University of Hawaii at a depth of 1,200ft. The starboard side of the conning tower had one shell hole in it from a 4in round from *Ward*'s No. 3 gun. The depth charging had not damaged her hull.

back. But the remaining 167 planes successfully got aloft and turned to head towards Pearl Harbor.

In all, a total of 353 planes had now been launched in two waves. Of these, some 154 were assigned to attack US warships whilst the remaining 199 aircraft were tasked to strafe and bomb the US airfields and destroy any US aircraft present on the ground and in the air. The Japanese intended to secure undisputed local air superiority.[1]

0740 – Pearl Harbor
Some 20 minutes after *Ward*'s Contact Report was made, Admiral Husband E. Kimmel, Commander-in-Chief, US Fleet (CINCUS) was alerted – and as staff waited for Admiral Kimmel to arrive at his submarine base, they sought confirmation of the morning's events. The warships in the Naval Base were not alerted however – nor was army command on Oahu advised that the navy had just sunk an enemy submarine that had been attempting to enter the Naval Base. US crews aboard ships and shore personnel at barracks and airfields, on what appeared to most to be just another sleepy Sunday morning, were given no warning to man their AA weapons and break out ammunition boxes. No order was issued for aircraft to be launched from airfields.

(I) 0749: The First-Wave Planes Attack

The first wave of 183 planes, carrying most of the weapons designed to attack capital ships, was split into three groups:

1st Group: 49 Nakajima B5N Kates would operate as level bombers, tasked to attack battleships and carriers. They carried Type 99 # 80 Mk 5 1,760lb AP bombs and large naval AP shells with stabilising tail fins welded on. Another 40 Kates carried modified Type 91 aerial torpedoes.

2nd Group: 51 Aichi D3A Val dive bombers armed with 550lb Type 99 #25 550-lb (250kg) general-purpose (GP) bombs – tasked to target Ford Island and Wheeler Field, northwest of the harbour.

3rd Group: 43 Mitsubishi A6M Zero fighters, tasked to win and maintain air superiority by strafing and destroying as many parked-up US aircraft on the ground as possible.

When Commander Mitsuo Fuchida of the *Akagi*, supreme air commander of the attack, arrived with the first wave planes over Oahu's north shore near Kahuku Point, he banked his flight west and flew along the northwest coast. Fuchida then issued the order to all his pilots over or approaching Pearl Harbor: 'All aircraft immediately attack enemy positions.' [2] Fuchida slid back the canopy of his B5N Kate and fired a single blue flare, the signal that *surprise had been achieved* – and to attack.

0749

As the first-wave planes arrived over Oahu, thinking that some of his planes may have missed the single blue flare, Commander Fuchida fired another single blue flare. The leader of the Val dive bombers had however spotted both single flares, and whilst they were separated by a gap in time, two flares fired together was the signal to attack in the formation that would apply *if surprise had not been achieved*. He led his Val dive bombers into the requisite immediate attack position for that scenario.

Lieutenant Commander Shigeharu Murata, leading the Kate torpedo bombers, had also spotted both single flares fired by Commander Fuchida. Realising the Val dive bombers had misunderstood the signal, there was little option open to him – he led his torpedo bombers into their attack position. The first-wave planes began to divide so that the Val dive bombers and the Kate level bombers would lead the attack and draw fire from the slower torpedo bombers – which attacked at low level.

The Kate torpedo bombers from the *Hiryū* and *Sōryū* moved to attack US warships west of Ford Island whilst those from *Akagi* and *Kaga* flew to the southeast before turning in a large arc around and across Hickam Field in order to have a clear run against the battleships moored in Battleship Row, on the east side of Ford Island. The low, slow Kate torpedo bombers were using the first moments of complete surprise to make unchallenged runs at the US battleships.

Meanwhile, off the entrance to Pearl Harbor, the midget submarine *Ha-19* grounded and failed to penetrate the Naval Base. It would eventually wash ashore in Waimanalo Bay on the east side of Oahu (where it was captured on 8 December.)*

0753

Realising that his air groups were attacking as though surprise had not been achieved, and that nothing could be done about it now,

---

* *Ha-19* Ensign Kazuo Sakamaki swam ashore and was captured by Hawaii National Guard to become the first Japanese POW of the war. Another midget submarine was damaged by depth charging and abandoned before its crew could fire its torpedoes. It was located outside Pearl Harbor in 1960. Nagumo received a radio message from a midget submarine at 0041 on 8 December claiming damage to one or more large US warships inside Pearl.

Commander Fuchida in overall charge of the attack ordered the code words 'Tora! Tora! Tora!' sent by wireless to Vice Admiral Nagumo's flagship *Akagi*. Tora is the Japanese word for tiger – and was the code word that confirmed: 'We have succeeded in the surprise attack.'[3] The signal was received aboard *Akagi* – and also picked up aboard the battleship *Nagato*, Yamamoto's flagship in the Inland Sea, off Japan, where the raid was being monitored.

Just before 0800, the first wave of 183 Japanese torpedo bombers, dive bombers and fighters swept across the Pearl Harbor Naval Station – taking everyone by complete surprise.

The fundamental rule of any air battle is to gain immediate control of the local air space by eliminating the defensive activities of enemy fighters.[4] As Japanese aircraft headed for the US airfields, hundreds of largely unprotected US planes were neatly lined up in rows, parked wingtip to wingtip in the open to prevent sabotage. These planes would be easy pickings – as the base AA guns were unmanned and ammunition lockers were secured.

Under Commander Fuchida's control, thirty-five Val dive bombers of 2nd Group attacked Wheeler Army Airfield in central Oahu, which Japanese intelligence had assessed was the main centre of US fighter operations. The Vals were tasked to destroy US fighters on the ground – before they could get aloft – and they found some 140 US fighters parked up there, mainly Curtiss P-36 Hawks and the more recent Curtiss P-40 Warhawk. Nearly two-thirds would be destroyed or put out of action.

Almost simultaneously, twenty-six Val dive bombers of 2nd Group swarmed over Hickam Field, adjacent to the Pearl Harbor Navy Yard on the east side of the southern entrance channel, which was believed to be the major US heavy bomber base for the US Army Air Force (AAF). About two-thirds of the heavy B-17 bombers, and the B-18 and A-20 Havoc medium bombers, found there were destroyed or rendered incapable of getting aloft.

Simultaneously, a portion of 2nd Group detached to attack Ford Island, which was believed to be a base for navy carrier fighters. Of some fifty US planes present, very quickly more than thirty had been shot up. The smaller Bellows Field on the eastern tip of Oahu was also hit, destroying several Curtiss P-40 Warhawk fighters. Ford Island and Kaneohe on the east coast of Oahu were home to several squadrons of long-range PBY seaplanes, which were also heavily attacked.

The devastating attacks by Japanese planes successfully secured initial air superiority – and few US planes would subsequently get off the ground. The Japanese bombers over Pearl Harbor were thus relatively free from attack by US fighters – whilst at sea, 200nm to the north, the six vulnerable carriers of the *Kidō Butai* were now also protected against a possible US counterattack by air.

As the Val dive bombers plunged from the sky towards their targets, Commander Fuchida's level and torpedo bombers vectored to attack the US battleships. The torpedo-carrying planes began their low, slow runs towards the US battleships, which were lined up singly or rafted up in pairs in Battleship Row, which ran along the southeast side of Ford Island.[5]

As the dive bombers, level bombers and torpedo bombers began their attacks, forty-three Zekes carried out a low-level strafing sweep – shooting up AA positions, ground installations and any planes, ships or targets of opportunity spotted in the harbour. The Zekes intercepted and destroyed four US fighters which had got airborne and were trying to disrupt the bombing operations.[6]

(II) 0800–0815: Battleship Row, Pearl Harbor Naval Base

Whilst the Val dive bombers attacked airbases across Oahu, starting with the largest, Hickam Field in the south and Wheeler Field in central Oahu, the bulk of the Japanese air groups headed to attack the US Pacific Fleet battleships, seven of which were lined up in Battleship Row, either singly or in pairs with their bows pointed southwest – roughly towards the southern entrance to Pearl Harbor.

The flagship of Admiral Husband E. Kimmel, Commander in Chief US Pacific Fleet (CINCUS-CINCPACFLT) based in Pearl was the 608ft-long, 31,400-ton battleship *Pennsylvania* (BB-38), which normally was berthed in Ten-Ten Dock across from Battleship Row. Unknown to the Japanese however, *Pennsylvania* was meantime undergoing a refit in Dry Dock No. 1 at the Navy Yard on the east side of the entrance channel, where three of her four propellers had already been removed.

Of the seven battlewagons tied up on Battleship Row, the 624ft (oa), 32,300-ton battleship *California* (BB-44) was moored in isolation, at the southmost head of Battleship Row opposite the Navy Yard, with her port beam unknowingly exposed to a torpedo attack. Astern of *California*, the 553ft-long, 7,470-ton oiler *Neosho* (AO-23) lay at the fuel dock.

Astern of *Neosho*, the 624ft-long, 32,600-ton battleship *Maryland* (BB-46) lay moored with her starboard beam towards Ford Island – with the slightly smaller 583ft-long, 27,500-ton battleship *Oklahoma* (BB-37) rafted up outboard of her on her port beam.

A photograph looking east taken from a Japanese plane during the torpedo attack on ships moored on both sides of Ford Island. A torpedo has just hit USS *West Virginia* on the far side of Ford Island. Other battleships moored nearby are, left to right: *Nevada*, *Arizona*, *Tennessee* (inboard of *West Virginia*), *Oklahoma* (torpedoed and listing) alongside *Maryland*, and *California*. On the near side of Ford Island to the left are the light cruisers *Detroit* and *Raleigh*, target and training ship *Utah* and seaplane tender *Tangier*. (NH 50930 courtesy of the US Naval History & Heritage Command)

Astern of *Maryland* and *Oklahoma*, the 624ft-long, 32,300-ton battleship *Tennessee* (BB-43) lay in the inboard position with her starboard beam towards Ford Island. The similarly sized 624ft-long, 32,692-ton battleship *West Virginia* (BB-48) was moored alongside in the outboard position on *Tennessee*'s port beam.

Astern of these two battleships the 608ft-long, 29,158-ton battleship *Arizona* (BB-39) was moored with her starboard beam towards Ford Island. The smaller repair ship *Vestal* (AR-4) was secured alongside her port beam in the outboard position whilst her repair crew carried out minor works to *Arizona*. Although *Vestal* was dwarfed by the *Arizona*, the hull of the 465ft-long repair ship nevertheless offered a considerable degree of protection against torpedo attack, screening the most critical parts of the neighbouring battleship: her magazines, engine spaces and boilers. *Arizona* would be bombed.

The 585ft-long, 27,500-ton battleship *Nevada* was moored in isolation astern of *Arizona* at the other end of Battleship Row. *Nevada* would be the only battleship able to manoeuvre as the attack developed.

Of the seven battleships moored in Battleship Row immediately before the Japanese attack, *Oklahoma* and *West Virginia* were each rafted up to another battleship in the outboard position, and thus presented their port beams to a torpedo attack. Tucked in towards the interrupted quays at Ford Island alongside and inboard of *Oklahoma*, *Maryland* was protected from torpedo attack – and would thus be bombed. Likewise, *Tennessee* was moored in the inboard position against the quays at Ford Island, abeam of *West Virginia*. She was therefore also protected from torpedo attack and would be bombed.

The much smaller 521ft-long, 21,825-ton vintage ex-battleship *Utah* (BB-31) was also present, moored on the other side of Ford Island. Launched in 1909, *Utah* had been demilitarised in 1931 and converted into a target ship and redesignated AG-16. All her main and secondary battery weapons had long since been removed and by the eve of the Pearl Harbor raid, she had been converted to train AA gunners.

0800

Moored on her own at the northeast most end of Battleship Row astern of *Arizona*, *Nevada*'s starboard side faced towards Ford Island. With all the ships' bows pointing southwest towards the southern entrance into the Naval Base, *Nevada* was essentially moored at the aft end of the row of battleships.

Just before 0800, as the *Nevada* ship's band began playing 'Morning Colors' for the ceremonial hoisting of the national ensign, the Japanese air raid began with the dive-bombing of the Air Station on Ford Island. This was followed immediately by the torpedo-plane attack on the battleships. General Quarters sounded immediately.

As the torpedo bombers began their low-level attack runs against the exposed port beams of the accessible battleships and prepared to drop their Type 91 aerial torpedoes, those Kates of the 1st Group carrying 1,760lb Type 99 # 80 Mk 5 AP bombs and adapted naval shells began their high-level attacks at an estimated 9,800ft. The AP bombs were fitted with a delayed fuze – so that the bomb would not explode on contact with the ship but would punch down through multiple decks before the delayed fuze detonated the bomb deep in the bowels of the ship. About eight of the 49 Type 99 AP bombs and adapted naval shells dropped by the Kates would hit their intended battleship targets. At least two of those bombs broke up on impact, whilst another detonated before penetrating an unarmoured deck – one was a dud and several were found unexploded inside the ships during subsequent salvage work. Approximately thirteen of the forty Type 91 torpedoes dropped by the Kates hit battleships, with four torpedoes hitting other ships.

Men still asleep aboard US ships were suddenly awakened to the sounds of alarms, bombs exploding and gunfire as General Quarters was sounded. (The famous message, 'Air Raid Pearl Harbor. This is not a drill.' was sent from the headquarters of Patrol Wing Two, the first senior Hawaiian command to respond.)

Within a few minutes of the low-level torpedo attacks beginning, three US battleships would be critically hit – *California*, *Oklahoma* and *West Virginia*. The major part of the torpedo attack was over by 0805.

The battleship *Oklahoma*, moored in Berth Fox 5 in the outboard position alongside *Maryland*, was targeted by Kate torpedo planes from the *Akagi* and *Kaga* – and three Type 91 aerial torpedoes struck her port beam in relatively quick succession.

The first and second Type 91 torpedoes hit seconds apart just before 0800, striking amidships approximately 20ft below the waterline between the smokestack abaft the foremast, and the mainmast (situated forward of the after superfiring pair of main-battery turrets). The torpedoes blew away a large section of the ship's anti-torpedo bulge and spilled oil from the adjacent fuel bunkers' sounding tubes, but neither torpedo penetrated the inner hull.

About eighty crew scrambled to man the AA guns but were unable to bring them into action because the firing locks were in the armoury. Most of the men manned their action stations below the ship's waterline or sought shelter in the third deck – as they had been trained to do during an aerial attack to gain protection under the horizontal armour deck.

The third Type 91 torpedo struck at 0800, hitting close to where the first two did. This torpedo penetrated the hull, destroying the adjacent fuel bunkers on the second platform deck and rupturing access trunks to the two forward boiler rooms as well as the transverse bulkhead to the aft boiler room and the longitudinal bulkhead of the two forward firing rooms. Water began flooding into the great battleship.

The battleship *Maryland* lay against the concrete interrupted Ford Island quays, inboard of *Oklahoma*. As the attacks began, many of the crew were preparing for shore leave at 0900 or eating breakfast. As the first Japanese aircraft swept over the harbour and explosions rocked

7 DECEMBER 1941 – 'A DATE WHICH WILL LIVE IN INFAMY'

the outboard battleships, *Maryland*'s bugler blew General Quarters. Seaman Leslie Short had been addressing Christmas cards near his machine gun as the attack began. He brought the first of the ship's guns into play, shooting down one of two Kate torpedo bombers that had just released its torpedo against *Oklahoma*. Gunners aboard *Maryland* would soon bring all her AA batteries into action.

Meanwhile, as *Oklahoma* flooded with water through the three torpedo holes in her port hull and torpedo blister, she began to list to port. Two more Type 91 aerial torpedoes then struck her port side. As she rolled further to port, men began to abandon ship – and those below deck frantically tried to make their way out of the ship. But as part of their protection system against shells and bombs, battleships only have a limited number of exit points onto deck and many were unable to get out of the ship in time. Those men fortunate enough to be able to clamber clear of the ship found themselves being strafed as they abandoned ship.

In less than 12 minutes, *Oklahoma* had rolled over, capsizing until her top hamper, upperworks and two masts hit the seabed. The midsection of her starboard beam projected above the water and part of her starboard keel was exposed. It is thought that as many as eight torpedoes may have struck her in all.

As their ship listed, many of *Oklahoma*'s crew clambered aboard *Maryland* to help man her AA batteries. However, 429 men of the *Oklahoma* died – many trapped inside the ship as it capsized.

Astern of *Oklahoma* and *Maryland*, the battleship *West Virginia*, tied up alongside and outboard on the port side of *Tennessee*, was hit by seven or more Type 91 torpedoes on her port side, whilst her rudder was blown off by another. Bombers hit her from above with a pair of AP bombs adapted from large-calibre naval shells with tail fins welded on to give the characteristics of a spiralling bomb. The first AP bomb hit the port side, penetrating the superstructure deck and causing extensive damage to the casemates below. Secondary explosions of the ammunition stored in the casemates caused serious fires there and in the galley deck below.

The second adapted AP bomb hit *West Virginia* on the roof of the rear superfiring 16in No. 3 turret. The bomb penetrated but failed to explode – although it nevertheless destroyed one of the 16in guns. The OS2U Kingfisher floatplane on the catapult atop the turret was destroyed whilst a second Kingfisher was knocked down to the main deck, spilling aviation gasoline onto the deck that then caught on fire.

Of the seven or more Type 91 torpedoes that hit her, at least three torpedoes hit the anti-torpedo side-protection system below the vertical

The capsized hull of Oklahoma, with a barge alongside to support rescue efforts, probably on 8 December 1941. *Maryland* is at right, and *California* is in the centre distance. (*80-G-32453 courtesy of the US Naval History & Heritage Command*)

armour belt. These torpedoes opened two large holes in the hull beneath the armour belt – and at least one torpedo passed through these holes after the ship began to list and exploded, completely breaking through the ship's multi-layered anti-torpedo side-protection system. At least one torpedo hit the armour belt itself, damaging several plates.

The torpedo hits caused extensive internal damage and the ship avoided capsizing only through prompt damage-control efforts. Captain Mervyn S. Bennion of the *West Virginia* was struck by bomb fragments from a hit nearby on *Tennessee*. Mortally wounded, he remained aboard *West Virginia* assisting in its defence until he died – and would be posthumously awarded the Medal of Honor.

As *West Virginia* filled with water, slowly settling into the water on an even keel, the majority of the crew were able to abandon ship, although some crew returned to the ship to fight the fires that had broken out. Fuel oil leaking from the *Arizona* astern, after she was destroyed by a

7 DECEMBER 1941 – 'A DATE WHICH WILL LIVE IN INFAMY'

Sailors in a motor launch rescue a survivor from the water and burning oil alongside the foremast of *West Virginia* during or shortly after the air raid. USS *Tennessee* is inboard of the sunken battleship. A 5in/25-cal. AA gun nearby is still partially covered with canvas, the boat crane is swung outboard. *(80-G-19930 courtesy of the US Naval History & Heritage Command)*

bomb hit, caught fire and engulfed *West Virginia* in a wall of flames, which was also fed by her own leaking fuel oil.* By the time the attack was over, a total of 106 *West Virginia* crew had been killed.

Nevada was moored on her own abaft *Arizona*. Fortuitously, earlier that morning, a second boiler had been lit on *Nevada* with the intention of switching the power load from one boiler to the other at about 0800. As the Japanese planes began their attack, *Nevada's* AA gunners opened fire and her engineers scrambled to raise steam to allow her to cast off and begin to manoeuvre.

---

* The fires were eventually put out the following day.

0803

The battleship *California* was the southernmost ship moored at the head of Battleship Row. At the time of the attack, 2 of her 5in guns and 2 of her .50-cal. machine guns were designated as ready guns, with 50 5in ready use shells and 400 .50-cal. rounds near the guns.

As the attack began, the ship went to General Quarters and as the ship was prepared to get underway, at 0803 the crews of the ready AA guns began to engage the attacking Japanese aircraft, which included Mitsubishi A6M Zero fighters that strafed the ship. The gunners quickly expended the ready ammunition – and the magazines had to be unlocked before they could be resupplied. As the guns were being resupplied, two Kate torpedo bombers approached and dropped their Type 91 aerial torpedoes. At 0805, both torpedoes hit *California*, one forward and the other further aft.

The forward torpedo detonated below the armour belt between No. 2 turret and the bridge, creating a hole 10ft high and 24ft long and destructively deforming the first inner torpedo bulkhead and transverse stiffeners of the multi-layered anti-torpedo side-protection system and holing the second torpedo bulkhead with splinters.

The aft torpedo strike blew open a hole that was 40ft long below the armour belt. The interior anti-torpedo bulkheads of the side-protection system however held and helped to contain the flooding.

The side-protection system could have handled these two torpedo hits when the ship was at action stations, with all doors and openings dogged down and closed. However, *California* had unluckily been prepared for inspection at the time of the attack – and most of the internal watertight doors had been opened. As the attack began and the ship went to the Battle Closure Condition Z, the crew began closing the doors to make her watertight – but before that could be accomplished, the two torpedoes had struck. As uncontrolled flooding started to spread throughout the ship, *California* took on a list to port of 5° to 6°. Many of the portholes and exterior doors were also open for the inspection, allowing water to enter the ship as it listed. Counterflooding of spaces on the starboard side of the ship reduced the list to 4°, but the flooding on the lower port side continued to spread.

The torpedo blasts ruptured the forward fuel tanks, allowing water to enter the fuel system, shutting down the ship's electrical system and hindering the efforts of the damage-control teams.

Moored alongside Ford Island inboard of *West Virginia* and protected from torpedo attack, *Tennessee* had quickly gone to General Quarters, her AA guns being manned within a few minutes. *Tennessee* received

7 DECEMBER 1941 – 'A DATE WHICH WILL LIVE IN INFAMY'

At the southeastern side of Ford Island, USS *California* lists to port after being hit by Japanese torpedoes and bombs. (*80-G-32463 courtesy of the US Naval History & Heritage Command*)

orders to get underway – but before her crew had got steam up in her boilers, she had been hemmed in and trapped in her berth as the other battleships around her received crippling damage. *West Virginia* outboard of her was torpedoed and sinking – whilst ahead of her, *Oklahoma* was capsizing.

Meantime, as the torpedo planes carried out their runs against *California*, *Oklahoma* and *West Virginia*, the other battleships were receiving their own attention from Japanese bombers. On board the battleship *Arizona*, shortly after 0800, ten Kate torpedo bombers, five each from the carriers *Kaga* and *Hiryū*, arrived overhead, some carrying a delayed fuze Type 99 # 80 1,760-lb AP bomb, whilst others carried adapted 15in naval shells with stabilising fins welded to them.[7]

The Kates approached *Arizona* at an estimated altitude of 9,800ft with the Kates from *Kaga* initially targeting *Arizona* from amidships to the stern, followed by *Hiryū*'s bombers targeting the forward part of the ship.

The Kates scored four hits and three near misses on *Arizona*. One was a near miss off the port bow whilst the aftmost bomb ricocheted off the face of No. 4 turret and penetrated the deck to detonate in the captain's pantry, causing a small fire. Another bomb hit the port edge of the ship, abreast the mainmast, probably detonating in the area of the anti-torpedo bulkhead. The next bomb struck near the port rear 5in AA gun.

The last bomb hit in the vicinity of No. 2 Turret in the foreship. What happened next has never been fully explained, since the delayed fuze bomb apparently did not pierce the armour deck above the magazines – but about 7 seconds after the hit, the forward magazines detonated in a violent and catastrophic explosion, that vented mostly through the sides of the ship and destroyed much of the interior structure of the forward part of the ship. A fireball exploded from the ship and a column of black smoke and fire erupted for almost a thousand feet directly upwards. Blazing furiously, *Arizona* quickly settled on the bottom – fierce fires erupted that would burn for two days.

Debris from the destroyed *Arizona* showered down on Ford Island. The forward turrets and conning tower collapsed downwards some 25–30ft and the foremast and smokestack sagged forward. Of the 1,512 crewmen on board at the time, 1,177 were killed – approximately

View from the north looking down Battleship Row on 7 December 1941. The sunken and burning *Arizona* is in the centre, although her tripod mainmast still stands her foremast has sagged forward. To the left are *Tennessee* and the sunken *West Virginia*. (NH 97377 courtesy of the US Naval History & Heritage Command)

7 DECEMBER 1941 – 'A DATE WHICH WILL LIVE IN INFAMY'

half of the total lives lost during the whole raid. The explosion on *Arizona* showered burning oil over *Tennessee*'s stern, which was quickly surrounded by fire that was fed by oil leaking from *West Virginia*.

0810

At about 0810, a single Type 91 aerial torpedo struck *Nevada*'s port bow about 14ft above the keel, between the second and first platform decks. The hit was 5–6ft below the bottom edge of the vertical main armour belt – and about 15ft below the waterline.

The outer steel plating of the torpedo bulge detonated the torpedo as intended, the steel plating of the bulge being ripped open and allowing water to rush into the now exposed internal void spaces of the bulge. The blast opened up the bulkheads to the first (or outer) oil-filled space of the underwater side-protection system and the bulkheads to the inner ring of fuel tanks also gave way. But the system of voids and oil-filled compartments was designed to behave in this way and protect the final innermost watertight anti-torpedo bulkhead.

But although the final bulkhead of the anti-torpedo underwater protection system held, it was dished in by about 2ft over a large area of about 400sq ft and gaps some 7in long had been sprung between joints in the plating. Water immediately began to leak through these split joints and flood the port-side compartments below the first platform deck.

An ordnance storeroom on the second platform deck flooded quickly, whilst the 5in powder magazine began to flood slowly. Above the ordnance storeroom on the first platform deck was a powder magazine for the main-battery 14in guns. Oil and water from the ruptured side-protection system voids and tanks below began to enter the magazine and the ship began to take on a list, which steadily increased to about 4–5°. The first platform deck voids and smaller triangular voids just above them were accessed by manholes. The watertight covers to the manholes were sprung open by force of the explosion or were loose – and oil and water began to spout up from them.

As *Nevada* listed and her bow settled, in the crew spaces between the main-battery barbettes along the centre line of the ship, oil and water was spurting out from the sounding tubes that led to the fuel tanks. Counterflooding of compartments on the starboard side of the ship successfully reduced the list – although her head was soon down by about 3ft.[8]

Admiral Kimmel's flagship *Pennsylvania* was on blocks in Dry Dock No. 1 with the destroyers *Cassin* (DD-372) and *Downes* (DD-375) also in the dock, side by side on blocks ahead of her. As the Japanese attack began, *Pennsylvania*'s crew rushed to their battle stations, and her AA gunners opened fire on the attacking planes. Japanese torpedo bombers unsuccessfully attempted to torpedo the side of the dry dock to flood it, before strafing *Pennsylvania*.

0820

By now, *California* was crippled, *West Virginia* was slowly sinking – and *Oklahoma* had capsized. *Arizona* had blown up and *Nevada* was torpedoed and listing.

Japanese bombers now attacked the trapped *Tennessee* hitting her twice with the same adapted AP bombs as had destroyed *Arizona* – but neither of these two bombs detonated properly. One bomb hit the starboard yard of the mainmast, smashing the catapult atop the aft superfiring No. 3 Turret before partially penetrating the 5in-thick roof armour of the turret and breaking apart without detonating. The left gun was knocked out of commission by the fragmenting bomb whilst a small fire was started.

A fragment of the second bomb penetrated the 5in roof armour of the three-gun forward superfiring No. 2 Turret – and hit the centre gun barrel, disabling the gun. Lethal splinters were flung around by the bomb's impact on the turret roof and it was a shrapnel shard from this that struck and killed the captain of *West Virginia*, Mervyn S. Bennion, on the open bridge of his own ship, moored alongside *Tennessee*.

Neither bomb inflicted serious damage to *Tennessee* itself, but the ship's magazines were flooded to avoid the risk of the fires raging aboard and around the vessel from spreading to them and igniting the propellant charges stored there.[*]

Moored forward of *Tennessee* and inboard of *Oklahoma*, with her starboard side towards Ford Island, *Maryland* was hit by two AP bombs, which detonated low on her hull. The first struck the forecastle and made a hole about 12ft x 20ft. The second exploded forward after entering the hull at the 22ft water level. The ship began to take on water – two officers and two men had been killed in the attack.

California, already hit by two Type 91 aerial torpedoes, was now repeatedly attacked by Val dive bombers. One 550lb bomb hit on the starboard side and another was a near miss on the port side that caused minor damage.

---

[*] By 1030 the crew had suppressed the fires aboard the ship, though oil still burned in the water around the ship for another two days. In an effort to push the burning oil away from the ship, she slowly turned her screws at a speed of about 5 knots.

7 DECEMBER 1941 – 'A DATE WHICH WILL LIVE IN INFAMY'

0830

Several high-altitude Val dive bombers began a series of attacks on the dry-docked *Pennsylvania*. During the next 15 minutes, five aircraft attempted to hit her from different directions. One bomb was a hit on *Pennsylvania* and passed through the boat deck and exploded in casemate No. 9. In the course of the attack on *Pennsylvania*, eighteen men were killed (including her executive officer) and thirty-eight wounded.

Fragments of a bomb that exploded between the two destroyers *Cassin* and *Downes*, side by side and forward of *Pennsylvania*, easily penetrated the destroyer's thin plating to the fuel bunkers, releasing fuel oil that then caught fire. In an effort to help extinguish the fires, shore crew flooded the dry dock – but burning fuel on the rising surface of the water would eventually burn both destroyers out. As the water in the

The destroyers *Downes* (DD-375), at left, and *Cassin* (DD-372), capsized at right, burned out and sunk in the Navy Yard dry dock on 7 December 1941. The relatively undamaged *Pennsylvania* is in the background. (*80-G-32511 courtesy of the US Naval History & Heritage Command*)

dock rose, *Cassin* became partially afloat, slipped from her keel blocks and rolled against *Downes*. About 10 minutes later, explosions began as the fires reached magazines and ammunition began to cook off.

0840

It had taken until 0840 for crew on *Nevada* to raise enough steam to enable her to move. But with steam now up, *Nevada* was able to back away from her berth F-8 at the north end of Battleship Row. By this time, her gunners had shot down four enemy aircraft.

As the flooding from the torpedo hit forward became more pronounced, *Nevada* was ordered to proceed to the west side of Ford Island. She was not to leave the harbour and not to be sunk in the narrow entrance channel where she could bock the entire Naval Base.

Nevada began moving slowly southwest down Battleship Row, past the destroyed *Arizona*, as she headed for the southern channel entrance. By mistake, her after magazines were flooded by direct sea connection rather than by the sprinkler system – and as they rapidly filled with water, the added weight aft raised her bow.

0843

Having successfully entered Pearl Harbor, a Japanese midget submarine fired a first torpedo at the seaplane tender *Curtiss* (AV-4) on the northwest side of Ford Island. The torpedo missed – and continued until it impacted a dock. The destroyer *Monaghan* (DD-354) spotted the submarine and attacked at speed to ram. The midget submarine fired a second torpedo at the attacking *Monaghan* – but missed by 50yd. *Monaghan* successfully rammed the midget submarine and then dropped two depth charges. It was assumed she had been sunk – but there was no time to investigate.

(III) 0845: The Second-Wave Planes Attack

Just minutes after *Nevada* began to move out of her berth, at 0845, the second wave of 167 Japanese level bombers, dive bombers and fighter aircraft swept over Pearl Harbor, 3 planes having aborted. The second-wave planes flew in 3 groups and comprised 54 Nakajima B5N Kates operating as level bombers, 78 Aichi D3A Val dive bombers and 36 A6M Zero fighters. The separate sections of the second wave arrived at their attack positions almost simultaneously from several directions.

In the 1st Group, 54 Kate torpedo bombers were armed with 550lb and 132lb General Purpose (GP) bombs. Of these, 27 Kates attacked

7 DECEMBER 1941 – 'A DATE WHICH WILL LIVE IN INFAMY'

US fighter and bomber bases, hitting aircraft on the ground and hangars on Kaneohe NAS, Ford Island and at Ewa Mooring Mast Field at Barbers Point. The other 27 Kates attacked hangars and aircraft on Hickam Field to the east of the southern entrance channel.

The 78 Val dive bombers of the 2nd Group were armed with 550lb GP bombs – tasked to target battleships and cruisers. With one plane having aborted, the 3rd Group, comprising 35 A6M Zero fighters, targeted aircraft parked at Ford Island, Hickam Field, Wheeler Field, Barbers Point and Kaneohe in a combined strafing and air-strike mission.[9]

At about 0845, the crippled *California* was struck by a bomb from a Val dive bomber near the forwardmost casemate on the starboard side. After penetrating the upper deck, the bomb ricocheted off the second deck and detonated in the ship's interior, where it caused extensive damage, started a serious fire, and killed about fifty men. By 0915, the fire had spread to casemates No. 3, 5 and 7 – and by 1000, smoke from the fire had reached the forward engine room and forced the men inside to evacuate the area. The crew might have kept her afloat but were ordered to abandon ship just as they were raising power for the pumps, ending pumping efforts. In the course of the attack, ninety-eight men had been killed and sixty-one wounded. Despite subsequent pumping efforts over the next three days the hull slowly filled with water and the ship would eventually settle into the muddy seabed.

Already damaged by a torpedo, as *Nevada* got underway she became a prime target for the second-wave Val dive bombers – whose pilots hoped to sink her in the entrance channel to the Naval Base. Dreadnought battleships such as *Nevada* were however designed to withstand these sorts of hits – and it was in fact extremely unlikely that the Vals, carrying modest 550lb bombs, would be able to sink her.

The *Nevada*, down 3ft by the head, moved slowly south down Battleship Row, past the destroyed *Arizona*, then past the burning *West Virginia*, which was by now sitting partially submerged on the bottom. *Nevada* then moved past the capsized *Oklahoma* and past the stricken *California*.

As the flooding inside *Nevada* became more pronounced, once she was off Ten-Ten Dock, which lies opposite the southeasternmost side of Ford Island and was normally reserved for the dry-docked flagship *Pennsylvania*, her crew prepared to drop anchor. As they were doing this however, several flights of Val dive bombers from the second wave attacked her – and she was struck by a total of some five 550lb delayed fuze bombs.

One bomb exploded over the crew's galley whilst another struck the port director platform and exploded at the base of the smokestack on the upper deck. A third bomb hit near No. 1 turret inboard from the port waterway that guided water off the deck – and blew large holes in the upper and main decks.

Two bombs struck the forecastle – one passing out through the side of the second deck before exploding. The other bomb however detonated inside the ship near the gasoline tank – and leaking fuel and vapours from this tank caused intense fires to ignite around the ship.

The gasoline fires that took hold around No. 1 Turret had the potential to cause a catastrophic magazine explosion as had just happened on *Arizona*. However, the main shell rooms and magazines on *Nevada* were in fact virtually empty – as over the last few days, the 14in-gun battleships had been replacing their standard-weight main-battery projectiles with a new heavier projectile that offered greater penetration and a larger explosive charge. All of the older projectiles and their potentially volatile powder charges had already been removed from *Nevada*'s magazines – the crew was to begin loading the new powder charges later that day.

0907

By now, *Nevada* was on fire, down by the head and still flooding with water from the single torpedo hit forward. In addition, she had now been hit by some five 550lb GP bombs from the Val dive bombers. She was now attacked heavily again – and hit by a sixth 550lb GP bomb, which started further fires. Gasoline fires were now preventing damage-control parties from containing the flooding in the forward spaces of the torpedo defence system.

The flooding of the main 14in magazine and counterflooding to correct her trim had further lowered her bow – and this allowed more water to enter the ship at the second deck level through the exit hole made by one of the 550lb bombs. Lack of watertight subdivision between the second and main decks allowed water entering through bomb holes in the forecastle to flow aft through the ship's ventilation system and flood the dynamo and boiler rooms. Through all this time, her AA gunners had remained in action and managed to down three more Japanese planes.

The attack slackened at 0908.

0910

The southbound *Nevada* beached with her bow on the shallows at Hospital Point, south of the southernmost end of Ford Island, on the

7 DECEMBER 1941 – 'A DATE WHICH WILL LIVE IN INFAMY'

east side of the entrance channel. As she ran onto the shallows, her stern was in deeper water and soon began to swing around to the south, creating a hazard to navigation in the narrow entrance channel. Shortly after beaching, the magazines of the destroyer *Shaw* in a floating dry dock nearby exploded – and showered the decks of *Nevada* with debris. As a result, it was decided to move *Nevada* to the other western side of the channel.

A tug pushed *Nevada*'s stern further round and the bow floated off. Tugs then moved the ship most of the way across the channel, with *Nevada*'s own engines only being used at the last moment, when they were backed until her stern was hard aground at Waipi'o Point at about 1030. With only her stern sitting on the shallow coral shelf on the west of the entrance channel, she continued to take on water to her bow and middle section, settling further into the water with an 8° list to starboard. During the attack, *Nevada* had suffered a total of 50 killed and 109 wounded.

Although the Japanese had concentrated on the battleships, they also attacked other targets of opportunity. The light cruiser *Helena* (CL-50), alongside Ten-Ten Dock in *Pennsylvania*'s usual berth, was hit by a Type 91 torpedo and the minelayer *Oglala* moored alongside outboard of her was hit by bombs and capsized. The light cruiser *Raleigh* (CL-7) was holed by a Type 91 torpedo whilst the light cruiser *Honolulu* (CL-48) was damaged. The repair vessel *Vestal*, moored alongside *Arizona*, was heavily damaged as the *Arizona* blew up. The seaplane tender *Curtiss*, targeted earlier by a midget submarine, was also damaged. The destroyer *Shaw* (DD-373) was badly damaged when three bomb hits started fires that caused her forward magazine to explode just after 0930. The disarmed ex-battleship target ship *Utah* (BB-31/AG-16) was holed twice by Type 91 torpedoes and capsized.

(IV) 0930: The Second-Wave Attack Ends

The two waves of the Japanese air assault had been completed within 90 minutes. As the last planes of the second wave delivered their weapons, the air groups turned to head back to their carriers – flying due south as fast as possible at first, instead of north, to conceal the true position of their carriers from US eyes.

Down on the ground at Pearl Harbor Naval Base it was a scene of utter devastation. During the 90 minutes of the raid, 2,403 Americans had been killed – of which, 1,177 had been killed aboard *Arizona* when

PEARL HARBOR'S REVENGE

she blew up. Of this total, 2,008 were sailors, 218 were soldiers and AAF personnel, 109 were Marines and 68 were civilians; 1,178 had been wounded.

All 8 Pacific Fleet battleships present had been hit – with 4 sunk. In addition, 3 light cruisers, 3 destroyers, the training ship (ex-battleship) *Utah* and other smaller vessels had been sunk or damaged, a total of some 21 naval units.

Of the 402 US aircraft present in Hawaii, 188 aircraft had been destroyed and 169 damaged – mostly on the ground. Hardly any had actually been ready to take off to defend the base when the raid began. However, during the attack 8 Army Air Forces pilots managed to get aloft and 6 were credited with downing at least 1 Japanese aircraft. Of 33 Consolidated PBY Catalina flying boats stationed in Hawaii, 30 were destroyed. The other 3 had been out on patrol at the time of the attack – and they returned undamaged

Several Japanese junior officers, including the air commander of the attack Commander Mitsuo Fuchida of the *Akagi* and Commander Minoru Genda, an air operations officer on the staff of the 1st Air Fleet who had helped Yamamoto plan the attack, are claimed to have urged Vice Admiral Nagumo to carry out a third strike in order to destroy as much of Pearl Harbor's fuel and torpedo storage, maintenance and dry dock facilities as possible.

Commander Genda, who had previously unsuccessfully advocated a ground invasion of Hawaii after the air attack, believed that without an invasion, three strikes were necessary to completely disable the Naval Base. The captains of the other five carriers in the task force reported they were willing and ready to carry out a third strike, which could have destroyed oil-depot fuel tanks that were full to capacity – and the docks and power station.

Controversy about a possible third strike has whirled around since the war – and provoked a range of views. Many fine military historians have suggested that the destruction of these shore facilities would have completely destroyed Pearl Harbor as a naval base. The ability of the US Pacific Fleet to interdict Japan's expansionist plans would have been degraded far more effectively than the loss of its old Standard-Type battleships.

Vice Admiral Nagumo, however, decided to withdraw – and no doubt an array of factors weighed upon him. His orders from Yamamoto were peremptory and did not give him discretionary powers and freedom of action. His assigned targets did not include the base facilities at Pearl. The two waves of the attack had inflicted all the damage hoped for to the assigned targets – and another attack could not be expected to greatly increase the extent of that damage.[10]

There were also logistical problems to confront. After the second wave of the strike was completed, the Japanese planes had headed south to mislead the enemy, before returning to their carriers, which were still on station 200nm north of Oahu. Recovery of the returning strike aircraft was completed at 1215.

A full deck load strike, in 2 waves, of some 350 planes had already been carried out that morning – and no reserve planes had been carried for a third strike. If there was to be a third wave, then the carriers would have to wait until the planes returned from the first and second waves of the attack – the sky would be thick with planes circling the six carriers as the individual planes waited their turn to land. The sheer process of landing so many planes on six carriers would be complicated and time consuming.

But even once the planes were landed on the carriers, deck crews would have to refuel and rearm the planes whilst pilots were debriefed – and then briefed on their new targets. The refuelled and rearmed planes would then have to be respotted on the flight decks before a third wave could launch.

Such a complicated process from landing so many planes to finally having them refuelled, rearmed and spotted on the flight decks would have taken 2–3 hours – just to get to the point where the planes could launch for the 200nm flight back to Pearl Harbor. Any third wave would need to make that 200nm flight – and then spend time delivering the attack before embarking on the return 200nm flight to the carriers. A third strike would thus take at least 6 hours.

Sunset in Hawaii in December is at about 1800 – so a third strike and return to the carriers could not be carried out during daylight. Returning pilots would need to find their carriers in darkness and attempt night landings. It was particularly difficult for Japanese fighter planes to fly long distances at sea – as they were not equipped with homing devices and radar, as were the larger planes. The bombers were to rendezvous with the fighters on completion of their missions at a designated point – and then lead the fighters back to the carriers. But how could that be done in darkness? It thus seems that a third follow-up strike could not be carried out until the following morning – but had a third strike been delayed to the next day, the Japanese escort destroyers would have been critically low on fuel.

Nagumo was also still unaware of the whereabouts of the US carriers. He had achieved surprise, hit all his assigned targets and won a seemingly great victory. If he lingered for a third strike, he would be risking the *Kidō Butai* possibly being engaged the next day by swarms of US carrier planes. Nagumo's force was also now within range of US land-based bombers on Hawaii, where intercepted US messages indicated that at least fifty large planes were still operational. Had enough US planes based in Hawaii escaped destruction to be able to launch an attack against his carriers?

If Nagumo launched a third wave, he would be risking three-quarters of the IJN Combined Fleet's strength to wipe out targets that were not in his orders. US AA performance on land batteries and on naval units present in the harbour had increased significantly by the time of the second wave that morning – with AA guns being manned and supplied with ammunition.

Two-thirds of Nagumo's aircraft losses had been incurred during the second wave. If he launched a third wave, US gunners aboard ships and in shore AA batteries would be waiting, armed and ready. US combat air patrols of fighters would be in the air above Pearl Harbor – waiting. Any third wave would have to fight its way in.

Nagumo had already lost the element of surprise – and higher casualties could therefore be expected. Could he risk higher losses of planes and pilots, and possibly the precious carriers themselves, at the very beginning of the war for seemingly less important targets? It is clear Nagumo had a number of dilemmas facing him – just as he would have once again in six months' time, at the Battle of Midway.

As history records, for many and complicated reasons, Nagumo did not instruct a third strike. The US fuel dumps and vital shore facilities for torpedo storage, repair, maintenance and dry dock facilities, destruction of which would have rendered the whole base at Hawaii useless, were not attacked. Hawaii would remain a powerful naval base; a submarine and intelligence base which was later instrumental in Japan's defeat. Rather than crippling US naval power in the Pacific for long enough to allow Japan to secure her position, the raid had left Hawaii – and US naval power in the Pacific – to fight another day.

Although an apparently stunning success for Japan that resonated around the world, strategically the attack was less significant. The *Kidō Butai* had withdrawn, taking a northerly route across the empty expanses of the North Pacific back to Japan, rendezvousing and refuelling from the oilers at the designated points en route. The vast fuel storage facilities for the US Pacific Fleet had not been damaged and none of the US carriers deployed in the Pacific had been present or damaged. The US carriers had escaped destruction and within six

7 DECEMBER 1941 – 'A DATE WHICH WILL LIVE IN INFAMY'

months would play a pivotal role in halting Japanese expansion at the Battle of the Coral Sea and at Midway.

Back in Pearl Harbor however, no one knew if the Japanese carriers were withdrawing or whether further attacks would be made. The scale of midget submarine operation was unknown. One midget submarine had been fired on by the destroyer *Ward* in the early morning hours before the attack had begun. The destroyer *Monaghan* had rammed a sub during the attack in the harbour – and after depth charging, it was assumed she had been sunk – but no one knew for sure. Another midget submarine in the entrance channel had fired torpedoes at the light cruiser *St Louis* (CL-49) (and missed) as she emerged from the channel during the attack. The midget submarine *Ha-19* was unsuccessful in its efforts to penetrate Pearl Harbor and drifted around the southeasternmost tip of Oahu where it grounded the next day, on 8 December, a few hundred yards off the beach near Bellows Field on the southeasternmost shore of Oahu. One of the sub's crew swam ashore and was captured.

Japanese Type A midget submarine photographed on 8 December 1941 aground on eastern Oahu beach, following attempts to enter Pearl Harbor during the attack the day before. (*NH 91331 courtesy of the US Naval History & Heritage Command*)

A Japanese Type A midget submarine at the Navy Yard, December 1941. This submarine was sunk by the destroyer *Monaghan* (DD-354) in Pearl Harbor during the attack on 7 December 1941. The hull shows damage from depth-charging and ramming. A hole is visible in the after part of the conning tower, likely from a 5in shell. (*NH 54302 courtesy of the US Naval History & Heritage Command*)

As the dry docks would be invaluable to the repair of the damaged battleships and other vessels, target rafts were placed in front of dry-dock caissons and a torpedo shield made from interlocking sheet piling was placed in front of Dry Dock 2 and the incomplete Dry Dock 3.

Enemy submarines were reported off Haleiwa Point on 8 December and another off Kaena Point on the 9 December. Meantime, destroyers patrolled offshore and repeatedly dropped depth charges on sound contacts. But it was aircraft, not submarines, that had caused the damage at Pearl and consequently AA defences were strengthened. Battleships sitting on the bottom of the harbour could still provide AA cover. *California* and *Nevada* were each ordered to organise AA defence groups of 450 men per ship to man the shipboard machine

7 DECEMBER 1941 – 'A DATE WHICH WILL LIVE IN INFAMY'

guns and 5in/25-cal. AA batteries, power for which was provided from the shore or attendant salvage vessels. *California*'s AA gunners were billeted in the lightly damaged *Maryland* whilst *Nevada*'s men bunked on the *Pennsylvania*.

Reports of air raids had everyone agitated, leading to shooting down of *Enterprise* planes trying to make a night landing on Ford Island later on the day of the attack. Many reports of groups of planes approaching Oahu were received and AA fire was frequently opened – but all contacts were non-existent, or friendly planes. But as the days after the attack passed, eventually the beleaguered military and civilian populations of Hawaii realised that the Japanese were gone.

All eight US battleships present had been damaged, with four sunk. All but the *Arizona* were later raised, although the *Oklahoma* was so badly damaged that she was never fully repaired and returned to service. The other six battleships would be repaired, modernised and returned to the war. Their big guns would wreak a terrible revenge as they carried out pre-invasion bombardments of shore positions across the Pacific, tangled with Japanese warships at Leyte and provided task-force AA cover, their armour providing crucial protection during the latter stages of the war as attacks by kamikazes intensified.

Of the battleships present, the final tally for the Pearl Harbor raid was:

1. *Arizona* (BB-39) – hit by 4 AP bombs. Exploded – destroyed. 1,177 KIA.
2. *Oklahoma* (BB-37) – hit by 5 torpedoes. Capsized. 429 KIA.
3. *West Virginia* (BB-48) – hit by 2 bombs, 7+ torpedoes. Sunk. 106 KIA. Returned to service July 1944.
4. *California* (BB-44) – hit by 2 bombs, 2 torpedoes. Sunk. 98 KIA. Returned to service January 1944.
5. *Maryland* (BB-46) – hit by 2 bombs. 4 KIA. Returned to service February 1942.
6. *Nevada* (BB-36) – hit by 6 bombs, 1 torpedo, beached. 50 KIA. Returned to service in October 1942.
7. *Pennsylvania* (BB-38) – hit in dry dock by one bomb and debris from dry-docked destroyers. 18 KIA. Undocked on 12 December – remained in service.
8. *Tennessee* (BB-43) – hit by 2 bombs. 5 KIA. Returned to service February 1942.

(V) Aftermath

The Pacific

When the last planes of the second wave of the *Kidō Butai* left the air space above Pearl Harbor – they headed south at maximum speed to hide their destination, and the location of the six carriers from US eyes. Once a safe distance away, they swung around to head north and rendezvous with the carriers. The *Kidō Butai* now began its extraction passage west to Japan, on a more direct route to the south of their insertion passage – but still well to the north of Midway and Wake.

Pearl Harbor meanwhile was a scene of devastation. *Arizona* lay a shattered wreck on the muddy seabed with her hull completely submerged and almost torn in two at her foreship by the magazine explosion. Her forward turrets and conning tower had collapsed down by some 25–30ft whilst her foremast and smokestack had collapsed forward. Fuel oil covered the water around her, fires raged and thick, black smoke billowed upwards.

Oklahoma lay capsized on her port side with the starboard side of her keel projecting above the water. She too was surrounded by burning fuel oil that billowed clouds of black smoke. There were still 436 *Oklahoma* men unaccounted for – killed or missing, many trapped inside the hull as the battleship capsized. Some had been able to find air spaces above the water level inside the ship. They tapped on the hull or called out for help. Rescue crews topside on the hull heard voices coming from below – and cut into the hull, freeing men from their steel prison many hours afterwards. One team of civilian yard workers freed a group of thirty-two *Oklahoma* sailors after cutting open the hull.

West Virginia sat on the bottom, upright, but part submerged to the main deck and burning. She had settled slowly into the water allowing most of her crew to be evacuated – but 130 of her crew were unaccounted for. Fuel leaking from the destroyed *Arizona* astern of her had engulfed *West Virginia* in flames, which were also fed by her own fuel leaking from ruptured tanks and pipes. As clouds of black smoke billowed upwards, firefighting teams would take until the following day to extinguish the fires. Tapping was also heard from inside her hull.

California, hit by two torpedoes and several bombs and near misses, was slowly settling towards the muddy seabed with a list to port. She slowly filled with water over the next three days.

Maryland had been hit by two AP bombs and hemmed in in her berth by the capsized *Oklahoma* alongside – but she had escaped serious damage and lost just four crew. *Pennsylvania* had escaped serious damage in dry dock, being hit by one bomb on the boat deck aft on the starboard side – and by debris from explosions aboard the two destroyers forward of her in the same dry dock. The damage was all superficial but eighteen of her crew, including her executive officer, had been killed. The two destroyers *Cassin* and *Downes* were total wrecks.

Tennessee had been hit by two bombs and had been trapped in her berth against her interrupted mooring quays at Ford Island by the *West Virginia*, which had taken on a dramatic 28° port list after being torpedoed. *West Virginia*'s starboard hull had risen up against the bottom edge of *Tennessee*'s port-side armour belt, which possibly stopped *West Virginia* from rolling further to port before counterflooding reduced her list. But as *West Virginia*'s port list was reduced, her starboard beam had pinned *Tennessee* against the top of the forward concrete mooring quay.

Tennessee herself was slightly down by the bow but largely undamaged – although fuel-oil fires burned in the water around her for two days. Forward of *Tennessee*, the capsized *Oklahoma* lay outboard, with the trapped *Maryland* inboard. Astern of *Tennessee*, the shattered burning remains of the *Arizona* blocked any way out. *Tennessee* would remain wedged in her berth, pushed up against the quays, until *Maryland* could be pulled free from her berth in front.

Nevada, hit by a torpedo and some six bombs, lay beached by the stern opposite Hospital Point. She was ablaze, down by the bow and well settled into the water with a 3° list to starboard.

Hard-hat divers soon began sounding the submerged hulls of the battleships to establish if any crew were left alive inside. Divers were lowered by rope 20ft beneath the surface near the bow. After banging on the hull with a hammer three times – the diver listened for any response before moving 25ft aft and repeating the process as he moved towards the stern. At the stern, the diver was lowered to the muddy seabed and the entire hull was then sounded again from stern to bow.[11]

The diver sounding procedure was repeated on both sides of each battleship – except for on the hull of *West Virginia*, where several hundred feet of her starboard shell plating was rammed hard against the hull of the *Tennessee*. No sounding had proved possible in this area when divers examined her hull on 12 December. But sadly unknown to the divers, far below the surface in a pair of unflooded compartments, some *West Virginia* sailors were in fact still alive, forlornly waiting for rescue. When the ship was finally dewatered six months later, three bodies were found in a completely dry storeroom dressed in blue uniforms with supplies of fresh water and food. One carried a wallet-size calendar, which had the days checked off from 7–23 December, when it is believed they finally ran out of air.[12]

As the fires were extinguished and the smoke cleared from the skies above Pearl Harbor Naval Base, a great clear up began. However, despite the magnitude of the disaster, damage to the naval base itself appeared relatively slight.

The Naval Base may have survived, but as the Battle Force Material Officer Captain Homer Wallin later noted: 'It seemed very doubtful whether any of the vessels which were sunk could be returned to effective service, or whether some of them could even be refloated.'[13] Over half of the battleship force was out of action.

On the day of the attack, the Fleet Maintenance Officer Commander D.H. Clark reported the condition of *Oklahoma* and *Arizona* as 'beyond repair', whilst he noted about the *Nevada*: 'Doubtful if can be refloated.

The burned-out, sunken wreck of USS *Arizona* photographed a few days after the attack. The top of the three-gun superfiring Turret 2 is visible at left. The foremast and tower have sagged forward and the superstructure is devastated. The tripod mainmast remains standing and the floatplane crane is visible at right. (*80-G-1021538 courtesy of the US Naval History & Heritage Command*)

7 DECEMBER 1941 – 'A DATE WHICH WILL LIVE IN INFAMY'

18 months to repair if floated.' The *West Virginia* was 'doubtful' with a time estimate of a year to eighteen months for repair.[14]

In his subsequent update of 9 December, the Material Officer Captain Homer Wallin commenting about both *Arizona* and *West Virginia* stated: 'So far as the ship proper is concerned, these vessels may be considered as total wrecks.' He recommended removing anything of value from them.[15]

Kidō Butai

Meanwhile, as frantic salvage and repair work began at Pearl Harbor, the *Kidō Butai* continued their extraction passage west across the Pacific towards Japan.

Out at the distant Wake Atoll outpost, far out into the Pacific, the same day as the Pearl strike, 27 Japanese Mitsubishi G3M Nel medium bombers flying from Kwajalein in the Marshall Islands, suddenly swept over the atoll and bombed it. Four days later, on 11 December 1941, as the *Kidō Butai* headed west far to the northeast of Wake, 450 Japanese Special Naval Landing Force troops made a first attempt to seize the atoll and its airfield. The escort squadron of light cruisers, destroyers, a submarine tender and armed merchantmen opened a naval bombardment at first light on 11 December at a range of just over 5 miles. The US Marines garrisoned on Wake sunk the destroyer *Hayate* with their 5in/51-cal. coastal defence guns and hit the destroyer *Yayoi*. Four Wildcat fighters then sank the destroyer *Kisaragi*. *Hayate* and *Kisaragi* were the first Japanese warships to be sunk in the war, and the strong defence put up by the Wake garrison caused the Japanese naval force to withdraw without landing. It was the first Japanese failure of the war.

Whilst the IJN South Seas landing forces was meeting such determined resistance on Wake, the *Kidō Butai* was closing Wake on its way back to Japan. On 16 December, when almost halfway between Midway Island and Wake Island but well to the north, the carriers *Sōryū* and *Hiryū* were detached from the *Kidō Butai* along with an escort of seaplane cruisers and destroyers. This powerful task group was then sent on a more southwesterly bearing to close Wake.

As the 2-carrier detachment reached a flying off position 350nm off Wake, on 21 and 22 December 1941, *Hiryū* launched 29 Val dive bombers and 18 Zero fighters whilst *Sōryū* launched 14 Vals and 9 Zeros – the last of Wake's aircraft were eliminated.

At 0235 on 23 December 1941, the second Japanese invasion attempt of Wake then began with landings by 1,500 marines after a preliminary bombardment and strikes by carrier aircraft.

The beleaguered US Marines fought on through the night and into the next morning – but by mid-afternoon they had no option but to surrender. As all US resistance on Wake ended, *Sōryū* and *Hiryū* and their escorts were free to turn and head northwest once more towards the Japanese home islands.

The other four carriers, *Akagi*, *Kaga*, *Zuikaku* and *Shōkaku*, arrived at Kure in southern Japan on 25 December 1941. *Hiryū* and *Sōryū* arrived at Kure four days later on 29 December 1941.

US Pacific Fleet
The USA declared war on Japan on 8 December 1942, the day after the Pearl Harbor attack. Japan's Axis partner Germany then declared war on the USA – which led to the USA declaring war on Germany on 11 December 1941. The USA had suddenly been plunged into a war in two oceans, the Pacific and the Atlantic.

The eight older 21-knot Standard-Type battleships at Pearl had been sunk or damaged, whilst the ninth, *Colorado*, was still undergoing a refit at Puget Sound Naval Yard. There were six heavy fast carriers capable of 33 knots in the US Fleet as war began in December 1941 – excluding the smaller *Ranger*. But they had to be split between the Atlantic and Pacific theatres – and as the attrition of 1942 wore on, US carrier numbers would get thin – and those battleships lightly damaged at Pearl were desperately needed back in fighting condition. Those that could be, would be salvaged and repaired as a matter of urgency.

In the first half of 1942, as salvage attempts got under way at Pearl, the Japanese aggressively attempted to expand their hold on the Pacific. The USA did what it could with its available ships to delay Japanese efforts until new planes, new carriers and new battleships could be built and commissioned – and the war taken back to Japan with vengeance.

Chapter 3

Salvage – Pearl Harbor

Pearl Harbor was a Naval Base not a salvage yard – and the sunk, damaged or trapped battleships were, with the exception of the beached *Nevada* and dry-docked *Pennsylvania*, still in their berths. They were not close to cranes, repair and fabrication yards and salvage infrastructure – and other than *Pennsylvania*, they weren't conveniently on blocks in dry docks. A salvage organisation would therefore have to be created from scratch to coordinate the complicated process of patching up the battleships sufficiently to allow them to be floated from their berths and moved into dry dock where more detailed – but still temporary – repair works could be carried out.

For the damaged battleships, Pearl Harbor was now an emergency repair yard – the final repairs necessary to get the battleships back in the war could only be properly carried out at the Naval Shipyards on the West Coast of the USA. The Salvage Organization would need to operate independently and let the Pearl Harbor Navy Yard get on with the vital task of keeping the remainder of the fleet operational.

The Base Force was chosen as the salvage organization, it was the obvious choice, as its tenders and repair ships carried out routine repairs and maintenance to the fleet ships. Navy Yard Pearl would be in operational, but not administrative, control of the Base Force Salvage Organization. 'It has been tentatively agreed to that the Base Force Salvage Organization will be considered, for the time being, an outside force of the Navy Yard, Pearl Harbor.'[1] The mission for the Salvage Organization was to do just what was necessary to deliver the ships the few hundred yards across the oily water of Pearl Harbor to the Navy Yard. The Salvage Organization would formally begin work on Tuesday, 9 December 1941.

Monday, 8 December 1941 – *Maryland* **is Assessed**
Tennessee, Pennsylvania and *Maryland* had only been lightly damaged and were almost ready for action. *Maryland* stood the best chance of getting back into the fight first. She was boxed in by the capsized hull of *Oklahoma* outboard of her – but it seemed she could be manoeuvred clear. But for now, salvage workers planned to repair her as much as possible where she lay, in her berth F-5. She had a bomb hole 23ft below the waterline on the port side at Frame 8, with split seams in her hull and splinter holes. A second bomb had hit on the fo'c'sle deck, wrecking anchor chains and destroying deck wiring, but otherwise the ship was undamaged – although she was 5ft down by the head.

Divers measured the submerged bomb hole the day after the attack, Monday, 8 December, and found that the bomb had detonated in a canvas and life-jacket storage area, the contents absorbing many of the fragments. But an estimated 1,000 tons of water had flooded the ship from the holes and split seams, and by intentional flooding of the forward magazines. This water could not be pumped out as hatches had been sprung by the blast – eight submersible pumps had already been burnt out in attempts. A portable caisson would be installed over the hole, to allow the flooded compartments to be pumped dry.[2] The Navy Yard sent out a party to sound the depth of the water around and forward of *Maryland* and assess how she could be towed out.

Dry Dock 1 – *Pennsylvania, Cassin* **and** *Downes*
Kimmel's flagship *Pennsylvania* was sitting on blocks in Dry Dock 1 along with the two burnt-out destroyers *Cassin* and *Downes*. *Pennsylvania* herself however was only lightly damaged from a bomb hit, by debris from explosions aboard the destroyers and by fierce fuel oil fires. The Navy Yard quickly began to refit the three propeller shafts and screws of *Pennsylvania*, previously removed for maintenance, and her lightly damaged superstructure was repaired as necessary.

Tuesday, 9 December 1941 – *California* **Continues to Flood**
Meanwhile, as immediate work began on *Pennsylvania* in Dry Dock 1, *California* continued to flood with water and settle lower. By Tuesday, 9 December, she was down by the bow and listing to port – but with some sixteen pumps running, she was still afloat for the time being. An estimated 9,500 gallons of seawater was entering her per minute, and the pumps could only remove just over 8,000 gallons per minute. She was thus taking on more than 1,000 gallons every minute, the water

searching through her innards and filling her compartments one by one.[3] With Dry Dock 1 presently occupied by *Pennsylvania* and the two burnt-out destroyers *Cassin* and *Downes*, it was quickly decided that the lightly damaged *Maryland* could wait and that *California* would be towed to Dry Dock 2 as quickly as possible – before she settled on the bottom. Dry Dock 2 had been incomplete at the time of the attack – but could be made ready within days.

California would however have to wait until emergency works could be carried out in Dry Dock 2 to the light cruiser *Helena* (CL-50), which it was believed at the time had taken a near miss that burst her plating and badly flooded her. *Helena* had lost all power, the fresh water supply for her boilers had been salted up and the evaporators were inoperative, but she was still afloat and could be moved by tugs.[4] *Helena* was given first priority into Dry Dock 2 just as soon as it could be made ready.

Nevada – Salvage Works Begin

Salvage work started on *Nevada* within days after the attack. She lay grounded with her stern on the shallows on the west side of the entrance channel. Striking between the two forward turrets, about 14ft above the ship's keel, a single torpedo had blown in the anti-torpedo blister shell plating of the hull and inner bottom. The hole in the torpedo blister was 16ft long and 27ft high. Crews went out to *Nevada*'s capsized sister ship *Oklahoma* to lift a template from the same spot on her hull to use in fabricating a wooden patch for *Nevada*. Five 550lb bombs from Val dive bombers had struck her during the second wave of the attack, since when she had continued to flood.

To prevent the enormous weight of the *Nevada* sliding her off the shelf into the deeper water of the channel, battleship anchors were sent out and fastened to the stern chains. Divers surveyed the ship and reported she was sitting on a large lava rock underneath Turret 3 on the starboard side – and that her starboard screw was in about 4ft of silt and mud.[5]

Divers cut away the jagged edges around the torpedo hole so the patch could be placed flush against the hull – finding that a significant part of the torpedo hole now lay under the muddy seabed. A dredge was called in to remove the mud – and allow divers access to measure the hole. As divers explored the hull, members of *Nevada*'s crew who knew her compartments and corridors and machinery were given a crash-course introduction to diving, before descending inside the ship to secure watertight doors, close valves and isolate oil tanks.

Wednesday, 10 December 1941 – *California* is Lightened in Preparation to Enter Dry Dock 2

As the days went by after the attack, *California* continued to settle deeper into the water. Although given priority for Dry Dock 2 after *Helena*, when it began to look unlikely that *California* could be successfully dry-docked before she touched bottom, the Navy Yard began to prepare to dry-dock *Maryland* in her place so that the hole in her bow could be patched. Meanwhile, to lighten *California* and give her a chance of being floated into dry dock, removal of usable material began.

Two days after the attack, on Tuesday evening, 9 December, when it became clear that *California* would soon be on the bottom, crew and civilians from the Navy Yard began to remove four of *California's* five port side 5in/51-cal. guns – before the water rose over them. On Wednesday morning, 10 December, increased efforts began to remove all accessible ordnance, guns, ammunition and fire-control equipment. The 5in/51-cal. guns on the upper deck were removed then the port 5in/25-cal. AA guns. The 3in/50-cal. AA guns were removed, along with the catapults, 36in battle searchlights and 12in signal searchlights, rangefinder mounts and gun directors. The *West Virginia*, which was too badly damaged for immediate salvage, was receiving similar attention.

Despite the sixteen pumps running, *California* was still inexorably filling up with an estimated 72,000 gallons per hour and as the water altered her trim, she listed. Her eight 8in Manila mooring lines went taught, the strain snapping a mooring bollard on the quay and part of a quarter deck chock.[6] Lines parted all day Tuesday, 9 December and Wednesday, 10 December – and to prevent her from capsizing, tugs were called to push her gently against the quay so additional cables could be run.

Dry Dock 2 may have been incomplete at the time of the Japanese attack, but within days it had been made ready. On Wednesday, 10 December, tugs were able to ease the light cruiser *Helena* away from her berth at Ten-Ten Dock and manoeuvre her into Dry Dock 2. The water was drained from the dock and work began immediately to patch her and get her seaworthy. She was wanted out of the dry dock as quickly as possible and on her way east to the West Coast of the USA for permanent repair.

10 December 1941 – *Maryland* is Freed, Whilst *California* Settles on the Bottom

At noon on 10 December, the same day *Helena* entered Dry Dock 2, *Maryland* was eased forward beyond the capsized hull of *Oklahoma* and taken over to the Navy Yard. That afternoon, a dredge came alongside *California*'s starboard side and removed an anchor chain, dropping the anchor to the seabed below. The *California*'s crew ran the chain around Turret 1 and then secured it to the forward quay. As more wires parted, only the anchor chain eventually held the bow in place, the stern continuing to pivot out a few inches at a time.[7]

By 1600 on Wednesday, 10 December, it was believed that *California* was now on the bottom – but the yielding soft silty seabed couldn't support her weight and she continued to settle into the muddy seabed. Water entering the hull through the torpedo holes now carried mud and fuel oil into the ship at third-deck level. Later in the day, the quarter deck was abandoned as water came up over the gunwales to swirl around the after turrets. As the main-deck catapult and stern crane began to submerge, pumping was called off.

Throughout the night *California* continued to sink further into the mud. Turret 4 disappeared altogether with only the three 14in barrels visible, elevated and trained to starboard as during the attack. The deck catapult disappeared.

Finally, during the night of 10 and 11 December, the ship came to a halt, with a port list of 5.5° and her hull settled some 16–17ft into the muddy seabed. Nearly all the fo'c'sle was submerged, with the port side 5ft underwater and only the higher starboard gunwale of the fo'c'sle deck dry. The port side of her quarter deck was 17ft underwater whilst the starboard side was 7.5ft underwater.

Tennessee – Removal of Quay

Once *Maryland* was moved clear at noon on 10 December, the way was now open to get the lightly damaged *Tennessee* out of her berth, astern of *Maryland*'s berth. But *Tennessee*'s starboard side between her two forward main-battery turrets was wedged hard against the forward interrupted mooring quay at her Berth F-6. To move *Tennessee*, either the *West Virginia* on her port side would have to be pulled outboard – or the concrete F-6 mooring quay on *Tennessee*'s starboard side would have to be removed. *West Virginia* had taken three torpedo hits, flooded and settled on the bottom of the harbour with her decks awash. She wasn't going anywhere quickly – so removal of *Tennessee*'s F-6 mooring quay was the obvious way to get her out. The order was quickly given.

Tennessee had been hit by two bombs, which had done relatively little damage. A fragment of one bomb had hit the centre gun of the superfiring forward Turret 2, whilst the second bomb had hit the starboard yard of the mainmast, smashing the catapult atop Turret 3 before penetrating the roof of Turret 3 and breaking apart without detonating. The port gun was knocked out of commission by the fragmenting bomb whilst a small fire was started.[8] The worst damage however was caused by burning debris from the devastated *Arizona*, which had started fires on *Tennessee*'s wooden deck abaft Turret 4, and by burning oil on the water that had cracked and warped hull plating on both port and starboard sides of *Tennessee*'s hull as far as Turret 3, the red-hot hull prompting crew to flood three magazines lest they ignite.[9]

However, if any Japanese ships appeared on the horizon, all bar one of the ship's six forward main-battery guns were able to fire, whilst five of the six after turret guns were also able to fire. Officers looked to the sinking *California* for replacement parts for the two inoperable guns. Once the fires aboard *Tennessee* had been extinguished, she was ready for action – except that she could not move until the quay was removed.

12 December 1941 – *Pennsylvania* Leaves Dry Dock No. 1
With her propellers reinstalled, Kimmel's flagship *Pennsylvania*, in Dry Dock 1, was refloated and un-docked on 12 December 1941. With only light damage from the attack, she was immediately ready for action. By Sunday, 14 December 1941, just one week after the attack, stores and provisions were being loaded back aboard *Pennsylvania* – as her crew got her ready for sea.

16 December 1941 – *Tennessee* is Freed
Blasting to remove the forward mooring quay at F-6 was completed by 16 December 1941, when *Tennessee* was pulled slowly out of her berth, forward past *West Virginia* alongside. She moved through *Maryland*'s now empty berth, passing alongside and inboard of the capsized *Oklahoma* before being moved across to the Navy Yard for repairs to begin. The heat from fierce fires had warped some of her hull plates, damaging seams and loosening rivets, all of which needed to be repaired to make her hull watertight before she could get underway for permanent repairs. A patch cover was fitted to the roof of Turret 3.

Tennessee, *Pennsylvania* and *Maryland* Ready for Action
The Battle Force may have been crippled on 7 December, but within a week, by 16 December 1941, the big guns and AA weaponry of the lightly damaged *Tennessee*, *Pennsylvania* and *Maryland* were now all nearly ready for action, should another strike by Japanese fast carrier planes roar over Oahu, or should enemy warships appear off the coast.

California and *West Virginia*

California and *West Virginia* had both been too badly damaged for immediate salvage. With *California* now sitting on the bottom of Pearl Harbor, men began to strip what they could from these two battleships – removal of *California*'s main-battery guns would take about 2,000 tons of weight off the ship. Guns would also be removed from *West Virginia* – and the guns from both ships would be allocated for island defence ashore or to replace those damaged on other ships.

On Friday, 12 December, one of the 5in/25-cal. guns removed from *West Virginia*'s undamaged starboard side was lifted aboard *Pennsylvania* and installed to replace one with a damaged barrel. Of the other seven of her battery of eight 5in/25-cal. guns, four were set up as a shore battery at West Loch in Pearl Harbor, one went to the heavy cruiser *Chicago* (CA-29), two went to the heavy cruiser *Salt Lake City* (CA-25) whilst a range keeper went to *Maryland*. A 5in/51-cal. gun was removed from *West Virginia* and taken aboard *Pennsylvania* to replace one damaged by the bomb hit near the galley. Six were turned over to the army to use in defence of Oahu. A pair of machine guns went to *Tennessee*.

20 December 1941 – *Pennsylvania*, *Tennessee* and *Maryland* Go to Sea

On Saturday, 20 December 1941, less than two weeks after the attack, a simple message came at 1548 from the signal tower: '*Maryland* under way'. The great battleship slowly made her way out of Southeast Loch, followed 12 minutes later by *Tennessee*. Less than half an hour later, *Pennsylvania* made her way out of the Navy Yard and headed for sea, having completed repairs the day before.

Four destroyers escorted the three battleships east to navy yards on the West Coast of the USA. *Pennsylvania* arrived in San Francisco Bay on 29 December 1941 and headed north to Mare Island, whilst *Tennessee* and *Maryland* headed up the West Coast to Puget Sound. Once repairs were completed, the three battleships would return to the fleet to defend the West Coast of the USA from attack.

20 December 1941 – *West Virginia*

Meanwhile, *West Virginia* was sitting on the bottom of Pearl Harbor with the water level almost up to her main deck. No one yet knew how badly she was damaged below the waterline. And as the three temporarily repaired battleships *Pennsylvania*, *Tennessee* and *Maryland* left Pearl Harbor that Saturday afternoon, 20 December 1941, divers planned a survey of the damage to *West Virginia*'s port side. The *West*

Virginia executive officer had reported three rapid heavy shocks during the attack, which were presumably three torpedo hits – before he was thrown to the ground by another explosion, which could have been either a fourth torpedo or a bomb. There was possibly a fifth torpedo hit – as well as hits from several bombs.

30 December 1941 – *West Virginia* Underwater Examination
On 30 December, from a float tied up near Frame 46, abreast Turret 2, divers began the underwater exploration of the port side of *West Virginia*. Another float was moored 220ft aft, at Frame 102 just forward of Turret 3. These two fixed datum floats would allow investigation of the 220ft span between them, the site of the likely foremost and aftmost torpedo damage.

Five dives were made directly under the forward float on the first day. As they descended, in very poor underwater visibility, the divers began initially to explore a little forward from the hole at Frame 46 float. Finding no damage, they began to move aft.

Between Frames 46 and 52, the divers found a split in the hull, just above the bilge, that was about 2ft wide and 10ft high – well below the bottom edge of the vertical armour belt. They also located several small ruptures, which had their edges bent outwards, as though from internal explosions.

Working their way further aft, during four to five dives a day, they located a number of smaller holes before finding a large hole 25ft long and 17ft high – roughly between the two smokestacks, far above. The bottom edge of the hole was about 37ft below the main deck and was pushed inwards – this was the likely impact point of the torpedo.[10]

The divers continued working their way aft – and an 8ft x 4ft hole was located at Frame 92, roughly under the mainmast. Plumb lines were rigged at each of the holes to allow for easy return to make further detailed measurements.[11]

As a result of the survey dives, the destruction on her port side, though bad, was less than had been assumed in the immediate aftermath of the attack. The battleship could be 'floated in a reasonable length of time by patching and dewatering'.[12]

Divers began to seal up the smaller holes in her hull, whilst salvage workers began to design and fabricate patches for the two large torpedo holes on *West Virginia*'s port side. Topside, other workers began clearing the ship to reduce the fire hazard by cleaning up the oily trash and getting it off the ship. By the last day of December 1941, some 50 tons of debris and damaged equipment had been assembled in piles to await removal.

Now that the ship had been cleared up, work could begin to lighten her for dewatering. On 20 December, orders went out from the Navy Yard to the Salvage Organization, that once *California*'s main battery had been removed, the eight main-battery 16in guns on *West Virginia* were to be removed – along with both masts, both smokestacks, cranes and catapults. Parts of damaged superstructure were removed whilst stanchions and lifelines were removed from the quarter deck and fo'c'sle and lifeboat cradles, davits and skids were removed. Doors and hatches were removed where possible along with 150 fathoms of anchor chain.

1 January 1942 – *Nevada* Begins to be Patched

The 'big patch' for *Nevada*'s port-side torpedo damage, being fabricated using a template from *Oklahoma*'s hull, took weeks to construct. In the interim, small patches were placed on the fragment holes in the hull. On New Year's Day 1942, a 10ft x 12ft patch was placed over the rupture in the starboard side and the first of the large salvage pumps was hoisted aboard *Nevada* and tested.

On 3 January 1942, the salvage crew rigged 17ft slings and shackles on A-frames to receive the 'big patch' – which arrived alongside *Nevada* at 0900 on 8 January 1942.

7 January 1942 – *Nevada* Begins to be Dewatered

Pumping out of *Nevada* began on 7 January 1942 – and by the first night, the water level had been reduced by 9in. This lowering of the water level allowed a start to be made on clearing out compartments on the main deck. By 12 January, *Nevada* had been dewatered down to the second deck, the crews working methodically through each compartment and deck to clean the ship. Salt water, heated by a boiler on deck, was used to wash the spaces and passageways clean of mud and oil, the sludge being skimmed up and removed. Men wiped down her innards with rags, washing bulkheads and decks.

By 14 January, the forward end of the 'big patch' was nearly in place with the aft end 7ft out from the hull. Tough coral was blocking the bottom of the patch being seated and had to be chipped away with pneumatic hammers and wedges by divers working in shifts.

By 23 January 1942, as divers continued to remove coral beneath the bilge keel, two 10in pumps were installed on the second deck forward, which was now dry. Five days later, pumping of the third deck began. A careful plan had been conceived for dewatering the ship, fore to aft, deck by deck, except for the flooded area between Frames 20 and 48 to ensure a safe head of water on the patch.

7 February 1942 – *Nevada* Salvage Fatalities

On 7 February 1942, a lieutenant in a trunk at first platform level unscrewed the air test cap at a doorway – and as water squirted out, he suddenly collapsed. A machinist rushed to his aid – and he also collapsed, falling into the water and dying. More men rushed over to help and another four collapsed almost immediately. The four were taken to the Naval Hospital and recovered, but the lieutenant who had first unscrewed the air test cap later died at the hospital. The cause of the two deaths was hydrogen sulfide, which presents with a rotten-egg sewer smell and is caused by rotting and disintegrating organic material within the confines of the hull. It had been noticed previously as ever-present during the dewatering – but dissipated quickly as it rose. But in these lower compartments, under pressure, the gas was odourless – it was lethal, and able to kill in minutes. Blowers and ventilation pipes had soon been installed deep into the *Nevada*'s innards to draw in fresh air and expel contaminated air.

13 February 1942 – *Nevada* is Afloat and Enters Dry Dock on 18 February 1942

At 1300 on 13 February 1942, *Nevada* lifted off the bottom and was once again afloat. As she continued to be dewatered, her 14in powder could now be unloaded to ammunition lighters from her magazines low down in the ship.

By 17 February 1942, *Nevada* had been sufficiently dewatered to allow lines to be run out from tugs to her stern, above the shallows. The battleship was now towed out to deeper water in the channel.

Early on the morning of 18 February, tugs came alongside the battleship. Her cables were slipped, and the tugs pushed *Nevada* across the entrance channel towards the Navy Yard, the pumps still running to keep pace with leaks of buoyancy. The lightened ship now drew 31ft aft – but almost 42ft forward. Ballast tanks aft were flooded to bring the deeper bow up – and she was able to pass over the sill of Dry Dock 2 just before 1000.

Once in dry dock, temporary repairs were completed to make her seaworthy. She was then undocked and sent east to Puget Sound Navy Yard where she would undergo repairs and modernization that would take until October 1942 to complete.

20 February 1942 – *Pennsylvania* Sorties

Repairs to *Pennsylvania* at Hunter's Point, San Francisco, were completed on 12 January 1942 and *Pennsylvania* was able to leave San Francisco Bay on 20 February 1942 and begin gunnery training and manoeuvres off the coast of California. During her time in San Francisco, her AA battery was considerably strengthened with the addition of ten Bofors 40mm quad-mount cannons and fifty-one rapid-fire Oerlikon 20mm single mounts. To improve fields of fire for the AA guns, the tripod mainmast was removed, with the stump replaced by a deckhouse above which the aft main-battery director cupola was housed. One of the new CXAM-1 radars was installed above the cupola.

The older 5in/51-cal. secondary battery casemate guns and the 5in/25-cal. AA guns were replaced with modern 5in/38-cal. Dual Purpose guns in eight twin-turret mounts. The new 5in/38-cal. DP guns could elevate to 85° and fire at a rate of one round every 4 seconds.

Tennessee and *Maryland* were also repaired and modernised, at Puget Sound Naval Yard. The portions of *Tennessee*'s fire-damaged hull plating and electrical wiring were replaced, and her lattice mainmast was replaced with a small tower. In place of her .50-cal. machine guns, she received a battery of sixteen 1.1in guns in quadruple mounts and fourteen 20mm Oerlikon autocannon. New Mark 11 versions of her 14in guns replaced the old Mark 4 barrels.

25 February 1942 – *Tennessee* and *Maryland* Sortie

With repair and modernisation works to *Tennessee* and *Maryland* now completed, *Tennessee* sortied on 25 February 1942 to be shortly joined by *Maryland* and the newly refitted battleship *Colorado*, the ninth battleship that had escaped damage at Pearl whilst undergoing a refit at Puget Sound Navy Yard.

Pennsylvania, Tennessee and *Maryland* Join Task Force 1

The three repaired and refitted battleships, *Tennessee, Maryland* and *Colorado*, moved to San Francisco, where they undertook a series of shakedown exercises and cruises to West-Coast ports as they made ready to join TF 1, the West Coast Patrol Force commanded by Vice Admiral William S. Pye, Commander Battle Force (COMBATFOR), which comprised the battleships *Mississippi*, *New Mexico* and *Idaho* and escorts. It was still only a few months since the Japanese raid had devastated the US Pacific Fleet at Pearl Harbor – but already the powerful West Coast Patrol Force fielded the seven battleships, *New Mexico, Idaho, Mississippi, Tennessee, Maryland, Colorado* and *Pennsylvania*, and was supported by the thirty plane escort carrier *Long Island* (CVE-1) and a screen of destroyers. The ships of TF 1 began a series of training manoeuvres that lasted for several months to prepare for the coming campaigns in the Central Pacific.

25 March 1942 – *California* **Afloat**
Meantime, back in Pearl, salvage workers had been continuing to clear up and lighten the *California*, which was fully submerged to main deck level and partially underwater at the upper deck. Her hull was patched – and wooden cofferdams fitted around her deck edges to bring the ship's effective waterline above the water. Pumping then began to dewater the ship – and she was finally refloated on 25 March 1942. But work was set back on 5 April 1942, when an accidental explosion of hydrogen sulfide gas, possibly mixed with fuel-oil vapour, dislodged a hull patch and watertight doors, leading to partial reflooding. The hull had to be laboriously repatched and pumped out again but on 9 April 1942, *California* was manoeuvred into Dry Dock 2.

After completing temporary repairs, she was undocked on 9 June 1942, and on 10 October 1942, she was able to head to sea to rendezvous with her destroyer escort for the passage east to Puget Sound for permanent repairs and modernisation.

17 May 1942 – *West Virginia* **Afloat**
Once *West Virginia* had been cleared up, lightened and her hull made watertight, dewatering began and she was refloated on 17 May 1942 and manoeuvred by tugs into Dry Dock No. 1 on 9 June 1942.

At the time of the attack, it had been thought that she had been hit by five aerial torpedoes, whilst a sixth impact had been discovered during the temporary patching. The inspection of her hull in dry dock revealed damage from a seventh torpedo hit. Six of them had run quite shallow, the deepest only 11ft beneath the surface, whilst the seventh was 19ft down and struck her aft, nearly destroying her steering gear. The shallow runners struck on or even above her belt armour and so were relatively ineffective with armour damage being minimal. But the compression wave had pushed in the shell plating below the belt so far that it had split. The inner torpedo bulkhead was dished in and torn loose at its lower edge – and this had allowed water to flood the fire rooms and cause the ship to list. The list had led to two torpedoes striking the upper part of the side of the ship, leading to extensive flooding across and down through the second and third decks.

In dry dock, as shipyard workers began temporary repairs to make the ship seaworthy, they discovered the remains of between sixty-six and seventy men who had been trapped below decks as she sank. Some of these men had survived for several days in air pockets with emergency rations and fresh water, but the air and supplies had run out long before the ship was refloated. Three bodies were found in a dry compartment, having survived for sixteen days.

After completing temporary repairs in dry dock, *West Virginia* was undocked and got underway for the Puget Sound Navy Yard, Washington for a thorough reconstruction.

Modernisation of the OBBS

Almost immediately after the attack, the navy began to consider the extent to which the heavily damaged old First World War-era battleships such as *West Virginia* and *California* could be modernised. They had been constructed in the dreadnought era – before the advent of the aerial torpedo – when the main threat to capital ships was the big guns of other capital ships. The older style of dreadnought did not have the extensive subdivision and internal watertight compartmentalisation that newer battleships had and was vulnerable to torpedo attack. This had been starkly demonstrated when HMS *Royal Oak*, commissioned in 1916, had been attacked on 14 October 1939 in the British naval base at Scapa Flow in the Orkney Islands by the German submarine *U-47*. *Royal Oak* had been hit by 4 torpedoes – and had capsized and sunk within some 15 minutes with the loss of 837 crew – most of whom were trapped below decks and struggling to get out of the few openings to deck as the ship went over.

Contrast this rapid sinking of a dreadnought-era battleship to torpedo strikes, with the brand-new battleship HMS *Prince of Wales*, commissioned in 1941, which was attacked by eighty-seven Japanese level and torpedo bombers off the east coast of Malaya, 200 miles north of Singapore, on 10 December 1941, just days after the Pearl Harbor raid. Despite being hit by four Japanese aerial torpedoes, the extensive compartmentalisation of this modern battleship meant she took some 100 minutes to sink and most of her crew were able to abandon ship safely, the wounded being placed in boats that were gently floated off her deck as she settled slowly into the waters of the South China Sea.

As *West Virginia* and *California* had both been badly damaged and could not be quickly returned to service like the other battleships, to improve underwater protection, they would have the anti-torpedo bulges fitted that had been planned before the war but not installed. The additional buoyancy of the bulges would offset the loss of freeboard incurred by the addition of 1,400 tons of additional deck armour against bombing and falling shot. Proposals were considered to replace the lattice masts of the US battleships with other structures that could accommodate the heavier radar equipment now being fitted to the fleet's ships.

The limited number of dry docks on the West Coast however limited the pace of reconstruction, and *West Virginia* had to wait until *Tennessee* and *California* were rebuilt; work on *West Virginia* would not complete until September 1944.

Operations in Relation to the Battle of Midway, 4–7 June 1942
In the immediate aftermath of the Battle of Midway, on 5 June 1942, Vice Admiral Pye deployed TF 1 to defend against a possible incursion by the heavy capital ships of the Japanese fleet. TF 1 took up a position some 1,200nm west of San Francisco – but when the anticipated Japanese naval attack had not materialised by 14 June 1942, Pye was able to take TF 1 back to San Francisco.

By May 1942, as the three hastily repaired veteran battleships of the Pearl Harbor raid, *Pennsylvania*, *Maryland* and *Tennessee*, returned to active duty, the Japanese expansion had reached Guadalcanal in the Solomon Islands, east of Papua New Guinea and northeast of Australia and the Coral Sea. But now that the US fast carriers had successfully stopped the Japanese advance at the Battle of Midway, the course of the war had changed. The Allies were no longer on the defensive and were able to consider a limited offensive. The situation however became critical when in early July 1942, US reconnaissance revealed that the Japanese had begun construction of a strategic airfield on Guadalcanal. This Japanese airbase lay only 555 miles from the large island of Espiritu Santo, in Vanuatu, which the Allies had occupied a few months before in March 1942, and which was being developed into a major Allied supply and support base. An airbase on Guadalcanal would give Japan air superiority over the proposed Allied areas of operation – and also threaten the sea lines of communication from the West Coast of the USA to the east coast of Australia. Admiral Ernest King, Chief of Naval Operations (CNO) announced an accelerated timetable for the first Allied land offensive of the Pacific War, Operation WATCHTOWER, the Guadalcanal campaign. It would begin in just three weeks' time at the start of August.

Following the crushing Japanese loss of four fleet carriers at Midway, there was no longer a significant naval threat to the West Coast of the USA – and there was no need to keep the old battleships of the West Coast Patrol Force on the West Coast. They were powerful fighting weapons and as the US posture in the Pacific War morphed from defending against the Japanese onslaught – to the opening of the first Allied offensive campaign at Guadalcanal, the ships of TF 1 would be redeployed to the forward base at Pearl Harbor for the first time since the raid of 7 December 1941. As the commencement of the Guadalcanal campaign neared, on 1 August 1942, elements of the former TF 1 departed the West Coast of the USA for Pearl Harbor.

As the veteran battleships of the Pearl Harbor attack, *Pennsylvania*, *Tennessee* and *Maryland*, reached and entered Pearl Harbor Naval Base on 14 August 1942, it was the first time that the three battleships had been back at Pearl since the Japanese attack the year before on 7 December 1941. It must have been a moving spectacle for those ashore to behold the great fighting ships re-entering the harbour as the crews of the three returning battleships eagerly scanned their old home.

So much had changed since the three battleships had left Pearl for the West Coast on 20 December 1941. *Nevada* had been refloated from the channel and was now back on the West Coast of the USA for repair and modernisation, *California* had been refloated on 9 June – but was still present at Pearl undergoing repairs before she too could be sent back to the West Coast for permanent repair. *West Virginia* remained under repair in Dry Dock 1. *Oklahoma* still lay capsized in her berth along Ford Island, with plans to parbuckle and right her being formulated. *Arizona* lay mostly submerged, destroyed where she had exploded and sunk at her berth during the attack.

Notwithstanding that the old battleships of TF 1 had now been forward deployed to Pearl Harbor, the Commander-in-Chief of the Pacific Fleet Admiral Chester Nimitz (CINCPAC-CINCPOA) chose not to deploy the old battleships to the Guadalcanal campaign – owing to their heavy use of fuel oil. At this time in the war, the Pacific Fleet had just seven available tankers, too few to operate both the fast carriers and Pye's old battleships.

Thus, as the Guadalcanal campaign began, there was a pause in operations for the old battleships at Pearl that allowed *Tennessee* to be sent back east to Puget Sound for reconstruction. Her heavily damaged sister *California* was slated to be shortly sent to Puget Sound on 10 October 1942 to be rebuilt and modernised – and the navy decided that *Tennessee* should be similarly modernised. The work on *Tennessee* would last nearly a year and would see the ship radically altered. The more heavily damaged *California* would be out of the war undergoing her refit from 20 October 1942 for some fifteen months until 31 January 1944.

The threat posed to battleships by torpedoes fired from submarines or aircraft was by now fully realised. In addition to the torpedoing of British battleship HMS *Royal Oak* at Scapa Flow on 14 October 1939, the Italian Regia Marina battle fleet had lost almost half its capital ships in one night on 11/12 November 1940 when attacked at Taranto harbour by twenty-one Fairey Swordfish biplane torpedo bombers from the British carrier HMS *Illustrious*. On 26 May 1941, Swordfish torpedo bombers from the carrier HMS *Ark Royal* played an important role in disabling the German superbattleship *Bismarck* in the Atlantic following the Battle of the Denmark Strait. Although it may have been the British battleships that delivered the *coup de grâce* with their big guns and torpedoes, the vulnerability of a modern super battleship to an aerial torpedo delivered by a slow British bi-plane torpedo bomber had been exposed. Then on 10 December 1941, *Prince of Wales* and the reconstructed First World War-era battlecruiser HMS *Repulse* had been bombed, torpedoed and sunk in one action in the South China. The torpedo damage to the US battleships at Pearl had by now also been carefully studied as salvage and repair took place.

The underwater protection schemes on the US battleships would therefore be improved before they returned to service. New antitorpedo bulges would be installed on *California* and *Tennessee* and internal compartmentalization improved. Superstructures would be completely revised, with the old First World War-era heavily armoured conning towers being removed and a smaller tower erected in its place to reduce interference with the fields of fire of AA guns. Horizontal protection would be considerably strengthened to improve resistance to air attack; 3in of special treatment steel (STS) would be added to the deck over the magazines and 2in STS elsewhere.

The ships' weapons suites would also be overhauled with new firecontrol systems installed for main and secondary batteries. The mixed battery of 5in/51-cal. and 5in/25-cal. guns would be replaced by a uniform battery of sixteen modern 5in/38-cal. DP guns in eight twin mounts that were controlled by four Mk 37 directors. The light AA battery was altered to ten quadruple 40mm Bofors guns and forty-three 20mm Oerlikon rapid-fire autocannons.

The free-swinging Oerlikon 20mm cannon was fitted in a flexible mount and was manually aimed by a gunner. The Oerlikon began to be installed aboard US Navy ships from 1942 onwards to replace the Browning M2 machine gun, which had limited range and stopping power. The Oerlikon became an iconic sight aboard naval vessels during the Second World War, and in its role as an AA gun it provided effective dense fire at around 300 rounds per minute (rpm) at short ranges of up to 1 mile, at which range heavier guns had difficulty tracking targets. Many versions of it are still in use by navies around the world today.

SALVAGE – PEARL HARBOR

But as the war progressed, and as ranges to attacking aircraft increased and the Japanese turned to night attacks, it was found that the Oerlikon performed poorly in comparison with the 40mm Bofors autocannon. The powerful and effective 40mm Bofors autocannon were controlled by Mark 51 optical directors with integrated gyro gun-sight lead-angle indicators. The Bofors could knock down an enemy aircraft at long range, before it could release its weapon, whereas the Oerlikon could only knock down an aircraft when it was a lot closer and had possibly released its weapon. There was a saying in the US Navy at the time that when the 20mm Oerlikons opened fire, it was time to hit the deck. The Oerlikon was largely abandoned later in the war due its lack of stopping power against heavy Japanese aircraft and kamikaze attacks.

After *Nevada*'s repair was completed in October 1942, she sailed for Alaskan waters where she provided fire support from 11–18 May 1943 for Operation LANDCRAB to recapture the Aleutian island of Attu, seized by Japan at the beginning of the war.

In mid-1943, *Nevada* then went on Atlantic convoy duty before being chosen as Rear Admiral Morton Deyo's flagship for the Normandy Invasion, where she would bombard shore positions in support of the landing forces on D-Day.

With her reconstruction and modernisation completed, *Tennessee* returned to service on 7 May 1943 and on 22 May 1943 departed for San Pedro to rejoin the fleet. *Maryland* was forward deployed with *Colorado* in early November to Fiji whilst *Pennsylvania* remained at Pearl Harbor. *California* would be ready for service by 31 January 1944.

The heavily damaged *West Virginia* took until September 1944 for her repair and modernisation work to be completed. Like *Tennessee* and *California*, she too had new torpedo bulges added, along with a new superstructure in place of the old heavy conning tower. With new weapons and new fire control, she would go on to serve in the Philippines campaign and take part in operations from the Battle of Leyte until the surrender of Japan on 2 September 1945.

After *Oklahoma* had been parbuckled and righted, she was towed into Dry Dock 2 at Pearl Harbor on 28 December 1943. Once she was on blocks and with the water drained away, it, was found that she had been too badly damaged to be repaired and returned to service. She was stripped of her main guns, machinery, ammunition and stores and made watertight to be moved to the mainland of the USA where she was subsequently decommissioned on 1 September 1944.

The devastated *Arizona* had been so badly damaged by the magazine explosion that she did not merit salvage. She was left to rest where she lay on the bottom of Pearl Harbor. Her surviving superstructure was removed in 1942 and most of her main-battery guns were subsequently salved and installed ashore as coastal defence batteries on Hawaii.

Of the eight Pacific Fleet battleships sunk or damaged at Pearl Harbor on 7 December 1941, six would return to service to wreak their revenge: *California, Maryland, Nevada, Pennsylvania, Tennessee* and *West Virginia*.

For *Oklahoma* and *Arizona*, there would be no revenge.

Chapter 4

The US Standard-Type Battleship

By the time of the *Kidō Butai* raid on Pearl Harbor on 7 December 1941, the US Navy had seventeen battleships – but with both Germany and Japan threatening to bring the USA into the war on two fronts, the battleships had been of necessity split between the Atlantic and Pacific theatres.

Nine of the seventeen battleships were stationed at Pearl Harbor – although only eight battleships would be actually present when the Japanese attacked, as *Colorado* was undergoing overhaul at Puget Sound Navy Yard. All eight US battleships present at Pearl were hit – with four sunk and the other four damaged, with one beached.

The US battleships damaged or sunk at Pearl were all older battleships, broadly constructed to a standard design in the dreadnought era during or just after the First World War. Between 1912 and 1917, the US Navy produced twelve battleships of five classes that had broadly similar characteristics – the design concept coming to be known as the *Standard Type*.

The Standard-Type battleship used oil fuel, was protected by 'all-or-nothing' armour with main-battery weapons in four two- or three-gun turrets, set in two superfiring pairs, one pair in front of the superstructure and one pair abaft. Although each of the succeeding Standard-Type classes incorporated a series of improvements on the preceding class, the battleships were sufficiently similar that they could operate as a homogenous whole in the line of battle.

The Standard-Type battleships had been modernised and refitted to varying extents in the inter-war years – but by the Second World War they were all already twenty to twenty-five years old and only capable of making the standard First World War-era battleship speed of 21 knots. The new breeds of fast aircraft carriers could make 33 knots and after a twenty-year gap in US battleship building, six months before the Pearl Harbor raid, the first modern fast US battleships entered the fleet: the two 28-knot North Carolina-class units *North Carolina* (BB-55) and *Washington* (BB-56) in April and May 1941 respectively.

US battleships were given the ship designation 'BB' – and as the new fast battleships began to appear, the old 21-knot First World War-era Standard-Type battleships came to be talked about in the navy as the 'old battleships', or OBBS. Initially almost dismissed as being too old, slow and of little use, the 'old battleships' of Rear (later Vice) Admiral Jesse B. Oldendorf's Fire Support Groups would go on to provide vital and effective support for many operations in the Pacific – most notably, forming line of battle at the Battle of the Surigao Strait in the Philippines in October 1944 when they crossed the T of the Japanese battle line in the last clash of battleships in history.

The first Standard-Type battleships were the two revolutionary 25,500-ton Nevada-class Battleship 1912 units, *Nevada* (BB-36) and *Oklahoma* (BB-37) – ordered in March 1911. These units set the pattern for the Standard Type by moving to ten 14in/45-cal. main-battery guns in four turrets. They were the first to use the triple turret – and introduced the single-sleeve turret – where all guns could elevate together. The ten guns were arranged in two pairs of superfiring turrets fore and aft of the superstructure, with a two-gun turret superfiring above a lower triple turret.

The Nevadas introduced the 'all-or-nothing' armour protection scheme. Battleships had traditionally protected their most important and vulnerable parts from enemy shellfire, underwater mines and torpedoes inside an armoured box called the citadel, which ran from just in front of the forward gun turrets all the way back to abaft the after turrets. Along either side of the citadel, on either side of the ship at the waterline, ran the main waterline vertical armour belt of which, about one half of the vertical belt was below the waterline. The floor of the citadel was the double bottom of the ship itself – buried deep in the water.

In older dreadnoughts, above the heavy waterline belt, was another medium thickness belt designed to prevent light and medium calibre shells penetrating the casemate secondary batteries ranged along either beam. Forward of the citadel, thinner medium armour protected the bow whilst aft above the steering gear, the armour thickened again to medium thickness.

The continuing advances of larger calibre guns with greater muzzle velocities and greater range led to the phenomenon of plunging fire, or falling shot, and demanded significant improvement in armour protection. It was believed that at very long ranges, ships would be attacked primarily with Armour-Piercing (AP) shells – since hits could be anywhere on the ship and High-Explosive (HE) shells would be ineffective against belt or deck armour. Thus, to survive against the heaviest AP shells, only the heaviest armour should be used.[1]

The whole ship however could not have the heaviest armour, so to save weight, the large areas of relatively light armour outwith the citadel used in earlier battleship designs were dispensed with in the Nevadas. The most vital life critical areas of the ship, the ammunition and propellant magazines, the propulsion machinery, fire-control and command and communications sections would be protected within the armoured citadel by armour thick enough to resist the heaviest shells. The non-vital areas such as crew berthing, stores and offices, where a hit would not be critical to the ship's survivability, would be outwith the citadel and not be protected. The unarmoured parts of the ship would not offer resistance to AP shells to trigger their firing mechanisms, which were designed to explode after penetrating armour – an AP shell might pass right through the unarmoured parts of the ship without exploding. Armour was used at its greatest possible thickness – or not at all – and this concept allowed 'all-or-nothing' ships to have thicker armour covering a smaller portion of the hull.

Changes in deck armour were also made to protect from the developing phenomenon of plunging fire. A total of 4.5–5in of deck armour was provided throughout the citadel – and the additional weight was minimised by reducing the armoured length of the ship, by introducing triple main-battery turrets that allowed a reduction in the number of turrets to four from the awkward five and six turret arrangements of the previous two classes.

The Nevada-class Standard-Type battleships displaced some 27,500 tons (S) and 28,400 tons (F) and were 583ft long (oa) with a beam of some 95ft 2.5in and a draft of 27ft 7.6in. The adoption of oil fuel enabled overall length to be shortened. The vertical waterline armour belt along either side of the citadel was 13.5in thick but tapered to 8in thick at the lower edge. Turret face armour was 18in thick on the triple turrets and 16in on the superfiring twin turrets.

The *Nevada* and *Oklahoma* were commissioned in early 1916 and set a new standard for armament, armour and propulsion. The Standard-Type design concept produced ships of a 21-knot maximum speed with roughly a 700yd tactical diameter at that speed and an operating endurance of 8,000nm at 10 knots. This made the Standard Type compatible with the earlier Wyoming and New York classes – and gave the interwar US battle line broadly homogenous handling characteristics, in stark contrast to the battle lines of Britain and Japan, whose ships had varying speeds from 23 to 31 knots. Whilst tactically coherent, the US battle line however ended up being several knots slower than Britain or Japan, whose fleets nevertheless were hobbled by the speed of their slower ships. The sacrifice of speed was a tactical decision of little consequence in the First World War when the Standard-Type battleships were designed – but with the subsequent advent of the fast aircraft carrier capable of 33 knots, by the Second World War, the 'old' Standard-Type battleships were unsuitable as carrier escorts – when high speed became of value for battleships.

The second Standard-Type battleship design produced the two Pennsylvania-class units – *Pennsylvania* (BB-38) and *Arizona* (BB-39), sometimes referred to as Battleship 1913 and Battleship 1914. The Pennsylvania class would move from the *two triple* and *two dual* mount turrets of the Nevada class, to *four triple* single-sleeve turrets that gave a total of twelve 14in/45-cal. main-battery guns. Whilst the Nevada-class units had a waterline length of 575ft and a beam of 95ft, the increased displacement necessary to support the increased firepower of the Pennsylvania-class units extended the length of the ship to 600ft with a beam of 97ft. This would be the last increase in the physical size of the Standard Type. The *Pennsylvania* was fitted with a two-level conning tower to allow her to serve as fleet flagship, her higher conning tower distinguishing her from her sister ship *Arizona*. The Pennsylvania-class units had improved underwater side-protection schemes against torpedo hits. *Pennsylvania* and *Arizona* were brand new when the USA entered the First World War in 1917 – and both were present at Pearl when the Japanese attacked in December 1941.

The third Standard-Type design was the New Mexico-class Battleship 1915. They repeated the Pennsylvania-class arrangement but had improved underwater side-protection systems, an extra half inch of deck armour and a clipper bow. The amidships secondary battery guns were moved to a higher drier position on the fo'c'sle deck.

Twelve 14in/50-cal. main-battery guns were set in four three-gun turrets, as with the 14in/45-cal. guns of the preceding Pennsylvania-class units but were fitted with individual sleeves that allowed each gun to elevate independently.

The fourth Standard-Type design saw the two Battleship 1916 Tennessee-class units *Tennessee* (BB-43) and *California* (BB-44). Both Tennessee-class units were launched after the First World War had ended, *Tennessee* on 30 April 1919 and *California* on 20 November 1919 – being completed in 1920 and 1921 respectively. Both would be present at Pearl Harbor on 7 December 1941.

The Tennessee-class units were a repeat of the New Mexico-class design – except that the bow and stern casemate guns were removed and the superstructure was more built up. New fire-control equipment was added giving 'fighting tops' on the heavier cage masts. Adoption of turbo-electric drive allowed an intricate subdivision of the machinery spaces and permitted more space outboard for a new improved torpedo defence system. The layered system of voids, liquid-filled tanks and thin armour bulkheads together with the improvement in fire control were the most significant improvements on the New Mexico class.

The two Tennessee-class super-dreadnoughts *Tennessee* and *California* carried the same main battery of twelve 14in/50-cal. Mark IV guns in *four three-gun turrets* placed on the centre line in two superfiring pairs of turrets, one pair forward and one pair abaft the superstructure. These improved mounts allowed each barrel to elevate independently to 30° giving a range of 35,100yd with the standard 1,500lb AP shell – and an increased range of 36,650yd, some 20 miles, with the lighter 1,275lb high-capacity shell. They had the same top speed and general armour scheme as the preceding classes.

The fifth and last Standard-Type battleship design, Battleship 1917, were the up-armed 32,600-ton Colorado-class units *Colorado* (BB-45) (commissioned on 30 August 1923), *Maryland* (BB-46) (commissioned 21 July 1921) and *West Virginia* (BB-48) (commissioned on 1 December 1923).

The Colorado class was a duplicate of the previous Tennessee-class design in practically every respect other than carrying eight more powerful 16in/45-cal. Mark 1 main-battery guns in four two-gun turrets in place of the 14in main-battery guns installed on the preceding *Nevada, Pennsylvania, New Mexico* and *Tennessee* classes.

(I) Deck Armour

In the years since the ships had been constructed towards the end of the First World War, the threat from aircraft and aerial bombs had grown. For if a bomb is heavy enough and dropped from high enough, no practical armour in the citadel could stop it – thus it became necessary to detonate the bomb as high, and as soon, as possible. A number of different designs were trialled, some departing from the all-or-nothing concept by added a 'decapping' surface of light armour or thick hull plating outboard of the main armour belt, to keep out HE aerial bombs and decap AP shells before they could reach and penetrate the armour deck. Many different schemes of horizontal protection were developed, some with a single thick deck, others with a thick armoured deck with a thin 'splinter deck' below to catch fragments. A bomb striking the unprotected ends of the ship could easily pass out the bottom of the ship without detonating. Deck armour was extended aft from No. 4 turret and increased in thickness over the vulnerable propulsion areas, the steering machinery, shafts and screws.

When the first generations of dreadnoughts were developed, the less powerful guns of the day had a restricted range – and so fired in a shell that followed a relatively flat trajectory, from relatively close range. Until 1905, the normal battle range for capital ships was about 6,000yd (3–4 miles) with long-range engagements perhaps out to 10,000yd, or 6 miles. At both these relatively short ranges, a horizontally fired shell would not be able to strike the deck of the enemy ship – and so, to save unnecessary weight, decks were more lightly armoured than the vertical waterline belt along the side of the citadel where a hit would allow water into the ship. The deck armour of the early dreadnoughts was just 1in thick – and was primarily designed to provide protection against splinter damage from shells bursting above the deck.

As battleship design developed however, new and improved guns could hurl their shells further and further. Soon shells were being fired with a range of 21,000yd – some 12 miles. More powerful guns firing from greater distances increased the height of the shell's trajectory and produced a new phenomenon: 'plunging fire' or 'falling shot' that was more likely to strike the lightly armoured deck rather than the thick vertical side-armour belt. Battleship armour and protection systems thus had to evolve to meet the threat of plunging fire – and from the *Nevada* onwards, two decks totalling 4.5–5in of armour were installed throughout the length of the citadel.

The *uppermost horizontal armour deck* on US battleships of the era was Special Treatment Steel (STS) of up to 3.5in thick that connected to the tops of the waterline vertical armour belt on either side of the citadel. STS was a type of Krupp steel developed in about 1910, a nickel-chrome-vanadium-steel alloy that was used on all parts of a US warship that required direct-impact armour protection.

When laid down in 1912, the 575ft (wl) long Nevada class had 3in of horizontal deck protection in three different layers, covering the 400ft of citadel, with the armour deck extending further aft with increased thickness above the steering machinery and shafts. As the threat from aircraft materialised, during the 1927–9 modernisation, the upper armoured deck was increased with the addition of an extra 2in to give 5in.

A *lower watertight armoured splinter deck* was added on the Standard-Type battleships that ran from the bottom of the vertical waterline armour belt at an inclined angle upwards for about 20ft inboard, before covering horizontally the important spaces below – such as boilers, engines, magazines and shell rooms. This horizontal splinter deck with sloping sides was expected to trap and stop the splinters of shells burst by the vertical side-armour belt or by the horizontal armour deck above. The 20ft distance inboard was to provide sufficient space to be certain that AP shells would explode before striking the internal STS bulkhead. Initially on the Nevadas, the horizontal mid-section of the splinter deck was 1.5in thick in two layers – with the sloping sides being 2in thick in two layers.

The upper platform deck and the lower platform deck were situated directly beneath the armoured deck and below the waterline. The upper platform deck housed the shell rooms clustered around the shell hoists, the anchor capstan drive motors and the steering machinery for the rudders. The lower platform deck below housed fresh-water tanks and the magazines containing the cordite propellant charges.

The gun turrets themselves were also heavily armoured, with the heaviest armour being on the turret face and sides – some 11–12in thick on the earlier dreadnoughts and 18in thick by the launch of the Tennessee-class units in 1919.

The same thinking that had given vertical side-armour belts great thickness but left decks more lightly armoured carried forward to the turrets, where, unlike the thick face and sidewalls, the turret roof was only given 3–4in of armour in early ships, and 5in by the time of the Tennessees. As the range of bigger guns opened, turrets too became vulnerable to plunging fire.

(II) Transverse Armour Bulkheads

Both ends of the waterline vertical armour belt were connected by transverse armour bulkheads that ran athwartships, across the ship from one side of the hull to the other. The Nevada-class units had 13in-thick transverse STS armour bulkheads tapering to 8in, situated forward of the fore turrets – and abaft the after turrets.

(III) Conning Tower

When not in action, a capital ship would be navigated from the command bridge. In action, the ship could be controlled entirely from the relative safety of the armoured conning tower, which was located at the front of the superstructure and in early dreadnoughts had simple slit windows on three sides that gave a field of view for officers during battle. The conning tower was essentially a heavily armoured upright cylinder, with armour varying on different ships but being up to 16in thick on the Standard-Type battleships. The conning tower was fitted out with engine order telegraphs, speaking tubes, telephones, compass and helm.

As the dreadnought evolved, the conning tower developed to become a massive structure weighing hundreds of tons. A Royal Navy analysis of First World War combat, however, revealed that officers were unlikely to use the conning tower during battle, preferring the open superior views of the unarmoured command bridge, despite the risks. Thus, in the run-up to the Second World War, the heavily armoured conning tower was abandoned and replaced with lighter structures in many navies.

(IV) Underwater Side-Protection System

The real danger to dreadnoughts came with the advent of reliable torpedoes and mines during the First World War – capital ships had to have better protection beneath the waterline. Trials revealed that the effectiveness of the internal watertight torpedo bulkhead varied according to its distance from the outer skin of the ship and its thickness. A blast penetrating the outer skin of the ship could be dissipated in empty or oil-filled compartments inboard. As dreadnoughts evolved therefore, they were extensively subdivided below the waterline into multiple watertight compartments – so that if the hull was holed by shellfire, mine, torpedo or collision, only one area of the ship would flood, and the ship would not sink.

The First World War saw the development of the *anti-torpedo bulge* (or blister) and in 1915, the Tennessee-class units were designed with improved Torpedo Defence Systems. Earlier ships would later be retrofitted as needed with blisters.

The layered *torpedo belt*, or Side-Protection System, was introduced in 1922 following the Washington Naval Treaty and was a series of lightly armoured voids and water or oil-filled compartments that extended laterally along the ship's waterline. Both the anti-torpedo bulge and the torpedo belt were attempts to protect against damage underwater by absorbing the force of a hit below the waterline well away from the internal watertight torpedo bulkhead of the internal hull itself.

As battleship design progressed, a three-layer Side-Protection System was developed that ran along both sides of the ship beneath the waterline vertical armour belt. The Side-Protection System comprised air spaces immediately inboard of the shell plating of the torpedo bulge or belt, into which an explosion could dissipate. Inboard of these air spaces was a water or oil-filled partition that was designed to bend or buckle and absorb any remaining explosive force. Inboard of this partition were further spaces to dissipate any residual explosive force that penetrated the partition. Then came the 1½in-thick anti-splinter torpedo bulkhead of the ship proper itself. By the beginning of the Second World War, these multi-layered systems had come to be known as the Liquid Sandwich. British battleships constructed in the immediate run up to the Second World War were designed to withstand torpedoes with up to a 750lb (340kg) warhead.

(V) Armament

(A) Main Battery

Before the dreadnought era, capital ships had no centralised fire control. Each gun was fired independently of the others from its respective turret. From 1906 onwards capital ships were fitted with the latest in rangefinding techniques, sighting and fire control. Crucially, for the first time, all available main-battery guns in a broadside could be aimed and fired by one gunnery control officer positioned in an armoured chamber at the top of the conning tower just in front of the bridge – and also by a secondary gunnery control centre towards the stern of the ship. Officers in the spotting top, an armoured compartment situated well up the foremast, observed the fall of shot – the splashes from shells landing beside the enemy ship far in the distance. They could then give suitable corrections to walk the guns in on their target.

Gunnery

The task of hitting an enemy warship in First World War-era battleships was complicated – as opposing ships could be manoeuvring at their top speed of about 21 knots on battleships and 25–30 knots on battlecruisers. Opposing ships could be 10–15 miles apart, and if steaming at full speed towards each other, could have a closing velocity of 40–60 knots.

To increase the complexity of the task, the ships would often be fighting in difficult seas, the ships pitching and rolling. If nothing was done to correct pitch and roll, one minute guns could be pointed at the enemy, the next they could be pointed into the sea. Sudden changes of course and alterations in speed were made by both sides to try and avoid shells that would arrive sometime after flashes from the enemy guns on a distant horizon were sighted. Hitting another ship was extremely complicated. Imagine trying to fire a shell 10 miles as your ship pitched and rolled – and hit something that is coming towards you at 60mph and making sudden changes of course.

(a) Rangefinding
Before the radar era, battleships had turret and main-battery director optical rangefinders. The main optical rangefinders were situated high up on either side of the forward superstructure with another aft. US main-battery turrets were also equipped with individual rangefinders, periscope sights and gun-laying positions for local fire control. Viewing ports were installed on the front of the turret to avoid blast damage from the guns of a super-firing turret.

(i) Finding the *True Range*
There were competing systems of a basic optical rangefinder used to measure the true distance from the gun to its target – and fire-control systems on capital ships became very elaborate. By the outbreak of the First World War, the British favoured the Barr & Stroud *coincidence rangefinder*, which brought two images into coincidence by rotating the compensating wedge prism. The US Navy originally used coincidence rangefinders, but adopted a different stereoscopic system in the 1930s.

The Barr & Stroud coincidence rangefinder consisted of a 9ft-long horizontal tube with an eye piece for the operator in the middle. At each end of the tube was a pentaprism, one of which was fixed at 90°, whilst the other could be pivoted by turning a hand knob or hand wheel. The operator would see either a true image of the target and a ghost image, or the target image could be split horizontally. In the former version, turning the range knob or wheel would move the ghost image until the operator felt it had converged with the true image – at which point, the target was properly triangulated, and the range could be read off a scale around the hand wheel. The split-image type worked similarly to close the right triangle with the operator lining up the upper and lower images.

(ii) Finding the *Gun Range*

The *optical rangefinder* (and latterly in the Second World War, radar) provided the *true range* to a target – not the *gun range* – for an enemy ship could move some distance after the shells were fired. It became necessary to be able to work out where the enemy ship would actually be when the shells arrived.

To calculate the gun range, it was necessary to factor in and compensate for the range and bearing of the enemy ship by taking into account:

1. The enemy vessel's movement throughout the water.
2. The attacking ship's own movement.

Target range and bearing measurements were taken over a period of time and manually plotted on a chart. The speed and course of the target could then be computed using the distance travelled over a certain period of time. The target course was difficult to ascertain – and many systems measured a relative quantity called *angle on the bow*, the angle made by the ship's course and the line of sight – usually estimated by observational experience. To confuse human observers, ships used dazzle camouflage with painted lines and geometric shapes on the hull – but dazzle camouflage was useless when radar arrived.

The US Navy's first deployment of an electromechanical fire-control computer rangekeeper was on *Texas* (BB-35) in 1916. The rangekeeper performed three functions:

1. Target tracking: by continuously computing the current target bearing. A difficult task as both ship and target are moving.
2. Target position prediction: predicting where the target will be at the time of projectile arrival, which is the point the guns are aimed at.
3. Gunfire correction: a number of corrections have to be applied, such as azimuth, gun elevation, wind speed and direction, air resistance, gravity, projectile type amongst others.

(b) Local Control and Director Fire

Firing of the main-battery guns could be controlled either by *local control* at the turret itself or by *director fire*. In local control, both pointing of the guns and training were done at the gun itself. In director fire, training and pointing were sent to the guns by gunnery officers from centralised gun-control systems.

The gunnery officer was in direct control of the guns and was based in the fire-control tower – an armoured chamber which formed the rear portion of the conning tower. The gunnery officer was supported by lower ranking gunnery officers (who controlled the secondary battery), by men on the rangefinder, by men on the director and by a number of men for transmitting orders.

The spotting top was at first a small simple armoured chamber with viewing slits around it, high up the foremast, with often an additional top on the mainmast. The spotting top accommodated the observer for the main armament, a lieutenant and the spotting officer for the secondary armament who observed the splashes from the fall of shot around the enemy. The spotter had to judge the amount each shell was short, or over, by visually estimating the small distance between the splash and the waterline of the target, many miles distant – a difficult task if the waterline was below the horizon or if the pattern of splashes was off in deflection. Patterns had to be brought in on deflection before accurate range spotting could begin and allow corrections to be transmitted to the gunnery officers through head telephones. One technique was to fire short and then fire salvos as quickly as possible at small increments of range until the target had been crossed. Spotting could also be carried out by aircraft – and capital ships were soon equipped with catapults and float planes. After its invention in 1935, radar was also employed for spotting.

Although fire-control systems varied from nation to nation and ship to ship, it was common for all orders from the gunnery officer or direction layer to go by telephone and speaking tube to a transmitting station situated beneath the armour deck below the waterline. From there orders and information were transmitted to individual guns.

As soon as the gunnery officer had selected an enemy ship to fire at, he would focus the cross hairs of his periscope sight on that ship – on German ships it was the same periscope as on a submarine. This allowed the small observation slits in the armoured conning tower to be completely closed by armoured caps.

A director was situated on the periscope of the gunnery officer, and this enabled all the guns of the ship connected to the director to follow every movement of the gunnery officer's periscope. Guns more than 100m apart, at bow and stern, could be trained on exactly the same spot 12 miles away or more, in the direction fixed by the periscope, the distance of which had been established by the rangefinders.

Where the director was in operation, the guns were kept on the enemy without any crew actually working the guns needing to see the target. The director operated an indicator in every turret – which gave all the corrections for range and deflection. The enemy could be close or far away – ahead or astern. The ships could be passing each other side by side. As long as the periscope was on the target and as long as the range – or distance to the target – had been established, each gun was aiming at exactly the part of the enemy ship that the periscope was pointing at. Even when the ship turned sharply, as long as the periscope was kept on the enemy all the guns remained on target.

(c) Elevation Telegraph
Once the range was known, the guns themselves had to be elevated or lowered ccordingly. In the transmitting station deep in the bowels of the ship was situated the *elevation telegraph*. When the telegraph was moved to the desired elevation, an *elevation repeater* or indicator on each gun (linked to the elevation telegraph) moved to the figure indicated by the elevation telegraph – in much the same way as when an engine order telegraph on a ship's bridge was moved to full speed or half speed, a repeater in the engine room (connected by chain to the bridge telegraph) would ring up the required instruction. The elevation repeater moved an indicator on the gun sight and the gun was trained to the proper elevation.

(d) Range Clock
The range clock was situated on the elevation telegraph. If the gunnery officer had calculated that the range to the enemy was decreasing by say 750yd per minute, an order would be given 'rate 750 minus'. The range clock was then set at a speed of minus 7.5 and the range given on the elevation telegraph gradually diminished by that amount automatically.

The gun now had the required elevation and was trained accurately on the enemy by the director periscope. But the ship could be rolling heavily – one minute the guns could be pointed at the water and the next minute they could be pointed at the sky. The *gun-layer* was tasked to ensure that the sight of the gun was always kept trained on the enemy. This was a drill practised almost daily to hone individual skills. Even when the ship was anchored in port, gun-layers could practise shooting from a rolling ship as small targets were moved around in front of the ship. The target would move – but not the ship or its guns – the target moving in curves that corresponded to the rolling of the ship.

The gunnery officer operating the director on his periscope sight provided the necessary firing impulse for a simultaneous salvo from the main-battery guns– firing when the roll of the ship brought the crosshairs of his sight across the horizon when the guns were on target. None of these pre-radar optical methods could be confidently used at night, in poor weather or in any other situation when the directors could not clearly see the horizon.

After Jutland, warships developed a device that automatically enabled the loaded gun to be fired at the moment when the telescopic sight was on the enemy. True continuous aim of the big guns, which employed gyroscopic instruments, to determine level and cross level without visual observation of the horizon, became available in the mid to late 1930s. In smooth seas, these new systems were capable of sending corrective signals to the guns on a continuous basis so that the guns remained correctly pointed and oriented – essentially the ship rolled and pitched around the guns.

(e) Gunhouse

The upper part of the main turrets, called the *gunhouse*, consisted of a heavily armoured revolving turret and platform turned by electricity on which the guns were situated. The ammunition hoists emerged close to the guns and turned as the turret revolved.

The hoists descended down, inside an armoured cylinder called a *barbette*, to shell and powder-handling rooms directly below the gunhouse and from there separate hoists ran down to shell rooms and powder magazines below the horizontal armoured splinter deck deep in the bowels of the ship. Behind the guns was a relay of ready ammunition, about four to six rounds for each gun.

The gunhouse was heavily armoured, with the heaviest armour being on the turret face and sides – some 11–12in thick on the earlier dreadnoughts and 18in thick by the launch of the Tennessee class in 1919. The turret roof was only given 3–4in of armour in early ships, and 5in by the time of the Tennessees.

The interior of the turret gunhouse was subdivided into individual two- or three-gun chambers that were separated from the turret officer's booth and sight stations by a transverse bulkhead welded to the turret roof. The turrets were essentially divided into two or three individual gas and flame-tight compartments.

The floor of the gunhouse formed a complete deck, broken only by the wells into which the gun breeches descended when the guns were elevated. Access to the turrets was from below by way of two hatches in the gunhouse deck or via the embarkation hatch for the shell room. Shells were brought aboard via the embarkation hatch and down a trunk into the shell room.

The turret officer's booth was located in the rear overhang of the turret above the shelf plate, to the rear of a transverse gas and flame-tight bulkhead. The turret officer's booth held the rammers, the rammer power units, the rangefinder periscopes, sprinkling tanks and fire-control switchboards. The entrance doors to the gun chambers and powder hoist operators' stations were located in the transverse bulkhead. The control switchboard and microphone units were located in the booth adjacent to the ready light panel.[3]

The turrets were trained electrically by a single electric motor situated below the pan plate. The electrical control room held the turret switchboard and the motors for the main ammunition hoists. The turrets could be trained from any of three positions to the centre and either side, each position having a trainer's sight. The turret could also be trained from the officer's position.

Although the guns were trained electrically, they were elevated and rammed hydraulically. Elevation was by a vertical hydraulic cylinder driving a rod which connected to the gun cradle. All the gun machinery was designed to be operated manually if necessary.

In early twin-mount turrets, the two guns could be clutched together to allow them to elevate as a pair – allowing turrets to fire their guns together. Salvos could be fired as full salvos, where all the guns were fired simultaneously, or as partial salvos where half the main battery, usually either the forward or after group, fired together. A split salvo could be fired where one gun of each turret fired together, roughly every 15–20 seconds.[4]

Many of the older classes of dreadnoughts were equipped with guns in single slides in each turret – where all the guns of a turret were attached to a single elevating mechanism. This required only one elevation operator to point all of the guns in a turret – meaning that the guns were mechanically aligned with great precision. A single slide however reduced the rate of fire of the entire turret to that of the slowest individual gun crew – and a failure of a single component in the slide mechanism put the entire turret out of action. Single slides would be abandoned for the installation of multiple slides that allowed each gun to elevate independently.

(f) Barbette
The revolving gunhouse platform sat on a circular ball race or roller path ringing around the top of a large armoured cylinder – the barbette – that ran down through the bowels of the ship to the magazines below. The walls of the barbette were 13in thick on the Standard-Type

US battleships and gave protection down through multiple deck levels to the lower horizontal armoured splinter deck above the magazines. The ammunition hoists led up from the magazines and shell rooms at the bottom of the ship inside the barbette to the shell and powder-handling rooms directly below the gunhouse.

(g) Ammunition Hoists, Shell-Handling Flats and Powder-Handling Room
Situated beneath the gunhouse and electric deck and forming the top of the barbette were the upper and lower projectile-handling flats, which accommodated the bottoms of the shell hoists that led up into the gunhouse. The lower projectile flat was separated from the powder-handling room immediately below by a flame-tight compartment.

The function of the shell-handling flats and powder-handling room below was to send ammunition up to the guns, and only a small stock of ammunition and cartridges was kept there as the reservoir from which the gun was supplied.

The ammunition hoists ran up from the shell rooms and propellant magazines far below to the shell-handling flats and powder-handling transfer rooms, which then sent the shell or propellant to the gunhouse above. The ammunition hoists were essentially broken at the shell and powder-handling flats below the turret for safety. There were no ammunition hoists running directly from the magazines all the way up into the gunhouse, to avoid a strike on the turret causing a potentially catastrophic flash or explosion that could penetrate all the way down such a direct hoist and touch off the magazines – and destroy the ship.

(h) Shells, Propellant and Firing
The main-battery shells and propellant for battleships guns were kept in shell rooms and magazines situated near the very bottom of the ship, where they were protected by their depth in the surrounding water and by the horizontal upper armoured deck and the lower armoured splinter deck. They were also protected by the vertical waterline armour belt above and outboard.

(a) Shells
There were two main types of shell, Armour Piercing (AP) and High Explosive (HE). AP shells were made of the best nickel steel and had only a small high-explosive charge. The shell was base-fuzed with a delayed fuze and had a heavy cap on its front end that deformed on impact but served to protect the shell so that it could penetrate the enemy's thick armour and then burst inside the ship.

HE shells had a comparatively thin steel case and contained a large amount of high explosive. This shell had its fuze on its front end and was designed to burst on contact, its explosive effect being devastating on unarmoured or lightly armoured targets; but the shell was unable to penetrate heavy armour.

(b) Propellant
Cordite is a smokeless propellant developed in the late nineteenth century to replace gunpowder in artillery and naval guns. Consisting of nitroglycerine, gun cotton and petroleum jelly manufactured in thin spaghetti-like rods, it was known initially as 'cord powder' – a name quickly abbreviated to 'cordite' or simply 'powder'. Cordite was not designed to be a high explosive such as gunpowder – it was developed to *deflagrate*, or burn, and produce high-temperature gases. It was the rapidly expanding gas inside the breech that accelerated the projectile up the barrel – the shell was still accelerating as it left the barrel, unlike gunpowder where the shell was decelerating from the moment of detonation.

The propellant magazines deep in the ship were clustered around the main-battery barbettes and ammunition hoists. The early versions of cordite required to be kept at a temperature of less than 50°F (10°C) by a cooling system lest it become unstable, so on all warships, the temperature of propellant magazines had to be monitored.

The first Standard-Type US battleships, the two Nevada-class units ordered in 1911, were armed with the 14in/45-cal. main-battery gun and could fire a 1,402lb projectile out to a maximum of about 23,000yd – about 13 miles. The propellant charge was contained in four silk bags of smokeless powder, each of which weighed about 105lb. Each 14in/45-cal. gun could fire comfortably every 1¼ to 1¾ minutes. When the turrets were subsequently modernised, they could fire out to just over 19 miles.

By the time the last class of four Standard-Type battleships was being constructed, the Colorado-class battleships *Colorado*, *Maryland*, *Washington* and *West Virginia* (laid down from 1917–20), they had been up armed with 16in/45-cal. Mark 1 main-battery guns. Firing a 2,110lb shell to a maximum range of 34,300yd, almost 20 miles, these guns offered a 50 per cent increase over the 1,402lb shell of the preceding 14in/45 cal. guns of the earlier Standard-Type battleships.

(B) Secondary Battery
The secondary armament of battleships consisted of smaller calibre, rapid-firing weapons arranged along either beam of a battleship above the waterline vertical armour belt, mostly in casemate armour in early designs.

(a) 5in/51-cal.
As constructed, on the first Nevada, Pennsylvania and New Mexico classes of Standard-Type battleships, the secondary battery consisted of twenty-one or twenty-two 5in/51-cal. guns. At the beginning of the Standard-Type series, *Nevada* had fourteen of her secondary battery weapons mounted one deck higher than on previous battleship designs as it had been found in practice in the North-Sea clashes between British and German warships that casemate guns mounted lower in the hull were badly affected by moderate or heavy seas. Additionally, as the range of warship clashes opened, the low mountings of casemates became less useful, limiting the gun's effective range. By 1916, the Royal Navy had begun removing lower casemate guns on some warships and plating over the firing ports.

The secondary 5in/51-cal. low-angle (LA) guns had a rate of fire of eight to nine rounds per minute – firing a 50–55lb shell out to an effective range of 17,000yd – just over 9 miles. The mount allowed elevations of -10° to +20° to protect the battleship against smaller ships such as torpedo boats, destroyers or light cruisers that might try to close for a broadside torpedo shot. They would also be the primary armament in a night action when the main battery would not be firing. With a maximum elevation of +20° they were of little use against aircraft.

(b) 5in/38-cal.
Increased awareness of the need for AA protection led to the mounting of improved Dual Purpose (DP) 5in/38-cal. guns on the First World War-era US battleships during post-First World War refits. These DP guns entered service in 1934 and were designed with an elevation of -15° to +85° so as to be effective against both surface targets and aircraft. These guns had a rate of fire of fifteen rounds per minute but could reach twenty-two rounds per minute for short periods. They were arguably the best US DP naval gun of the Second World War, particularly when under the control of the improved Mark 37 Gun Fire Control System director.

(C) 21in Beam Submerged Torpedo Tubes
The Standard-Type battleships as built were fitted with two 21in submerged torpedo tubes, mounted one on each beam towards the bow.

A beam torpedo could not simply be fired out laterally from a vessel underwater when under way because the force of water passing down the hull would deflect it and possibly jam it in the tube. Consequently, when a torpedo was to be fired, the torpedo hatch was opened, and a ram mechanically extended outwards from the hull to protect the torpedo. The torpedo was completely outside the ship in the ram before it was fired. The torpedo tubes on the Standard-Type BBs would be removed as obsolete during inter war modernisations.

(D) Keel
Battleships had a flat hull double bottom of unarmoured shell plating, which incorporated areas for storing oil and fresh water. The extra air space generated inside the hull provided additional buoyancy on the lower side of the ship and the flat bottom enabled convenient dry docking for repair.

Along either side of the central part of the hull just up from the flat bottom were *bilge keels*. These were long thin strips of steel about 3–4ft high, designed to give the flat hull a cutting edge for manoeuvring and to reduce rolling of the ship in poor weather.

Along the hull bottom were spaced several *docking keels* – long, thin, rectangular steel boxes running fore and aft, about 6in high and usually filled with oiled wood. When the ship was dry-docked, her whole weight rested on these docking keels, and they could absorb the weight and spread it out evenly along the athwartships hull frames of her double bottom, in the same way that skis spread the skier's weight on the snow.

(E) Machinery
During the First World War, the later classes of dreadnoughts moved from coal to oil fuel. The advantages of oil were obvious – when burned, oil provides 30 per cent more heat per pound than coal, and the use of oil negated the need to recoal every few days. Oil required no stokers and emitted much less smoke than coal, black clouds of coal smoke obscured gun-laying and made the ships much more visible on the horizon. Refuelling by oil was also much faster and easier.

The first US Standard-Type battleship, the *Nevada*, received direct-drive Curtis steam turbines that were fed by twelve oil-fired Yarrow water-tube boilers and a pair of reduction geared cruising turbines clutched to the high-pressure turbines for fuel economy at low speeds and to reduce overall consumption. Her sister Nevada-class unit *Oklahoma* however was fitted with two vertical triple expansion reciprocating engines fed by the same 12 boilers by way of a trial of the 2 methods of propulsion.

The *Oklahoma*'s reciprocating engines proved troublesome, generating excessive vibration. As a result, the direct-drive Curtis steam turbines, which generated 24,800shp on *Nevada*, would become standard in all following US battleships until the new turbo-electric drive system was introduced on one of the three New Mexico-class units commissioned in 1917–19.

The boilers, turbines and gyro compass rooms were situated at the very bottom of the ship. The boiler rooms, and forward and after turbine rooms were several deck levels high and began directly abaft the conning tower in front of the bridge and abaft Turret 2.

Before the switch to turbo-electric drive with *New Mexico*, boilers were set in rows of athwartships boiler rooms that began under the bridge superstructure forward of the foremost smokestack and filled the lower levels of the ship. Steam was produced by the Yarrow boilers on *Nevada* at around 295psi.[5]

High-pressure turbines were situated athwartships in turbine rooms abaft the aftmost row of boilers. As high-pressure steam was fed through the turbine blades the resulting change in direction turned the blades – not expansion of the steam as in a triple expansion engine. After steam had passed through the high-pressure turbines it was fed back to larger low-pressure and astern turbine in the aft turbine rooms. The spent steam exited the low-pressure turbines to condensers, the resultant water ready to be fed back to the boilers for the cycle to repeat.

The turbines, via reduction gearing, drove the two propeller shafts on the Nevada class, the shafts running aft through the bowels of the ship for some distance before they exited from their tubes into free water. From the succeeding Pennsylvania class onwards the larger Standard-Type battleships would have four shafts.

The first Standard-Type battleships carried a single smokestack to vent exhaust gases, however the turbo-electric drive introduced with one of the three New Mexico-class units and continued with the Tennessee-class units required two stacks. With the move to turbo-electric drive systems, this allowed much greater compartmentalisation, allowing boiler rooms and machinery spaces to be spread along the ship lengthwise. In this way, one or two hits would only flood a small fraction of the power plant and would not be able to immobilise the ship.

(F) Interwar Modernisation
In 1922, the Washington Naval Treaty led the US Navy to begin an upgrade of the combat abilities of their existing battleships. The treaty precluded new battleship construction as well as reconstruction, so

although major work on the main belt and main battery could not be undertaken, upgrades in firepower, protection and propulsion were still possible.

The Nevada, Pennsylvania and New Mexico classes were by now understood to be deficient in underwater protection – so all received anti-torpedo blisters.

The horizontal protection of the ships against plunging fire was also improved with the 3in STS armour deck being increased to between 4.75 and 5in. Firepower was also improved by increasing maximum gun elevations, which gave longer gun ranges.

Catapults were fitted on all battleships to allow spotter floatplanes to be carried and launched, most often one catapult would be installed on the quarter deck and another on top of the superfiring after turret. Once the floatplane had been launched and carried out its mission, it would land near the battleship and be recovered aboard by a deck crane.

The secondary battery was moved higher from First World War-era hull casemates to the deckhouse superstructure, where it could operate in all weather conditions. AA protection was upgraded with eight 5in/25-cal. DP weapons being fitted. Fire-control systems for the main, secondary and AA batteries were moved to control tops that were installed on two large tripod masts on the Nevada and Pennsylvania classes between 1927 and 1929 and on top of the large superstructure added to the New Mexico class between 1931 and 1934.

(G) Speed

Fleet speed of First World One-era battleships was 21 knots – but the new breeds of fast carriers such as the converted battle cruisers *Lexington* (CV-2) and *Saratoga* (CV-3), commissioned in 1927, and the next Yorktown class of fast carriers that joined the fleet in 1937–41, *Yorktown* (CV-5), *Enterprise* (CV-6) and *Hornet* (CV-8), could all make 33 knots. By the Second World War, with the older modernised First World War-era Standard-Type battleships only able to make 21 knots, the problem was obvious. The old battleships simply could not keep up with the new fast carriers.

The primacy in naval warfare of the fast carrier became clear in the early days of the Pacific War, as the opposing fast carriers clashed at the Battle of the Coral Sea in May 1942 and at the Battle of Midway in June 1942. The role of the modern battleship had morphed from being the primary striking weapon of a fleet – to that of providing armoured big gun and AA support for the fast carriers. The older, 21-knot First World War-era battleships such as those sunk or damaged at Pearl would play no part in these new-style carrier battles – but they were well suited to supporting amphibious assaults. They may be slow, but their big guns were still accurate and devastating when brought to bear – the OBBS remained powerful weapons of war, heavily armoured with guns able to destroy heavy enemy warships, bombard land positions and provide close support to landing forces. In the Pacific, the older US battlewagons would be used continually in this role from the invasion of Attu in 1943 through to the end of the war – with devastating effect at the Battle of the Surigao Strait. The *Nevada* would use her big guns to bombard the Normandy beaches on D-Day.

During the Second World War, as the Allied forces began their march west and north across the Pacific towards Japan, Japanese island holdings had to be assaulted sequentially. The Allied invasion forces would be led by the battleships, which would conduct softening up naval bombardments of Japanese defences before amphibious landings took place. Pre-invasion aerial photoreconnaissance of target islands would provide the location of Japanese defensive positions, which would be targeted by the big guns of the old battleships (OBBS).

At first, the early Allied amphibious assaults of Japanese-held islands began with a short naval bombardment, which would soon be found to be inadequate. At the first amphibious assault on Betio in the Tarawa Atoll in November 1943, the pre-invasion naval bombardment lasted 2½ hours and delivered some 2,400 tons of explosive. Although the shelling caused much damage and inflicted heavy casualties on the Japanese defenders, when the US Marines began their amphibious landings, they still faced a functioning Japanese defence, and it took three days of fighting and heavy US casualties before the island was secure.

Learning from the lessons of Tarawa, when Kwajalein Atoll in the Marshall Islands was invaded a few months later, the pre-invasion naval bombardment was increased to 6,000 tons of explosive with the battleships closing to under 1 mile from their targets.

By the invasion of Saipan in June 1944, the OBBS, along with TF 58 fast battleships, cruisers and destroyers, carried out a 2-day long bombardment, delivering 165,000 rounds. There were 13 days of naval bombardment prior to the landings on Guam on 21 July 1944, with a total of 274 ships firing roughly 45,000 rounds. The subsequent naval bombardment at Iwo Jima lasted a full 3 days before the landings on 19 February 1945.

As the war neared its finale, in the late stages of the invasion of Leyte and the end of the Okinawa campaign, the older battleships were exposed to the kamikaze. The modernised old battleship was by now supremely suited to defend against this new threat, being heavily armoured and fitted with large, effective AA batteries. Whilst the kamikaze could inflict deadly damage to more vulnerable carriers and unarmoured ships, against the large armoured battleship, kamikazes could damage the topsides but could not penetrate the deck armour, allowing a battleship, even after being hit, to remain on station.

Once ashore, assault troops depended on close fire support from the invasion fleet battleships. Gunfire Liaison Officers, trained in naval gunfire, would be ashore and able to call in artillery support from the battleships and direct the fire, which would often be in relatively close proximity to Allied troops.

Part II

Battleship Revenge

Chapter 5

USS *California* (BB-44)

USS *California* (BB-44). No major modifications were carried out from her commissioning until the Pearl Harbor attack. The large range clock on the foremast was set to the initial range to an enemy ship established by optical rangefinders to help squadrons of ships aim at the same target. Once some shots had been fired, spotters would report the fall of shot and the range could be corrected up or down, depending on whether the shots were short or over. (*NH 70814 courtesy of the US Naval History & Heritage Command*)

Specifications (as built): Tennessee class
Builder: Mare Island Naval Shipyard, Vallejo, California
Launched: 20 November 1919
Commissioned: 10 August 1921
Decommissioned: 14 February 1947
Displacement: 32,300 tons (S). 33,190 (F)
Length: 624ft (oa)
 600ft (wl)
Beam: 97ft 5.75in
Draft: 30ft 2in (S)
Speed: 21 knots
Endurance: 8,000nm at 10 knots (S)

Armament:
 Main Battery: 12 x 14in/50-cal. set in 4 triple turrets
 Secondary Battery: 14 x single 5in/51-cal.
 AA Battery: 4 x single 3in/50-cal.
 Torpedo Tubes: 2 x 21in (submerged)

Armour:
 Belt: 13.5in tapering to 8in on lower edge. 17ft wide
 Bulkheads: 13.5in
 Barbettes: 13in
 Turrets: Face: 18in. Roof: 5in. Sides: 10in. Rear: 9in
 Deck Armour: Uppermost armour deck: 3.5in in 2 layers with 4.5in over machinery
 Lower splinter deck: 1.5in in 2 layers
 Conning tower: 16in
 Sister ships in class: *Tennessee* (BB-43)
 Fate: Sold for scrap in 1959 and broken up.

California (BB-44) was the second of the two Tennessee-class battleships constructed as part of the Standard-Type series of twelve similar battleships.

After being authorised on 3 March 1915, the keel of the *California* was laid down on 25 October 1916 at the Mare Island Naval Shipyard in Vallejo, California. Work was halted however during the First World War whilst the shipyard focused on outfitting smaller craft, and her hull was eventually launched for fitting out one year after the end of the war on 20 November 1919. She was commissioned on 10 August 1921.

USS *CALIFORNIA* (BB-44)

The two Tennessee-class battleships *Tennessee* and *California* were mostly design copies of the preceding New Mexico-class battleships, the primary differences being enlarged bridges, greater elevation for the main-battery turrets and relocation of the secondary battery from hull casemates to the upper deck. She had a noticeably raked stem – in preference to the plumb stem of the early First World War-era dreadnoughts.

(a) Armament

(i) Main Battery
12 x 14in/50-cal.
California was armed with a main battery of twelve 14in/50-cal. guns, the 14in gun being the standard gun on US battleships since the Nevada class.

The twelve 14in guns were set in four three-gun turrets placed in two superfiring pairs on the centreline, one superfiring pair forward of the superstructure towards the bow and one superfiring pair abaft the superstructure towards the stern. Unlike earlier US battleships equipped with single-sleeve triple turrets, the Tennessee-class mounts allowed each barrel to elevate independently. The Tennessee class would be the last Standard-Type US battleship to carry the 14in gun – the next Colorado-class evolution would move to the more powerful 16in/45-cal. gun.

USS *California* forward superstructure and No. 1 and No. 2 three-gun 14in turrets, 1938. Also seen are the range clock just below the fire-control top, rangefinders atop the pilothouse and armoured conning tower, which is ringed by viewing slits. (*NH 80528 courtesy of the US Naval History & Heritage Command*)

(ii) **Secondary Battery**
14 x 5in/51-cal.
The secondary battery consisted of fourteen 5in/51-cal. breech-loading (BL) guns clustered mostly in casemates in the superstructure amidships. These BL guns had a rate of fire of eight to nine rounds per minute, firing a 55lb 5in shell with an effective firing range of 17,000yd (9.5 miles) at 20° elevation.

Initially, *California* was to have been fitted with twenty-two of these 5in/51-cal. BL guns, but before completion, the secondary battery was reduced to fourteen guns and the now empty redundant hull casemates were plated over to prevent flooding.

(iii) **AA Protection**
California was constructed with four 3in/50-cal. DP guns. These quick-firing (QF) guns used fixed ammunition, where the powder propellant charge and the projectile were housed in one case that looked like a large sporting cartridge. QF guns began to be fitted to warships when the need for AA protection began to be recognised, first entering service in 1915 as a refit to USS *Texas* (BB-35). The maximum range of the 3in/50-cal. QF gun was 14,600yd (approximately 8 miles) at 45° elevation and they had a ceiling of 29,800ft.

By 1922, two of the secondary battery 5in/51-cal. guns had been removed and *California*'s AA weaponry had been beefed up from four to eight 3in/50-cal. DP guns.

(iv) **Beam Torpedo Tubes**
As was fairly standard for the dreadnoughts of the day, *California* was fitted with two 21in submerged torpedo tubes, mounted one on each broadside towards the bow.

(b) Armour

The main vertical armour belt along the sides of the citadel was 13.5in thick, tapering to 8in at the lower edge. The belt was 17ft wide (or high) – with half the main belt being below the waterline.

The uppermost horizontal armoured deck was up to 3.5in thick in two layers with 4.5in over her steering. The lower horizontal armoured splinter deck was 1.5in thick, the concept being that the uppermost armour deck would detonate an incoming shell or bomb – and that the lower armour deck would catch any splinters caused by the explosion above.

The main-battery gun turrets had 18in-thick faces, with the roof being 5in thick, and the sides and rear being 10in and 9in thick respectively.

(c) Propulsion

A new style of turbo-electric power plant had been installed on one of the three ships of the preceding New Mexico class – and had proved to have many advantages including offering a greater steaming radius. Because of the reduced size of the turbo-electric drive machinery, greater internal subdivision of the battleship in the machinery spaces was possible, improving the underwater protection of the ship. A General Electric turbo-electric drive was therefore designed into both of the succeeding Tennessee-class units.

Eight oil-fired Babcock & Wilcox boilers generated steam at 280psi and developed 26,600 shaft horsepower (20,000 kW). Powered by this turbo-electric drive, *California*'s four propellers gave a top speed of 21 knots.

The new turbo-electric drive was an important addition to the ship's underwater protection system. The dreadnoughts of the day had traditionally used direct-drive steam turbines. This system was very efficient at generating mechanical power to turn the shafts – but its major drawback was the manner in which it paired a highly efficient rotation of the turbines – with the inefficient slow rotation rate of the propeller. Waste was inevitable when the propeller was operated too slowly or too quickly.

Traditional direct-drive turbines needed a lot of space, with multiple turbine stages required to achieve fuel-efficient cruising speeds, high speeds and astern propulsion. All this required a multiplicity of steam pipes to send power to the ship's machinery leaving the direct-drive system vulnerable to damage, and the ship itself susceptible to flooding through ruptured pipes if hit below the waterline. The need for so much machinery robbed the ship of space to accommodate weapons.

The new turbo-electric drive fitted to the trial New Mexico-class unit and both Tennessee-class units used a two-stage *mechanical to electric* process – instead of sending direct power from the turbines to the four propeller shafts. Like the direct-drive steam turbines, the first stage of the turbo-electric drive used boilers to send HP steam to move a turbine, returning spent steam to a condenser for reuse. The turbines were mounted in tandem and surrounded by eight boiler rooms in individual compartments. Even if one or more boiler rooms on one side were to be flooded by a torpedo hit, the turbines could continue to operate.

In the second stage of the turbo-electric system, the steam turbines drove one or two electric generators – rather than directly driving the prop shaft. The electricity from the generators was then sent to electric motors mounted on the propeller shaft heads, which could power the prop shafts at the most efficient rate. The turbines could therefore operate at a constant, highly efficient rotation speed, without having to abruptly slow down or speed up, risking damage. The propeller could be turned flexibly – according to the conditions of the environment or operational requirements. No longer was special piping required for a reverse stage for astern propulsion – the electric motors could be easily reversed. The turbo-electric system could be better compartmentalised, making it less vulnerable to damage in the event of accident or enemy attack.

Although the turbo-electric drive was adopted in a series of ships, turbo-electric systems were significantly heavier than direct-drive turbines and their use would be interrupted in the 1920s to comply with the Washington Naval Treaty of 1922 and the London Naval Treaty of 1930, which limited the gross weight tonnage of warships.

The two Tennessee-class units had a design cruising range of 8,000nm at 10 knots that required 1,740 tons of fuel oil. They carried 57 officers and 1,026 enlisted men.

(d) Topsides

As built, *California* was fitted with two lattice or cage masts with spotting tops for the gun battery. These lattice masts were common on US capital ships and armoured cruisers of the early to mid-twentieth century, the lattice work intended to make the masts less vulnerable to damage by shells from enemy ships, which might pass right through them. They could also better absorb the shock caused by firing the ship's heavy main-battery guns, by isolating the fire-control equipment and rangefinders mounted on top. Although a very clever idea – and one that the US Navy used up to the Second World War, the masts were found in practice to be easily damaged by weather in poor seas, typhoons and hurricanes. USS *Michigan*'s mast was bent right down to deck during a storm in 1918.

As the calibre and range of naval guns increased, heavier rangefinders were required, and the powerful guns and engines created shocks and vibrations. During the 1920s and 1930s it was considered uneconomical and unnecessary to replace the most modern and strongest lattice masts of warships with tripod masts. Only the oldest US battleships had replacement tripods fitted with new modern directors and rangefinders, which were too heavy for the existing older styles of lattice masts to support. Lattice masts were eventually phased out in favour of the more rigid tripod masts favoured by the Royal Navy.

The two ships of the Tennessee class sported two slender smokestacks in place of the single large smokestack of earlier classes.

Following her commission on 10 August 1921, *California* joined the fleet as its flagship. On 11 November 1924, Lieutenant Dixie Kiefer took off from the *California* for the first night aircraft launch from a warship in history when his Vought UO-1 bi-plane fighter was launched by catapult from the *California* in San Diego harbour with the only illumination being *California*'s searchlights, which were trained 1,000yd into the distance. Further experimentation with aircraft continued and in 1926 an aircraft catapult was installed on one of her main-battery turrets. *California* now carried up to three Vought UO-1 floatplanes.

As the threat of aircraft to battleships increased, in late 1929 and early 1930, *California* received a new battery of eight 5in/25-cal. guns on AA mounts in place of her original 3in/50cal. guns. In 1935–6, 0.50-cal. machine guns were placed in the foretops, two forward and four aft with two more being added adjacent to the foremast.

In December 1940, four 3in/50-cal. guns were added in tubs below the bridge wings and towards the stern.

PEARL HARBOR, 7 DECEMBER 1941

On the morning of 7 December 1941, *California* was moored on her own in Berth F-3 at the southeastern side of Ford Island, with her bow pointing towards the southern navigation channel that leads into Pearl Harbor from the Pacific. The oiler *Neosho* (AO-23) was moored at the fuel dock some way astern of her. *California* was the southernmost capital ship along Battleship Row.

As the *Kidō Butai* attack on Pearl Harbor began, an estimated eighteen Japanese Val dive bombers appeared over Hickam Field and some nine Val dive bombers swooped in from the northeast and began to bomb and strafe the hangars and planes at the Naval Air Station on the southern end of Ford Island. At 0750, *California*'s first lieutenant, Lieutenant Commander Marion Little, who was the senior officer aboard the ship at the time, issued the order to sound General Quarters, man battle stations and start setting the battle closure Condition Z.

Five planes swooped in from eastsoutheast and dived on the warships in Berths F-3 to F-8. With the dropping of the first bombs on Ford Island, at 0758, Commander Patrol Wing Two broadcast the warning to All Ships Present: 'AIR RAID, PEARL HARBOR. THIS IS NOT A DRILL.' There would be some four separate torpedo-plane attacks on the battleships.

As the raid began, twelve torpedo planes swung in to attack the battleships from the southeast, launching torpedoes from low altitude at short distance. Another wave of torpedo planes then came in from the southwest. All the outboard battleships, *California* (Berth F-3), *Oklahoma* (Berth F-5) and *West Virginia* (Berth F-6) were exposed to torpedo attack.

California had 2 of her 5in guns and 2 of her .50-cal. machine guns designated as ready guns, with 50 5in shells and 400 .50-cal. rounds at the guns. At 0803, the crews of the ready guns began to engage the Japanese torpedo planes – and *California* was quickly strafed by Mitsubishi A6M Zero fighters – no doubt in an attempt to suppress the AA fire her gunners were offering and allow the more vulnerable slow and low attack by torpedo bombers to take place. *California*'s AA gunners quickly expended the modest amount of ready ammunition – the magazines had to be unlocked before the guns could be resupplied.

As her ready guns ran out of ammo and went silent – and as resupply efforts began – a pair of Nakajima B5N Kate torpedo bombers began their attack runs from the east, dropping their Type 91 torpedoes toward *California*. Both specially adapted torpedoes ran true and at 0805, one hit her port side forward between Turret 2 and the bridge whilst the other hit further aft on the port side.

The torpedo strike on the fore part of the ship detonated below the armour belt at Frame 52, creating a hole 10ft high and 24ft long. The explosion deformed the first torpedo bulkhead and transverse stiffeners between Frames 47 and 60 and holed the second bulkhead with fragments. The other torpedo opened up a hole in her hull at Frame 101 that was 40ft long, and extended from the first seam below the armour belt to the bilge keel.

The underwater side-protection scheme of the Standard-Type battleships had a sequence of thin vertical bulkheads forming four compartments along the inside of the ship – that were roofed by the lower armoured splinter deck. The outermost space, immediately inside the shell plating of the hull, was about 4ft wide and was left empty or void. Then came three separate 3ft-wide fuel tanks, abreast of each other. These middle spaces were filled with fuel or water. There was then another 4.5ft-wide void space before the inner bulkhead of the ship proper, which was also left void. In all the ship was protected by 17.5ft of empty space and fuel tanks between the shell plating of the skin of the ship and the interior compartments located behind the inner anti-torpedo bulkhead.

A torpedo striking the ship under the main vertical armour belt would detonate and produce a blast of gas and a shower of splinters. The expanding gas from the blast would vent into the empty outer space and be dissipated in deforming the three liquid-filled middle compartments, which would bend, and also absorb the splinters. The walls of the ship and these compartments were made as thin as possible to minimise the production of splinters by the torpedo explosion.

Neither of the Type 91 torpedoes that hit *California* was particularly destructive – and neither would have been fatal to the ship had they hit whilst the ship was at General Quarters and ready for action. The outer shell plating of the hull and first bulkhead were punctured – whilst the second bulkhead was dished in with two large holes punched in it. But in the case of each torpedo, the third and fourth bulkheads were dished in but had held as intended – whilst the fifth bulkhead, the inner anti-torpedo bulkhead protecting the inside of the ship, was nearly undamaged.[1] Oil bubbled out from the ruptured outer tanks and rose to the surface, forming a slick as the ship listed to port.

This was however ostensibly peacetime – and the ship had been prepared for inspection at the time of the attack: internal watertight doors had been opened. The voids below the waterline of the anti-torpedo system were accessed for maintenance and inspection by manholes above. The voids had been slated for inspection for possible leakage from adjacent fuel tanks – and several manhole covers on each side of the ship had been removed and others loosened.

Once dogged down, these manholes would have been watertight. But with some covers removed and others loosened, as the attack began and General Quarters was sounded at 0750, the crew rushed to close up the ship for action – and close the watertight doors and manhole covers. They were still in the process of dogging these down when the two torpedoes struck about 0805 – and flooding began. Although the crew were able to dog the covers down on the disengaged starboard side, as the ship was hit and began to list to port, flooding prevented those on the port side being dogged down. Four large ventilation fans flooded, and with many watertight fittings open, the spread of water down was rapid.[2]

An uncontrolled flooding began as water started to spread throughout the ship. By 0815, *California* had taken a list to her damaged port side of 5.5–6°, putting the third deck on the port side about 8ft below the waterline.[3] Damage-control teams began to counterflood compartments on the opposite starboard side of the ship, reducing the list to 4° to port. Despite this, water continued to flood into the ship on her lower port beam. Many of the portholes and exterior doors of the ship had been open for the inspection, and as the ship listed, water began to enter the ship through these.

The torpedo hit forward had ruptured the forward fuel tanks, which had allowed water to enter the fuel system. The ship's electrical system shut down, hindering the efforts of the damage-control teams.

Between 0815 and 0915, as damage-control teams frantically worked to stop the flooding and redress the port list, the ship was repeatedly attacked by Aichi D3A Val dive bombers. At 0820, a near-miss bomb forward opened a hole in her port bow and flooding brought her head down by about 3.5ft. At about 0840, the ship was shaken by four near bomb hits.

At 0845, Commander Earl Stone, the ship's executive officer, boarded the ship and took command of the vessel. Between 0840 and 0915, after a lull in the attacks, horizontal bomber attacks at high altitude by about fifteen planes began. At about 0900, *California* was struck forward by a bomb that penetrated the upper armour deck near the forwardmost casemate on the starboard side. The bomb then ricocheted off the lower second armoured deck – detonating inside the ship and killing about fifty men and starting a serious fire. The bomb was believed at the time to be a delayed fuze 250kg SAP bomb – and it left an entry wound in the deck that was 13–14in in diameter and travelled about 20ft from point of impact.[4] Whilst the ship was under attack, the boiler room crew succeeded in getting four of the boilers restarted, allowing power to be restored.

By 0915, the fire had spread to casemates No. 3, 5 and 7, by which time Captain Joel Bunkley and Vice Admiral William S. Pye, the Battle Fleet commander, had returned to the ship, which was Pye's flagship. Smoke from the fire eventually reached the forward engine room at 1000, forcing the men inside to evacuate the area and putting an end to pumping efforts.

After the Japanese planes of the second wave had broken off their attack at about 0945, vessels came alongside the stricken *California* to begin firefighting efforts and pumping water out. The portable pumps used by these vessels however lacked the power necessary to handle the volume of water flooding into her hull – and the great battleship, flagship of the Battle Fleet, continued to slowly flood and settle into the waters of the harbour. Over the next three days, she eventually

USS *CALIFORNIA* (BB-44)

Crew abandon USS *California* as oil burns on the water at about 1000 on 7 December 1941. The capsized hull of USS *Oklahoma* is visible astern at the right. (*NH 97399 courtesy of the US Naval History & Heritage Command*)

settled onto the muddy seafloor. In the course of the attack, in total ninety-eight men had been killed and sixty-one wounded.

Several men were awarded the Medal of Honor for their actions during the attack. Lieutenant (then Gunner) Jackson Charles Pharris, one of the ship's gunners, organised a group of men to carry ammunition up from the magazines and rescued several sailors who had been overcome by fuel-oil fumes. Ensign Herbert C. Jones and Chief Radioman Thomas Reeves both organised similar parties to carry ammunition, but both were killed during the attack. Machinist's Mate First Class Robert Raymond Scott was also killed after he refused to leave his battle station which contained the air compressor, but which was flooded as a result of the torpedo hit, saying words to the effect: 'This is my station and I will stay and give them air as long as the guns are going.'[5]

USS *California* lists after the Japanese attack. Astern is the oiler *Neosho* (AO-23), which survived the attack but would be sunk at the Battle of the Coral Sea in May 1942. (*Courtesy of National Archives & Defense Visual Information Distribution Service*)

Salvage

In the days that followed, after inspections by divers, a number of plans were formulated by the Salvage Division committee to lift *California*. One idea was that a cellular watertight cofferdam could be installed around the whole ship by driving sheet piling into the muddy seabed to form a watertight fence. But Public Works reported that the mud surrounding the ship was too deep and too fluid to provide a good support for the piles.[6]

The alternative was to float *California* – without using patches over the two torpedo holes. Two smaller wooden cofferdams would instead be installed around the main deck and the starboard side of the upper deck, one towards the bow on the port side and the other being a larger cofferdam that would be erected around the quarterdeck aft.

Divers began working on the ship to seal smaller holes and ruptures in the hull plating on 19 December 1941 – patching splinter holes and scuppers and closing any portholes that were hanging open. Missing manhole covers to the anti-torpedo underwater defence system voids were replaced and loose covers tightened. Broken pipelines were secured and isolated.

The ship was still taking on some water however, and a stream of bubbles bled steadily from her higher starboard quarter through missing rivets and seams, which the divers had to seal with caulk and sheet lead. But once these repairs had been carried out, and once the damaged areas had been isolated by closing boundaries using existing ship's fittings, there was almost no inflow of water into the ship.[7]

The cofferdams were required to reduce the head of water, estimated at 17ft, over the main deck. This head would have caused the main deck to collapse if the ship had been dewatered by standpipes from below, without shoring the deck.

On 27 December 1941, divers discovered another hole in the hull on the port side at Frame 12. The *California*'s salvage officer James Rodgers wrote in the Base Force Salvage Memorandum of the same date: 'This is believed to have been caused by a third torpedo hit that many people spoke of but were not sure of.'[8] Subsequent inspection would reveal this to be hull damage from a near miss bomb.

The ship would be lightened as far as possible to assist with refloating and getting her into dry dock. Work began to remove her main battery, and the heavy armour plates of Turrets 1, 2 and 3 were detached and removed and ordnance men carefully lifted 14in shells out to barges. *California*'s most accessible forward main-battery 14in/50-cal. guns of Turrets 1 and 2 were successfully removed in mid-January, whilst the 14in guns of Turret 3 were removed in early February 1942. The guns of the aftmost low Turret 4 had been trained to starboard as the ship listed to port. That turret was now fully submerged and out of sight, save for the tips of the barrels.

The patch for the near miss bomb hole in the port bow arrived on 25 January 1942 and was hung on an A-frame. It was then lowered into place on chains and secured by divers to the hull with some difficulty over the course of the next two days. A foundation was built on the upper deck for a boiler, water tanks and oil burners so that steam could be produced and provide power for lights and cleaning equipment.

Plans were meanwhile finalised for the two single-wall cofferdams, one along the port side of the fo'c'sle and one around the entire quarter deck. Once watertight, water over the main and upper decks of the ship

USS *California* refloating operations, Pearl Harbor. The cofferdam installed along port bow and forward turrets is seen here. The roofs and barrels of both forward turrets have been removed. (*NH 55036 courtesy of the US Naval History & Heritage Command*)

and the dams would be pumped out. Then, without a huge weight of water overhead, the ship would then be dewatered deck by deck. Once the ship had been refloated, it would be moved to dry dock for more extensive repairs, sufficient to allow the ship to transfer back to the West Coast of the USA for permanent repair.

The quarter deck cofferdam would consist of nine sections along the port side of the stern, nine corresponding sections along the starboard side and one section at the stern that would link the port and starboard sections. The sections ranged from 19.5–30.5ft wide and were fabricated from vertical planks that were 8in thick x 12in wide and varied from 16–20ft in length. These planks would be shored by sturdy 8 x 8in beams on the starboard side and 10 x 10in beams on the deeper port side where the head of water was greater.

These shoring beams would be set at about 45° to the deck and be secured to beams bolted to the deck or to the turrets. The barbettes would have a band of steel welded to them to which would be welded L-shaped stiffeners with the shoring beams bolted to them. The sections of buoyant wood would be weighted down with sandbags in boxes built into the inside of the cofferdam.

The fo'c'sle cofferdam was less technical as it only required to surround the deeper port side – as the higher starboard side of the fo'c'sle deck was above the waterline. There would be eight sections of 4 x 12in beams, the sections ranging in length from 26–31ft. One section would join the other seven to the superstructure deck. The sections were to be anchored by 6 x 10in beams bolted to the deck with only a few shoring beams requiring to be run to Turret 2 and none to Turret 1.[9] The fo'c'sle cofferdam had been erected by 23 February 1942 and secured to the ship. As this was being done, the lattice mainmast was cut and lifted off the ship on 12 February 1942.

Divers from the Navy Yard continued to work inside the ship, closing openings and manhole covers. A fuel barge was brought alongside and 5,400 gallons of *California*'s fuel oil was pumped out. Work went on to break both armoured conning towers free of their mounts, which would remove a considerable weight – although removal was not required for flotation at this point, it became necessary in time to reduce the ship's draft sufficiently to allow it to enter dry dock.[10]

The fo'c'sle pumps were started on 25 February 1942, once manholes were closed and broken pipelines secured. This allowed 20,000 gallons of water a minute to begin being pumped out from behind the cofferdam fence. Divers went to work again – locating leaks in the cofferdam, revealed by tell-tale bubble streams, for sealing. The conning tower was finally detached from its mounts and more fuel oil removed from the ship.

Within two days, the fo'c'sle deck had been cleared of water – but the main deck would not be dewatered until the quarter deck cofferdam was set in place, which was expected to be in a few weeks' time. Men got to work cleaning mud and debris and removing unnecessary fitments from those parts of the *California* that were now exposed and dry.

By 12 March 1942, the cofferdam surrounding the port and starboard sections of the quarterdeck was fully in position. With the fo'c'sle already dry, the pumps began to lower the water level on the main deck – and by 17 March 1942, the uppermost starboard side was dry.

By 20 March, the water was below the second-deck centreline hatches. The following day, pumping from the interior began after the main deck had been cleared of water.[11] During the course of the attack, some ninety-eight men had been killed – but as yet, forty-five had not been recovered from inside the ship. Most remains were expected to be found on the starboard second deck, where the bomb hit had killed a number of men – and in the third-deck crew spaces, where those overcome by fuel fumes in the darkness had drowned. As pumping from the interior began on 21 March, the first of the missing crew were located on the second deck.

The large quantity of heavy wood fence sections, shores and braces of the quarter deck cofferdam had increased the overall buoyancy of the ship – and this helped raise her stern first and break the ship out of the grip of the clinging mud. As more of the ship became dry, crew went to work with steam-pressure cleaning guns to rid the ship of the mud and oil that had accumulated inside over the three to four months it had been submerged. Small pumps then collected the resulting water and oil slurry and pumped it overboard. Tens of thousands of gallons of sludge were removed from the ship in this way – a time-consuming job to clean the ship to a standard sufficient for her to sail to the West Coast of the USA.

By 23 March 1942, the water level had been reduced to just 2ft above the third deck – the stern of the ship was now buoyant and off the seabed. As the water receded here on the third deck, fifteen more bodies were found – badly decomposed after three months inside the wreck. On 24 March, more bodies were found. As remains were discovered, they were carefully moved into canvas body bags and removed.

California was by now fully afloat – being held there off the seabed by delicate pumping, to allow a full search of the inside to be completed. Over the coming days more remains were discovered and removed.

By 30 March 1942, although a number of crew were still missing, it was felt that recovery of the bodies was complete as far as possible in

USS *CALIFORNIA* (BB-44)

the cleared areas. With the pumps handling leaking of the cofferdams, further dewatering of the ship began again.

By the following day, the forward engine room, motor rooms and port firerooms had been pumped dry. The ship was practically on an even keel with only a slight list to port – and was drawing just over 43ft.[12] By 3 April, *California* was sufficiently high in the water to be moved to enter dry dock.

Of the available dry docks at Pearl Harbor Naval Base, Dry Dock 1 presently accommodated the 9,950-ton heavy cruiser *Minneapolis* (CA-36) and the destroyers *Maury* (DD-401) and *Phelps* (DD-360). The large fleet carrier *Lexington*, back from the Gilbert and Marshall Islands raids, was currently occupying Dry Dock 2 – undergoing a quick refit before being despatched to the Coral Sea. It was decided that when the *Lexington* was undocked on 8 April, *California* would take her place – as Dry Dock 3 was simply too small to host a battleship. In preparation, floating cranes removed the fo'c'sle cofferdam – and pumps continued to dewater the ship. The plan was to begin removing the quarterdeck cofferdam sections on Monday, 6 April 1942.

Astern view of USS *California* after being refloated in March 1942. An extensive wooden cofferdam has been erected around the stern and the ship lists to port. (*NH 83070 courtesy of the US Naval History & Heritage Command*)

At 1315 on 5 April 1942 however, as pumps and cofferdams kept *California* afloat and slowly dewatered her further, there was an explosion aboard the ship – possibly the result of a mixture of fuel-oil vapor and hydrogen sulfide gas caused by rotting marine organics inside her hull. The explosion dislodged the temporary patch that had been fitted in January to cover the near-miss hole at the port side of the bow. Watertight doors were also damaged, causing serious flooding – and within 2 hours, the bow was down 5ft and the stern had risen 3ft.

Divers isolated the damaged area that afternoon – and within a day, the bow was being dewatered and raised. Over the next few days, the salvage team repatched the hull and pumped the ship out again.

On 9 April, with *Lexington* undocked and now bound for the Coral Sea, *California* was finally towed by four tugs to Dry Dock No. 2, watched by crowds of hundreds of people. Once inside the dry dock and positioned over the blocks, the caisson was pumped dry to expose the whole underside of the hull and allow repairs to the two torpedo holes.

By 9 June 1942, just two months later, the dock was able to be flooded and the temporarily repaired ship was refloated, removed from dry dock and moved to Berth 22 along the seawall. *California* may have been afloat – but there was still much to be done to allow her to sail for Puget Sound, Washington State for reconstruction and modernisation.

Four months later, on 10 October 1942, *California* was finally able to depart Pearl Harbor and rendezvous at sea with her escort, the new recently commissioned Benson-class destroyer *Gansevoort* (DD-608). The two vessels then made their way to Puget Sound, Washington State, a distance of some 2,600 miles. In the Navy Yard, the repair and modernisation works would last some fifteen months from 20 October 1942 to 31 January 1944, by which time it was more than two years since she had been sunk at Pearl Harbor.

At Puget Sound, all of the ship's guns save her main battery were removed – and her superstructure was completely removed in preparation for reconstruction. Her hull was widened by the addition of torpedo blisters on either beam, which increased her overall beam to 114ft – rendering her now too wide in the beam to pass through the Panama Canal. To further improve the underwater protection scheme against torpedoes and mines, additional longitudinal bulkheads were added, allowing further internal subdivision and watertight compartmentalisation.

The main-battery 14in/50-cal. guns were modified to automatic control and the new Mark 34 director fitted on the two new towers. Her older CXAM radar was removed and installed ashore on Oahu.

USS *CALIFORNIA* (BB-44)

Forward torpedo damage to the hull of USS *California* at about Frame 52, in April 1942, soon after entering dry dock. The vertical armour belt is visible above the hole and the deformed bilge keel below. (*80-G-32917 courtesy of the US Naval History & Heritage Command*)

California's aging secondary battery 5in/51-cal. and 5in/25-cal. guns were replaced with sixteen modern 5in/38-cal. Dual Purpose guns in eight new twin turrets, four on each beam with fire controlled by four Mark 37 directors and associated radars. These DP guns had a barrel elevation of -15° to +85° and were thus effective at long range against surface targets whilst also being an effective AA weapon. The increased 38-cal. barrel length compared with the previous 5in/25-cal. weapon gave greatly improved performance in both AA and surface roles, firing a 53–55lb shell with an average rate of fire of twelve to fifteen rounds per minute.

The light AA battery was also improved to forty Bofors 40mm autocannons in ten quadruple mounts and fifty-two single rapid-fire Oerlikon 20mm guns.

PEARL HARBOR'S REVENGE

Horizontal armour protection was also considerably strengthened to improve resistance to air attack and plunging fire. There were 3in of special treatment steel (STS) added to the deck over the magazines and 2in STS added elsewhere. The roofs of the turrets were increased to 7in.

In place of the original heavy First World War-era conning tower, she received one of the more modern lighter towers that had been removed from the recently rebuilt *Brooklyn*-class cruisers.

Both old First World War-era cage masts were removed, with a modern tower mast installed in place of the cage foremast and the cage mainmast being replaced by a small superstructure to accommodate the second main-battery fire-control director. A single enlarged smokestack took the place of the two original stacks.

The reconstruction had increased the ship's full load displacement to almost 41,000 tons – and although new boilers had been installed

USS *California* (BB-44) underway in January 1944 after repair, probably in Puget Sound. The two lattice masts are gone, she has a new superstructure and a single enlarged stack in place of the previous two stacks. (*80-G-166187 courtesy of US Naval History & Heritage Command*)

to boost power, the increase in her displacement kept her post-modernisation speed at 20.5 knots. The ship's crew had doubled to a total of 114 officers and 2,129 enlisted men.

Once the repairs and modernisation work had been completed, *California* was able to depart Puget Sound on 31 January 1944 and begin a series of sea trials followed by a shakedown cruise off San Pedro and training exercises to prepare her crew, many of whom were fresh from initial training, for combat operations in the Pacific. Then, before final deployment, the ship underwent a machinery overhaul in San Francisco in April 1944.

It was time for the great battleship to get back into the war.

BATTLESHIP REVENGE

Return to Service – 1944

(I) The Mariana and Palau Islands Campaign
Battle of Saipan, 15 June–9 July 1944

On 5 May 1944, now some two-and-a-half years after being sunk at Pearl Harbor, *California* departed the West Coast of the USA to join the fleet assembling in the Central Pacific for Operation FORAGER – the Mariana and Palau Islands campaign, slated to begin in June 1944.

In the campaigns of 1943 and those of the first half of 1944, the Allies had successfully captured the Solomon Islands, the Gilbert Islands, the Marshall Islands and the Papuan peninsula of New Guinea. The Japanese however still held the Philippines, the Caroline Islands, the Palau Islands and the Mariana Islands – with the islands of the Palau and Mariana archipelagos forming the principal strongpoints in a chain of islands that Japan's military regarded as its last line of defence to the east.

From an Allied perspective, the Palaus and Marianas represented important targets for several reasons:

1. Palau was a strategic Japanese barrier to deployment to the Philippines.
2. The Marianas airfields provided the Japanese with land-based air cover – and an air capability to strike at Allied operations.
3. If the Marianas could be seized, then the Allies would gain airfields from which the new US ultra-long-range Boeing B-29 Superfortress strategic heavy bomber could be deployed directly against the Japanese home islands.
4. Allied air assets and supplies could be staged westwards from the Marianas as Allied forces advanced.

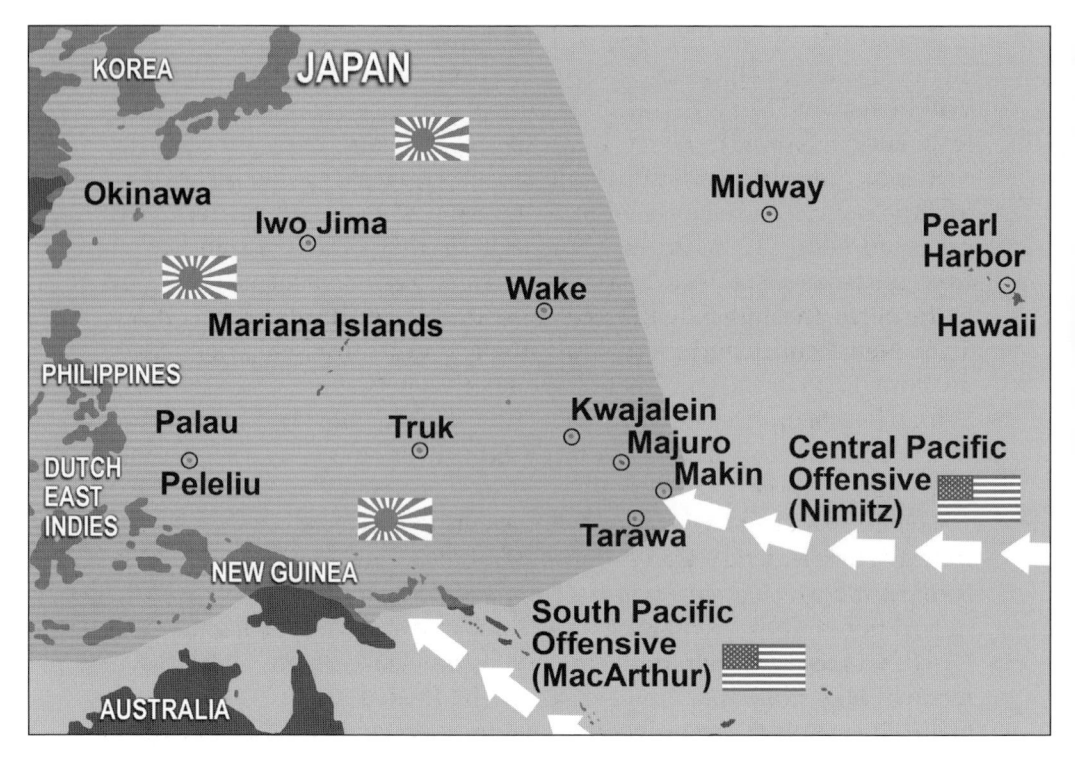

A general chart of the Pacific showing the extent of Japanese holdings in November 1943.

The Mariana Islands, also called the Marianas, are a crescent-shaped north–south archipelago of the summits of fifteen mostly dormant volcanic mountains rising out of the abyssal depths of the western Pacific. They lie to the southsoutheast of Japan, north of New Guinea and east of the Philippines. Lying about 1,000 miles from the US forward base at Eniwetok Atoll, Saipan is the largest and most northerly of the Northern Mariana Islands with Tinian and Rota to its south – and the US territory island of Guam furthest south.

The Northern Marianas had been administered by Japan under her League of Nations South Pacific Mandate of 1919, which granted her control of the Pacific Ocean islands that had been part of German New Guinea. The large southern island of Guam was separate from the Northern Marianas and had been a US territory since the conclusion of the Spanish-American War in 1898. Japanese troops had invaded and seized Guam on 8 December 1941, shortly after the attack on Pearl Harbor.

Saipan's location, 120 miles northeast of Guam at the north of the chain, made it a logical and crucial first target for the Allied operation. With Saipan in US hands, Guam and Tinian to its south would be cut off from support from the north, and from Japan itself.

Saipan was the Japanese Command Post for the western Pacific – and the centre of its island network of unsinkable aircraft carriers. With many airfields strung throughout the Marianas, Japan staged aircraft from the home islands and the Bonin-Volcano islands, such as Iwo Jima to the north, through Saipan to all of its southern outposts such as Wake, Truk, New Guinea and the Palaus. IJN fleet units used Saipan as a safe anchorage. As part of the last line of defence of the Japanese homeland, Saipan had been strongly fortified with coastal artillery batteries, shore defences, underground fortifications and an airstrip. Some 30,000 troops were stationed there by mid-1944.

The US 5th Fleet by now included the fifteen carriers of TF 58 – and for any surface action that required the Battle Line of battleships to be formed, the 5th Fleet now had seven new state-of-the-art fast battleships, in addition to the older modernised battleships such as *California*.

After a passage from the West Coast of the USA of some 2,400 miles, in early May 1944 *California* arrived at the Pearl Harbor Naval Base in Oahu. It must have been an emotional homecoming as she once again entered the great naval harbour.

Once at Pearl, in anticipation of her new fire-support duties for the Mariana and Palau campaign, she took part in shore-bombardment practice off the volcanic island of Kahoolawe, which lies about 7 miles southwest of the Hawaiian island of Maui. Kahoolawe had always been lightly populated due to its lack of fresh water and during the Second World War, and in the post-war period, it was used as a training ground and bombing range.

After stopping over at Pearl, *California* then continued her westward deployment – departing Hawaii on 31 May 1944 and moving a further 2,500 miles west to Kwajalein Atoll in the Marshall Islands, seized by the Allies five months earlier in January 1944.

California arrived at Kwajalein Atoll on 8 June 1944 and joined Fire Support Group 1 (TG 52.17), under the command of Rear Admiral Jesse B. Oldendorf. Fire Support Group 1 now consisted of four of the old, modernised battleships, *Tennessee, California, Maryland* and *Colorado*, along with heavy and light cruisers and a screen of destroyers. Fire Support Group 2 (TG 52.10), under the command of Rear Admiral Walden L. Ainsworth, comprised the three old battleships *Pennsylvania, Idaho* and *New Mexico* along with cruisers and their screen. In all, the

Fire Support Groups now comprised seven old battleships, of which, four, namely *Tennessee, California, Maryland* and *Pennsylvania*, were all survivors of the Pearl Harbor raid.

From Kwajalein, the US 5th Fleet deployed northwest towards the Mariana Islands to begin Operation FORAGER, arriving off the initial target, Saipan, late on 13 June 1944 in anticipation of D-Day Saipan on 15 June.

As the operation developed, the great quandary faced by the Allies was whether Japan would commit her fleet to defend the Marianas. US analysts believed that a major naval battle would develop – but planning for such an engagement would require a different strategy from that formulated for the Gilbert and Marshall Islands campaign, where contact with the Japanese fleet had been planned for – but was not really expected. Knowing that the Marianas formed a bastion of Japan's last line of defence, the Allied naval Commander-in-Chief, Admiral Chester Nimitz, expected that the Japanese would use every asset and tactic available. He was right, Japan would attempt to defend its precious Saipan base at all costs.

Before any landings in the Marianas began, a heavy naval and air bombardment would soften up enemy positions. For the Marianas operation, more than 600 vessels would take part – including the fast-carrier strike force TF 58. As the battleships of the Fire Support Group were en route to Saipan, TF 58 carrier aircraft pounded the Marianas for three days following a fighter sweep on the afternoon of 11 June.

13 June 1944
The softening up naval bombardment of Saipan began on 13 June 1944 when Vice Admiral 'Ching' Lee's 7 TG 58.7 fast battleships (attached to the fast-carrier TF 58), 11 destroyers and 10 fast minesweepers opened fire from a distance of 10,000yd (more than 5 miles), remaining well offshore to avoid near shore minefields. The 16in guns of the famous battleships *Washington* (BB-56), *North Carolina* (BB-55), *Iowa* (BB-61), *New Jersey* (BB-62), *South Dakota* (BB-57), *Alabama* (BB-60) and *Indiana* (BB-58) all went into action, along with the 8in guns of the heavy cruisers *Wichita, Minneapolis, New Orleans* and *San Francisco* and the lighter batteries of the screen of destroyers.

14 June 1944
By early on the morning of 14 June 1944, the two OBB Fire Support Groups of the main landing support bombardment force had arrived from Kwajalein and were in position off Saipan, under Rear Admiral

Jesse B. Oldendorf's command from his flagship, the *Northampton*-class cruiser *Louisville* (CA-28). The seven Fire Support Group modernised, old battleships were accompanied by eight escort carriers, heavy cruisers, light cruisers and a screen of twenty-six destroyers.

After launching spotting aircraft to observe the fall of shot, *California* and the six other OBBS, along with attendant cruisers and destroyers, commenced a naval bombardment that would continue throughout the landings on 15 June – with devastating accuracy. The training that the OBB gunners had undergone with Marine Corps fire-control experts at the shore bombardment range at Kahoolawe, southwest of Maui, now paid dividends. Their gunners had more experience and training in shore bombardment than the gunners aboard Vice Admiral Ching Lee's fast battleships, which were trained for naval engagements.

California opened fire at 0558 with her 14in main-battery guns at a range of 14,500yd (just over 8 miles) – engaging targets in the area around the capital, Garapan. *California* however had moved within the 17,500yd range of Japanese 4.7in (120mm) coast-defence guns – and at 0910 a Japanese 120mm counter-bombardment shell struck *California* abaft the fire-control platform, killing one man, injuring ten, starting a fire and disabling the ship's air-search radar. This was however precisely the sort of hit that battleships had been designed to deal with – the fire was brought under control and she was able to continue firing unaffected until later in the day, when *California* departed the area for the night. She would close Saipan again the next morning.

D-Day Saipan, 15 June 1944
The US invasion fleet transport vessels moved into place off Saipan just after 0500 on 15 June – and the pre-invasion naval bombardment commenced at 0530. As the invasion troops afloat readied to begin the attack, a diversionary force of Marines carried out a dummy landing at the large village of Garapan, on Saipan's west coast – moving to within 5,000yd of the shore. *California* supported the Garapan dummy assault, opening fire at 0612.

For the initial phase of the main landing, more than 300 amphibious LVTs carrying some 8,000 Marines moved forward from their mother ships at 0700. As this was happening, the naval big-gun bombardment of Saipan paused briefly between 0700 and 0730 to allow for an air strike. Once completed, the big guns began firing again – with *California* now switching fire to the landing beaches.

By 0900, the Marines were ashore and engaging the enemy on the west coast of Saipan as dug-in defenders attempted to repel the landing.

California targeted Japanese artillery on Afetna Point, which had been shelling the US Marines.

At 0954, US observers spotted a group of Japanese Type 95 Ha-Go light three-man tanks and Type 97 Chi-Ha medium four-man tanks in Garapan. These manoeuvrable tanks were used for infantry support – and despite many shortcomings, they were a serious threat to the light US Marine landing forces. *California* engaged the tanks, destroying at least one – before going on to bombard a battery of Japanese guns which had been engaging the battleship *Maryland*. *California* continued to bombard Japanese positions throughout the day, before withdrawing for the night at 1830.

In all, the combined 14 battleships (new and old) and supporting warships fired an estimated 165,000 shells, destroying land targets, conducting counter-battery missions, destroying AA gun emplacements and burning all unburnt cane fields that would offer the enemy cover.

The bombardment had however failed to degrade the entrenched enemy fortifications significantly – and strategically placed barbed wire, artillery and machine-gun emplacements and trenches inflicted a heavy toll on the Marines. But despite this, by nightfall, the 2nd and 4th Marines had established a 6-mile-wide beachhead that stretched inshore for half a mile.

The Japanese counterattacked that night – but were fought back with heavy losses. *California* remained offshore overnight, and after establishing radio communications with the marines ashore, provided fire support to break up Japanese night counterattacks. *California* would remain on station off Saipan for several days, bombarding Japanese defences as the Marines pushed inland and engaging Japanese aircraft with her powerful AA batteries. She was lightly damaged by friendly fire on 18 June.

In all, some 71,000 US troops of V Amphibious Corps successfully landed on Saipan, meeting opposition from more than 30,000 well dug-in Japanese troops. The presence of the 5th Fleet off the Marianas prevented Japanese re-enforcement troop convoys from arriving after the US landings began.

Despite difficulties with liaison and control, close air support had combined excellently with the precision shore-bombardment gunnery of Oldendorf's older battleships to lay down an excellent barrage. The three-and-a-half days of pre-invasion bombardment was an unprecedented amount of heavy support for the Marines. Japanese records narrate that all the main body of Japanese defenders could do during the bombardment was to watch helplessly from their defensive positions as they were remorselessly pummelled.

USS *CALIFORNIA* (BB-44)

22 June 1944
After nine days of operations off Saipan, *California* was able to withdraw with *Tennessee* to replenish depleted ammunition and stores and undergo repairs at Eniwetok in the Marshalls. The same day, *Maryland* was damaged by an aerial torpedo off Garapan and would withdraw to Pearl Harbor for repair. *Pennsylvania* was detached on 25 June for Eniwetok to prepare for the Guam/Tinian landings in the Marianas.

Battle of Guam, 21 July–10 August 1944
The next strategic target for the Allies after Saipan was Guam, the westernmost territory of the USA and the largest island of the Marianas chain. Sitting at the south of the Marianas, Guam is some 32 miles long and 4–12 miles wide.

Guam had been invaded by Japan on 8 December 1941, immediately following the Pearl Harbor attack, and now held a garrison of some 19,000 personnel. If Guam could be seized by the Allies, then Apra Harbor could host the largest Allied ships – whilst Consolidated B-24 Liberator heavy bombers could fly north to bomb Iwo Jima and the Bonin Islands. The new Boeing B-29 Superfortress long-range bomber, which began to enter service in May 1944, would be able to hit targets such as Tokyo itself, some 1,500 miles to the north.

Commencing on 18 July, the pre-invasion bombardment by some 274 Allied ships fired almost 45,000 rounds against Guam's defences – whilst planes from the 13 aircraft carriers of TF 58 hit Guam from 18–20 July, the day before the invasion began. Every building that could be spotted – and all the palm trees near the landing beaches that could offer cover to the enemy – were destroyed.

On 19 July 1944, the two battleships *California* and *Tennessee*, and a screen of four destroyers, arrived off Guam following repair and resupply at Eniwetok. They joined Rear Admiral Jesse B. Oldendorf's Fire Support Group TG 53.5 battleships *Colorado*, *Pennsylvania*, *Idaho* and *New Mexico*, which had arrived from Eniwetok a week earlier on 12 July with six heavy cruisers, three light cruisers and a screen of destroyers and started shelling Japanese positions ashore.

The naval bombardment intensified in the days before the landings began on 21 July 1944 in a determined attempt to neutralise Japanese defences around the landing beaches. From its assigned position offshore, *California* brought her main-battery 14in guns to bear on Japanese defensive positions around the possible landing beaches of Tumon Bay, on the northwest coast of Guam, and the capital city of Agana, further south on the west coast.

At 0830 on D-Day Guam, 21 July 1944, the 3rd Marine Division landed near Agana to the north of Orote peninsula whilst the 1st Provisional Marine Brigade landed near Agat to the south. *California*'s guns fired in initial support for the amphibious assault, but the Marines were quickly ashore at both beaches and supported by the 77th Infantry Division had soon established a beachhead 6,600ft deep. *California* was detached later that day at 1500 and sent back up north to Saipan, which was now under Allied control following the end of the Battle of Saipan on 9 July 1944.

Battle of Tinian, 24 July–1 August 1944
Back at Saipan, *California* replenished her ammunition before moving towards the next Mariana island to be attacked – the small island of Tinian, where Allied amphibious landings were slated for 24 July. At some 40 square miles, Tinian lies just to the south of Saipan and well to the north of Guam – and held a garrison of almost 5,000 Japanese troops in well-prepared defensive positions.

Although naval gunfire had been hitting Tinian for almost a month, an intensive pre-invasion bombardment of the small island had opened on 16 July, broadly simultaneously with the naval bombardment of Guam, some 120 miles to the south.

Task Unit 53.1.16 of *California, Tennessee* and escort destroyers arrived off Tinian from Saipan on 23 July – the day before the landings began. Once in position, the main 14in battery guns and the secondary battery 5in guns of the two Pearl Harbor survivors opened a bombardment of Japanese positions around the large village of San Jose, which is situated on the southern end of the island and holds Tinian's main harbour and three beaches. This was in fact a diversionary bombardment – as the actual landing beaches were on the other northern end of the island. The two veteran battleships fired a total of 480 shells from their main guns and 800 rounds from their 5in guns, completely obliterating the town of San Jose. At 1700, as dusk approached, the two ships ceased their fire and withdrew for the night. The feint towards San Jose had worked – successfully diverting Japanese defenders from the actual intended landing site on the northwest coast.

The next morning, 24 July 1944, Task Unit 53.1.16 closed Tinian once again to provide close support as the 4th Marine Division began their D-Day landings. Tinian had two small beaches and low coral on the northwest coast – whilst the rest of the island had coral cliffs 15ft high at the water's edge. The two small, narrow beaches were almost certainly heavily guarded by the Japanese, whilst the 15ft-high jagged coral cliffs ringing around the rest of the island shoreline formed an apparent perfect barrier to landing heavy equipment, tanks and motorised artillery. But using materials found at an abandoned Japanese sugar mill on Saipan, and LVTs to supply flotation and mobility, two Seabee US Navy construction battalions on Saipan ingeniously fabricated landing ramps, nicknamed 'Doodlebugs', to scale the 15ft-high cliffs. The LVTs were fitted out to each carry its own ramp or ladder, which was made up of thick wooden beams connected with thick rope running through drilled holes in each beam. The wooden beams were strung across two longitudinal steel supports that were connected to the front leading beam of the ramp – the long steel supports being carried along either side of the LVT, suspended by chains to the other beams.

As the LVT approached the cliffs, hooks attached to the front end of the landing ramp caught firmly on the cliff tops. The LVT then reversed, backing out from under the landing ramp to let the back end of the two longitudinal steel beams fall into the water to rest on the coral bottom – with the wooden beams now resting on the two steel side supports and forming the ramp. The Doodlebugs could then move forward and rumble out of the water, driving up the ramps and over the cliffs. The ingenious ramps now in place then allowed the might of US mechanised units to mount the cliffs and outflank the prepared Japanese defences on the landing beaches, pouring into the island and driving the Japanese defenders out from their beach positions.

The 2nd Marine Division landed the following day and fighting raged for several days as *California* patrolled off the island, her powerful guns being called in to shell Japanese defensive positions as required in support of the ground troops. The Japanese adopted the same tactics as they had at Saipan, retreating during the day and attacking at night, making probes and counterattacks into the Marines' positions. By 29 July, US landing forces had captured half the island.

On 30 July the 4th Marine Division occupied Tinian town and Airfield No. 4. The remaining Japanese forces concentrated to make a last stand in the caves and ravines of a limestone ridge at the southern half of the island. On 31 July, *California* and the other fire-support ships began a heavy bombardment of these last Japanese positions before survivors launched a determined suicide banzai charge, which resulted in heavy casualties. The main fighting lasted until 3 August, although several hundred Japanese troops would hold out in the jungles for months.

With the main hostilities on Tinian now over, *California* was sent back down south to provide fire support at Guam, where the fighting was still going on. *California* provided big-gun support to the landing forces on Guam until 8 August, when she was detached with *Tennessee* and the heavy cruiser *Louisville* (CA-28) to head some 1,200 miles east to Eniwetok where she would replenish her depleted ammunition and fuel.

Organised resistance ended on Guam on 10 August 1944 and Guam was declared secure – although some 7,500 Japanese soldiers were estimated to still be at large in the jungles and ravines of the island.*

Espiritu Santo Naval Base – Dry Dock, 19 August–17 September 1944
After replenishment at Eniwetok, and just ten days after closing her fire-support duties off Guam, *California* departed Eniwetok with a task force of battleships, cruisers and destroyers heading some 1,900 miles southeast for the important US supply and support harbour base of Espiritu Santo, the largest island in the nation of Vanuatu, in the New Hebrides archipelago, southeast of the Solomon Islands chain.

En route, on 23 August 1944, her sister battleship *Tennessee* suffered a steering malfunction that caused her to veer out of line and collide with *California*, tearing a hole in *California*'s bow and killing seven of her crew. Bent and buckled bulkheads trapped several crew for some time until they could be cut through. Damage-control teams shored up the affected areas and were able to pump the water out of the hull. Although *Tennessee* had been more seriously damaged and had to leave the group for Pearl Harbor for more extensive repairs, the temporarily patched *California* was able to continue on with the remainder of the task force.

On arrival at the Espiritu Santo Naval Base, *California* entered the large ten-section, 927ft-long auxiliary floating dry dock *Artisan* (ABSD-1) for repairs that lasted from 25 August–10 September 1944. The collision damage prevented the ship from taking part in the Battle of Peleliu, which began on 15 September 1944.

(II) The Philippines Campaign
Battle of Leyte, 17 October–26 December 1944
On being undocked from the floating dry dock *Artisan*, *California* left Espiritu Santo Naval Base a few days later on 17 September 1944 and made her way northwest for some 1,600 miles – past the Solomon Islands and along the coast of New Guinea to Manus Island, in northern

---

* A number of Japanese soldiers held out in the jungle on Tinian for a long period. After the war ended on 2 September 1945, three US Marines were ambushed and killed on 8 December 1945. Sergeant Masashi Ito surrendered on 23 May 1960 after the rest of his colleagues were captured. On 24 January 1972, Sergeant Shoichi Yokoi was discovered by hunters – having lived alone in a cave for twenty-eight years.

Papua New Guinea. She arrived there five days later on 22 September, as preparations were under way for the next Allied operation.

The sea area between Formosa (Taiwan)-Luzon-China formed a natural bottleneck through which much of Japan's supplies of raw materials for her war passed – it became known as the Luzon bottleneck. If the Luzon bottleneck could be corked, an indirect blockade of Japan could begin to cut off her natural resources.

To initiate the corking of the Luzon bottleneck, the Allies planned to land in strength on Leyte, an island directly west across the Philippine Sea from the Mariana Islands. Leyte lies towards the eastern side of the Visayas group of the central Philippines and is one of the larger Philippine islands that has a number of deep-water approaches and sandy beaches suitable for amphibious assault and fast resupply. If Leyte was taken, then US air forces based there could then hit enemy positions and airfields anywhere in the Philippines archipelago.

The Allied landings on Leyte would trigger the 2nd Battle of the Philippine Sea, more commonly known today as the Battle of Leyte Gulf. Taking place over four days from 23–26 October 1944, and involving more than 200,000 military personnel, the battle is widely considered to have been the largest naval clash of the Second World War.

Allied operations in the Philippine Islands fell within the Southwest Pacific theatre under the command of the charismatic US General Douglas MacArthur – whose original campaign plan had provided for the recapture of Mindanao Island, in the southern Philippines, on 15 November and for land-based aircraft to support the Leyte assault on 20 December. However, the plan was subsequently changed, with the landing on Mindanao cancelled and the Leyte landings brought forward to 20 October – there would now be no land-based air support or ground troops from Mindanao available to support the Leyte operation. Air support would therefore have to come from the sea – and as at Saipan, the fast carriers and fast battleships of TF 38, from Nimitz's 3rd Fleet, would join MacArthur's 7th Fleet escort carriers to provide close air support – and engage the enemy fleet if it sought battle.

There would therefore be two Allied fleets in Philippine waters under separate commands for the Leyte operation:

1. Admiral William Halsey's 3rd Fleet of fast carriers, fast battleships and escorts, under Nimitz's overall command, would provide the *offensive* power.
2. Vice Admiral Thomas C. Kinkaid's 7th Fleet (which included units of the Royal Australian Navy), under the Southwest Pacific

command of General MacArthur, would have a *defensive* role in providing close naval support for landing troops with escort carriers and lighter warships. Rear Admiral Jesse B. Oldendorf's Fire Support TG 77.2, under Kinkaid's overall command, comprised the six older Standard-Type battleships, *West Virginia*, *Maryland*, *California*, *Tennessee*, *Mississippi* and *Pennsylvania*, operating with cruisers, destroyers and small fast PT torpedo boats. Air support was available from eighteen small escort carriers.

But crucially however, no single unified command structure for the two distinct fleets was established. And with Halsey and the 3rd Fleet reporting to Nimitz and Kinkaid and the 7th Fleet reporting to MacArthur, this fundamental defect would produce a crisis – and near catastrophe.

Although the Leyte operation was an army operation under MacArthur's command, Halsey would be free to use the 3rd Fleet to draw out and fight the Japanese Mobile Fleet. Nimitz made his fighting orders to Halsey clear, issued without reference to General MacArthur: 'In case opportunity for destruction of major portion of enemy fleet is offered or can be created, such destruction becomes the *primary task* [author's italics].'[13]

Halsey was thus authorised by Nimitz to seek out and destroy the IJN 1st Mobile Fleet, despite other mission commitments of search and support of the landings. This simple command would play a pivotal role as the battle developed. Halsey's orders were to first neutralise Japanese 2nd Air Fleet planes and infrastructure north of the Philippines, principally at Kyushu, Okinawa and Formosa. He was then to move southward towards the IJN 1st Air Fleet bases under Vice Admiral Ōnishi on the large north Philippine island of Luzon and in the Visayas in the Central Philippines.

It was the six carriers of 1st Air Fleet, the *Kidō Butai* (created in April 1941), that had attacked Pearl Harbor back on 7 December 1941. After the disastrous loss of four carriers at the Battle of Midway in June 1942, 1st Air Fleet had been disbanded – but it had subsequently been recreated on 1 July 1943 as an exclusively land-based naval air fleet of some 1,600 aircraft, flying from a network of unsinkable island airbases.

By June 1944, the IJN Second Fleet was made up of battleships, cruisers and destroyers under the command of Vice Admiral Takeo Kurita. Vice Admiral Jisaburō Ozawa commanded the more powerful Third Fleet

The Philippines

and had operational control of both fleets, which formed the combined 1st Mobile Fleet. By June 1944, the IJN Third Fleet now included 9 aircraft carriers carrying some 450 planes in total – and 2 battleships that had been converted to be half carriers, the 29,980-ton *Ise* and *Hyūga*.[14]

After the landings at Leyte, the Allies planned to seize Mindoro Island in the west of the central Philippines on 5 December 1944 – followed by a landing on 20 December 1944 at Lingayen Gulf, on the northwest side of Luzon, facing the South China Sea.

The invasion of Mindoro had been scheduled for 5 December 1944 – and was a major concern for Halsey. If the Japanese fleet carriers did not fight for Leyte, or survived a battle at Leyte, they would be free to strike at US shipping off Mindoro. Hundreds of Japanese aircraft could shuttle from airfields in China to carriers operating in the South China Sea and strike Mindoro. They could potentially trap MacArthur's amphibious forces and TF 38 on the west side of the Philippines. Halsey felt that the dangerous Japanese carriers needed to be eliminated at the earliest opportunity.

The invasion of Leyte by combined US and Australian forces would begin the isolation of Japan from the territories it occupied in southeast Asia, which were a vital source of oil and industrial materials such as rubber – and the aluminium ore known as bauxite, vital in aircraft manufacture. Japan's oil came primarily from the Dutch East Indies (modern-day Indonesia), then the fourth largest exporter of oil in the world – and which she had seized in March 1942.

By autumn 1944, the Japanese had been driven from many of their island bases in the South and Central Pacific, in the Gilberts and Marshalls. Most of the Mariana Islands, situated east of the Philippines, such as Saipan, Guam and Tinian had now been seized by Allied troops. Many other garrisoned islands had been hit, neutralised and bypassed – such as Truk and Palau. Japanese troops on these bypassed outposts were now beginning to starve. The USA had breached Japan's strategic inner defence ring and controlled airbases from which long-range Boeing B-29 Superfortress bombers could now directly attack the Japanese home islands themselves.

Japan by this stage had fewer aircraft carriers and battleships combined than the Allies had carriers. Admiral Soemu Toyoda, Commander-in-Chief of the IJN Combined Fleet, thus reorganised his forces as best he could, anticipating how to best meet the next Allied assault.

After analysing the options open to the Allies, the IJN prepared four plans. *Shō-Gō* 1 would be a major naval operation in the Philippines, whilst *Shō-Gō* 2, *Shō-Gō* 3 and *Shō-Gō* 4 were planned responses to attacks on Formosa, the Ryukyu Islands and the Kuril Islands respectively. These plans were complex and would commit much of the available Japanese naval forces towards a decisive battle – and would substantially deplete Japan's remaining thin reserves of fuel oil for her navy.

6 October 1944
In preparation for the Leyte landings on 20 October 1944, the four fast-carrier task groups of TF 38 sortied from Ulithi on 6 October 1944 and rendezvoused 375 miles west of the Marianas to begin pre-landing strikes against Japanese airfields that threatened the Leyte landings. Each of the 4 carrier task groups comprised 2 heavy carriers, 2 light carriers, 2 fast battleships and a screen of 3 cruisers and 14 destroyers – a total of 23 ships per task group. TF 38 was at its maximum unparalled strength, able to field more than 1,000 aircraft.

TF 38 aircraft attacked Okinawan airfields and shipping to the north with great success, followed by further strikes that culminated in four days of heavy air attacks against Formosa (Taiwan). These triggered Japanese command into initiating Operation *Shō-Gō* 2, the planned response to an Allied attack on Formosa, committing land-based aircraft to the destruction of the US fleet. Admiral Toyoda ordered 300 undertrained carrier pilots and their aircraft to airfields on Formosa to join the attack. Instead of having his carrier air power available to protect the Philippines, it would now be an all-or-nothing battle at Formosa.[15]

At Manus, *California* joined the battleships, cruisers and destroyers of Rear Admiral Jesse Oldendorf's 7th Fleet Fire Support TG 77.2, which departed on 12 October bound for the Philippines. In Formosa meanwhile, the aerial contest was gathering pace as Japanese pilots flew hundreds of sorties against US forces on 13, 14 and 15 October.

But the Japanese pilots were largely green, undertrained and inexperienced – and despite the large numbers of aircraft committed, Halsey's battle-hardened F6F Hellcat fighters shot down most of the Japanese fighters and destroyed hundreds of aircraft on the ground along with their land installations. In all, more than 500 Japanese planes were wiped out in the 4 days at Formosa. Admiral Toyoda had gambled – and lost. By doing so, he had prematurely sacrificed his air strength at Formosa – which had been ear marked for the defence of the Philippines.

With the air battle over Formosa so convincingly won, the carriers of TF 38 were now able to shift focus to the Philippines and begin the isolation of the beachhead at Leyte for the beach assault on A-Day, 20 October. Beginning on 15 October, TF 38 planes began five days of strikes against Luzon.

17 October 1944

In preparation for the Leyte landings, the Philippines campaign began on 17 October with initial landings by the 6th Ranger Battalion on three islands that stretch across the approaches to Leyte Gulf. Dinagat (situated northeast of Mindanao) and the small island of Suluan in eastern Samar were seized first of all – with a third island, Homonhon, taken the next day. The Rangers began to erect navigation lights to guide Allied forces into the Gulf. The same day, minesweepers began clearing channels into Leyte Gulf in preparation for the main landings on Leyte Island. The navy's underwater demolition teams (UDT) got into action, reconnoitring the waters off the proposed landing beaches – and finding that they were clear of submerged obstacles.

These preliminary Allied operations alerted the Japanese to the impending assault on the Philippines – and led to the activation on 18 October 1944 of Operation *Shō-Gō* 1 for the defence of the Philippines, where 432,000 Imperial Japanese Army (IJA) troops were now stationed.

Shō-Gō 1 was a typically elaborate Japanese plan, in which success depended on the precise movements and coordination of four naval forces. *Shō-Gō* 1 was daring and almost suicidal – but the twists and turns of the Pacific War had led to this moment where only a decisive Japanese naval victory in a large-scale fleet action would save the Philippines and keep her supply lifeline of resources open. Japan would commit its surface fleet in an all-or-nothing gamble with a coordinated attack on the Allied shipping and invasion forces at Leyte Gulf on the morning of 25 October 1944.

Shō-Gō 1 would employ a decoy **Northern Force** that included the fleet carrier *Zuikaku* and the light carriers *Zuihō*, *Chitose* and *Chiyoda* under the command of Vice Admiral Jisaburō Ozawa, which would sortie from the Inland Sea in the home islands of Japan. The two half-battleships *Ise* and *Hyūga* were attached to give 14in big-gun support along with a screen of light cruisers and destroyers. The Northern Force would deliberately attempt to be detected up north in the open expanses of the Philippine Sea to lure the fast carriers and fast battleships of Halsey's TF 38 away from Leyte Gulf, where they were now on station approximately 250 miles east of the Philippines. Although the Northern Force would be centred around several carriers – unknown to the Allies, these would have very few aircraft or trained air crew.

As the virtually planeless carriers of Ozawa's decoy Northern Force lured the US fast carriers and battleships away from Leyte, simultaneously, two other big-gun naval forces, the **Central Force**, under Vice Admiral Takeo Kurita and the **Southern Force**, commanded by Vice Admiral Shoji Nishimura, would approach the Philippines from the west. The Southern Force would be supported by the **Second Striking Force** under the Commander-in-Chief of the IJN 5th Fleet, Vice Admiral Kiyohide Shima, which would come down from the north to rendezvous with Nishimura's Southern Force in the Sulu Sea in the southwest Philippines.

Kurita's **Central Force**, based at the Lingga Roads anchorage south of Singapore, included the two superbattleships *Yamato* and *Musashi*, each with nine 46cm (18.1in) guns in three 3-gun turrets, the battleship *Nagato* with eight 41cm (16in) guns, two older battleships *Kongō* and *Haruna*, ten heavy cruisers, two light cruisers and 15 destroyers. It was by far the strongest of the three forces.

The Central Force would pass eastwards across the Sibuyan Sea in the central Philippines before transiting east through the San Bernardino Strait, which lies between Luzon to the north and Samar Island to the south. Once safely though the San Bernardino Strait, Kurita's Central Force would turn south and head down the east coast of Samar towards Leyte Gulf, which lies southwest of Samar Island.

The **Southern Force**, commanded by Vice Admiral Shoji Nishimura, would consist of the two older modernised 14in main-battery battleships *Fusō* and *Yamashiro*, the heavy cruiser *Mogami* (armed with fifteen 6in main-battery weapons) and escort destroyers. The Southern Force would cross the Sulu Sea from the west and then cross the adjoining Mindanao Sea before transiting northeast through the Surigao Strait, which lies between the islands of Leyte and Mindanao. Once through the Surigao Strait, the Southern Force would strike at Leyte Gulf from the south as the Central Force attacked from the north.

The **Second Striking Force** would sortie from the Pescadores, west of Taiwan and head south through the Sulu Sea to rendezvous with the Southern Force for the final push through the Surigao Strait to Leyte. It comprised the two heavy cruisers *Nachi* and *Ashigara* (with 8in main battery), the light cruiser *Abukuma* and seven destroyers.

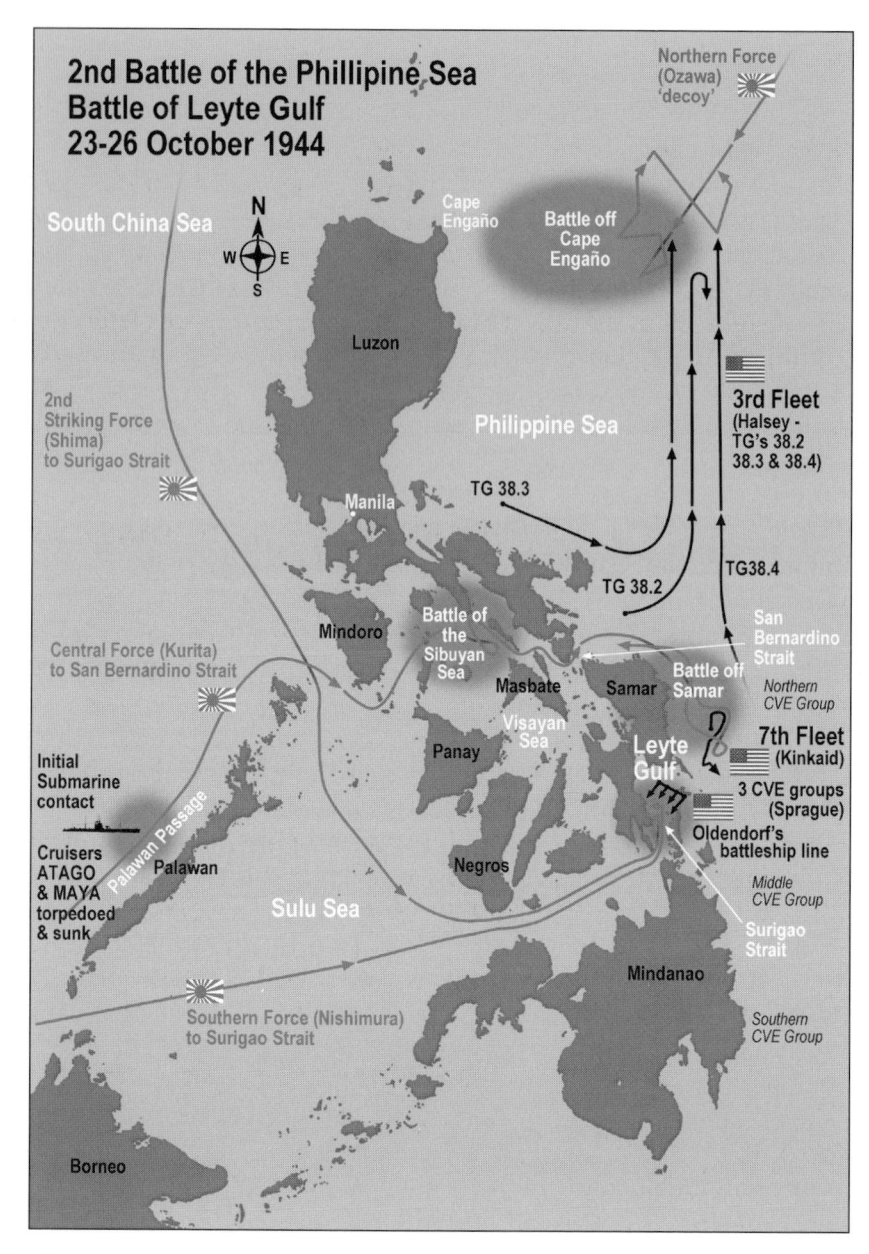

Battle of Leyte Gulf, 23–26 October 1944. This shows the insertion routes of the Japanese Northern Force, Central Force, Southern Force and 2nd Striking Force, disposition of Vice Admiral Kinkaid's 7th Fleet CVE groups east of Samar and Admiral Halsey's 3rd Fleet TG 38 fast-carrier forces. The separate actions involved are shown: Battle of the Sibuyan Sea, Battle off Samar, Battle of the Surigao Strait and the Battle off Cape Engaño.

18 October 1944

Kurita's Central Force and Nishimura's Southern Force sortied from the Lingga Roads, off Singapore, on 18 October 1944, two days before the Allied landings on Leyte began on A-Day, 20 October 1944.

The daring Japanese plan was very much a last throw of the dice in which Ozawa's virtually planeless carriers of the decoy Northern Force were going to be sacrificed as bait to lure the US TF 38 fast carriers away from the Philippines. Nishimura's Southern Force would face off against a strong battle line of the older Standard-Type battleships of Oldendorf's Fire Support Group at the Surigao Strait. But if the deception worked and Kurita's Central Force battleships *Yamato, Musashi, Nagato, Kongō* and *Haruna*, along with their powerful cruisers and destroyer escort, managed to avoid contacting the fast carriers and battleships of TF 38, they could wreak havoc amongst the vulnerable Allied shipping off Leyte – and devastate the landing beaches with a big-gun naval bombardment. But if Halsey and TF 38 didn't take the bait, the powerful US fast carriers and their fast-battleship screen could still cut off the Central Force's northward withdrawal back towards the San Bernardino Strait after the strike at Leyte Gulf. If that happened, and the Japanese fleet was destroyed (as seemed entirely possible), Japan's main naval strength would be reduced to land-based air and submarines. It was clear to Japanese commanders that if it all went wrong, the bold plan could turn out to be the end of the Japanese surface fleet.

Hundreds of additional planes had been requested from China and Japan – and would begin arriving within days. Vice Admiral Takijirō Ōnishi, commander of land based naval 1st Air Fleet assigned to the defence of the Philippines, had little faith however in these largely green pilots. He activated the Kamikaze Corps of suicide planes on 19 October.[16]

20 October 1944 – A-Day

The wide expanse of Leyte Gulf is bounded on the north and east by the large island of Samar, and on the west by the island of Leyte. On 19 October, A-Day -1, with minesweepers having cleared the approaches, the Allied naval bombardment warships began softening up Leyte, the bombardment continuing through to the next day, A-Day 20 October 1944.

On A-Day, after 4 hours' bombardment, US 6th Army forces began their landings at 1000 on the beaches fronting Leyte Gulf, of Dulag to the west (on the east shore of Leyte) and at San Pedro Bay (at the northwest end of Leyte Gulf).

After the beachheads were secured, at 1330 the Supreme Allied Commander General Douglas MacArthur was able to make his dramatic entrance from a landing craft through the surf onto Red Beach, near the municipality of present-day Palo on the east shore of Leyte and make his prepared statement: 'People of the Philippines, I have returned! By the grace of Almighty God, our forces stand again on Philippine soil.'*

The Battle of Leyte was the first battle in which Japan deployed organised kamikaze attacks – and later that day, with troops now ashore on Leyte, one of the first kamikazes, a Mitsubishi A6M Zero fighter, dived toward *California* in her bombardment station. Heavy AA fire from gunners aboard *California* and the screen deflected the plane off course – and it crashed harmlessly off her starboard bow. Over the following days, *California* remained off the invasion beaches, pounding Japanese defensive positions as US forces pushed their way inland.

Meanwhile, as the Allied landings proceeded, the four Japanese naval forces were moving towards Leyte Gulf for their planned Operation *Shō-Gō* 1 counterattack. After Allied reconnaissance aircraft and submarines sighted the Japanese forces as they moved towards the Philippines, Oldendorf's bombardment group of old battleships withdrew towards the Surigao Strait, south of Leyte every night to block any Japanese surface attack on Allied shipping.

The 2nd Battle of the Philippine Sea
The Battle of Leyte Gulf, 23–26 October 1944

The Battle of Leyte Gulf is considered to have been the largest naval battle of the Second World War, involving more than 200,000 belligerents. It began with a submarine engagement in the Palawan Passage and was followed by four main engagements over several days at different locations in the Philippines that came to be known as:

(i) Battle of the Sibuyan Sea.
(ii) Battle off Samar.
(iii) Battle of the Surigao Strait.
(iv) Battle off Cape Engaño.

---

* Today General MacArthur's Red Beach landing site at Palo on Leyte is enshrined by the MacArthur Landing Memorial National Park, the focal point of which are seven double-life-sized bronze statues set in a shallow artificial pool that depict MacArthur with the Philippine president-in-exile Sergio Osmena and accompanying officers striding ashore through the surf from their landing craft.

The US Standard-Type battleships would triumph at the Battle of the Surigao Strait, which would prove to be the last naval gunnery exchange between battleships in history. The IJN would suffer heavy losses in the engagements – their Mobile Fleet would essentially be destroyed and would never sail in such strength again. Successfully cut off from their fuel supplies by the subsequent corking of the Luzon bottleneck, the surviving IJN fleet units became stranded in their bases due to a lack of fuel.

As US troops were landing at Leyte on A-Day, 20 October 1944, the 4 Japanese carriers of the Northern Force loaded 116 aircraft, enough for a single strike on Luzon, in an attempt to trick Halsey into believing the Northern Force was also heading for a rendezvous with the 2 battleship forces down south, for a combined strike on Allied shipping and the beachhead at Leyte Gulf. Admiral Halsey, in command of the 3rd Fleet, had no way of knowing that Admiral Toyoda had sacrificed his main land-based and carrier-based air strength in the preceding disastrous air battle over Formosa.

At 1700 on 20 October, just hours after General MacArthur stepped ashore at Red Beach on Leyte's eastern shore, Ozawa's decoy Northern Force of four carriers, two half-battleships, light cruisers and destroyers sortied from the Inland Sea of Japan.

22 October 1944
Vice Admiral Thomas C. Kinkaid's 7th Fleet, operating with General MacArthur, had eighteen CVE escort carriers of the Escort Carrier TG 77.4, under the command of Rear Admiral Thomas L. Sprague. The CVE escort carriers were smaller and could make at best 24 knots. They were slower, more lightly armed and armoured and carried fewer planes than the large 33-knot fast carriers, which carried between eighty and ninety planes each.

Sprague's eighteen small CVE escort carriers were divided into three task units that were stationed up and down the east of Samar and Leyte and flying off Hellcat and Wildcat fighters and TBF Avenger bombers for close support of troops ashore on Leyte. Meanwhile, the planes of TF 38 patrolled the skies and attacked enemy airfields. The TF 38 planes were soon able to use two captured airfields on Leyte for emergency landings.

Now ashore, MacArthur's 6th Army troops moved inland under this powerful air cover, aiming to gain as much ground as possible before an anticipated Japanese counterattack on land, sea and air could develop. The waters offshore in the wide expanses of Leyte Gulf thronged with

Allied shipping – whilst equipment piled up on the landing beaches as transport ships raced to unload their cargoes and clear Leyte Gulf before any Japanese counterattack.

The apparent absence of Japanese fleet units in the area allowed Halsey to concentrate his naval forces on guarding the San Bernardino Strait, north of Samar, and the Surigao Strait, south of Samar. These two straits are the only channels from the west that enemy warships could use to get close to Kinkaid's vulnerable 7th Fleet shipping at Leyte Gulf.

Movements of major Japanese fleet units northward from the Singapore area were detected by the Allies on 21 and 22 October 1944 – these were elements of the Central and Southern Forces. Kinkaid was relying on protection against any surface threat from the 16in and 14in big guns of the six older Standard-Type battleships *West Virginia, Maryland, California, Tennessee, Mississippi* and *Pennsylvania* of Oldendorf's Fire Support TG 77.2, which were operating with 4 heavy cruisers, 4 light cruisers, 28 destroyers and 39 small fast PT torpedo boats. In addition, Kinkaid had air support from the eighteen small TG 77.4 CVE escort carriers – as well as the planes of the fast carriers of TF 38. TF 38 had a screen of six fast battleships, cruisers and destroyers and was still stationed 250 miles offshore to the east. Kinkaid had – for the time being – powerful support.

Thus protected, the 6th Army made good progress inshore at Leyte. With an apparent absence of Japanese naval units, and with Oldendorf's TG 77.2 battleships and cruisers and the TG 77.4 CVE escort carriers in position, Halsey felt the situation safe enough to detach the carriers of TG 38.1 and TG 38.4 and send them more than 1,000 miles east to Ulithi for replenishment.

(a) Initial Submarine Action in the Palawan Passage, 23 October 1944
Kurita, the Central Force commander, and Nishimura, the Southern Force commander, both now at Brunei Bay, received their orders the same day – and both forces sortied separately for the Philippines on 22 October 1944. The same day, Shima's Second Striking Force of cruisers and destroyers left Japanese waters, heading south to join and strengthen Nishimura's Southern Force.

Kurita's powerful Central Force of the 5 battleships *Yamato, Musashi, Nagato, Kongō* and *Haruna* along with 10 heavy cruisers, 2 light cruisers and 15 destroyers headed northeast from Brunei Bay for the Palawan Passage, which runs up the northwest side of Palawan Island. The east coast of Palawan forms the western boundary of the Sulu Sea of the Central Philippines.

Kurita intended that his Central Force would pass around the northern tip of Palawan Island and then head northeast across the Sulu Sea and enter the Sibuyan Sea. After crossing the Sibuyan Sea, his force would transit eastwards through the San Bernardino Strait, between the southern tip of Luzon Island and the north of Samar Island. Once through the San Bernardino Strait, the Central Force would head south down the east coast of Samar to strike Allied shipping and the beachhead at Leyte Gulf, southwest of Samar. By midnight on 22 October, the Central Force was moving in darkness northeast along the Palawan Passage prior to entering the Sulu Sea.

Palawan Island is 264 miles long and 25 miles wide and is the fifth largest island of the Philippines. The long, narrow, mountainous island runs northeast–southwest on the western periphery of the Philippines, essentially forming part of the archipelago's northwestmost boundary. To its west are the open expanses of the South China Sea.

Two US submarines, *Darter* (SS-227) and *Dace* (SS-247), were stationed in the Palawan Passage in close proximity on picket duty. Just after midnight on 23 October, whilst surfaced, *Darter*'s radar detected Japanese naval units at a range of about 30,000yd (roughly 17 miles) – and soon afterwards, visual contact was made by lookouts.

The two submarines sent three contact reports back to Halsey and shadowed the Japanese naval force on the surface for several hours as they manoeuvred to achieve a firing position ahead of what was Kurita's Central Force – for a submerged attack at first light. *Dace* and *Darter* achieved their firing positions just after 0500 in the nautical half-light of dawn. They attacked with devastating effect.

Darter fired a salvo of six torpedoes at Kurita's flagship, the 9,850-ton heavy cruiser *Atago* – at least four torpedoes were hits. *Darter* then scored two hits on *Atago*'s sister ship, the 9,850-ton heavy cruiser *Maya*, 10 minutes later. Both heavy cruisers sank quickly, the *Atago* sinking so quickly that Kurita himself ended up in the water, swimming for his life. He was picked up by the destroyer *Kishinami* before transferring to the battleship *Yamato*.

A third 9,850-ton heavy cruiser, *Takao*, was also hit and so badly damaged that it had to turn to limp back southwest with two destroyer escorts to refuge in Borneo. The two US submarines followed, looking to finish her off – but *Darter* however ran aground on a shoal. After all efforts to get her off failed, she had to be abandoned and her entire crew transferred to *Dace*.

Armed with the submarine contact reports, Admiral Halsey could now assume that the Japanese 1st Mobile Fleet was going to offer battle.

Whilst he recalled the TG 38.4 carriers which were on their 1,300-mile passage southeast to Ulithi, he would wait for further intelligence before recalling the TG 38.1 carriers, which were now some 600 miles away to the east, well on their way to Ulithi.

The fleet carrier *Bunker Hill*, central to Rear Admiral G.F. Bogan's TG 38.2, had also retired on 23 October for Ulithi to pick up more fighter aircraft, leaving TG 38.2 now weakened and comprising only one heavy carrier, *Intrepid*, and the light carriers *Cabot* and *Independence*. From originally having seventeen TF 38 fast carriers, Halsey was now left with eleven for the battle that now appeared imminent.

To protect the beachhead and shipping at Leyte, Halsey ordered his three remaining task groups to close the eastern Philippine islands and launch search planes the next morning in a fan that would cover the western approaches for the entire length of the Philippines archipelago. The three task groups reached their stations that night, 23 October, covering the three possible enemy approaches to Leyte – via the Surigao Strait, the San Bernardino Strait and from the Philippine Sea to the north.

Rear Admiral F.C. (Ted) Sherman's TG 38.3, comprising *Essex*, *Lexington*, *Princeton* and *Langley*, would cover the northern area, taking station near Polillo Island, east of Luzon and covering the open waters of the Philippine Sea well to the north of the San Bernardino Strait.

Following *Bunker Hill*'s departure for Ulithi, Bogan's weakened TG 38.2 would take station 140nm southeast of Sherman's TG 38.3 and cover the San Bernardino Strait. The planes of TG 38.3 and TG 38.4 would be able to come to TG 38.2's aid if required.

Rear Admiral R.E. Davison's TG 38.4, *Franklin*, *Enterprise*, *San Jacinto* and *Belleau Wood*, 120nm southeast of Bogan's TG 38.2, would cover the Surigao Strait.

(b) Battle of the Sibuyan Sea, 24 October 1944
TF 38 search planes launched at daybreak – and shortly after 0800, one of Bogan's TG 38.2 planes reported sighting 5 enemy battleships, 9 cruisers and 13 destroyers leaving the north of the Sulu Sea, south of Mindoro Island, bearing 050° and making 10–12 knots. This was Kurita's Central Force, which was heading roughly northeast for the Sibuyan Sea, having already lost two of its heavy cruisers and had a third damaged in the submarine night action off Palawan earlier.

The Sibuyan Sea, through which the Central Force was soon to pass, is a small sea some 175 miles across that separates the central Visayan Islands from the large northern island of Luzon. The sea is ringed by the large islands of Mindoro to the northwest, the southern coastline of Luzon to the northeast and the islands of Masbate and Panay to its south. Continuing eastwards between Masbate and Luzon, the San Bernardino Strait is reached, which leads to the Philippine Sea.

In light of the contact reports, at 0827, Halsey ordered Sherman's TG 38.3 and Davison's TG 38.4 to close at their best speed on Bogan's weakened TG 38.2, which was nearest the line of approach of the powerful enemy battleship force. At 0837, he ordered all task groups by TBS: 'Strike! Repeat: Strike!! Good luck!'[17] At 0846, Halsey now recalled McCain's distant TG 38.1, perhaps the strongest of the fast carrier Task Groups – but TG 38.1 was hundreds of miles away en route Ulithi and might not be back in time to participate in any contact with Japanese naval forces.

At 0943, Halsey's TF 38 search planes detected a second enemy force heading northeastward in the Sulu Sea, far to the south. This was Nishimura's weaker Southern Force of 2 battleships, 3 heavy cruisers, 1 light cruiser and 8 destroyers. It was clearly heading for the Surigao Strait.

Ted Sherman's TG 38.3 was the furthest north of the three carrier task groups, on station off Polillo Island. His aircraft were raiding Japanese airfields on Luzon to prevent enemy land-based air attacks by Vice Admiral Ōnishi's 1st Air Fleet on Allied shipping and the beachhead at Leyte Gulf.

In response to Sherman's TG 38.3 raids, Ōnishi launched three land-based 1st Air Fleet waves of fifty to sixty strike aircraft each to hit Sherman's carriers. These heavy Japanese air attacks forced Sherman to break off his Luzon strikes to concentrate on defending his own carriers.

Most of the Japanese planes attacking Sherman's TG 38.3 were successfully downed or damaged. However, a single Yokosuka D4Y3 Judy dive bomber managed to get through the CAP and AA screens and at 0938, successfully hit the TG 38.3 light carrier *Princeton* (CVL-23) with a 550lb AP bomb, which easily penetrated the wooden flight deck and exploded on the hangar strength deck below. The carrier's sprinkler system was damaged and as fires took hold and spread, a series of secondary explosions began.*

At 1000, up north in the Sibuyan Sea, lookouts on the Central Force superbattleship *Musashi* spotted the first wave of forty inbound planes

---

* Later, at 1524, the carrier was rocked by a large explosion as her magazine blew up, killing more than 100 of her crew and more than 200 crew of the light cruiser *Birmingham* (CL-62), alongside *Princeton* to provide firefighting support. *Princeton* was later scuttled by torpedoes – she was the largest US ship sunk during the battle and the first fast carrier the navy had lost since *Hornet* (CV-8) at the Battle of Santa Cruz two years earlier.

from Gerry Bogan's TG 38.2. Shortly afterwards, at 1025, Japanese AA gunners opened fire as Bogan's planes attacked. Meanwhile, down south, Davison's TG 38.4 planes attacked the Southern Force – aircraft from all three TF 38 task groups were now heavily engaged.

Nishimura's weaker Southern Force was pressing eastwards across the Sulu Sea towards the Surigao Strait. Screened by destroyers, the two sister battleships *Fusō* and *Yamashiro* both carried twelve 14in main-battery guns whilst the heavy cruiser *Mogami* carried fifteen 6in main-battery guns. The Southern Force was to rendezvous in the east of the Sulu Sea with Shima's Second Striking Force of the two heavy cruisers *Nachi* and *Ashigara*, the light cruiser *Abukuma* and seven destroyers. The two naval forces would then make the final push through the Surigao Strait to Leyte. But Shima was still well to the north, heading south through the Sulu Sea for the rendezvous.

Halsey assessed that by midnight the combined Southern Force and Shima's Second Striking Force would be in range of the OBBS of Rear Admiral Jesse B. Oldendorf's Fire Support TG 77.2 at Leyte Gulf. But satisfied that the weaker Southern Force could be dealt with by Oldendorf's battle line of Standard-Type battleships – and the planes of Kinkaid's eighteen 7th Fleet CVE escort carriers – he discontinued TF 38 air strikes against the Southern Force. He would concentrate his planes up north on the more powerful and more dangerous superbattleship Central Force, which was clearly heading for the San Bernardino Strait for an attack on Leyte Gulf.

More than 250 TF 38 planes attacked the Central Force in the Sibuyan Sea. 'Our planes hit the Central Force again and again throughout the day.' wrote Halsey later.[18] The battleships *Nagato*, *Yamato*, *Musashi* and the cruiser *Tone* were all damaged whilst the heavy cruiser *Myōkō* was hit by a Mark 13 torpedo from an *Intrepid* TBF Avenger at 1029 that put her starboard screws out of action. Her speed dropped to 15 knots and she had to retire to Borneo via Coron Bay, escorted by the destroyer *Kishinami*.

Japan's newest and largest battleship, the 71,659-ton (F) *Musashi*, became a primary target for TF 38 aircraft. At 1027, eight Curtiss SB2C Helldiver dive bombers from *Intrepid* made the first attack, scoring four near misses around the bow and amidships that blew in some of her plating and allowed the two forward peak tanks to slowly flood. *Musashi* was also hit by a 1,000lb bomb on the roof of No. 1 turret, which bounced off and failed to penetrate.

A few minutes later, as other aircraft joined the attack, *Musashi* was hit on her starboard side amidships, slightly abaft the bridge, by an aerial torpedo from an *Intrepid* TBF Avenger. She had soon flooded with an estimated 3,000 tons of water and taken on a 5.5° list to starboard. This was subsequently reduced to 1° by counterflooding compartments on the other side of the ship – and the speed of the battleship was not affected.

Just after noon, another attack by a division of eight *Intrepid* Helldivers scored further bomb hits – one of which penetrated two decks before exploding on the horizontal armour deck above one of the engine rooms. Fragments from the explosion shattered a steam pipe in the engine room, forcing it and an adjacent boiler room to be abandoned. Power to the port inboard propeller was lost and the great battleship's speed dropped to 22 knots on her three remaining shafts.

Nine TBF Avengers attacked from both sides of the battleship 3 minutes later, scoring three torpedo hits on the port side. *Musashi* fought on, but one torpedo explosion flooded another engine room. More counterflooding reduced her list to 1° to port – but the combined flooding had now reduced her freeboard by 6ft.

At 1330, a third strike by a combined twenty-nine aircraft from *Essex* and *Lexington* resulted in four bomb hits and four more torpedo hits. As a fourth strike went in against the Central Force, *Musashi* was seen to be trailing astern of the battle line at 20 knots, her bow now down by 13ft.

A fifth attack on the Central Force was made 2 hours later by sixty-nine carrier planes from *Enterprise* and *Franklin*. Nine *Enterprise* Helldivers scored four hits with 1,000lb semi-armour-piercing bombs – the first hitting the command bridge and killing nearly everyone there. *Musashi* was then hit by three more torpedoes from Avengers, which opened up her starboard bow. As she flooded further, her speed dropped to 16 knots and then to 13 knots, forcing Kurita to slow the rest of his fleet. She began to list further to port and her electrical power failed.

At 1525, a sixth attack on the Central Force was made by 75 aircraft from *Intrepid*, *Franklin* and *Cabot*, 37 of which targeted *Musashi* and scored 13 bomb hits and 11 more torpedo hits. *Musashi* had now been hit by an estimated 19 torpedoes and 17 bombs and her speed had dropped to 6 knots. Further counterflooding succeeded in reducing her port list from 10° to 6°.

Confronted by these attacks and concerned about the danger to his fleet if he entered the San Bernardino Strait in daylight, at 1530 Kurita ordered his Central Force to come to a new westnorthwest course of 290°. Kurita was in apparent retreat – getting out of the range of US carrier aircraft. The Battle of the Sibuyan Sea was over.

Shortly after beginning to withdraw, Kurita's Force approached the beleaguered trailing *Musashi*, which by now had come about and was slowly heading north to escape the Sibuyan Sea. Japan's largest battleship was listing to port, with her head now down by 26ft and her fo'c'sle deck awash.

As the flooding continued, *Musashi*'s engines eventually had to be stopped – and by 1915 her list had increased to 12°. Her crew was ordered off – and by the time they had completed her abandonment, the list had increased dramatically to 30°.

Just 20 minutes later, at 1936, in darkness and unseen by US eyes, *Musashi* finally succumbed and capsized. One of the heaviest and most powerfully armed battleships ever built by man then disappeared below the surface. Her captain, Toshihira Inoguchi, chose to go down with his ship – but more than 1,300 of her crew of 2,399 were saved.

The loss of *Musashi* was a spectacular Japanese naval loss – to add to the two cruisers *Atago* and *Maya* sunk and the cruiser *Takao* badly damaged by the American submarines *Darter* and *Dace* early the day before in the Palawan Passage. But Kurita still had four battleships and seven cruisers in his Central Force in the Sibuyan Sea that still posed a threat to the Leyte landing forces and shipping.

US pilot combat reports on 24 October of the damage to *Musashi* and other enemy units passed to Halsey in his flagship, the battleship *New Jersey*, led him to believe that Kurita's Central Force was no longer as potent a threat as it had been. But when the Central Force turned to head west in apparent withdrawal just after 1500, Halsey still did not discount the possibility that Kurita might yet turn his Central Force around towards the San Bernardino Strait. Halsey and his 3rd Fleet staff aboard *New Jersey* prepared a contingency plan to deal with the potential threat from Kurita's Central Force – the San Bernardino Strait would be covered by a powerful task force of fast TF 38 battleships supported by two fast-carrier task groups.

At 1512, Halsey sent a preparatory battle-plan despatch to his task-group commanders. If a surface engagement offered, he would detach 4 of the 6 fast battleships, 2 heavy cruisers, 3 light cruisers and 14 destroyers. A battle line 'WILL BE FORMED AS TF 34 UNDER V.ADM. LEE, COMMANDER BATTLE LINE. TF 34 WILL ENGAGE DECISIVELY AT LONG RANGES.'[19]

Halsey copied this despatch to Admiral Nimitz, CINCPAC-CINCPOA, at Pacific Fleet HQ in Pearl and to Admiral Ernest King, the Chief of Naval Operations (CNO), in Washington – but as there was no unified command structure, he did not copy it to Vice Admiral Kinkaid, commanding the 7th Fleet at Leyte Gulf.

Halsey's despatch was in fact picked up by 7th Fleet – but as the despatch didn't say *when* TF 34 would be formed, or under what circumstances, Kinkaid assumed that TF 34 *had* been formed – and would take station off the San Bernardino Strait. Nimitz at Pearl took the same understanding from the despatch.

To support the invasion forces at Leyte, Kinkaid had deployed his 18 CVE escort carriers in 3 task groups of 6 CVEs each – called 'Taffies' – that were protected by destroyers and destroyer escorts. Each CVE escort carrier carried an average of 28 planes – and 2 of his 18 CVEs had already departed for Morotai carrying defective aircraft for transfer ashore and repair.

The Northern CVE Group of six carriers was stationed off the east coast of Samar Island. The Middle CVE Group was stationed broadly to the east of Leyte Gulf whilst the Southern CVE Group was stationed east of Mindanao, to the south of the Surigao Strait. With Oldendorf's battleships stationed in Leyte Gulf, there were no battleships in Kinkaid's three escort carrier groups that could deal with a direct attack by Japanese battleships. It was a potentially fatal situation – and as it transpired, Kurita's superbattleship force would almost overwhelm Kinkaid's lighter, and exposed, forces close to the Leyte beachhead the next day.

In numbers of big-gun warships, both opposing sides up north at the San Bernardino Strait appeared about even – each had 4 battleships, whilst the Japanese had 6 cruisers to TF 38's 5, but crucially, Halsey, even with *Princeton* mortally wounded (but still afloat) at this point, still had 10 carriers – whilst the Japanese had almost no aircraft.

At 1710, Halsey issued a further clarification by short-range TBS voice radio to his subordinate commanders of his position regarding TF 34: 'IF THE ENEMY SORTIES, TF 34 WILL BE FORMED WHEN DIRECTED BY ME.'

But as this was a voice radio transmission, with the limitations of the day, it wasn't picked up by 7th Fleet – nor was a telegraphic copy sent to Admiral Nimitz, CINCPAC-CINCPOA, at Pearl or Admiral King, CNO, at Washington. Kinkaid, Nimitz and King were therefore none the wiser about what Halsey was doing and still believed that TF 34 had already been formed.

To US eyes, both passages that allowed an approach and attack on Leyte, the San Bernardino Strait to the north of Samar and the Surigao Strait to the southwest of Leyte, now appeared to be well covered. But the critical question of concern to all US commanders was the whereabouts of the Japanese carriers – they hadn't been spotted yet. Halsey believed they were to the north and Ted Sherman, CTG 38.3, faced with attacks by Japanese naval planes up north off Polillo Island, was 'strongly suspicious of the presence of Jap carriers to the northeast'.[20]

After the war, Halsey learned that as Kurita's Central Force headed northwest that afternoon, away from TF 38 air attack, Kurita had received a despatch from Admiral Toyoda, Commander-in-Chief of the Combined Fleet: 'WITH CONFIDENCE IN HEAVENLY GUIDANCE, THE ENTIRE FORCE WILL ATTACK.'[21]

At 1715, as dusk approached, Kurita obeyed the order and turned his Central Force back eastwards towards the San Bernardino Strait, hoping to transit the strait in darkness so that early the following morning, the Central Force could emerge from the strait and head down the east coast of Samar to surprise the Americans and smash the landing forces at Leyte. The plan still depended on Ozawa's decoy Northern Force carriers luring the US TF 38 carriers north – and away from Samar.

Ozawa's Northern Force, however, was still far to the north in the open expanses of the Philippine Sea – and had not yet managed to get itself detected.

Earlier that morning, 24 October, the day of the Battle of the Sibuyan Sea, well to the north of the Philippines, Admiral Ozawa was implementing the deception battle plan and doing what he could to get his Northern Force of virtually planeless carriers detected.

Ozawa sent the half-battleships *Ise* and *Hyūga* south with a screen of four destroyers as a vanguard that moved out some 50 miles ahead of the main body of his force, seeking out contact. Ozawa put out bogus radio transmissions and sent out regular air searches.

At 1145, Ozawa launched a seventy-six-plane strike from his four carriers – and at about 1330, the planes located and attacked the northmost of the three TF 38 carrier groups, Ted Sherman's TG 38.3. The TG 38.3 Hellcats and the AA guns of Sherman's screen wrought havoc with the Japanese strike – but rather than taking the bait that this was a carrier strike, the Americans concluded that this was yet another attack by 1st Air Fleet land-based navy planes, like the one had seriously damaged the *Princeton*.

Finally, at 1515 the vanguard of Ozawa's force was spotted by a US search plane. Then, at 1640, a *Lexington* Helldiver spotted the main body of Ozawa's Northern Force and reported the presence of the enemy carrier force heading south approximately 200 miles off Cape Engaño, at the northeastern tip of Luzon. At 1730, Sherman informed Halsey: '3 CARRIERS 2 LIGHT CRUISERS 3 DESTROYERS 18-32 N 125-28 E COURSE 270 SPEED 15.'[22]

As US aircraft contact reports came in, it seemed that there was a 17-ship-strong Japanese force to the north that included 1 heavy carrier, 3 light carriers, 2 half-battleships with a flight deck aft, a heavy cruiser, a light cruiser, 3 other AA cruisers and a screen of 6 destroyers.[23] But the position, 200 miles northeast of Cape Engaño, was too far for Halsey's planes to reach, before the imminent sunset.

Despite the fatal damage to the carrier *Princeton*, in his subsequent Action Report 0900, Ted Sherman, CTG 38.3, explained:

> The carrier forces to the north were our meat; they were close enough so that they could not get away if we headed to the northward ... As the sun went down the situation was entirely to my liking and I felt we had a chance to completely wipe out a major group of the enemy fleet including the precious carriers which he could ill afford to lose.[24]

Halsey had a dilemma before him. With the whereabouts of Ozawa's Northern Force now apparent, if Kurita and his still powerful Central Force did reverse course, coming about to head east toward the San Bernardino Strait, he would have two powerful Japanese naval forces to contend with, the Northern and Central Forces.

That evening, Vice Admiral Willis A. 'Ching' Lee, commander of the TF 34 Battle Line, advised Halsey that in his view, the Northern Force was playing decoy – and that he should form his line of battle off the San Bernardino Strait.[25] The US commanders discussed the possibility of leaving Lee's Battle Line and one carrier group to guard the San Bernardino Strait and sending the other two task groups north after the carriers of Ozawa's Northern Force. Halsey however, having already lost the *Princeton* to Luzon-based aircraft, determined that 'he would keep his fleet together because the entire operation would be under potential land-based air attack'.[26] By concentrating his forces, he would maximise AA protection. At this point however, Kinkaid down at Leyte and Nimitz at Pearl believed that the TF 34 battle line had *already* been formed at San Bernardino.

If TF 38 remained concentrated and went north after the carriers of Ozawa's Northern Force, then it was obvious that Kurita's apparently retiring and damaged westward-bound Central Force might come about and pass through the San Bernardino Strait to attack the vulnerable Leyte landing forces and 7th Fleet shipping. Whilst Halsey believed the Central Force might inflict damage, in his subsequent Action Report, he indicated that with the damage the Central Force had reportedly taken, he believed that 'its fighting power was too seriously impaired to win a decision'.[27]

PEARL HARBOR'S REVENGE

Halsey felt that the three separate Japanese naval forces were likely converging for a predetermined rendezvous with the Northern Force carriers off Samar the next day – for a combined attack on the transports at Leyte.[28] He felt the weaker Southern Force could safely be ignored and be dealt with by the Standard-Type battleships under Oldendorf's command and by the planes of Kinkaid's CVE escort carriers. The fresh and undamaged fleet carriers of the Northern Force had the potential to execute air strikes over hundreds of miles – they would be the paramount prize.

Halsey and his staff assessed that if the Central Force did turn around and head east through the San Bernardino Strait overnight, it would not enter Leyte Gulf until 1100 the next morning at the earliest. Unsupported by transport or supply ships, 'it could hope only to harry the landing operation [at Leyte]. It could not consolidate any advantage … It could merely hit and run.'[29] By then, Oldendorf's battleships would have obliterated the weaker Southern Force at the Surigao Strait and would be able to move to meet the battleships of Kurita's Central Force.

After listening to his officers after dinner, and mulling over the various options, with the carriers of Ozawa's Northern Force now just 300 miles away, Halsey made his decision. He would keep his fleet together because the entire operation would be under potential land-based air attack. Addressing his Chief of Staff, Rear Admiral Robert Bostwick (Mick) Carney, he put his finger on the charted position for the Northern Force: 'Here's where we're going. Mick, start them north.'[30] Halsey later wrote: 'It preserved my fleet's integrity, it left the initiative with me, and it promised the greatest possibility of surprise.'[31]

At 1950, Halsey radioed Vice Admiral Kinkaid, aboard his command ship *Wasatch* at Leyte, and also Nimitz, at Pearl, with a brief despatch, that was short of detail: 'CENTRAL FORCE HEAVILY DAMAGED ACCORDING TO STRIKE REPORTS x AM PROCEEDING NORTH WITH 3 GROUPS TO ATTACK CARRIER FORCE AT DAWN.'[32]

From the wording of this despatch, Kinkaid, Nimitz and King assumed that as Halsey was taking 'three groups' north after the enemy carriers, that the TF 34 Battle Line had now been formed as a separate entity and that those battleships, cruisers and destroyers were being left to guard the San Bernardino Strait and cover the 7th Fleet flank. It appeared that Halsey was taking the two fast battleships, not delegated to the battle line, north with him to deal with the two Japanese half-battleships *Ise* and *Hyūga* in the Northern Force.

But in reality, unknown to Kinkaid, Nimitz and King, TF 34 had not been formed and *all* of Lee's TF 34 battleships and cruisers would shortly be on their way north with the TF 38 carriers. Shortly after the war, the US historian Comer Vann Woodward wrote: 'Everything was pulled out from San Bernardino Strait. Not so much as a picket destroyer was left.'[33]

Then, at 2006, a night Hellcat from *Independence* spotted Kurita's Central Force in the Sibuyan Sea – it had indeed come about and was now heading back east toward the San Bernardino Strait at 12 knots. But having already decided to head north in pursuit of the Japanese carriers, TF 38 continued on its mission to hit the enemy carriers the next day. Halsey had taken the bait.

At 2022, after passing on the contact report to Kinkaid at Leyte, Halsey ordered Bogan and Davison's TG 38.2 and TG 38.4 to join Sherman's TG 38.3 up north off the east coast of Luzon, for the run to the north. He sent orders to McCain's distant TG 38.1 to return for battle. He then went to bed, having been without sleep for two days.

After the *Independence* night-fighter sighting of the Central Force was received by Kinkaid at 2024, he heard nothing more from Halsey. As there was no common chain of command, Halsey did not keep Kinkaid automatically informed of his plans. When he sent his despatch that he was proceeding north 'with three groups' he did not say how he was going to deal with the Kurita's Central Force or of his plans for the San Bernardino Strait.

After successfully getting themselves spotted earlier that afternoon, just after 1500, the two half-battleships *Ise* and *Hyūga* and their screen in the vanguard of Ozawa's Northern Force turned back towards the main body at 2230, shrouded in darkness. Meantime, at 2300, far down south, Nishimura's Southern Force entered the western end of the Surigao Strait.

In Leyte Gulf, essentially sandwiched between Kurita's Central Force headed for the San Bernardo Strait to his north and Nishimura's Southern Force entering the Surigao Strait to his south, Kinkaid was now unknowingly exposed and vulnerable. Believing that Lee's TF 34 Battle Line had already formed at San Bernardino, Kinkaid expected that two night big-gun duels were about to take place:

1. Lee's battle line of four fast battleships, cruisers and destroyers would take on the four battleships and escorts of Kurita's Central Force at the San Bernardino Strait.
2. Oldendorf's battle line of six older battleships, cruisers, destroyers and PT Boats would face off against Nishimura's two battleships, a heavy cruiser and destroyer escorts of the Southern Force at the Surigao Strait.

At midnight, the three TF 38 task groups rendezvoused off Luzon and the reformed TF 38 surged north at 16 knots to achieve a good striking position the next day.

(c) Battle of the Surigao Strait, 24–25 October 1944
Meanwhile, southwest of Leyte Gulf, the southernmost action in the complicated Battle of Leyte Gulf, the Battle in the Surigao Strait, began shortly before midnight on the evening of 24 October 1944. Although no one knew it at the time, the battle would prove to be the last big-gun clash between battleships in history – as Oldendorf's 7th Fleet battleships, *Pennsylvania, Tennessee, California, West Virginia, Maryland* and *Mississippi*, along with his cruisers, destroyers and PT Boats, decimated Nishimura's Southern Force as it tried to break through the Surigao Strait into Leyte Gulf. Of the six old Standard-Type battleships in action, five had been damaged or sunk at Pearl Harbor on 7 December 1941.

Nishimura's Southern Force of the two sister battleships *Fusō* and *Yamashiro*, along with the heavy cruiser *Mogami* and four destroyers, had crossed the Sulu Sea eastwards and began to enter the western entrance to the Surigao Strait. Shima's Second Striking Force of two heavy cruisers, one light cruiser and seven destroyers was meantime far to the north in the Sulu Sea – heading southeast to rendezvous with Nishimura for the passage through the Surigao Strait. But as a result of strict radio silence, the two forces failed to coordinate their activities correctly and would never link up. As the Southern Force approached the Strait, Shima's Second Striking Force was 25 miles astern – the Battle of the Surigao Strait would be fought entirely by Nishimura's Southern Force, which was running into a trap.

In preparation for the coming battle, when he received Vice Admiral Kinkaid's order to prepare for a night action, Oldendorf positioned his Battleship Force of six Standard-Type battleships across the northeast exit from the Surigao Strait off Hingatungan Point. This gave him maximum sea room but restricted the enemy's movements.[34] He hoped to cap the enemy 'T' when Nishimura's Southern Force approached.

Oldendorf's battle line was screened by a Left Flank Force of the three 8in main-battery heavy cruisers *Louisville*, *Portland* and *Minneapolis* and the two light cruisers *Columbia* and *Denver*. A Right Flank Force screened the other side of the strait and comprised the heavy cruiser HMAS *Shropshire* and the two light cruisers *Boise* and *Phoenix*. Some twenty-eight destroyers were present along with thirty-nine small fast PT Boats ready to make torpedo attacks as the enemy

USS *CALIFORNIA* (BB-44)

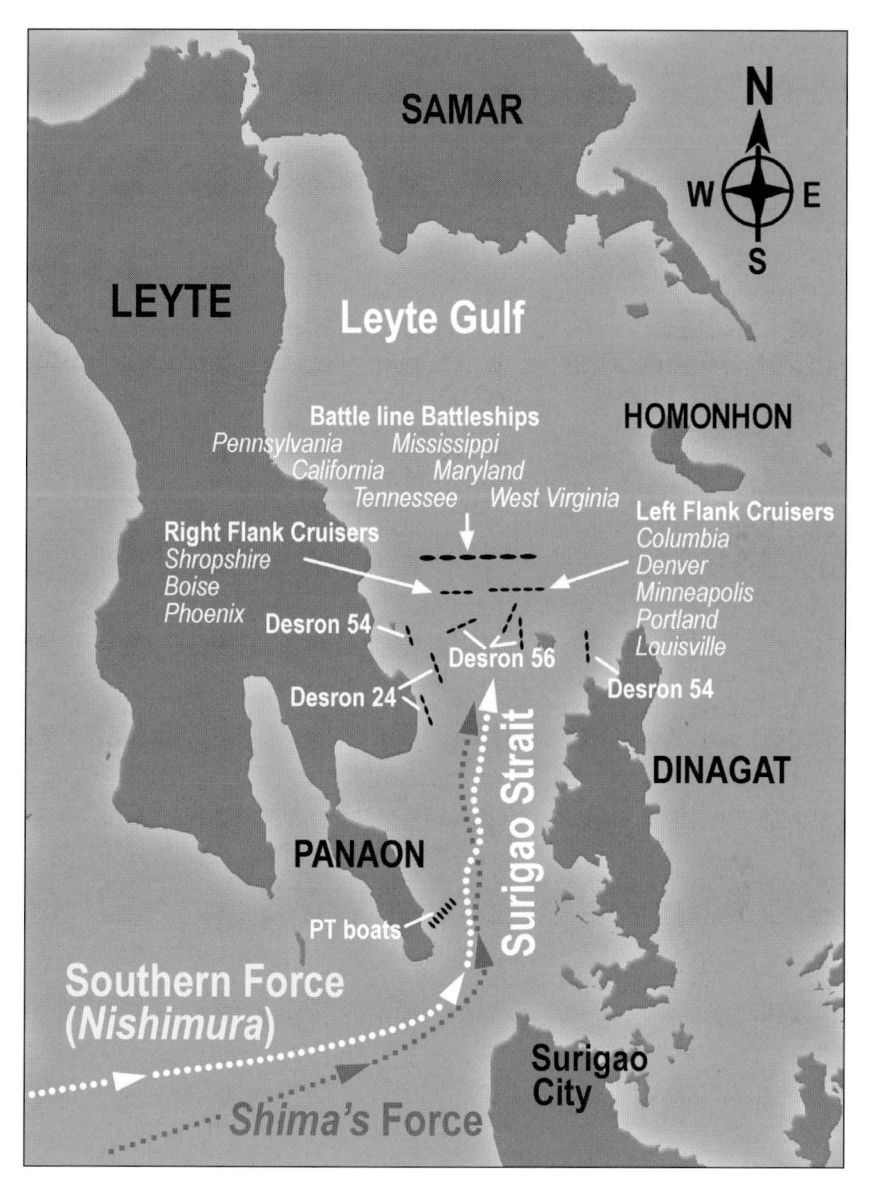

Battle of the Surigao Strait. The Japanese Southern Force of battleships, cruisers and destroyers, approaching from the west, attempts to pass through the Strait but runs into a well-prepared deployment of Allied warships. The US PT torpedo boats, deployed at the south of the Strait, engage first. The Japanese Force in line astern pushes through them – and runs into torpedo attacks by US destroyers. The big guns of the US standard type battleships arranged in line of battle across the Strait and flanked by a powerful cruiser force, then open up. The Japanese Southern Force is annihilated in the engagement.

warships advanced. The PT Boats could make more than 40 knots and were armed with Mark 8 torpedoes with a 466lb warhead. Oldendorf sent his PT Boats southwest down the strait to scout for the Japanese warships.

The Battle of the Surigao Strait began at 2236 when the first PT torpedo boats encountered and engaged Nishimura's oncoming Southern Force warships at the western entrance to the strait. Repeated torpedo attacks by the small PT Boats would take place over the next 3½ hours – although no hits were scored. Nishimura's Southern Force beat off the PT Boats, and passing through them, continued north along the strait.

In anticipation of breaking into Leyte Gulf, Nishimura's Southern Force began to alter formation to line ahead at 18 knots with the destroyer *Michishio* in the lead, and the destroyers *Asagumo*, *Yamagumo* and *Shigure* following. The flag battleship *Yamashiro* followed behind the destroyers – with *Fusō* and then *Mogami* following astern.

At 0236, Oldendorf ordered his BattFor ships to General Quarters – and the approaching Japanese ships were picked up on radar at 0240. Five destroyers of DesRon 54 were already heading south in attack formation, increasing speed to 25 knots before launching their attack with Mark 15 torpedoes. The Japanese ships would soon be subjected to devastating torpedo attacks from large numbers of US destroyers deployed on both sides of their axis of advance.

At about 0300, the battleship *Fusō* was hit on her starboard side amidships by one to three torpedoes from the DesRon 54 destroyer *Melvin*. *Fusō* began to lose speed and list to starboard – she then fell out of formation. Mortally wounded, at 0345 *Fusō* capsized, exploded and sank.

The flag battleship *Yamashiro* was initially hit by a torpedo, which was no impediment to her battle cruising. But then she was hit again – causing her speed to initially drop to 5 knots. By 0348 however, she was making 15 knots again and was firing at the Allied destroyers as they withdrew after their attacks.

The destroyer *Yamagumo* was hit by three torpedoes – and exploded and sunk. The destroyers *Michishio* and *Asagumo* were both badly damaged, with *Asagumo*'s bow being blown off by a torpedo. Nishimura was now left only with the battleship *Yamashiro*, the heavy cruiser *Mogami* and the destroyer *Shigure* – but he nevertheless pressed on with the advance. Shima's Second Striking Force was some 40 miles astern.

Nishimura's ships were detected on the US battleship radars at a range of 44,000yd – about 25 miles. In the darkness, the remaining

Japanese ships were tracked on radar as the range closed. As Oldendorf sent the destroyers of DesRon 56 into attack, he gave the order for his heavy warships to open fire to cover the destroyer attack. At 0350, the big guns of the Allied cruisers flanking Nishimura's Force to port and to starboard commenced firing – whilst just a few minutes later at 0352, the main-battery guns of the Standard-Type battleships opened fire.

The *West Virginia* had just emerged from her three-year long refit and modernisation the month before to become flagship of Rear Admiral Theodore D. Ruddock, commander of BatDiv 4. She now sported the latest air-search radar and fire-control radar for her main and secondary batteries. Her main battery of eight 16in guns was now controlled by Mk 37 directors – and having the most modern fire-control systems, she was the first of the battleships to commence firing at a distance of almost 23,000yd, just over 12 miles. *West Virginia* hit the Japanese flag battleship *Yamashiro* with her first salvo – *Yamashiro* returned fire with her No. 1 and No. 2 main-battery 14in guns and a gunnery duel developed. A few minutes later, *California* and *Tennessee* opened up with their big guns, *California* engaging the leading Japanese vessel at a range of just over 11 miles with a six-gun salvo.

A classic big-gun duel now developed – the US battleships, strung across the strait, had crossed the T of the Japanese battle line. Japanese fire control proved less effective and little threatening fire was returned. Several torpedoes launched by the Japanese vessels approached the US line, but none of them struck Oldendorf's battleships.

Operating under radar fire control, *Tennessee* went on to fire sixty-nine 14in AP shells during the battle, whilst *California* fired sixty-three 14in AP shells and *West Virginia* fired ninety-one 16in AP shells. *California* suffered a misfire in the right gun of her aftmost Turret 4, and concussion from the third salvo disabled the rear Mk 8 radar and damaged the scope for the forward radar, but the gun-layers nevertheless continued to accurately direct the guns. Sixteen minutes after opening fire, *California* checked her fire as the surviving Japanese ships turned and fled.

The other three of Oldendorf's battleships had less advanced gunnery radar and struggled to hit the Japanese ships. *Maryland* visually ranged the Japanese ships from the splashes from the fall of shot and fired forty-eight 16in shells. *Pennsylvania* was unable to find a target and her guns did not fire. *Mississippi* only fired once – with a full broadside salvo from her twelve 14in guns. Unknown at the time, this would be the last salvo ever to be fired by one battleship at another battleship – the era of these great steel titans was over. The Allied heavy cruisers, fitted with the latest radar equipment, fired over 2,000 rounds of armour-piercing

6in and 8in shells. *Yamashiro* and *Mogami* took a savage beating from this murderous hail of big shells – and from the torpedoes from US destroyers.

After the opening exchange of fire, in the confines of the strait, the eastbound US battle line prepared to come about to head west – and checked fire. The order was given to make simultaneous starboard turns of 150° – but the skipper of the *California* misinterpreted the order to 'turn one five' (meaning to turn 150°) and took it as an instruction to turn 15°. As the great ship made its slight turn to starboard, the *Tennessee*, ahead of *California* in the battle line, made the full 150° turn. Realising the confusion, *California* turned hard to starboard as *Tennessee* moved out of line. The two ships narrowly avoided each other – but as a result, *California* masked *Tennessee* from the enemy, blocking her from firing for several minutes until the battle line sorted itself out and could recommence firing.

At 0409, Oldendorf gave the order to cease fire, having received reports that he was hitting his own ships in the darkness. *Yamashiro* and *Mogami*, both heavily damaged, took the opportunity to come about and retire southwest down the strait, along with the destroyer *Shigure*, which lost steering and slewed to a halt temporarily – before being able to make way again.

Shortly after, at 0419, after being hit by two more torpedoes fired by the destroyer *Bennion*, Nishimura's flagship, the battleship *Yamashiro*, rolled to port and capsized within 5 minutes – before plunging to the seabed. Nishimura went down with his flagship, along with most of her 1,400 crew.

The heavy cruiser *Mogami*, although badly damaged, managed to limp away from the battle and eventually rendezvoused with Shima's Second Striking Force, which by now was less than 10 miles away and heading northeast up the strait. *Abukuma* was hit by a torpedo and fell out of formation.

As Shima's Second Striking Force advanced up the Strait, his ships came across the floating debris of one, possibly two, sunken ships. Believing it was two separate sunken ships, one being the battleship *Fusō*, Shima determined that there was now little point in sacrificing his own lighter force of cruisers and destroyers. At 0506, he retired his cruisers from the strait along with the damaged *Mogami* and the destroyers *Asagumo* and *Shigure*. His flagship, the heavy cruiser *Nachi*, collided with *Mogami* in the darkness, flooding *Mogami*'s steering room and causing her to fall behind.

After the big-gun duel, Oldendorf's battleship force headed south down the strait in a stern chase of any Southern Force surviving warships – supported by fighters and torpedo planes. The destroyer *Asagumo* was sunk at 0721 and *Mogami* was bombed in the Bohol Sea by TBF Avengers from the CVE escort carriers and subsequently had to be abandoned. She would be scuttled by torpedoes from a Japanese destroyer the next day. Of Nishimura's seven ships, only the destroyer *Shigure* had escaped.

Nevertheless, despite the apparent overwhelming success of the contact, as dawn approached on 25 October, as a result of the stern chase, Oldendorf's force of six battleships and escorts had been drawn 65 miles south and away from the Leyte beachhead. Leyte was now very exposed should an attack from the north develop.

Meanwhile, back off Leyte, as the battle in the Surigao Strait raged to the south, Vice Admiral Kinkaid called a 7th Fleet staff meeting at 0400 – to check for anything that had been omitted or could be actioned. Although no one could think of anything that was awry, Captain Richard H. Cruzen remarked to Kinkaid: 'Admiral, I can think of only one other thing. We have never directly asked Halsey if TF 34 is guarding San Bernardino.'[35]

At 0412, Kinkaid sent a message to Halsey asking for confirmation: 'AM NOW ENGAGING ENEMY SURFACE FORCES SURIGAO STRAIT x QUESTION IS TF 34 GUARDING SAN BERNARDINO STRAIT.'[36] But with the communication restrictions of the day, it would take more than 2 hours for the message to reach Halsey in *New Jersey* and be decoded.

No one knew that, in fact, Kurita's Central Force, after reversing course in darkness, had already successfully passed in darkness completely unopposed through the San Bernardino Strait and emerged into the Philippine Sea at 0300 that morning. The Central Force was now steaming south along the east coast of Samar, heading for Leyte Gulf.

The superbattleship *Musashi* had been sunk in the Sibuyan Sea the day before, but the Central Force still boasted the 4 battleships *Yamato*, *Nagato*, *Kongō* and *Haruna*, 6 heavy cruisers, 2 light cruisers and 11 destroyers. The contest was still afoot.

Halsey and the TF 38 carriers, which could have dealt with the Central Force, were by now far away to the north – chasing Ozawa's virtually planeless decoy Northern Force.

The scene was set for an epic showdown off Samar.

PEARL HARBOR'S REVENGE

(d) Battle off Samar, 25 October 1944

By dawn on 25 October, as Kurita's Central Force battleships headed south down the east coast of Samar towards Leyte, Allied intelligence as to the whereabouts of the Japanese naval forces was still sketchy.

At 0648, Halsey was surprised to receive Kinkaid's despatch, sent at 0412, seeking confirmation as to whether Lee's TF 34 Battle Line had been formed at San Bernardino. Halsey replied at 0705: 'NEGATIVE x IT IS WITH OUR CARRIERS NOW ENGAGING ENEMY CARRIERS.'[37] But it was too late for Kinkaid to do anything – and at this point, no one knew the exact location of the Central Force or the Northern Force.

With Halsey's entire force now far away to the north, the only remaining US forces near San Bernardino Strait were the three 7th Fleet CVE Task Units, totalling sixteen escort carriers, each carrying twenty-eight planes. The CVEs relied on their own CAP and a screen of destroyers and smaller destroyer escorts for protection – and those would be virtually impotent against the fast, powerful Japanese battleships that were, unknown to the Americans, heading their way.

The CVEs and their destroyer escorts were more used to screening convoys from submarine attack. They carried few anti-ship aerial torpedoes as they normally relied on protection by the 3rd Fleet from enemy warships. Many of the planes aboard the CVEs were armed for combat air patrol, anti-submarine work and close infantry support. With no torpedoes and bombs, they would be largely ineffectual against the heavily armoured enemy warships.

The Northern CVE Task Unit 77.4.3 (Taffy 3) was patrolling northeast of Samar, safe in the mistaken belief that Lee's battle line was already positioned north at San Bernardino and protecting from an attack from that direction. No one afloat on Taffy 3 knew that Halsey's 3rd Fleet were now far away up north – and just how exposed they were.

With no prior warning, at 0645, the twenty-three southbound warships of Kurita's Central Force were sighted visually to the north of Taffy 3. It must have been a shocking blow to those aboard the US ships to see the unmistakeable silhouettes of the Japanese battleships heading their way at speed. For his part, Kurita was unaware that Halsey had taken Ozawa's bait, and assumed he had found a TF 38 carrier group. He ordered a 'General Attack', his fleet splitting into divisions to attack independently.

Many of Kinkaid's escort carrier planes, were far away pursuing the fleeing surviving Southern Force warships southwestward down the Surigao Strait. They were recalled and vectored to attack Kurita's Central Force. Oldendorf's battleships were by now 65 miles away in the Surigao Strait on their stern chase of the fleeing Southern Force. Even at their top speed of 21 knots, it would take 3 hours for them to get back to Leyte Gulf to provide big-gun support for the vulnerable escort carriers.

As Kurita's superbattleship force closed the six exposed Taffy 3 escort carriers for the kill, the CVEs launched their planes and began to hastily withdraw, covered by smoke from the screen of three destroyers and four destroyer escorts. At 0706, as a rain squall briefly shielded the carriers, the destroyers were ordered to launch a torpedo attack on the Japanese units to disrupt the enemy advance.

The superbattleship *Yamato* had by now closed sufficiently to commence firing with her main battery. Her fearsome 46cm (18.1in) shells, the largest ever on any battleship, began to fall in amongst the six unarmoured Taffy 3 escort carriers.

The Taffy 3 destroyers and destroyer escorts bravely turned to attack the Japanese capital ships, opening up with their much smaller 5in main-battery guns once in range. But these guns were not heavy enough to have much effect on the bigger and more heavily armoured Japanese battleships – nor did they have armour sufficient to defend against Japanese big-gun hits. Wildcat and Hellcat fighters, and TBM Avenger torpedo bombers, from the escort carriers attacked the Japanese warships – strafing, bombing, dropping what torpedoes they had and firing rockets until they ran out of ammunition.

At 0707, Kinkaid radioed Halsey to advise that his ships were being attacked by heavy Japanese warships – but the message like all others would take more than an hour to be transmitted, received and decoded. No help would come from Halsey.

Closest to the approaching Japanese units, the destroyer *Johnston* (DD-557) charged forward at flank speed, firing her main 5in battery and launching ten torpedoes at the heavy cruiser *Kumano*. One torpedo struck *Kumano* and blew her bow off, forcing her to withdraw out of line.

The two Taffy 3 destroyers, *Hoel* (DD-533) and *Heermann* (DD-532), along with the destroyer escort *Samuel B. Roberts* (DE-413) then attacked.

Hoel began a 35-knot attack from about 10 miles on the nearest enemy battleship, the *Kongō*, which was leading a column of four battleships. Within a few minutes, she had closed to 8 miles and was able to commence firing with her 5in battery – *Kongō* replied with her own 14in main battery. Continuing to close, once the range was down to about 5 miles, *Hoel* launched a salvo of torpedoes that forced *Kongō* to turn sharply to comb the tracks – losing ground on the fleeing escort carriers.

Hoel was hit minutes afterwards and three of her guns were knocked out along with the port engine.

Notwithstanding the damage, *Hoel* turned to engage the battleships *Haruna* and Kurita's flagship *Yamato*, firing a half salvo of torpedoes and hitting *Yamato*, which was forced to turn to evade the torpedoes. *Hoel* however was by now crippled and was quickly surrounded by a number of Japanese destroyers who fired at her remorselessly, even as her crew abandoned ship. After the small ship had taken more than 40 hits, she capsized and sank at 0855 with the loss of 253 officers and men. There were only 86 survivors.

The destroyer *Heermann* began her 38-knot torpedo run at the heavy cruiser *Haguro*. She launched her torpedoes and opened up with her 5in battery as the heavy cruiser *Chikuma* came in range. *Heermann* then altered course to fire three more torpedoes at the lead battleship *Kongō* – before switching her targeting again and launching three torpedoes at the battleship *Haruna* from 4,400yd. She then withdrew, laying another smoke screen to cover the carriers – before re-entering the fray once more to engage four enemy heavy cruisers and begin another gunnery duel with the better armed and armoured heavy cruiser *Chikuma*.

Heermann was struck by a number of 8in shells from *Chikuma* and was holed in the bow. Flooding caused her bow to settle until her anchors were awash – but her brave attack, allied to hits from aircraft, had forced *Chikuma* to withdraw. The heavy cruiser would subsequently sink during the Japanese retreat. The heavy cruiser *Tone* then attacked *Heermann*, which withdrew to lay more smoke. Taffy 2 planes then began to arrive to assist their Taffy 3 comrades, hitting *Tone* and forcing her to withdraw.

The 24-knot Taffy 3 destroyer escort *Samuel B. Roberts* then charged towards the heavy cruiser *Chōkai* on a torpedo run, getting in so close to the heavy Japanese cruiser that the cruiser's guns could not depress sufficiently to hit her. The diminutive destroyer escort launched three Mark 15 torpedoes – one blowing off *Chōkai*'s stern.

Samuel B. Roberts fought on for another hour, setting the bridge of the heavy cruiser *Chikuma* on fire with hits from its 5in gun – before she was hit by a 14in shell from the battleship *Kongō*. The effect of the hit on such a small unarmoured ship was devastating. A hole 40ft long x 10ft wide was opened up on her port side at her engine room aft. The order to abandon ship was given at 0935 and she sank 30 minutes later, taking ninety of her crew with her.

As Japanese warships dealt with the daring destroyer attacks and attempted to close Kinkaid's escort carriers, the planes of the escort carriers attacked with whatever weapons they had. Crucially, Kurita's Central Force had no CAP fighter cover – and the US aircraft could attack unopposed other than by shipborne AA fire.

The CVE escort carriers could make 19 knots at most – they could not outrun the fast Japanese warships, which were capable of almost 30 knots. The range steadily closed, allowing the CVEs to open up with their meagre armament of a single 5in DP gun mounted on the stern. The Avenger's bombs and torpedoes were by now expended, and so the planes bravely made dummy runs to distract the enemy battleships.

Just after 0800, the heavy cruiser *Chikuma* opened up with her 5in guns on the escort carrier *Gambier Bay* (CVE-73) at a range of 5 miles. Shells struck *Gambier Bay*'s flight deck – and after further hits, she slewed to a stop. Three Japanese cruisers closed the disabled carrier to point-blank range and shelled her until she capsized and sank just after 0900. She was the only US carrier sunk by direct gunfire during the Second World War.

Vice Admiral Ōnishi, commander of the land-based 1st Air Fleet on Luzon, sent in the first organised flight of kamikaze suicide planes, which crashed into several CVEs. At about 1050, the Taffy 3 jeep carrier *St Lo* (CVE-63) was struck by a A6M Zero kamikaze on her flight deck, which set off secondary explosions and set her ablaze. She had to be quickly abandoned at 1100 and sank shortly afterwards at 1125 with the loss of 114 crew. *Yamato* closed the Taffy 3 escort *Gambier Bay* (CVE-73), disabled by shell hits and dead in the water, to point-blank range and sent her to the bottom.

In the action, 5 US ships were sunk: the 2 escort carriers, 2 destroyers and a destroyer escort. TG 77.4 had lost 105 planes.[38] But such was the damage and confusion caused by the US defensive actions, that Kurita still believed that he was engaging major US fleet units, rather than lighter CVE escort carriers and destroyers.

At about noon, Kurita received an inaccurate contact report by radio that US carriers were closing from the north. With US land-based aircraft operating out of Leyte, he feared being trapped in Leyte Gulf. He had already lost three of his heavy cruisers – and he decided that he must now head out to sea to engage what he believed was the remainder of the US fast carriers. Interviewed after the war he remarked: 'The destruction of enemy aircraft carriers was a kind of obsession with me, and I fell victim to it.'[39] He made his decision to clear Leyte Gulf at 1230.

At 1310 McCain's TG 38.1 planes arrived from extreme range – such that after striking Kurita's Central Force they had to land and rearm on airfields on Leyte. Together with planes from the CVE escort carriers, they sank a light cruiser and a destroyer and damaged most of the other ships.

Kurita's force however found no US fleet carriers – and by 1730 his ships were running low on fuel. Kurita turned the Central Force for home, in full retreat north towards the San Bernardino Strait.[40] He had chosen to go after the illusory US carriers with his big guns – but the US carriers were in fact much further north. By not pressing on with his powerful battleships against the escort carriers to Leyte Gulf, Kurita had lost the opportunity of hitting the beachhead and destroying vulnerable shipping offshore. A golden opportunity had been squandered.

In the battle, more than 1,000 US service personnel had been killed in action – more than had been killed at the Coral Sea and Midway combined. But the light US forces had acquitted themselves with great valour – and had prevented a serious attack on the Allied forces at Leyte Gulf.

Halsey later wrote: 'I opened my hand and let the bird fly away off Luzon. So did the enemy off Samar.'[41]

(e) Battle off Cape Engaño, 25 October 1944
After the carriers of the Northern Force were spotted in the late afternoon of 24 October, some 300nm distant to the north and east of Cape Engaño on the northeast tip of Luzon, Halsey had taken the bait. His 5 TF 38 fast carriers *Intrepid, Franklin, Lexington, Enterprise* and *Essex*, with the 5 light carriers *Independence, Belleau Wood, Langley, Cabot* and *San Jacinto*, the 6 fast battleships *Alabama, Iowa, Massachusetts, New Jersey, South Dakota* and *Washington*, 8 cruisers and more then 40 destroyers had surged through the darkness of a tropical night into the early hours of 25 October – chasing the enemy carriers.

The TF 38 air groups together could field more than 600 combat aircraft – and were overwhelmingly more powerful than Ozawa's Northern Force of the heavy carrier *Zuikaku*, the 3 light carriers *Chitose, Zuihō* and *Chiyoda*, the 2 half-battleships *Ise* and *Hyūga*, 3 light cruisers and 9 destroyers. Crucially, the Japanese carriers had few planes.

At 0100 on 25 October, radar equipped night Hellcats were launched from *Independence* to search 350 miles out from the TF 38 carriers. Just over an hour later, at 0208, a series of reports came in – five enemy warships had been detected just 80 miles to the north of TF 38. At 0214, another report came in correcting the number of ships and giving their course as 110°, they were running roughly eastsoutheast. This was the vanguard force of the half-battleships *Ise* and *Hyūga* and escorts, which were still deliberately trying to get themselves spotted and trigger a night engagement to lure Halsey further north. At 0220, one US plane reported another group of enemy ships 40 miles astern of the first force – it was the main body of the Northern Force. Another report at 0235 confirmed the sighting. Halsey wrote later: 'We had them!'[42]

At 0255, Halsey ordered Lee to form his line of battle 10 miles ahead of the carriers and ordered his task-group commanders to arm the planes of their first deckload strike at once – he would launch at earliest dawn, with a second strike to follow as soon as possible. The radar on the night Hellcat that had been shadowing the Northern Force however unfortunately chose that moment to break down – and radar contact with the enemy ships was lost.

In Ozawa's decoy Northern Force, when lightning strikes were misidentified as TF 38 being attacked by land-based aircraft, Ozawa recalled the vanguard force of the two half-battleships *Ise* and *Hyūga* and their four destroyer escorts, to rendezvous with his nearly empty carriers. As a result of the *Independence* night Hellcat radar failure, when the time of the battle expected by the Americans came, with nautical daylight at 0430, the southbound Japanese warships spotted in the early hours by the Hellcat were nowhere to be seen.

However, as daylight approached, although there was no surface contact for Lee's battlewagons to engage, aboard the US carriers, preparations were made for a daybreak launch. The CAP was cleared off the deck – followed by the search planes.

At 0630, as search planes fanned out in their search pattern, 10 deckload strikes of a total 180 strike aircraft launched. The strike divisions headed northeast to await contact flashes from the search planes once a sighting of the enemy was made. A total of 60 Hellcats, 65 Curtiss SB2C Helldiver dive bombers and 55 Avenger torpedo bombers roared down the flight decks to orbit ahead of the task force. Meantime, on the Japanese carriers, Ozawa was launching 75 of his own aircraft to attack the US Task Force.

At 0648, Halsey received Kinkaid's despatch from Leyte Gulf: 'AM NOW ENGAGING ENEMY SURFACE FORCES SURIGAO STRAIT x QUESTION IS TF 34 GUARDING SAN BERNARDINO STRAIT.' Halsey replied: 'NEGATIVE x IT IS WITH OUR CARRIERS NOW ENGAGING ENEMY CARRIERS.'[43]

The four Japanese carriers of the Northern Force had steamed south to a position some 100 miles northeast of TF 38 before the US search aircraft registered on their radar screens. Once detected, Ozawa immediately turned his four carriers and their escorts around to draw Halsey north – successfully opening the distance by 40 miles before US aircraft were visually sighted at 0710.

At 0735, US aviators reported sightings of the enemy fleet 140 miles northeast of TF 38. The two half-battleships, destroyers and cruisers formed a protective ring around the four carriers to provide AA cover. Ozawa began launching his last twenty-nine planes as Lee's fast battleships sprinted forward to the fight. It seemed that Halsey had succeeded in catching the enemy carrier fleet and would deliver a crushing blow off Cape Engaño that might change the course of the war.

At 0802, Halsey received another despatch from Kinkaid: 'ENEMY VESSELS RETIRING SURIGAO STRAIT x OUR LIGHT FORCES IN PURSUIT.'[44]

TF 38 aircraft closed Ozawa's Northern Force and began attacking just after 0800 – the F6F Hellcat fighters quickly destroying Ozawa's CAP of twenty-nine aircraft. The exposed Japanese carriers were attacked, with most TF 38 planes initially targeting the light carrier *Chitose*. By the intensity of the air attack, Ozawa knew that his decoy mission had succeeded – he had lured the American carriers north, away from Leyte.

At 0822, aboard his flagship, the battleship *New Jersey*, Halsey received a further despatch from Kinkaid: 'ENEMY BBS AND CRUISER REPORTED FIRING ON TU 77.4.3 FROM 15 MILES ASTERN.'[45] This was the beginning of the Battle off Samar as Kurita's Central Force surprised Kinkaid's CVE escort carriers. But Halsey was confident of Kinkaid's ability to look after himself: 'I figured that the eighteen little carriers had enough planes to protect themselves until Oldendorf could bring up his heavy ships.'[46]

At 0820, Air Group 15 from the carrier *Essex* were the first to engage the four Japanese carriers as Japanese AA fire opened up. The *Essex* planes hit *Chitose* with bombs and three aerial torpedoes, flooding the light carrier's boiler rooms and damaging her rudder. She quickly took on a 27° list, which was reduced to 15° by counterflooding. But with both engine rooms out of action, she slewed to a stop, dead in the water. Shortly afterwards, she would roll over to port and sink stern first with the loss of more than 900 of her crew.

The light carrier *Zuihō* was attacked in close succession to *Chitose* just after 0830. *Zuihō* took three near misses at her stern and one direct hit by a single 550lb bomb on the aft section of her flight deck that started several fires, bulged her flight deck and knocked out her steering – she took on a small list to port.

The fleet carrier *Zuikaku* was hit by three bombs on her flight deck on her port side amidships that started fires in her upper and lower hangars. She was then hit just minutes later by an aerial torpedo on her port side aft of amidships that damaged one of her two port shafts. The strike caused severe flooding that brought on an initial sharp port list, that was brought under control to 6°. She was left with two operational shafts and could still make 23 knots.

As the attacks went in against the Japanese carriers 140 miles northeast of TF 38, at 0830 Halsey received a fourth despatch from Kinkaid: 'URGENTLY NEED FAST BBS LEYTE GULF AT ONCE.'[47] The despatch surprised Halsey – who felt that his primary task was not to protect the 7th Fleet but to strike with his 3rd Fleet against the prize, the Japanese carriers.

At 0850, a flash report of the progress TF 38 planes were making with their attack on the Northern Force carriers reached Halsey aboard *New Jersey*: 'ONE CARRIER SUNK AFTER TREMENDOUS EXPLOSION x 2 CARRIERS 1CL (light cruiser) HIT BADLY OTHER CARRIER UNTOUCHED x FORCE COURSE 150 SPEED 17.'[48]

Although Halsey believed his attack on the four Japanese carriers was going well, with one carrier sunk, he needed more time to finish off the three remaining carriers. But nevertheless, with Kinkaid appealing for assistance, he ordered McCain's TG 38.1, which was refuelling to the east, to head south towards Samar at best possible speed, and ordered Kinkaid be notified. But the fast carriers and Lee's fast battleships, so desperately needed off Samar, were still with Halsey more than 300 miles north of Leyte Gulf.

At 0900, Halsey received a fifth despatch from Kinkaid: 'OUR CVES BEING ATTACKED BY 4 BBS 8 CRUISERS PLUS OTHERS x REQUEST LEE COVER LEYTE AT TOP SPEED x REQUEST FAST CARRIERS MAKE IMMEDIATE STRIKE.'

Then at 0922, a sixth despatch: 'CTU 77.4.4 UNDER ATTACK BY CRUISERS AND BBS 0700 … REQUEST IMMEDIATE AIR STRIKE x ALSO REQUEST SUPPORT BY HEAVY SHIPS x MY OBBS LOW IN AMMUNITION.'[49]

Kinkaid's 7th Fleet escort carriers, destroyers and destroyer escorts were, at the time the despatch was sent, fighting for their very survival down off Samar, making their heroic but almost suicidal attacks on the heavy Japanese warships as his escort carriers were pummelled.

Halsey responded within 5 minutes: 'I AM STILL ENGAGING ENEMY CARRIERS x MCCAIN WITH 5 CARRIERS 4 HEAVY CRUISERS HAS BEEN ORDERED TO ASSIST YOU IMMEDIATELY.'

Halsey later wrote that he gave his position so Kinkaid would know there was no possibility of the fast battleships reaching him.[50]

At 1000 Halsey received another clear, uncoded, despatch from Kinkaid: 'WHERE IS LEE x SEND LEE.'

Admiral King in Washington and Nimitz at Pearl Harbor also had no idea of the whereabouts of Lee and his battleships. Nimitz sent a coded terse message to Halsey: 'TURKEY TROTS TO WATER x FROM CINCPAC x WHERE IS, REPEAT, WHERE IS TASK FORCE 34 x THE WORLD WONDERS.'[51]

The first four words and the last three words of the message were padding used to confuse enemy crypto analysts. The communications staff on Halsey's flagship *New Jersey* deleted the first four words correctly – but left in the last three words. When Halsey read the message at 1000, he took the message as a stinging rebuke. Infuriated, he lost his temper – grabbing his cap and throwing it to the deck. But the meaning of Nimitz's message was clear – the fast battleships were not where Nimitz thought they should be.

Almost simultaneously with the confusion reigning on the flag bridge aboard *New Jersey*, the second wave of TF 38 strike aircraft arrived above the beleaguered Japanese Northern Force – this time concentrating mainly on the light carrier *Chiyoda*, scoring four hits and leaving her crippled and ablaze.

Second-wave TF 38 planes also attacked the light carrier *Zuihō* but were driven off with rocket batteries and AA guns. Several torpedo attacks were made on *Zuikaku*, but these were driven off by AA fire or avoided. Three Japanese carriers still remained afloat – along with the two undamaged half battleships *Ise* and *Hyūga*.

Faced with the developing situation for Kinkaid off Samar, Halsey ordered Lee's TF 34 battle line and Bogan's TG 38.2 to proceed south towards San Bernardino. Sherman's TG 38.3 and Davison's TG 38.4 would continue their attacks against the Northern Force carriers. Ted Sherman shared Halsey's frustration, writing in his subsequent Action Report: 'We ruled the sea in our vicinity, there were no enemy aircraft in the air to bother us, the enemy was in full retreat, and the only remaining objective was to prevent his cripples from getting away.'[52]

Halsey notified Kinkaid: 'TG 38.2 PLUS 6 FAST BBS PROCEEDING LEYTE BUT UNABLE ARRIVE BEFORE 0800 TOMORROW.'[53]

Halsey then informed Nimitz: 'TASK FORCE 34 WITH ME ENGAGING CARRIER FORCE. AM NOW PROCEEDING WITH TASK GROUP 38.2 AND ALL FAST BB TO REINFORCE KINKAID …'.[54]

At 1115, a frustrated and conflicted Halsey changed course from 000° to 180° – from due north to due south. The Japanese Northern Force lay just 42 miles from the muzzles of his 16in battleship guns – in an exposed position. *Chitose* had been sunk, *Chiyoda* was dead in the water, *Zuihō* was crippled and *Zuikaku* could only make 18 knots and had a damaged flight deck. The enemy carriers had few planes left to defend them.

Halsey had in the meantime been receiving another set of despatches from Kinkaid that included: 'ENEMY RETIRING TO NORTHEASTWARD.' Then finally at 1145: 'ENEMY FORCE OF 3 BB 2 CA 9 DD 11-43N 126-12 E COURSE 225 SPEED 20.'[55] This position put Kurita's Central Force 55 miles northeast of Leyte Gulf – likely heading for the San Bernardino Strait. Although all six US fast battleships were heading south, Halsey's best chance of intercepting Kurita was to send his fastest ships in advance – the only two battleships that could sustain high speeds were his flagship *New Jersey* and *Iowa*. With a screen of light cruisers and destroyers, the two-battleship vanguard force raced ahead at 28 knots, preparing for 30 knots. Bogan's three TG 38.2 carriers were also heading south to San Bernardino.

Halsey was sending all six fast battleships south, choosing not to split his force and leave two battleships behind to finish off Ozawa's half-battleships *Ise* and *Hyūga*. He wanted to have overwhelming force when Lee's battleships met Kurita's. The two *Ise*-class half-battleships would escape to fight again – and down south off Samar, Kurita's four fast battleships in the Central Force would also escape through the San Bernardino Strait.

Despite having turned his battleships and TG 38.2 to head south at 1115, aircraft flying from the remaining two TG 38.3 and TG 38.4 continued to pummel the Northern Force carriers. Ozawa's flagship *Zuikaku* was hit by seven torpedoes and nine bombs and began to list – forcing him to transfer his flag to the light cruiser *Ōyodo*. *Zuikaku* eventually rolled over and sank stern first just after 1400, taking Rear Admiral Kaizuka Takeo and 842 of her crew to their deaths with her.

The damaged light carrier *Zuihō* was repeatedly attacked and hit by a torpedo and two bombs. Both engine rooms and one boiler room flooded, and her speed slowed to 12 knots. At 1445, she slewed to a stop and lay dead in the water. She was attacked again, and her list increased to 23°. She was eventually abandoned at 1510, and finally succumbed and sank shortly afterwards at 1526 with the loss of 215 officers and men.

Earlier, the battleship *Hyūga* had attempted to take the crippled *Chiyoda* in tow. But the tow had to be broken off at about 1230 when the third US attack came in. At about 1630, *Chiyoda* was closed by the four US cruisers *Santa Fe*, *Mobile*, *Wichita* and *New Orleans* and their support destroyers – and sunk by gunfire.

The surviving units of the Northern Force retired in disarray late in the afternoon – with four US fast light cruisers in pursuit and two wolf packs of US submarines waiting across its course. That night just after 2100 the light cruiser *Tama* was torpedoed by the US submarine *Jallao* (SS-358) northeast of Luzon – she sank with all hands.

The final losses in the Battle off Cape Engaño for the IJN Northern Force were:

Sunk: 4 carriers, 1 light cruiser, 2 destroyers
Damaged: 2 battleships, 2 light cruisers, 4 destroyers

Japan's last attempt to win a decisive battle had failed. Her four carriers were gone. Kurita with his powerful battleship Central Force had not pushed on for the Leyte beachhead, where he could have attacked Allied shipping and bombarded Allied troops ashore on the beachhead.

But had Kurita pressed into Leyte Gulf, then by 1400 his Central Force, comprising not least the superbattleship *Yamato*, would have been engaged by Oldendorf's returning battle line of six Standard-Type battleships, cruisers and destroyers – and by the planes of McCain's five TG 38.1 carriers coming in from the east after their aborted passage to Ulithi.

After any such strike at Leyte Gulf, Kurita would then have had to face Lee's TF 34 battle line of six fast battleships and their escorts racing down from the north – and Halsey's three other fast-carrier Task Groups, 38.2, 38.3 and 38.4. In all, Kurita would have faced the full air power of TF 38 and the big guns of Lee's fast battlewagons. Kurita decided to save what he could of the Central Force – much to the relief of Kinkaid and his battered 7th Fleet CVE escort carrier force.

At about 2000, Halsey sent up six night Avengers from *Independence* and at 2200, the Avengers reported fifteen enemy ships passing along the east coast of Samar into the San Bernardino Strait. Kurita's Central Force was in full retreat re-entering San Bernardino Strait – the two fast battleships of Halsey's southbound TG 34.5 were still 2 hours away to the north.

Shortly after midnight, one of TG 34.5 scouting destroyers made contact with a Japanese Central Force straggler. Halsey watched from the bridge of his flagship *New Jersey* as his cruisers devastated the unfortunate enemy vessel with 6in shells – before a destroyer delivered the *coup de grâce* with torpedoes. This set off a secondary magazine explosion so violent that on his flag bridge, Halsey felt the shock arrive from 15 miles away.[56]

At dawn, McCain (TG 38.1) and Bogan (TG 38.2) launched strikes over the Sibuyan Sea that sank one light cruiser and damaged a heavy cruiser – but Kurita would eventually reach Manila safely.

The complicated and confusing Battle of Leyte Gulf was over – the Allied beachhead was safe. It had been a striking Allied victory – but at considerable cost. The light carrier *Princeton* had been lost, along with the two escort carriers *Gambier Bay* and *St Lo*, the two destroyers *Hoel* and *Johnston* and the destroyer escort *Samuel B. Roberts*.

But the IJN had lost 45 per cent of the ships engaged. The 3 Japanese battleships *Musashi*, *Yamashiro* and *Fusō* had been sunk – along with the heavy carrier *Zuikaku* and the 3 light carriers *Zuihō*, *Chiyoda* and *Chitose*. In addition 6 heavy cruisers and 4 light cruisers had been sunk along with 9 destroyers: a total of some 305,710 tons of shipping.[57]

The Japanese fleet had been sacrificed in a last-ditch and failed battle to save the Philippines.

The Battle of Leyte Gulf has long been argued – and caused much controversy. Some have argued that prime responsibility for letting Kurita's Central Force penetrate the San Bernardino Strait undetected and attack Kinkaid's vulnerable 7th Fleet escort carriers rested with Halsey. 'Bull' Halsey, true to his nickname, took Ozawa's bait and was lured north – denuding the San Bernardino Strait of Lee's battle line and the air power of TF 38. But there is much to be said in Halsey's defence, the primacy of the Japanese carriers was his priority in terms of his orders.

Halsey was subsequently able to write in his official report to Admirals King and Nimitz of 'the elimination of serious naval threat to our operations for many months, if not forever'.[58] He never admitted any error in leaving the San Bernardino Strait open and unprotected, advising King in January 1945 when he returned to Washington that instead of running south with Lee and Bogan to relieve Kinkaid's 7th Fleet, he should have stayed north to finish off Ozawa's Northern Force with his big guns when they were so close. King replied: 'No. It wasn't a mistake. You couldn't have done otherwise.'[59]

With the complicated battle now over, *California* and the other ships of Oldendorf's Fire Support Group moved back to their stations and resumed their ground-support operations for the next month.

On 20 November 1944, roughly one month after the Battle of Leyte Gulf, *California* left the Philippines and headed for repairs and replenishment some 1,700 miles southeast to the US Naval base at Seeadler Harbor, Manus. She remained there from 25 November until 15 December 1944, when she proceeded north to the Kossol Roads to the north of the Palauan archipelago, which had just been secured in November after many months of intense fighting. *California* remained off Palau until 1 January 1945 when she returned to Leyte Gulf to rejoin the bombardment group once again.

(III) 1945 – The Philippines Campaign Continues
The Invasion of Lingayen Gulf, 3–13 January 1945
The next major assault was the invasion scheduled for 9 January 1945 of the strategically important Lingayen Gulf on the northwestern side of Luzon Island, the largest and northernmost island of the Philippine archipelago. If the 34-mile long and 22-mile wide Lingayen Gulf could be secured then landing troops would have a 100-mile overland route south to approach Luzon's capital city of Manila. The operation was under the overall command of General Douglas MacArthur, who was embarked aboard the light cruiser *Boise* (CL-47).

Preliminary minesweeping and shore bombardment would begin on 6 January 1945, following which, 68,000 troops of the US 6th Army would land on 9 January at the southern end of Lingayen Gulf – with more than 200,000 troops planned to be ashore within several days. The 7th Fleet Commander, Vice Admiral Thomas C. Kinkaid, was in overall command of the 164 ships of TF 77, the Luzon Attack Force, the lead element of which was the Bombardment and Fire Support TG 77.2, under the command of Vice Admiral Jesse B. Oldendorf, embarked upon the *California*. Oldendorf had proved his mettle at the Battle of the Surigao Strait in October 1944, been promoted from Rear to Vice Admiral on 15 December 1944 and made commander of the Battleship Squadron. Oldendorf's Bombardment and Fire Support Task Group included the 6 Standard-Type battleships *West Virginia*, *Mississippi*, *California*, *Pennsylvania*, *Colorado* and *New Mexico*, along with 6 cruisers, 19 destroyers, 12 escort carriers and a screen of 14 destroyers and supporting craft – and would be supported by TG 77.4, the Escort Carrier Group.

The main elements of Oldendorf's Bombardment and Fire Support Group departed Leyte Gulf on 3 January, to transit the Surigao Strait, the Sulu Sea, Mindoro Strait and then pass up the west coast of Luzon to Lingayen Gulf. As they moved north, Japanese aircraft began conventional and kamikaze attacks on Oldendorf's Force.

USS *CALIFORNIA* (BB-44)

As the main part of Oldendorf's force passed through the Surigao Strait it divided into a van and rear group, each group centered around a nucleus of escort carriers to provide a CAP of about forty aircraft in daylight hours. By 4 January the force was in the Sulu Sea.

Although *California* was not damaged in the kamikaze attacks, at about 1700 on 4 January, approximately fifteen Japanese planes were picked up on radar at a range of about 45 miles, splitting into two attack groups. One enemy kamikaze dropped two bombs and then crashed into the island superstructure of the escort carrier *Ommaney Bay* (CVE-79). One bomb penetrated the flight deck and exploded amongst fully fuelled aircraft in the forward hangar bay, whilst the second bomb penetrated to the second deck before exploding. Fires were started that cooked off ammunition – and eventually the flames reached the torpedo-stowage area aft, where torpedoes blew up in a massive explosion at 1818, ripping the *Ommaney Bay* apart. The blazing hulk was eventually scuttled by torpedoes from the destroyer *Burns* (DD-588).

Vice Admiral Oldendorf's bombardment force arrived off Lingayen Gulf before dawn on 6 January 1945. Just before sunrise, the minesweepers entered the gulf first, followed by *California*, with Oldendorf himself aboard, and the bombardment ships, which would provide AA cover for the minesweepers and were repeatedly attacked by Japanese planes.

The naval bombardment of enemy positions ashore began at about noon. *California* launched her floatplanes to spot for her guns, and once her planes were aloft and in position, her 14in guns commenced firing on Santiago Island on the western side of Lingayen Gulf – targeting Japanese artillery that might endanger Allied forces once they entered the gulf.

Allied minesweepers then began to sweep two channels from the entrance of the gulf to the landing beaches. The minesweepers and bombardment ships were repeatedly attacked over the next few days by kamikazes flying from airfields close by on Luzon.

On the first day of the bombardment, 6 January 1945, the battleship *New Mexico* took a devastating kamikaze hit to the bridge on the port side that killed her commanding officer and twenty-nine other crew and wounded eighty-seven more. Amongst the dead was the British Lieutenant General Herbert Lumsden, Prime Minister Winston Churchill's personal representative to General MacArthur's HQ.

Shortly after 1715 on 6 January, a pair of A6M Zero kamikazes attacked *California*. As they closed the great battleship, AA gunners shot down one of the A6M Zeros, but the other kamikaze got through and crashed into *California*'s port side, abreast the mainmast. Gasoline from the kamikaze's fuel tanks started a fire whilst a 5in round from a friendly ship accidentally hit one of *California*'s 5in guns. The shell exploded inside the turret and started another fire. Both fires were quickly brought under control, but the kamikaze attack had killed 45 crew and injured another 151. The damage itself was however relatively minor – and temporary repairs were made whilst the ship remained on station and her guns continued to target Japanese positions ashore. Many other Allied ships were hit and damaged.

At 0655 on 7 January, minesweepers and the Bombardment and Fire Support ships re-entered Lingayen Gulf – and by the afternoon, six Underwater Demolition Teams (UDT) were in operation off the landing beaches as the naval bombardment continued. The UDT swimmers found no submerged beach obstacles.

Kamikazes attacked the invasion fleet ships in force. The light cruiser *Boise*, with MacArthur aboard, was damaged whilst the destroyer minesweeper *Hovey* (DMS-11) was sunk by aerial torpedo and the destroyer minesweeper *Palmer* (DD-161) was bombed and sunk.

Japanese air attacks continued as the main Allied invasion force closed Lingayen Gulf. Planes from the Allied 7th Fleet CVE escort carriers flew hundreds of sorties, knocking down kamikazes and bombing and strafing targets along the landing beaches. The escort carrier *Kitkun Bay* (CVE-71) was hit and disabled by a kamikaze and had to be towed away.

9 January 1945, S-Day
As previous Allied pre-invasion bombardments had been so devastating, the Japanese had decided not to defend the beaches and instead fight from inland positions in the hills. This tactic, allied to Oldendorf's devastating naval bombardment and the strikes from CVE escort carrier planes, meant that when the first of some 68,000 troops of the US 6th Army began going ashore at about 0930 on S-Day, 9 January, they encountered little opposition. Over the next few days, a total of more than 203,000 Allied troops were landed at Lingayen Gulf, quickly establishing a 20-mile beachhead.

10–18 January 1945
With the beachhead now secured, *California* left Lingayen Gulf on 10 January to patrol the South China Sea, west of the Philippines. The Japanese still held Vietnam, Malaya and Singapore to the west of

the South China Sea – from where it was possible the Japanese fleet could counterattack.

California then returned to Lingayen Gulf – before departing on 22 January for the long passage to repair and replenish at Ulithi Atoll in the Caroline Islands, which by now had been developed into a major Allied staging area. She arrived at Ulithi Atoll on 28 January 1945.

The battle-scarred *California* had soon departed Ulithi, heading some 3,600nm east for Pearl Harbor, where she paused briefly from 6–8 February 1945. She then departed eastwards from Hawaii, heading more than 2,000nm back to the West Coast of the USA for permanent repairs and modifications at Puget Sound Naval Shipyard, in Washington State.

(IV) Battle of Okinawa – Operation ICEBERG, 1 April–22 June 1945
10 May 1945
California departed the West Coast of the USA on 10 May 1945 – heading west to open sea to rejoin the fleet, which was by now operating off Okinawa, in the Ryukyu Islands, which had been assaulted the month before on 1 April 1945 and were still bitterly contested. Okinawa lies just 400 miles south of the main Japanese home island of Kyushu and once pacified, would be used as a supply base and an airfield for medium and heavy bombers to launch bombing raids directly against the Japanese home islands.

California steamed first to the Pearl Harbor Naval Base, where she was alongside from 16–29 May before departing for Ulithi, where she anchored up from 9–12 June before departing north towards Okinawa. The war in Europe may have ended with the surrender of Germany on 7 May 1945, but this was of little comfort to the beleaguered US troops on Okinawa itself. The Battle of Okinawa developed into one of the bloodiest in the Pacific War, lasting eighty-two days from 1 April–22 June 1945, as the US Army and Marines came up against fanatical Japanese troops.

15 June 1945
California arrived off Okinawa on 15 June, by which time the US forces had already been fighting on the island for more than two months. The Japanese had launched a major kamikaze campaign during the Allied operations, and these attacks continued whilst *California* was on station. On 17 and 18 June, she turned her 14in main-battery guns, together with the 8in guns of the heavy cruisers *New Orleans* (CA-32)

and *Tuscaloosa* (CA-37), to bombard Japanese shore batteries and fire directly against enemy ridge positions in support of the US 96th Infantry Division. Heavy fog hampered efforts by the ship's floatplanes to locate concealed Japanese positions, but *California* nevertheless conducted a heavy bombardment of the area over the two days.

By 22 June 1945, organised enemy resistance on Okinawa had ended, but at huge cost. There were approximately 160,000 casualties on both sides – at least 80,000 Allied, including 12,500 KIA. Some 110,000 Japanese had been killed in action – including drafted Okinawans wearing Japanese uniforms. Some 150,000 Okinawan civilians had died, almost half the pre-war population of 300,000.

Both sides had lost many ships and aircraft, not least the superbattleship *Yamato*, sent on a suicide mission in early April to be run ashore and then operate as an armoured shore battery. The attacks by kamikazes had been ferocious – and it was thought that the defence of the Japanese homeland islands would see even more determined resistance. But Okinawa was now in Allied hands and could provide a fleet anchorage, troop staging areas and airfields close to Japan in preparation for the eventual invasion of Japan itself.

The southern Japanese home island of Kyushu was now in easy range of Allied land-based bombers and fighters – and regular air strikes began in July. Boeing B-29 Superfortress bombers would be able to begin operating from Okinawa in August 1945.

California patrolled off Okinawa until 14 July 1945 to prevent any Japanese naval forces from attacking the Allied invasion fleet. From 15–22 July, she lay at the Kerama Islands, about 20 miles southwest of Okinawa, replenishing fuel and stores before joining TF 95 to provide armoured big-gun support to mine-clearing operations in the East China Sea.

The question of how to finally defeat Japan and end the war divided navy and army top brass. The army favoured invading the southernmost island of Japan, Kyushu – and the largest island of Honshū, on which Tokyo is situated. The navy admirals believed that Japan would surrender to an air and sea blockade, before Allied landings had to take place, with the feared huge loss of more than 500,000 dead or wounded Allied troops.[60] Despite their misgivings over landings, the navy made their preparations for the invasion of Japan.

(V) The Invasion of Japan – Operation DOWNFALL
On 25 May 1945, as the Okinawa campaign drew to a close, the Joint Chiefs of Staff (JCS) directed that the invasion of Japan should proceed,

the campaign being given the codename Operation DOWNFALL. It would begin on 1 November 1945.

Operation DOWNFALL was divided into two parts:

1. The 6th Army landings at Kyushu were codenamed Operation OLYMPIC and would take place with a target date set for 1 November 1945.[61] (Early in August the code name OLYMPIC was leaked – and so the JCS renamed the operation as MAJESTIC.)
2. The 8th Army landings on the coast of Honshū near Tokyo were codenamed Operation CORONET. These landings would allow for a drive across the Kanto Plain to Tokyo. The operation was scheduled tentatively for 1 March 1946.

The Allied Combined Chiefs of Staff planners assessed that organised resistance in Japan would cease by 15 November 1946.[62]

6 August 1945
Little Boy

On 29 and 30 July 1945, Allied shore bombardment and carrier air strikes against targets on the largest Japanese home island of Honshū continued, before being halted by typhoons and prolonged refuelling. And then, a special order arrived from Admiral Nimitz, instructing Admiral Halsey to take the 3rd Fleet well away from southern Japan.

On 6 August, the Boeing B-29 Superfortress bomber *Enola Gay*, flying from Tinian in the Northern Mariana Islands, dropped the first atomic bomb, *Little Boy*, on Hiroshima – on the southwestern end of the main island of Honshū. The possible effects of radiation fallout from the new weapon were unknown and so the Third Feet had been moved well clear. The bomb devastated Hiroshima with 70,000–80,000 people killed immediately – some 30 per cent of the population – and 19,700 injured and 170,000 rendered homeless. Over the next 2 to 4 months, the acute effects of the radiation would raise the number of dead to between 90,000 and 145,000 people.

Sixteen hours after the first bomb was dropped on Hiroshima, President Harry S. Truman called again for Japan's surrender, warning them to 'expect a rain of ruin from the air, the like of which has never been seen on this earth'.

On 8 August 1945, *California* was detached from operations and sent for maintenance work to San Pedro Bay in the Philippines. The work was scheduled to last from 11–15 August.

9 August 1945
Fat Man
On the evening of 8 August 1945, the Soviet Union declared war on Japan and soon after midnight on 9 August, invaded the Imperial Japanese puppet state of Manchuko. Hours later, on 9 August, the B-29 Superfortress *Bockscar* dropped the second atomic bomb on Nagasaki, this time a plutonium implosion bomb called *Fat Man*. Between 39,000 and 80,000 people died immediately and in the coming months from the effects of the radiation.

Following the Nagasaki bombing, Emperor Hirohito finally intervened and ordered the Supreme Council for the Direction of the War to accept the Allies' terms in the Potsdam Declaration for ending the war.

Ceasefire – 15 August 1945
Following a failed coup earlier that morning, Emperor Hirohito gave a recorded address across the Empire of Japan on 15 August 1945, announcing the surrender of Japan to the Allies. A ceasefire came into effect that day, 15 August, and the Japanese surrender was officially set for 2 September in Tokyo Bay.

On the day of the ceasefire, *California* was completing her maintenance works at San Pedro Bay, in the Philippines. That day *California* steamed north towards Nakagusuku Bay, on the south coast of Okinawa, where she remained from 23 August awaiting orders.

On 2 September 1945, the Empire of Japan formally surrendered unconditionally to the Allies aboard the fast battleship *Missouri*.

The Pacific War was finally over.

(VI) Occupation of Japan
Almost three weeks later, *California* departed Okinawa on 20 September 1945, bound for the port city of Wakayama, on the south of the main home island of Honshū. She arrived on 23 September and would support MacArthur's 6th Army troops as they began the formal occupation of Japan. The following week, *California* headed further north up the east coast of Honshū to Yokosuka, arriving there on 3 October and anchoring near the damaged battleship *Nagato*, which was still afloat.

Homeward Bound, 15 October 1945
California was attached to TG 50.5, which included that other veteran battleship of the Pearl Harbor raid *Tennessee* for the return passage to the Philadelphia Navy Yard, on the East Coast of the USA. With the addition of torpedo blisters to her hull during her post-Pearl Harbor modernisation, *California* was now too wide in the beam to transit the

Panama Canal. Thus, when the naval squadron departed Japan on 15 October 1945, the ships sailed initially south to Singapore, stopping there on 23 October, where they formed up with British, French and Italian warships slated to head west to European home ports.

The Allied task group set off from Singapore, heading west for Europe. The flotilla passed northwest up the Malacca Strait between the Malay Peninsula and Sumatra, and into the open waters of the Indian Ocean. En route westwards, the two US battleships stopped in Colombo, Sri Lanka, *California* leading *Tennessee* through a gap in the harbour boom on 30 October 1945 – as a boom defence vessel stood ready to close the gap after the two battleships had entered. The two battleships remained at Colombo replenishing for four days, with *California* embarking South-African troops for repatriation.

California departed Colombo on 3 November 1945, heading southwest for Cape Town, on the very southernmost tip of South Africa – where she disembarked her troops from 15–18 November. *California* then steamed westwards into the Atlantic on her way to Philadelphia.

7 December 1945 – Philadelphia
Almost two months after leaving Japan, *California* reached Philadelphia on 7 December 1945, where 754 officers and men were sent to discharge centres. As the ship was prepared to be laid up, another 40 officers and 1,345 men were discharged over the following months.

7 August 1946
California is placed in reserve, still in commission.

14 February 1947
California is decommissioned but remains in the navy's inventory.

10 July 1959 – Sold for Scrap
The Second World War had defined the end of the era of the battleship. The venerable and famous battleship *California*, which had served since shortly after the First World War and which had seen so much action in the Second World War, was now a relic of a bygone age. Aircraft carriers were now the supreme capital ship in any navy.

After twelve years languishing laid up, her time now long past, she was stricken from the Navy Vessel Register on 1 March 1959 and sold that year for scrapping to the Bethlehem Shipbuilding Corporation. She was subsequently broken up alongside her sister *Tennessee* at their east-coast scrapyard on the Patapsco River, Baltimore, just to the north of Washington.

Chapter 6

USS *Maryland* (BB-46)

USS *Maryland* (BB-46) off San Pedro, 19 November 1928. She is seen from astern. (*NH 75718 courtesy of US Naval History & Heritage Command*)

USS *MARYLAND* (BB-46)

Specifications (as built):	Colorado class
Builder:	Newport News Shipbuilding & Drydock Co., Virginia
Launched:	20 March 1920
Commissioned:	21 July 1921
Decommissioned:	3 April 1947
Displacement:	32,600 tons (S). 33,590 tons (F)
Length:	624ft (oa)
	600ft (wl)
Beam:	97ft 6in (wl)
Draft:	30ft 6in
Speed:	21 knots
Endurance:	8,000nm at 10 knots (S)
Armament:	
Main Battery:	8 x 16in/45-cal. Mark 1 in 4 2-gun turrets
Secondary Battery:	14 x single 5in/51-cal.
AA Battery:	4 x single 3in/23-cal.
Torpedo Tubes:	2 x 21in submerged beam tubes
Armour:	
Belt:	13.5in tapering to 8in on lower edge
Bulkheads:	13.5in
Barbettes:	13–4.5in
Turrets:	Face: 18in. Roof: 5in. Sides: 10in. Rear: 9in
Decks:	Armour deck (uppermost): 3.5in in 2 layers with additional layers aft over steering to give 6in
	Lower splinter deck: 1.5–2.25in in 2 layers
Conning tower:	16in
Sister ships in class:	*Colorado* (BB-45), *Washington* (BB-47: cancelled), *West Virginia* (BB-48)
Fate:	Sold for scrap – 8 July 1959

The Colorado-class units were broadly similar in size and performance to the preceding Tennessee-class units and the 'all-or-nothing' armour scheme, introduced with the Nevada class, was retained. The Colorado class would be the last and most powerful battleships built for the US Navy until the two North Carolina-class fast battleships entered service in 1941.

Known as 'Old Mary' or 'Fighting Mary', *Maryland* was designed in 1916 during the First World War and her keel was laid down by Newport News Shipbuilding & Drydock Company of Newport News, Virginia on 24 April 1917. Although four Colorado-class hulls were laid down, only three were completed, *Colorado*, *Maryland* and *West Virginia*. The fourth BB of the class, *Washington*, was over 75 per cent complete when construction was cancelled under the terms of the Washington Naval Treaty in 1922.

Maryland was launched for fitting out afloat on 20 March 1920 and commissioned more than a year later on 21 July 1921. As built, *Maryland* sported two lattice or cage masts with spotting tops for the main battery.

USS *Maryland* (BB-46) from the Brooklyn Bridge, 1923. (*NH 69055 courtesy of US Naval History & Heritage Command*)

USS *MARYLAND* (BB-46)

Her two smokestacks were situated in between the cage masts.* During her modernisation in early 1944, the cage mainmast was removed and replaced by a small tower.

Maryland would serve as the flagship of the fleet until 1923, when the flag was shifted to *Pennsylvania* (BB-38). *Maryland* was the least damaged of all the US battleships hit during the Pearl Harbor raid and would be the first to get back into the fight.

(a) Armament

(i) Main Battery
The preceding three classes of Standard-Type battleships had been armed with twelve 14in main-battery guns in four superfiring 3-gun turrets – but for the Colorado-class units the main battery was altered to eight larger 16in/45-cal. Mark 1 guns in four 2-gun turrets situated on the centreline of the ship. One superfiring pair of turrets was placed forward of the superstructure towards the bow whilst the after superfiring pair of turrets was placed abaft the superstructure towards the stern. Despite having fewer guns (12 reduced to 8) the broadside of a Colorado-class battleship was virtually similar to the broadside of the 12 14in guns of the preceding Tennessee class. The Mark 1 gun fired a 2,110lb 16in AP shell that delivered bigger hitting power and more penetration at distance than the 1,402lb 14in AP shell of the preceding classes.

The 16in/45-cal. Mark 1 gun had an effective range of 22,900yd (approximately13 miles) and a maximum range of 34,300yd (almost 20 miles).

(ii) Secondary Battery
The secondary battery consisted of fourteen 5in/51-cal. BL guns mounted in individual casemates clustered on either side of the superstructure amidships. None were set in the hull itself as with some earlier classes – and this gave the ship a cleaner, more modern appearance. The 5in/51-cal. BL gun had a rate of fire of eight to nine rounds per minute, firing a 50–55lb 5in shell with an effective firing range of 17,000yd (approximately 9 miles) at 20° elevation. The battery was reduced to twelve guns in 1922.

---

* For detail on cage masts, see Chapter 5 USS *California*.

(iii) AA Protection

Maryland was initially fitted with four 3in/23-cal. DP guns for AA defence, the number being increased to eight in 1922. These guns were the standard AA weapon for US Navy destroyers during the First World War and into the 1920s. The QF gun fired a fixed ammunition round where the case and 13lb projectile formed a single assembled unit, like a sporting cartridge. The weapon could depress to -15° and elevate to +75° in an AA mount and could fire eight to nine rounds per minute with an effective firing range of some 8,800yd, about 5 miles.

In 1928–9, the eight 3in/23-cal. guns were replaced by 5in/25-cal. QF heavy AA guns. The short barrel of the 5in/25-cal. DP gun made it much easier to train manually against fast-moving targets such as enemy planes.

(iv) Submerged Beam Torpedo Tubes

As was common for the dreadnoughts of the day, *Maryland* was fitted with two submerged 21in (530mm) torpedo tubes, one mounted in her hull below the waterline on each beam towards the foreship.

(b) Armour

Maryland was fitted with a vertical main waterline armour belt along the sides of her citadel that was 13.5in thick, tapering to 8in at the lower edge. The belt was 17ft wide (high) – with half the main belt being below the waterline.

As protection against plunging fire, the uppermost horizontal armour deck was 3.5in thick with additional layers of STS above the steering aft. The lower horizontal splinter deck was 1.5in thick in the middle with 2.25in-thick sloping sides and was designed to catch any splinters caused by an explosion on the armour deck above.

The main-battery gun turrets had 18in-thick faces with the roof being 5in thick, and the sides and rear being 10in and 9in thick respectively. The gunhouses rotated on barbettes that were 13in thick. The front of the conning tower was 16in thick.

(c) Propulsion

Maryland had four propellers that were driven by four General Electric turbo-electric drives with steam provided at 285psi by eight oil-fired Babcock & Wilcox boilers. The ship's propulsion system was rated at 28,900 shaft horsepower for a top speed of 21 knots. The eight boilers

USS *MARYLAND* (BB-46)

were set in individual compartments surrounding the turbo-electric drives, which were not directly connected to the propeller shafts – thus allowing additional compartmentalisation and increasing underwater protection.*

Maryland had a cruising endurance of 8,000nm at 10 knots, but additional fuel space could be used in wartime to increase her range to 21,000nm at 10 knots. Her crew numbered 64 officers and 1,241 enlisted men.

* * *

Starboard view of USS *Maryland* (BB-46) at Puget Sound Navy Yard dry dock, 2 July 1941. A crewman (in centre of shot) stands atop the newly added torpedo blister where it meets the top of the vertical waterline armour belt. (*UA.383.07.007 courtesy of US Naval History & Heritage Command*)

---
* For detail on turbo-electric propulsion systems, see Chapter 5, USS *California*.

In July 1941, *Maryland* was dry-docked in Puget Sound Navy Yard Base for overhaul and the installation of a torpedo blister on either beam that met the side of the ship just above the vertical waterline armour belt and had a flat top, sloped outward just enough to give drainage. The blister increased the beam of the ship to 108ft and increased her buoyancy. Four 1.1in quad mounts were added and the refit was completed on 1 August 1941.[1]

PEARL HARBOR, 7 DECEMBER 1941

On the morning of 7 December 1941, *Maryland* was lying with her starboard beam towards Ford Island, inboard of and alongside *Oklahoma*. Astern of *Oklahoma* and *Maryland*, the battleship *West Virginia* was tied up alongside and outboard on the port side of *Tennessee*.

Forward of *Maryland* and *Oklahoma* the 553ft-long, 7,470-ton oiler *Neosho* (AO-23) was tied up at the fuel dock. She had arrived the day before from the West Coast of the USA, discharged a full cargo of oil to Naval Air Station Ford Island and was now being prepared for the return passage to the West Coast.

As the attacks began just before 0800, many of the crew aboard *Maryland* had been preparing for shore leave at 0900 – or eating breakfast. As the first Japanese aircraft appeared and explosions rocked the outboard battleships, *Maryland*'s bugler blew General Quarters and the first AA guns went into action, shooting down one of two torpedo bombers that had just released its torpedo against *Oklahoma* alongside. Gunners aboard *Maryland* would manage to bring all her AA batteries into action and report seven enemy planes shot down.[2]

As *Oklahoma* flooded with water alongside through multiple torpedo holes in her port hull, she began to list heavily to port. In less than 12 minutes, *Oklahoma* had rolled over, capsizing until her top hamper, upperworks and two masts hit the seabed. The mid-section of her starboard beam projected above the water and part of her keel was exposed. Many of *Oklahoma*'s crew clambered aboard *Maryland* to help serve her AA batteries.

Maryland was hit by two AP bombs. One AP bomb struck her fo'c'sle deck creating a hole about 12ft x 20ft. The anchor and paravane chains were damaged along with hatches, coamings and some main-deck wiring but the operation of the ship and her guns were unaffected.

The second AP bomb hit 22ft below the waterline on the port side, towards the bow at Frame 10 – punching a hole through the hull plating and exploding inside the ship and causing split seams and splinter holes.

USS *MARYLAND* (BB-46)

Luckily the bomb had exploded in a canvas and life-jacket storage area and they absorbed many of the fragments. The ship began to take on water, an estimated 1,000 tons pouring into the ship and putting her head down by 5ft.

When the attack was over, although the lightly damaged *Maryland* was boxed in in her berth, her main, secondary and AA batteries were all still ready for action should enemy vessels appear off the horizon or should further waves of enemy aircraft come into view.

A portable caisson was soon altered to fit over the hole allowing the flooded compartments to be pumped out – although hatches sprung by the blast hindered pumping efforts.[3] Two officers and two men had been killed in the attack.

USS *Maryland* (BB-46) at berth F-5 with men working on the capsized hull of USS *Oklahoma* alongside during or immediately after the attack. (*NH 83065 courtesy of US Naval History & Heritage Command*)

Repair and Return to Service

On 10 December 1941, just three days after the attack, the relatively undamaged *Maryland* was eased forward from her berth alongside the capsized *Oklahoma*. Just before 1600 on 20 December 1941, less than a fortnight after the attack, she made her way slowly out of Pearl Harbor, with *Tennessee* following astern. About 30 minutes later, the recently repaired *Pennsylvania* moved out of the yard and turned her head towards the open sea to the south.

Escorted by a screen of four destroyers, the three battleships headed more than 2,000nm northeast towards San Francisco Bay for final repairs to be made in Navy Yards. *Maryland* and *Tennessee* were destined for the Puget Sound Navy Yard in Washington State whilst *Pennsylvania* would head north to Mare Island Navy Yard, north of San Francisco.

Maryland entered Puget Sound Navy Yard on 30 December 1941. Such was the urgent need for battleships that *Pennsylvania*, *Maryland* and *Tennessee* would be repaired as quickly as possible – to allow them to join the battleships *Colorado*, *Idaho*, *New Mexico* and *Mississippi*, which were operating as a defensive fleet that was kept at a 48-hour state of readiness due to invasion fears on the West Coast.

Over the course of the next two months, *Maryland* was repaired and her weaponry hastily improved, keeping to the 48-hour readiness order. Two of the original twelve 5in/51-cal. secondary battery guns were removed and the eight 5in/25-cal. AA guns received splinter shields. Splinter protection was added to the bridge, pilot house and radar. Sixteen single 20mm Oerlikon rapid-fire weapons were fitted and a new SC radar was fitted along with two Mk 3 fire-control radars.

Repairs were completed on 26 February 1942, following which she got under way with the newly repaired *Tennessee* and refitted *Colorado* for San Francisco – where the battleships would join TF 1, commanded by Admiral William S. Pye, guarding against any Japanese invasion. The ships carried out a series of shakedown manoeuvres and cruises to West-Coast ports before rejoining the fleet in June 1942.

It was time for *Maryland* to get back in the war.

BATTLESHIP REVENGE

As intelligence reporting alerted the Allies to the developing Japanese operation to invade the strategic US outpost and airbase of Midway Atoll, *Maryland* remained as part of a backup fleet on standby, awaiting orders to deploy if needed and protect the West Coast of the USA.

Battle of Midway, 4–7 June 1942

At the Battle of the Coral Sea, fought by opposing carrier forces between 4 and 8 May 1942, Japan won a tactical victory by sinking the fleet carrier *Lexington* (CV-2) along with the destroyer *Sims* (DD-409) and the oiler *Neosho* (AO-23), a survivor of the Pearl Harbor attack. Japan lost the light carrier *Shōhō*, a destroyer and some smaller ships. With only four operational US fleet carriers deployed in the Pacific, the battle had just robbed 25 per cent of US carrier strength.

Admiral Isoroku Yamamoto, Commander-in-Chief of the IJN Combined Fleet, was aware that whilst the raid on Pearl Harbor on 7 December 1941 had successfully sunk or disabled the US Pacific Fleet battleships, the US fleet carriers were still a threat he wanted eliminated. With *Lexington* sunk at the Battle of the Coral Sea, Yamamoto argued that another air attack on Pearl Harbor would trigger the US fleet, including the three remaining fleet carriers, to come out and fight. He assessed that *Yorktown* had been so badly damaged during the Battle of the Coral Sea that it perhaps would not be battle ready, or it may even have sunk. If that was the case, then the only carriers available to the Americans would be the *Enterprise* and *Hornet*. Either way, in addition to a superiority in battleships, Japan also had a superiority in numbers of carriers. Now was the time for the decisive battle that would buy time to allow consolidation of an advanced defence perimeter around the territories Japan had seized, which would be a barrier to any further direct attacks on Japan itself.

Yamamoto assessed however that Pearl Harbor was by now too well protected by land-based aircraft deployed there after 7 December 1941. He thus selected Midway Atoll, at the extreme northwest end of the Hawaiian island chain, as the bait to draw out the remaining US carriers. The tiny two-island atoll of Midway itself was not of any great significance to overall Japanese aims in the Pacific, but it did hold a US airfield – and Yamamoto felt that the Americans would view Midway as a vital outpost of Pearl Harbor and would defend it strenuously. Crucially, Midway lay some 1,300 miles from Hawaii – and was outwith the effective range of the US land-based planes stationed there.

Japanese commanders believed that with her battleships sunk or disabled at Pearl, the USA would be forced to commit the two or three remaining fleet carriers to defend Midway. With the US Pacific Fleet battleships out of action, in addition to having more fleet carriers, Yamamoto also had a much more powerful battleship fleet at his disposal. The chance was there for Yamamoto to draw out the US carriers from Pearl – into a trap where his own carriers and battleships would pounce and extinguish their threat once and for all. Then, with the US battleships *and* her carriers sunk, US naval power in the Pacific would be decimated. With Japan in control of Midway and the Aleutian Islands to the north, it would be game over for Pearl Harbor as a forward US base. Following a successful landing on Midway, the existing US airfield would be converted into a base from where bombing raids against Hawaii and the West Coast of the USA could be carried out.

Just some four weeks after the Battle of the Coral Sea, the two sides would clash once again in the Battle of Midway, fought between 4 and 7 June 1942. But unknown to Japan, US cryptographers had already broken the main Japanese naval code and deciphered some details of the plan and knew that Midway was the target. They also established the date of the attack as either 4 or 5 June.

Forewarned of the operation, the US Navy was able to plan its own ambush – with a good understanding that four enemy carriers were being deployed with supporting heavy warships and escorts. The subsequent Battle of Midway would be one of the most decisive battles in naval history – a complicated battle in which the IJN suffered crippling losses of the four carriers *Akagi*, *Kaga*, *Sōryū* and *Hiryū* (all part of the six-carrier *Kidō Butai* force that had attacked Pearl Harbor six months earlier) and the heavy cruiser *Mikuma*. On the US side, the battle-scarred *Yorktown* (CV-5) would be sunk – as well as the destroyer *Hammann* (DD-412).

Following the Battle of Midway, once the IJN fleet had fled west, the threat to the West Coast of the USA had been extinguished. *Maryland* was detached from TF 1 and sent to San Francisco on exercise for the next six months. On 1 August 1942, she set sail back to Pearl Harbor for her first visit to her old base since the Japanese attack eight months earlier. Too valuable to spend time being extensively refitted, her aft cage mainmast was hastily cut down at Pearl to half its original height to save weight and allow the installation of searchlights and four quadruple 1.1in light machine-gun mounts to augment her AA protection of eight 5in/25-cal. DP guns and sixteen Oerlikon 20mm cannons. The reconnaissance floatplane catapult mounted on No. 3 turret was removed, likely to increase AA firing arcs and save weight with the additional AA battery.

In early November 1942, *Maryland* departed Pearl Harbor with the battleship *Colorado* bound for the forward area, arriving in Fiji on 8 November 1942. *Maryland* and *Colorado* operated out of the Fiji Islands from November 1942 until February 1943, the two battleships patrolling the vast expanses of the Pacific to interdict any Japanese incursion from threatening Australia.

In February 1943, two more 1.1in quad mounts were added and the number of 20mm Oerlikon AA weapons was increased to forty-eight.[4] Her radar capability was improved with a SK radar whilst Mk 4 radars were fitted on the secondary battery directors. In March 1943, *Maryland* had ten 0.50-cal. heavy machine guns added.

Maryland then moved some 750nm west from Fiji to the New Hebrides (today known as the ocean nation of Vanuatu), which are situated southeast of the Solomons and on the east flank of the Coral Sea. After operating there initially off the island of Efate, in August 1943, *Maryland* and *Colorado* moved north to Aore Island, near Espiritu Santo.

Maryland then returned to the Pearl Harbor Naval Base in Hawaii for a five-week overhaul during which thirty-two more powerful 40mm Bofors AA autocannon were installed on the top decks and the foremast. Although *Maryland* mounted forty-eight Oerlikon 20mm weapons by this time, as ranges to attacking aircraft increased and the Japanese turned to night attacks, it was found that the Oerlikon performed poorly in comparison with the 40mm Bofors autocannon – and eight 20mm Oerlikons were removed, reducing the total number to forty.

The powerful and effective 40mm Bofors autocannon was controlled by Mark 51 optical directors with integrated gyro gun-sight lead-angle indicators. The Bofors could knock down an enemy aircraft at long range, before it could release its weapon, whereas the Oerlikon could only knock down an aircraft when it was a lot closer and had possibly released its weapon. The Oerlikon would be largely abandoned later in the war due its lack of stopping power against heavy Japanese aircraft and kamikaze attacks.

(I) The Gilbert and Marshall Islands Campaign, November 1943–February 1944

To be able to establish forward land-based airbases that would be capable of supporting US operations across the Central Pacific, towards the Philippines and Japan, US strategists determined to take the Mariana Islands, from where direct bombing raids on Japan itself could commence.

The Marianas are a crescent-shaped archipelago that lies southsoutheast of Japan, southwest of Hawaii, north of New Guinea and east of the Philippines. Saipan is the largest and most northerly of the Northern Mariana Islands with Tinian and Rota to its south – and the large US territory island of Guam furthest south.

The nearest islands capable of supporting the seizure of the Marianas, by providing land-based airfields, were the twenty-nine coral atolls of the Marshall Islands, situated well to the east of the Marianas, and northeast of the Solomon Islands. The Marshalls had been occupied by Japan as part of the South Pacific Mandate since the First World War and was home to many names that became iconic during the Pacific War – such as Kwajalein, Bikini and Majuro, the capital.

The Marshall Islands however were cut off from direct communications with the US naval base at Pearl Harbor by a Japanese garrison and airbase on the small island of Betio on the western side of Tarawa Atoll in the Gilbert Islands. The Gilbert Islands, now known as the Republic of Kiribati, are a 500-mile-long chain of sixteen main atolls and hundreds of small coral islands, straddling the equator in an almost north–south line. They lie short of halfway between Papua New Guinea and Hawaii – and southeast of the Marshall Islands. Thus, to be able to seize the strategically important Mariana Islands, the Allied advance westwards towards Japan had to begin far to the east – with the seizure of the Gilbert Islands.

On 6 August 1943, the Joint Chiefs of Staff authorised a two-prong advance across the Pacific. In the *first prong*, beginning on 15 November 1943, Admiral Nimitz (CINCPAC-CINCPOA) would first seize the Gilbert Islands, securing advance bases for initial photo-intelligence of the Marshalls before subsequent landings around New Year's Day, 1944.

Simultaneously with the first prong, in a *second prong*, General Douglas MacArthur, leading the Southwest Pacific Area offensive, would cross northern New Guinea moving towards the port of Hollandia, on the north coast, which had been held by the Japanese since 1942. New Guinea is the second largest island in the world and stretches over 1,500 miles from west to east, yet Hollandia was the only suitable anchorage on the north coast. Once secured, Hollandia would be developed into a staging post for the Allied advance along the north coast of New Guinea into the Dutch East Indies and then to the Philippines.

Once Nimitz's Central Pacific Force had seized the Gilbert and Marshall Islands, the Central Pacific Force could then neutralise the great Japanese fortress of Truk, the IJN Combined Fleet anchorage and powerful airbase situated in the eastern Carolines. After hitting Truk, Nimitz would continue on to the Palau Islands in the western Carolines, beginning on 31 December 1944.

With Truk neutralised, the Central Pacific Force could move to occupy Saipan, Tinian and Guam in the Marianas, to the northwest.

Then, in November 1944, the second phase of MacArthur's invasion of the Philippines would follow.

The three survivors of the Pearl Harbor raid *Pennsylvania*, *Maryland* and *Tennessee* would all bring their guns to bear on the Japanese during these operations.

Battle of Tarawa – Operation GALVANIC, 20–23 November 1943
Tarawa is a name synonymous with the first bloody US amphibious assault of the Pacific War. Tarawa Atoll lies almost two-thirds of the way to the north of the Gilberts chain of atolls and islands, whilst Makin is the northmost atoll of the Gilberts chain. None of these atoll islands has land higher than 12ft above sea-level, being formed of a coral bedrock overlaid by sand and poor soil.

Tarawa Atoll encompasses a large lagoon of almost 200 square miles that is surrounded by a wide reef. At the southwest point of Tarawa Atoll sits the tiny island of Betio, which is shaped like a long, thin triangle on its side, pointing in towards the centre of the atoll. Betio is only 2 miles long and some 800m wide at its widest point and has a shallow reef that extends 500m out from the shore around the whole island. The southern and west sides of the island open to the deep oceanic waters of the Pacific, from where it was believed any Allied assault would come.

In February 1943, Betio had been reinforced and fortified with some 500 pillboxes and stockades being constructed with interlocking fields of fire over the shore and across the water. A command post and a large number of bomb shelters were set up in the interior of the island to allow the Japanese defenders to survive an anticipated pre-invasion bombardment.

Fourteen coastal defence guns were set in concrete bunkers that guarded the approaches to the lagoon's sheltered anchorage. Forty field artillery pieces were deployed around the island, set into reinforced firing pits. An intricate trench system was constructed that would allow troops to move safely around the island under cover and an airfield was constructed straight down the centre of the island.

Betio was soon the base for some 4,500 Japanese troops who were well supplied, well prepared and well dug in, with fourteen Ha-Go Type 95 light tanks. As Rear Admiral Keiji Shibazaki, an experienced combat operations officer, took over command on 20 July 1943, he rallied his men by stating that it would take 1 million men 100 years to conquer Tarawa. The scene was set for the first great test of the US Marines amphibious assault capability.

The Allied plan for the invasion of the Gilbert Islands, code name Operation GALVANIC, brought together the largest gathering of ships yet assembled in the Pacific War. The bulk of the Central Pacific Force was redesignated as the 5th Fleet and on 5 August 1943 was placed under the command of Vice Admiral Raymond Spruance, the immediate subordinate of Admiral Nimitz (CINCPAC-CINCPOA). The huge invasion force comprised some 17 aircraft carriers, 12 battleships (including *Pennsylvania*, *Maryland* and *Tennessee*), 8 heavy cruisers, 4 light cruisers, almost 70 destroyers and 36 transport ships. The actual landings of about 35,000 US troops would be conducted by V Amphibious Force under the overall command of Rear Admiral Richmond Kelly Turner, flying his flag aboard the *Pennsylvania*.

The basic naval organisation for GALVANIC was issued on 25 October by Vice Admiral Spruance aboard his flagship, the heavy cruiser *Indianapolis* (CA-35) (which would later transport parts of *Little Boy*, the first nuclear device to be dropped on Hiroshima, to Tinian).

Rear Admiral Kelly Turner divided V Amphibious Force into two attack forces. The Northern Attack Force (TF 52), under Turner's own direct command, would capture Makin. The Southern Attack Force (TF 53), commanded by Rear Admiral Harry H. Hill aboard his flagship, the battleship *Maryland*, would seize Tarawa and Apamama. Of the approximately 35,000 invasion troops of V Amphibious Corps, the 27th Infantry Division (Army), under Major General Ralph C. Smith, would assault Makin – whilst the 2nd Marine Division, under Major General Julian C. Smith, would hit Tarawa.

The fast carriers would pound Japanese airfields in the Marshalls commencing on 23 November to establish and maintain air superiority over the Gilberts by intercepting any enemy aircraft from the Marshalls. The fast-carrier planes would then support the amphibious landing forces by neutralising Japanese defences, helping spot the fall of shot and flying observation missions over Makin, Tarawa and Apamama. The fast carriers would provide CAP fighter cover, search ahead of the invasion convoys and conduct Anti-Submarine Warfare patrols as the troop transports closed.

The **Northern Attack Force (TF 52)**, under Rear Admiral Richmond Kelly Turner in *Pennsylvania*, tasked to seize Makin, comprised thirty-five ships in total. The Fire Support TG 52.2 would deliver the pre-invasion naval bombardment and handle any surface threats that materialised and comprised the 4 battleships *Pennsylvania*, *New Mexico*, *Mississippi* and *Idaho* along with 4 heavy cruisers and 6 destroyers, arranged in 3 Fire Support Units. TF 52 sailed for the Gilberts from Pearl Harbor on 10 November 1943, refuelling at sea en route.

The **Southern Attack Force (TF 53)**, commanded by Rear Admiral Harry W. Hill in *Maryland*, and tasked to seize Tarawa, comprised some 56 ships and was much larger than the Northern Attack Force (TF 52). The Transport Group (TG 53.1) would embark the bulk of 2nd Marine Division in 12 attack transports, 3 attack cargo ships, 1 Landing Ship, Dock and 1 transport and would have a screen of 7 destroyers. The Fire Support TG 53.4 included the battleships *Tennessee, Maryland* and *Colorado*, with 2 heavy cruisers, 2 light cruisers and 9 destroyers. TG 53.4 departed Pearl Harbor on 21 October 1943 bound for the Efate Island staging area in modern-day Vanuatu, where rehearsals for the invasion began on 7 November. On 13 November 1943, TF 53 sailed from Efate for Tarawa.

The subsequent amphibious assaults on Makin, and particularly on Tarawa, were the first time that US amphibious forces had faced determined enemy opposition in force. In particular, the 4,500 Japanese defenders on Tarawa were well dug in, well supplied and well prepared – and they would fight with fanatical determination almost to the last man.

Softening up the target landing beaches at Makin and Tarawa by land-based air began several days before the two Attack Forces arrived. Then, as the Fast Carrier Pacific Fleet (TF 50) closed, carrier planes bombed Tarawa and Makin on 18 and 19 November, hitting airfields on Mili and Jaluit in the southern Marshalls and knocking out Japanese air capability at Nauru. On 19 November, TG 53.4, *Tennessee, Maryland* and *Colorado*, shelled Tarawa.

The plan was that 3 hours before the amphibious assault on D-Day, 20 November 1943, a pre-invasion naval bombardment and counter-battery fire designed to neutralise Japanese heavy coast defence guns would be delivered by the Fire Support Group battleships, cruisers and destroyers at moderately long range.

On 20 November, as the Fire Support Group ships prepared to commence their D-Day pre-invasion bombardment, the troop transports halted in the Transport Area at 0355. The tracked landing vehicles (LVTs) of the first assault waves at both Makin and Tarawa launched through the bow doors of the LSTs. Other Landing Craft, Vehicle, Personnel (LCVP or Higgins boat), were hoisted over the side of attack transports – and in darkness, Marines clambered down nets over the side of transport ships to board. The troop-laden LCVPs and LVTs then moved off to the Rendezvous Area to form up for the attack.

As the assembled might of the Southern Attack Force hove into view of Tarawa in the pre-dawn hours – and before the LVTs of the first three waves had reached the Rendezvous Area – four Japanese 8in coastal defence batteries on the southwestern point of Betio Island opened up, forcing the large attack transports to pull back out of range.

At 0507, in *Maryland*'s first offensive action of the war, her main-battery 16in guns and those of her sister *Colorado* commenced counter-battery fire against the four Japanese 8in coastal guns, tangling with them in a long-range gunnery duel. *Maryland* fired five salvos of her 16in main-battery guns – quickly knocking out three of the Japanese coastal defence guns. One shell hit a Japanese ammunition storage facility for the 8in guns – setting off a large explosion and fireball. With the Japanese 8in guns largely disabled, the approach to the lagoon was now open, although the one remaining Japanese 8in gun continued with intermittent and inaccurate fire.

Following the gunnery duel, the 3-hour pre-invasion naval bombardment of Tarawa began at 0610 to soften up Japanese defences ahead of the landings. The well-protected battleships *Maryland* and *Colorado* moved closer to shore to attract Japanese fire and locate artillery emplacements – delivering a punishing attack on Japanese gun emplacements, control stations, pillboxes and installations.

As the pre-invasion bombardment was taking place, the two minesweepers *Pursuit* (AM-108) and *Requisite* (AM-109) of Minesweeper Group (TG 53.2), covered by two destroyers, entered the Tarawa lagoon and swept the shallows of mines.

Once all landing craft were ready at the Rendezvous Area, they moved off at 0636 in line astern towards the Line of Departure, which was 6,000–6,600yd from the assault beaches RED 1, RED 2 and RED 3. Shells from the Fire Support Group ships continued to pound the beaches ahead of them.

The assault waves of some 125 LVTs and LCVPs were however beset by a strong westerly current which carried the slow-moving heavy craft away from the Line of Departure and their planned speed-over-the-ground could not be achieved. They arrived at the Line of Departure at 0825, 39 minutes late.

Precision strafing attacks and air bombardment by carrier aircraft began at 0749. When the carrier aircraft departed, the Fire Support Group warships recommenced their neutralisation fire and continued to shoot until 0855 – when the naval bombardment stopped and further strafing and bombing runs took place. The island was becoming increasingly shrouded in a pall of dust and smoke and it had become difficult to identify targets.

When the landing craft were finally abreast the beaches, the first three waves executed a simultaneous turn towards the beach, the first wave turning towards the beach at 0830, 44 minutes later than originally scheduled. The second and third waves followed across the Line of Departure at 33-minute intervals. With 3 miles to run to the beaches, and with the speed-over-the-ground now being less than 4 knots, the timetable, which allowed for a 40-minute run to the beaches slipped even further. As the assault waves moved from the Line of Departure, shells began bursting over the exposed Marines, although the air bursts proved ineffectual.

US planners had expected that the amphibious assault troops in their LCVPs and LVTs at Betio would meet a water depth of 5ft over the wide-fringing reef, which would allow their 4ft-draft untracked LCVP Higgins boats to pass over. Unfortunately, it was the time of the weaker *neap tides* and the water depth failed to rise to the expected 5ft, leaving just 3ft to a few inches over the reef. The Higgins boats were abruptly halted, unable to get over the reef and leaving the Marines stranded 500m off the beach. The Marines had to disembark from the LCVPs and wade across the reef chest deep under direct enemy fire.

The tracked LVTs however could lumber over the reef – but as the LVTs made their way over the reef and into the shallows, Japanese troops who had survived the naval shelling began to man their firing pits again and more troops were moved up the landing beaches from the southern beaches. Whilst the LVT cab had armour plates to protect the cox, the LVT cargo holds packed with Marines had no such protection. The LVTs began to face an increasing volume of incoming fire and eight of forty-two LVTs in the first wave were knocked out.

At 0900, as Marine landing forces encountered heavy Japanese resistance and began taking casualties to emplaced crossfire, *Maryland* provided covering fire to eliminate several Japanese machine-gun nests. Her scouting plane covered the progress of the Marines' assault, allowing *Maryland* to provide accurate direct close support. The scout plane was damaged, and the pilot wounded in this action.

Touch down for the Marines on RED 1 was at 0910 – and 0917 for RED 2 and RED 3. Those LVTs that had successfully crossed the reef and reached the beach however then encountered a sea wall, which they couldn't clear. As troops disembarked from the LVTs, they were pinned down along the wall.

Behind the first three waves, came waves of LCVPs and LCM landing craft carrying infantrymen, tanks and artillery. With standard drafts of 4ft, they were also barred from crossing the reef by the shallow depth of water. Many tracked LVTs went back out to the reef to pick up infantrymen and howitzer crews, whilst other troops, stranded offshore in their Higgins boats, had to wade ashore with their equipment. Japanese riflemen and machine-gunners caught them as they struggled through the water heavily laden.[5] By the end of the first day, half of the LVTs had been knocked out.

As night fell, 5,000 Marines were ashore and clinging to their beachhead – but 1,500 were already dead or wounded. Many Marines of the second wave had been unable to land – and spent the night floating out in the lagoon, trying to sleep in their Higgins boats. Meanwhile, Japanese marines were swimming out in darkness to some of the wrecked LVTs and to the wrecked Japanese steamship *Saida Maru*, which lay to the west of a pier. Hiding themselves away, they waited for dawn – when they would be able to fire on the landing troops from behind. The next three days would see intense fighting on this small island before it was declared secure at 1330 D+3.

After three days covering the offensive on Betio Island, *Maryland* then moved to Apamama Island, about 95 miles southeast of Tarawa, where she would support US Marine landings. The Marines there however met with only light resistance from thirty Japanese soldiers – and two prisoners were brought to *Maryland*. The sweep of the remaining islands of the Tarawa Atoll was completed on 28 November 1943.

The US 2nd Marine Division had suffered more than 997 Marines and 30 sailors killed in action on Tarawa with more than 2,000 wounded during the 76 hours of the battle – a total of some 3,407. Only 1 Japanese officer and 16 men surrendered out of the entire force of 4,500. It was a chilling portent of what was to come.

On 7 December 1943, *Maryland* left the waters off Tarawa Atoll – heading northeast on the long passage back to San Francisco, via Pearl Harbor, for repairs and replenishment.

Battle of Kwajalein and Invasion of Majuro – Operation FLINTLOCK, 31 January–3 February 1944
Having successfully seized Tarawa and Makin in the Gilberts, the Allies now had the land and naval territories necessary for the next stage of the war plan – the invasion of seven islands, in nine phases, of the twenty-nine coral atolls that make up the Marshall Islands, which are located

approximately 220 miles northwest of the Gilbert Islands. The other atolls and islands not seized would be bypassed.

The most strategically important atolls for US planners were Kwajalein, which had a Japanese airfield, and Majuro, which had a large lagoon of some 114 square miles that was suitable as a sheltered fleet anchorage. Majuro is situated at the southeast of the Marshalls and could also serve as an airbase for conducting air operations against the rest of the Marshall Islands and in time the Marianas, where Guam lay just over 1,600 miles distant. The initial operation to seize Kwajalein and Majuro was codenamed FLINTLOCK.

Kwajalein Atoll is the largest atoll in the Marshalls. It is an irregularly shaped boomerang atoll that stretches approximately 66 miles in a straight line from northwest to southeast and is surrounded by a barrier reef. The linked islands of Roi-Namur sit at the north of the atoll whilst Kwajalein Island, which gives its name to the atoll, is situated at the very south of the atoll.

The sixty-four small islands of Majuro Atoll have a total land area of just 4 square miles and ring around Majuro's fine lagoon. Majuro had been mandated to Japan by the League of Nations in 1920.

Kwajalein Atoll had been the hub of Japanese military operations in the Marshalls since August 1941 and was the closest major base to Truk. IJN airbases had been established on smaller Kwajalein Atoll islands – the airbase on Roi-Namur commanded all Japanese air forces in the Marshalls and Gilberts.

After the fall of the Gilberts to US forces in November 1943, the thousands of Japanese troops garrisoned in the Marshalls created what fortifications they could. Four twin-mount 127mm (5in) guns were installed on the northern ends of each of Roi-Namur and Kwajalein islands with 132mm DP guns, 80mm guns and 20mm AA guns. The beaches were covered by 7.7mm and 13mm machine guns and some 150 operational aircraft were available in the Marshalls.

Building on the lessons learned from recent operations in the Gilberts, US forces adopted a number of innovations. The assault would be preceded by several days, not hours, of naval bombardment – and day and night air attacks would give the Japanese no rest for at least a week prior to the landing. Immediately before the landing, the selected beaches would be subjected to a devastating naval and aerial bombardment.

With the assault on Kwajalein Atoll set for 31 January 1944, a few weeks before, on 13 January 1944, *Maryland* and other units of TF 53, the Northern Attack Force for FLINTLOCK, TF 53, set off from San

Pedro, California to form up at the Lahaina Roads anchorage in Hawaii – between the surrounding islands of Maui and Lanai. In this safe and sheltered naval anchorage, over the course of the coming days *Maryland* would be replenished and made combat ready with stores, fuel and ammunition.

The TG 53.5 Fire Support Group was commanded by Rear Admiral Jesse B. Oldendorf and was tasked to assault the northern Kwajalein Atoll linked islands of Roi-Namur. TG 53.5 comprised the battleships *Tennessee*, *Maryland* and *Colorado*, along with the heavy cruiser *Louisville* (CA-28), the light cruisers *Santa Fe* (CL-60) and *Mobile* (CL-63) and a screen of nine destroyers.

The Southern Attack Force would assault Kwajalein Island with the Fire Support Group TG 52.8 comprising the battleship *Pennsylvania* and the three modernised New Mexico-class Standard-Type battleships *New Mexico* (BB-40), *Mississippi* (BB-41) and *Idaho* (BB-42), along with heavy and light cruisers and destroyers.

Both the Northern and Southern Attack Forces deployed towards Kwajalein from Hawaii on 22 January 1944, in what was the last sortie in force from Hawaii – as on completion of the Marshall Islands campaign, Hawaii would be left far in the rear. The new forward base would be Majuro.

Rear Admiral Richmond Kelly Turner's 5th Fleet Amphibious Force, carrying V Amphibious Corps under the command of Major General Holland M. Smith, would execute the simultaneous landings on Majuro and Kwajalein atolls.

The 4th Marine Division and the 7th Infantry Division were assigned to the initial landings at Kwajalein, whilst the 2nd Battalion of the army's 106th Infantry Regiment was assigned to the simultaneous capture of Majuro Atoll. The remainder of the 106th and 111th Infantry Regiments along with the 22nd Marines were held in reserve for deployment as necessary.

The Invasion of Majuro Atoll, 31 January 1944
On 31 January 1944, the Reconnaissance Company of V Amphibious Corps and the army's 2nd Battalion of the 106th Infantry landed on Majuro for the opening act of Operation FLINTLOCK. The landing troops discovered that the Japanese had evacuated their fortifications to Kwajalein and Eniwetok some time previously, leaving only a single Japanese officer as caretaker. The US force took control of the atoll in that one day without any casualties, giving the US Navy the use of one of the largest anchorages in the Pacific.

The Invasion of Kwajalein Atoll

Kwajalein Island is only 2.5 miles long and 880yd wide – so the Japanese defenders had no alternative but to make plans to counterattack US troops on the landing beaches. But until the Battle of Tarawa, they had not appreciated that tracked US amphibious vehicles could cross coral reefs and land on the lagoon side of an atoll. They had concentrated their strongest defences on the other side of Kwajalein, facing the ocean, from where they expected the attack to come.

On 30 January 1944, 150nm east of Kwajalein, *Maryland* and the Northern Fire Support Group TG 53.5 opened fire en route on Japanese-held Wotje Atoll. By the early hours of the next day, 31 January, TG 53.5 was off the Marshalls with D-Day Roi-Namur slated for 1 February 1944.

In the pre-dawn hours of 31 January 1944, as softening up for the amphibious assault, the seven older battleships *Tennessee, Maryland, Colorado, Pennsylvania, New Mexico, Mississippi* and *Idaho*, along with their cruisers and destroyers, took their assigned stations. The 14in and 16in main-battery guns, along with the secondary batteries and the guns of the screen, swung towards Kwajalein Atoll and elevated.

Together with B-24 bombers flying from Apamama in the Gilberts, aircraft from eight CVE escort carriers and artillery now emplaced on Carlson Island, the powerful Fire Support Groups giving the low-lying Kwajalein Atoll islands a punishing pre-invasion bombardment – a softening up tactic that came to be known as a 'Spruance Haircut'.

The bombardment continued throughout the day – and accurate gunnery from *Maryland* destroyed numerous Japanese artillery weapons and pillboxes. In the course of the day, *Maryland*'s 16in guns fired so many times that the liners in the barrels of Turret 1 were split, putting the turret out of action for the rest of the day.

The pre-invasion air attacks and the heavy naval bombardment wreaked havoc on the beaches and airfield – such that resistance to the landing forces would prove to be much weaker than in the Gilberts. On Kwajalein, the pre-invasion bombardment was so effective that of some 3,000 troops garrisoned on Kwajalein, only about 300 were left alive to oppose the US invaders as they landed. The concentrated pre-invasion bombardment had so reduced US infantry casualties that it established the template for future assaults in the Pacific.

D-Day
1 February 1944

The amphibious assault on Kwajalein began at 0930 with successful landings on beaches Red 1 and Red 2 despite Japanese pillboxes, bunkers and infantry offensives. The US experience of amphibious landings was effective, the pre-landing naval bombardment had been devastatingly effective – and the main Japanese defences were positioned on the wrong side of the island. By sunset, the landing troops had reached halfway across the airfield runway. Although the Japanese launched counterattacks on each of the following nights, Kwajalein Island was nevertheless declared secure by the end of the fourth day.

The 4th Marines captured the airfield on the western half of the northmost islet in the atoll, Roi – the eastern half, Namur, was captured the next day. The whole atoll had been secured after eight days, on 7 February.

Of the 8,000 Japanese troops guarding Majuro and Kwajalein, less than 100 were taken prisoner (discounting Korean labourers) to US losses of 372 killed in action, 1,462 wounded and 183 missing.

On 5 February 1944, *Maryland* became the flagship for the Commander of the Northern Attack Force, Rear Admiral Richard L. Connolly. With the Marshalls now secure, and with no pressing need for the big guns of the Fire Support Group ships, TG 53.5 was able to depart from the Marshalls on 7 February 1944 for Majuro. With repairs required to her guns,

USS *Maryland* (BB-46) in Puget Sound, 25 April 1944. (*19-N-63821 courtesy of US Naval History & Heritage Command*)

Maryland was detached and with a task unit of carriers and destroyers she departed Majuro on 15 February 1944, bound for Bremerton Navy Yard, in Washington State on the West Coast of the USA.

At Bremerton, *Maryland* would undergo her first large-scale modernisation and overhaul. All the 1.1in Chicago Piano quad mounts and two 5in/51-cal. guns were removed. Two twin 40mm Bofors were replaced by quad mounts to give thirty-six Bofors 40mm guns in quad and twin mounts. Her 20mm Oerlikon guns were reduced in number to thirty-six single mounts with one quadruple 20mm mount in addition, a total of forty. All .50-cal. machine guns were removed. The previously cut-down cage mainmast was finally removed, and a new stump tower fitted to accommodate the Mk 11 cupola director formerly mounted on the maintop.[6]

(II) The Mariana and Palau Islands Campaign – Operation FORAGER, June–November 1944

Battle of Saipan, 15 June–9 July 1944
(A full account of Operation FORAGER can be found in Chapter 5, USS *California*)

Two months after entering Bremerton Navy Yard, *Maryland* sailed west from Puget Sound on 5 May 1944, bound for Kwajalein via Pearl. *Maryland* was joining the Fire Support TG 52.17, the main landing support bombardment force for Operation FORAGER, the Mariana and Palau Islands campaign, which would begin with the invasion of Saipan on D-Day, 15 June.

TG 52.17 was commanded by Rear Admiral Jesse B. Oldendorf, who flew his flag aboard the cruiser *Louisville* (CA-28), and comprised the 7 old Standard-Type battleships *California*, *Colorado*, *Idaho*, *Maryland*, *New Mexico*, *Pennsylvania* and *Tennessee* – with 6 heavy cruisers, 5 light cruisers and 26 destroyers. The Fire Support Task Group was split into a number of smaller Fire Support Units with *Maryland* and *Colorado* providing the main hitting power of Unit 4 of Fire Support Group 1.

Saipan is the second largest island in the Mariana archipelago after Guam and lies 120 miles northeast of Guam at the north of the chain. Saipan was the Japanese Command Post for the Western Pacific and was used as a safe anchorage for the Japanese fleet. The large island had been strongly fortified with coastal artillery batteries, shore defences, underground fortifications and an airstrip – and some 30,000 troops were stationed there by mid-1944. With Saipan in US hands, Guam and Tinian to its south would be cut off from support from the north, and from Japan itself.

Before any landings in the Marianas took place, a three-day heavy naval and air softening up bombardment began on 13 June as Vice Admiral Ching Lee's seven TG 58.7 fast battleships *Washington*, *North Carolina*, *Iowa*, *New Jersey*, *South Dakota*, *Alabama* and *Indiana* opened fire with their 16in main-battery big guns from a distance of 10,000yd (more than 5 miles), staying well offshore to avoid near shore minefields. The 8in guns of the heavy cruisers *Wichita*, *Minneapolis*, *New Orleans* and *San Francisco* and the smaller batteries of some thirteen destroyers of the screen also opened up.

The seven older Standard-Type battleships of Oldendorf's Fire Support TG 52.17 arrived with their escorts off Saipan from Kwajalein the following day on 14 June. Of the seven OBBS in the Fire Support Group, four of them were survivors of the Pearl Harbor attack – *California*, *Pennsylvania*, *Maryland* and *Tennessee*.

The naval bombardment by Oldendorf's Fire Support Group commenced at 0545 on 14 June 1944. The gunners aboard the seven old battleships were by now expert in shore bombardment, having trained with Marine Corps fire-control experts at the live-fire bombardment range on the volcanic Hawaiian island of Kahoolawe. They had more experience and training in shore bombardment than Lee's fast battleships, which were more suited to naval engagements. The accurate gunnery of Oldendorf's OBBS quickly destroyed Japanese coastal guns, ammunition dumps, small boats, storage tanks, blockhouses and buildings. In all, during the pre-invasion bombardment, the combined fourteen battleships, along with escort cruisers and destroyers, fired some 165,000 shells, destroying land targets, conducting counter-battery missions, destroying AA gun emplacements and burning all unburnt cane fields that would offer the enemy cover.

The US invasion-fleet transport vessels moved into place off Saipan the following day, just after 0500 on D-Day, 15 June. The pre-invasion naval bombardment commenced at 0530 and continued throughout the landings on 15 June – with devastating accuracy.

As the invasion troops readied to begin the attack, a diversionary force of Marines carried out a dummy landing at the large village of Garapan, on Saipan's west coast – moving to within 5,000yd of the shore. *Maryland* then turned her guns to Tanapag on Saipan's northwest coast, levelling it in heavy bombardment.

At 0700, under cover of the naval and air bombardment, more than 300 LVTs carrying some 8,000 Marines moved forward from their mother ships. Despite facing Japanese artillery that destroyed twenty inbound LVTs, by 0900 the Marines were ashore and engaging the enemy on

USS *MARYLAND* (BB-46)

the west coast of Saipan – where they faced strategically placed barbed wire, artillery and machine-gun emplacements and trenches. Despite this, by nightfall, the 2nd and 4th Marines had established a 6-mile-wide beachhead that stretched inshore for half a mile. The Japanese counterattacked at night – but were fought back with heavy losses.

The Japanese attempted to counter the devastating fire being rained down by the US battleships by air attack. On 18 June, AA guns on *Maryland* shot down their first Japanese aircraft, but on 22 June, a Mitsubishi G4M3 Betty medium bomber flew low over the still-contested Saipan hills and found *Maryland* and *Pennsylvania*. The Japanese plane dropped a torpedo, which struck *Maryland* on her starboard bow, opening a large hole and killing two crew.

Maryland was detached from the Fire Support Group and sent to Eniwetok. From there, escorted by two destroyers, she headed for the repair yards at Pearl Harbor – steaming in reverse the whole way so as not to do further damage to her bow. Once at Pearl Harbor,

USS *Maryland* (BB-46) entering dry dock at Pearl Harbor Navy Yard on 10 July 1944 for repair of damage to her bow following a hit by an aerial torpedo. (*National Archives*)

shipyard employees worked around-the-clock to repair *Maryland* and get her back in the fight. She would not however be ready to take part in the subsequent battles for Guam and Tinian in July and early August 1944.

Battle of Peleliu – Operation STALEMATE II, 15 September–27 November 1944

On 13 August 1944, the repaired *Maryland* departed Pearl for the Solomon Islands with a large task force, anchoring off the Florida Islands for two weeks before steaming for the Palau Islands on 6 September – where she joined Rear Admiral Jesse B. Oldendorf's Palau Bombardment and Fire Support TG 32.5. The tiny southern Palauan island of Peleliu was an important Japanese airbase airstrip – if that could be captured, the eastern flank of US forces preparing to attack Japanese forces in the Philippines would be secured. The commander of the US 1st Marine Division predicted that Peleliu, which was only 5 square miles, would be secured within four days. The island may have been small – but it was occupied by about 11,000 Japanese troops.

On 12 September, a three-day long pre-invasion naval bombardment of tiny Peleliu began as the battleships *Pennsylvania, Maryland, Mississippi, Tennessee* and *Idaho*, the heavy cruisers *Columbus, Indianapolis, Louisville, Minneapolis* and *Portland* and light cruisers *Cleveland, Denver* and *Honolulu*, led by the command ship *Mount McKinley*, opened up.

Oldendorf's bombardment ships initially covered minesweeping operations in the approaches and protected UDT teams of swimmers as they cleared the invasion beaches of underwater obstacles. The OBBS bombarded enemy shore positions – and by the evening of the second day of the bombardment, every enemy land target ashore was believed to have been destroyed. The bombardment was called off early as a result – but unknown to the naval commanders, the Japanese had adopted a new tactic of 'defence in depth', hiding their artillery and the bulk of their troops inland and underground, to withstand the bombardment.

On 15 September 1944, US Marines, and later the US Army's 81st Infantry Division, landed on Peleliu and nearby Angaur. Unknown to US commanders, the Japanese defenders were in fact well dug into pre-prepared and heavily fortified cave defences and would offer stiff resistance. The Battle of Peleliu would be a brutal, bloody and drawn-out affair, which raged for more than two months from 15 September until November. It was called the toughest battle of the war by some Marines.

USS *MARYLAND* (BB-46)

A reinforced Japanese command post on Peleliu that has taken two direct hits from 14in battleship AP shells during the three-day pre-invasion naval bombardment that began on 12 September 1944. It is believed the shells were fired by USS *Mississippi*. (*Author's Collection*)

Under cover of a naval bombardment, waves of US Marines head for the western invasion beaches of Peleliu in amphibious tractors on 15 September 1944, following the three-day pre-invasion naval bombardment. (*National Archives*)

201

Japanese construction crews had dug out and enlarged existing caves and created new tunnel complexes. Caves and bunkers were connected to an extensive subterranean system throughout central Peleliu, which allowed the Japanese to evacuate or reoccupy positions as needed. Multiple small tunnel entrances were created that could be used as firing positions. Gun emplacements, underground ammunition dumps and communication centres were all constructed.

The honeycomb cave system made maximum use of observation points and interlocking fields of fire. Communication tunnels ran between firing positions and deeper into the large underground system. Many caves were interconnected with larger tunnels so that heavy weapons and artillery could be moved from position to position.

The cave systems featured hidden escape routes, camouflaged entrances, multiple levels, built-in obstacles and sharp turns designed to protect Japanese troops from rifle fire, artillery fire and the feared flame throwers. Large quantities of water, food and ammunition were stockpiled in these underground positions to sustain a prolonged period of defence.

Japanese engineers added sliding armoured steel doors with multiple openings to accommodate both artillery and machine guns. Slanted cave entrances were constructed to thwart grenade and flamethrower attacks. Japanese defenders fought bravely for two months from their cave systems carved out of the limestone ridges of Umurbrogol, which soon had acquired the nickname Bloody Nose Ridge.

As brutal close-quarters fighting raged ashore, there was now little need for the Fire Support ships. They retired on 20 September 1944 towards Manus in the Admiralty Islands where at Seeadler Harbor, *Maryland* was assigned to the 7th Fleet commanded by Vice Admiral Thomas C. Kinkaid.

By October 1944, the 7th Marines on Peleliu had suffered 46 per cent casualties by the time they were relieved by the 5th Marines. US troops adopted siege tactics, burning the Japanese troops out – or collapsing and sealing the caves, trapping the IJA troops inside. US bulldozers rolled 55-gallon drums of aviation fuel into the caves and then set them on fire.

After two months of the most brutal defence, on 24 November 1944, Colonel Nakagawa, commander of the Japanese forces on Peleliu, proclaimed, 'Our sword is broken and we have run out of spears.' He solemnly burnt his regimental colours and performed ritual suicide – his remains were discovered in a sealed cave complex in 1993.

USS *MARYLAND* (BB-46)

The US Army declared Peleliu secure on 27 November 1944, ending the seventy-three-day long battle. The battle was controversial due to the island's lack of strategic value and the high casualty rate. Peleliu airfield, so cruelly fought over and so costly in casualties, never played a key role in subsequent Allied operations – Ulithi Atoll was instead used as a staging base for the invasion of Okinawa. The high casualty rate exceeded all other amphibious operations during the Pacific War. The battles for Peleliu and Angaur had highlighted the new Japanese tactic of defence in depth – which would be seen again at Iwo Jima and Okinawa.

(III) The Philippines Campaign, 20 October 1944–15 August 1945
Battle of Leyte, 17 October–26 December 1944
(For a full account of the Battle of Leyte, see Chapter 5, USS *California*.)

Meanwhile, as the brutal fighting continued on Peleliu, the Philippines campaign under General Douglas MacArthur, the Supreme Commander of the Southwest Pacific theatre, would open with the invasion of the island of Leyte. *Maryland* was assigned to the Fire Support TG 77.2, commanded by Rear Admiral Jesse B. Oldendorf.

At Manus, on 5 October 1944, the five Fire Support Group 77.2 battleships *Maryland*, *California*, *Mississippi*, *Pennsylvania* and *Tennessee* were joined by another veteran of the original Japanese strike on Pearl Harbor, *West Virginia*. She had only recently finished her extensive and lengthy repairs and modernisation and had steamed for Hawaii from Los Angeles on 14 September – before heading on to Manus. On arriving at Seeadler Harbor, she became the flagship of Rear Admiral Theodore D. Ruddock, the commander of BatDiv 4. Oldendorf's Fire Support Group of 7 battleships, 5 heavy cruisers, 5 light cruisers, destroyers and ancillary vessels departed Manus on 12 October 1944 bound for the Philippines.

At dawn on 17 October 1944, preliminary operations began for the Leyte invasion with landings by the 6th Ranger Battalion on strategic smaller surrounding islands straddling the gulf offshore where they would erect navigation lights for the amphibious transports to follow. Minesweeping operations began and UDT teams revealed clear landing beaches.

The Fire Support Group was split into two Fire Support Units: *West Virginia*, *Maryland*, *Mississippi* and escorts formed the core of the Fire Support Unit North (TF 78), commanded by Rear Admiral George L. Weyler. Fire Support Unit South (TF 79) was under the direct command of Rear Admiral Oldendorf and comprised *Tennessee*, *California*, *Pennsylvania* and escorts.

With preliminary minesweeping and UDT reconnaissance completed on 17 October, on the morning of 18 October, *Maryland*, along with four other battleships and cruisers and destroyers, steamed into Leyte Gulf. *Maryland* took up an advanced position between Red and White Beaches in the northwest of Leyte Gulf. The Fire Support Group units then began a naval bombardment.

On A-Day, 20 October 1944, after a 4-hour pre-invasion bombardment, 6th Army forces began landing on the assigned beaches at 1000. As the landing beaches were quickly secured, *Maryland* took up a sentinel position off Leyte Gulf to guard the landing beaches against Japanese counterattack by sea. Over the coming days, Japanese aircraft made repeated attempts to attack the Allied landing and naval forces – making widespread use of kamikaze suicide attacks for the first time.

Several days later, US submarines in the South China Sea spotted a number of separate Japanese naval forces heading for Leyte Gulf. A powerful Central Force including five battleships was heading toward the San Bernardino Strait. Another force of four Japanese carriers was reported north of Luzon, this was Ozawa's decoy Northern Force of almost planeless carriers that was actively trying to get spotted and lure Admiral Halsey's TF 38 fast carriers and battleships north away from Leyte Gulf. Meanwhile a Japanese Southern Force and a smaller Second Striking Force were converging to force a passage to Leyte Gulf through the Surigao Strait

As these separate Japanese naval forces closed on Leyte, the Battle of Leyte Gulf, fought between 23 and 26 October 1944, was about to begin. The battle would develop into a number of separate actions and battles:

1. The submarine action at the Palawan Passage (23 October).
2. The Battle of the Sibuyan Sea (24 October).
3. The Battle of the Surigao Strait (25 October).
4. The Battle off Samar (25 October).
5. The Battle off Cape Engaño (25–26 October).

Maryland was involved in the southernmost of these actions, the Battle of the Surigao Strait, fought as the Japanese Southern Force, which included the two battleships *Fusō* and *Yamashiro*, attempted to pass through the Surigao Strait and rendezvous with the Central Force to strike Allied shipping and troops ashore at the Leyte Gulf beachhead. The Central Force included the battleships *Yamato*, *Musashi*, *Nagato*, *Kongō* and *Haruna* and would successfully pass through the San Bernardino Strait, up north of Samar, and head south towards Leyte

Gulf. Although no one knew it at the time, the Battle of the Surigao Strait would prove to be the last big-gun clash between battleships in history.

Battle of the Surigao Strait, 25 October 1944
(For a full account of the Battle of the Surigao Strait, see Chapter 5, USS *California*.)

On 24 October 1944, four days after the Leyte landings began on A-Day, 20 October 1944, as Allied intelligence revealed the scale of the Japanese naval operation, Rear Admiral Oldendorf received Vice Admiral Kinkaid's order to prepare for a night action in the Surigao Strait. Oldendorf sailed his Fire Support Group to the southern end of Leyte Gulf and positioned his six battleships *Pennsylvania, California, Tennessee, Mississippi, Maryland* and *West Virginia* across the eastern exit from the Surigao Strait, off Hingatungan Point. This gave him maximum sea room but restricted the enemy's movements – he hoped to cap the enemy 'T' when the Japanese Southern Force approached.

Oldendorf positioned his four heavy cruisers *Louisville, Portland, Minneapolis* and HMAS *Shropshire*, and four light cruisers *Boise, Phoenix, Columbia* and *Denver*, in flanking positions to left and right of his battle line of battleships, which were strung out across the strait and the enemy axis of approach. He had twenty-eight destroyers ready to make torpedo attacks as the enemy warships advanced – and thirty-nine small fast PT motor torpedo boats that could make more than 40 knots and were armed with Mark 8 torpedoes that carried a 466lb warhead. Oldendorf sent his PT Boats southwest down the strait to scout for the oncoming Japanese warships.

The Battle of the Surigao Strait began at 2236 when the first PT torpedo boats encountered and engaged the oncoming Southern Force warships at the western entrance to the strait. Repeated torpedo attacks by the PT Boats took place over the next 3½ hours – but no hits were scored as the Southern Force passed through the PT Boats and continued north along the strait. In anticipation of breaking into Leyte Gulf, the Southern Force began to alter formation to line ahead with destroyers leading, followed by the flag battleship *Yamashiro*, the battleship *Fusō* and the heavy cruiser *Mogami*.

At 0236, early on 25 October 1944, Oldendorf ordered his ships brought to General Quarters – and then, as the Japanese ships approached, they were picked up on radar at 0240. Divisions of Oldendorf's destroyers attacked, increasing speed to 25 knots before launching their Mark 15 torpedoes. At about 0300, the battleship *Fusō* was hit on her starboard side amidships by several torpedoes from the destroyer *Melvin*. *Fusō* began to lose speed and list to starboard – she then fell out of formation.

The Japanese ships were picked up at 0302 on Oldendorf's battleship radars at a range of 44,000yd – and in darkness, the Japanese Force was tracked on radar until the flanking cruisers could open fire at 0350. The main-battery guns of the US battleships then commenced firing just a few minutes later, the most modern battleship *West Virginia*, sporting the latest air-search radar and fire-control radar for her main and secondary batteries, opened fire with her eight 16in guns at a distance of almost 23,000yd, just over 12 miles – hitting *Yamashiro* with her first salvo. *Yamashiro* returned fire with the 14in guns of her No. 1 and No. 2 main battery. A few minutes later, *California* and *Tennessee* opened up with their big guns – and a classic gunnery duel now developed. The US battleships had crossed the T of the Japanese battle line.

Operating under radar fire control, the more modern battleships *Tennessee*, *California* and *West Virginia* rained salvo after salvo of 14in and 16in shells onto the Japanese ships. The three older battleships *Maryland*, *Mississippi* and *Pennsylvania*, equipped with less advanced gunnery radar, struggled to hit the Japanese ships. *Maryland* visually ranged the Japanese ships from the splashes from the fall of shot and fired forty-eight 16in shells. *Pennsylvania* was unable to find a target and her guns did not fire. *Mississippi* only fired once – with a full broadside salvo from her twelve 14in guns. Unknown at the time, this would be the last salvo ever to be fired by one battleship at another battleship – the era of these great steel titans was over. Torpedoes from the destroyers sunk both Southern Force battleships *Fusō* and *Yamashiro*.

After the big-gun duel, supported by fighters and torpedo planes, Oldendorf's battleship force headed southwest down the Surigao Strait in a stern chase of surviving Southern Force warships. Of the seven Japanese ships, only the destroyer *Shigure* would escape.

Nevertheless, despite the apparent overwhelming success of the contact, as dawn approached on 25 October, as a result of the stern chase, Oldendorf's battleships had been drawn 65 miles southwest, and away from the Leyte beachhead. Leyte was now very exposed should an attack from the north develop.

As the Battle of the Surigao Strait was being fought, the powerful Japanese Central Force meanwhile had successfully transited east through the San Bernardino Strait, north of Samar. Heading south down the east coast of Samar in the hours before dawn, the 4 battleships *Yamato*, *Nagato*, *Kongō* and *Haruna*, 6 heavy cruisers, 2 light cruisers *Noshiro* and *Yahagi* and 11 destroyers pounced on the 16 lightly protected 7th Fleet

USS *MARYLAND* (BB-46)

CVE escort carriers and light escorts screening the Leyte landings. In the Battle off Samar, 5 US ships would be sunk: the 2 escort carriers *Gambier Bay* and *St Lo*, 2 destroyers and 1 destroyer escort. (For a full discussion of the Battle off Samar, See Chapter 5, USS *California*.)

Following the decisive victory at the Surigao Strait, *Maryland* continued to patrol the southern approaches to the Surigao Strait until 29 October 1944. But with the surviving units of the decimated Japanese naval forces now having left the Philippines, *Maryland* was then able to steam for the Admiralty Islands for a brief replenishment before resuming patrol duties around Leyte on 16 November – protecting Allied forces ashore on Leyte from continued Japanese air attacks.

On 29 November 1944, during another Japanese air attack, a kamikaze aircraft successfully got through the AA screen and crashed into *Maryland* between Turrets No. 1 and No. 2, piercing the forecastle, main and armoured decks. The strike caused extensive damage, started fires and killed some thirty-one men and wounded thirty others. Despite the damage however, the battleship's fighting ability had not been degraded and she was able to continue with her deployment until she was finally relieved on 2 December 1944.

USS *Maryland* (BB-46) is hit by a kamikaze suicide plane whilst operating off Leyte on the evening of 29 November 1944. (*80-G-270627 courtesy of US Naval History & Heritage Command*)

Maryland then left the Philippines for the Pearl Harbor Naval Base for repair, along with two heavily damaged destroyers. The flotilla reached Pearl Harbor on 18 December 1944, when it was determined that as a complete reconstruction of the old battleship would take seven to eight months, and as *Maryland* was needed back in the fight as soon as possible, only the damage from the kamikaze would be repaired and a new secondary battery installed. Over the next few months, all of her remaining ten 5in/51-cal. casemate guns were removed and replaced by sixteen 5in/38-cal. guns in eight new twin mounts, which would be better able to deal with the kamikaze threat.

(IV) 1945
With her second modernisation and repair completed, *Maryland* headed for the Western Pacific on 4 March 1945, arriving at Ulithi on 16 March. There on 17 March she joined the 5th Fleet and was assigned to TG 54.1 – the Gunfire Support Group, which was preparing for Operation ICEBERG, the invasion of the 66-mile-long island of Okinawa, slated to begin on 1 April 1945. *Maryland* was assigned with *Texas* (BB-35) to Fire Support Unit 1 – tasked to operate in the SouthernEast Shore sector of Okinawa.

The invasion fleet departed Ulithi on 21 March, bound for Okinawa.

Battle of Okinawa – Operation ICEBERG, 1 April–22 June 1945
By mid-February 1945, the Japanese surface fleet was largely destroyed and with the corking of the Luzon bottleneck, Japan was cut off from her major fuel stores. As Japan retreated to a grim defence of her homeland islands, the Allies closed in.

Okinawa lies 400 miles south of the Japanese home island of Kyushu, a primary target for the planned final assault on the Japanese home islands themselves – codenamed Operation DOWNFALL. Some 103,000 US Army troops would deploy for the invasion of Okinawa along with over 88,000 US Marines. The US forces would face more than 70,000 Japanese troops in well-prepared defensive positions. The invasion would turn into a particularly bloody eighty-two-day-long battle.

The Gunfire Support Group arrived in the Okinawa area on 25 March 1945 to begin covering minesweeping in the fire-support sectors. On 26 March the Gunfire Support Group began shelling Japanese positions ashore with *Maryland* and *Texas* of Fire Support Unit 1 being assigned targets on the southern coast of Okinawa to support a diversionary landing intended to distract Japanese forces away from the main landings on the west coast.

USS *MARYLAND* (BB-46)

The Japanese replied with several air attacks – and kamikazes hit two of *Maryland*'s radar picket destroyers. On 3 April 1945, two days after D-Day, 1 April 1945, *Maryland* was moved north to the west-coast invasion beaches to assist the cruiser *Minneapolis* (CA-36) of Fire Support Unit 2 in destroying several shore batteries at Naha City. Meanwhile heavy attacks by kamikazes on Allied shipping were taking place, with many ships being damaged.

Following the successful landings, *Maryland* remained off Bolo Point on the East China Sea coast, where the Japanese had previously established an airfield, her guns providing artillery support for the troops ashore as required.

Maryland continued fire-support duty off Okinawa until 7 April, when TF 54 was sent north to intercept a Japanese surface force. The IJN was committing much of its remaining naval strength in an operation to relieve Okinawa. The superbattleship *Yamato*, the cruiser *Yahagi* and eight destroyers had sortied from Japan on 6 April to close Okinawa, where operating with kamikaze and Okinawa-based army units they would attack the Allied forces. *Yamato* would then be beached to act as a devastating, heavily armoured and unsinkable gun battery – until she was destroyed.

The Allies however intercepted and decoded Japanese radio transmissions – and the Japanese warships were spotted by US submarines as they came out of the Bungo Strait between the Japanese home islands of Kyushu and Shikoku. Admiral Spruance ordered the battleships of TF 54 to prepare for a surface action against *Yamato* and sent them north to intercept.

On 7 April, as TF 54 headed north, 280 TF 58 fast-carrier dive bombers, torpedo bombers and fighters attacked the southbound Japanese naval force, sinking 6 of the 10 Japanese ships – including *Yamato*. Hit by multiple aerial torpedoes and bombs, *Yamato* rolled to port and capsized, her main 46cm turrets dropping from their mounts before two forward magazines exploded cataclysmically. The resulting mushroom cloud reached almost 4 miles high and was seen almost 100 miles away on the southernmost home island of Kyushu.

Kamikaze attacks meantime continued in strength, and at dusk on 7 April, about 18nm northwest of Okinawa, a kamikaze carrying a 551lb bomb successfully got through *Maryland*'s AA screen and crashed into the top of Turret 3 from starboard – destroying a number of Oerlikon 20mm mounts and starting a fierce fire. The fires began to cook off 20mm ammunition, which caused a number of casualties. In all, ten crew were killed, with thirty-seven injured and six missing.

Maryland's fighting capability was however unaffected, and she was able to remain on station for the next week, providing artillery support for troops ashore, despite several more air raids. Turret 3, which had been damaged in the kamikaze hit, was still operational – but did not fire for the remainder of this mission.

On 14 April 1945, *Maryland* was disjoined from the Fire Support Group at Okinawa for repair. She departed Okinawa, escorting several transports, and headed southeast to the Mariana Islands – and from there to Pearl Harbor. From Pearl, *Maryland* was sent back northeast to the West Coast of the USA, arriving at the Puget Sound Navy Yard at Bremerton on 7 May 1945 for extensive overhaul and reconstruction.

Whilst en route for Bremerton, with Berlin encircled, Adolph Hitler was believed to have shot himself on 30 April 1945 in his bunker. On 2 May 1945, as *Maryland* was five days out from Bremerton, the Battle of Berlin ended and nearly 1,000,000 German troops in Italy and Austria surrendered unconditionally. In the coming days German forces in other theatres surrendered. On 7 May 1945, as *Maryland* arrived at Bremerton, the Chief-of-Staff of the German Armed Forces High Command, General Alfred Jodl, signed an unconditional surrender document of all German Forces to the Allies with all active operations to cease on 8 May 1945.

The war in Europe was over – Japan was now left to fight on alone.

In Bremerton, Turret No. 3 was repaired, and the inadequate 3.5in-thick STS armour decks were improved with an extra 3in of STS over the magazines and 2in elsewhere over the protective deck. The turret tops were replaced and improved. The increased protection could now stop a 1,600lb AP bomb and better handle the kamikaze threat. The conning tower was replaced by a lighter STS structure with only 1.2in-thick armour to compensate for extra top weight.[7]

To compensate for the large increase in her weight, *Maryland* was fitted with a double-layer blister, which increased her beam to 114ft. As with *California*, she too was now too wide in the beam to transit the Panama Canal. The AA battery was further adjusted to give a total of thirty-six Oerlikon 20mm weapons in eighteen dual mounts whilst the twin Bofors 40mm mounts were replaced by quad mounts to give a total of forty 40mm weapons. The radar suite was modernised with an SK-2 air-search radar and a Mk 13 radar on the aft fire-control director.

Repairs and modernisation were completed in August 1945. She left Bremerton for sea trials, tests and training runs – her return to service post-refit coinciding with Japan's surrender. The war in the Pacific had finally ended.

With the war over, *Maryland* was assigned to the Operation MAGIC CARPET fleet – the repatriation of over 8 million US military personnel on active war service in the European, Asian and Pacific theatres.

During the remaining months of 1945, *Maryland* made five voyages between the West Coast and Pearl Harbor, returning more than 8,000 servicemen to the USA.

Post-War

Maryland arrived at Seattle, Washington for the last time on 17 December 1945. She entered Puget Sound Naval Shipyard on 15 April 1946 and was placed in commission in inactive reserve on 16 July 1946.

Maryland was decommissioned at Bremerton on 3 April 1947 and remained there as a unit of the Pacific Reserve Fleet before finally being sold for scrapping to Learner Company of Oakland, California on 8 July 1959.

Chapter 7

USS *Nevada* (BB-36)

USS *Nevada* (BB-36), 1920. Note the cage masts, hull casemate secondary guns, range clock and signal flags run up to dry. (*80-G-270627 courtesy of US Naval History & Heritage Command*)

USS *NEVADA* (BB-36)

Specifications (as built): Nevada class
Builder: Fore River Shipbuilding Co., Massachusetts
Launched: 11 July 1914
Commissioned: 11 March 1916
Decommissioned: 29 August 1946
Displacement: 27,500 tons (S) 28,400 tons (F)
Length: 583ft (oa)
575ft (wl)
Beam: 95ft 2.5in (wl)
Draft: 28ft 6in
Speed: 20.5 knots
Endurance: 8,000nm at 10 knots

Armament:
  Main battery: 10 x 14in/45-cal. in 2 pairs of turrets – lower triple turret and superfiring twin turret
  Secondary battery: 21 x single 5in/51-cal. guns (10 in casemates on each beam, 1 at stern)
  Torpedo Tubes: 2 x 21in submerged torpedo tubes

Armour: Belt: 13.5in tapering to 8in on lower edge
  Bulkheads: 13–8in
  Barbettes: 13in
  Turrets: Face: 18in and 16in. Roof: 5in. Sides and rear: 10in and 9in
  Decks: Armour deck: 3in STS and mild steel in 3 layers. Aft 4.5in STS plus 1.75in mild steel Splinter deck: 1.5in with 2in sloping sides to bottom of armour belt
  Conning tower: 16in

Sister ships in class: *Oklahoma* (BB-37)
Fate: Sunk as target ship on 31 July 1948

USS *Nevada* (BB-36) was the lead ship of the two Nevada-class Battleship 1912 units, *Nevada* and *Oklahoma*, whose basic Standard-Type design was characterised by a number of new features that would be incorporated into almost every succeeding US battleship until the end of the dreadnought period. *Nevada* is a particularly important ship: she was a leap forward in US battleship technology that brought several new features to battleship construction.

In all, twelve Standard Type battleships would be produced to the basic *Nevada* design – with each successive class having incremental improvements as naval technology progressed. Although the Nevada-class units were slightly smaller than those that followed, the size of the Standard-Type battleships would remain almost constant from the second evolution of the design onwards – the Pennsylvania-class Battleship 1913.

As the first of this new style of US Sstandard battleship, at 27,500 tons, *Nevada* was much larger than other contemporary US battleships. Her tonnage was nearly three times that of the now obsolete older pre-dreadnoughts, and almost twice that of the more recent 1904 16,000-ton battleship *Connecticut* (BB-18). *Nevada* displaced almost 8,000 tons more than one of the first US dreadnoughts, the 20,000-ton *Delaware* (BB-28) – constructed just seven years prior to *Nevada* and commissioned in 1910.

Nevada was the first US battleship to be driven by geared steam turbines using an oil-fired steam power plant in place of traditional coal, giving greater endurance and many practical advantages. Her main-battery guns were carried in four superfiring turrets, with the triple turret being installed for the first time. The four turrets were set in two superfiring pairs, one pair forward of the superstructure and one pair abaft. Whereas earlier dreadnought battleships often had a fifth turret situated in the middle of the ship, there would be no turrets located amidships. (For a detailed discussion, see Chapter 4, The US Standard-Type Battleship.)

Nevada sported 'all-or-nothing' armour that allowed increased deck armour over the citadel against plunging fire. Previous incarnations of US battleships had armour of varying thickness throughout the ship – the thickness varying in relation to the importance of the area to be protected. *Nevada* now had maximum armour over critical areas, such as the magazines and propulsion machinery, and none over less important places. This radical change in the protected length of battleship armour became known as the 'all-or-nothing' principle, which most major navies would later adopt for their own battleships.

The construction of *Nevada* was authorised in March 1911 and her keel was laid down on 4 November 1912 at the Fore River Shipyard operated by General Dynamics on Weymouth Fore River in Braintree and Quincy, Massachusetts. *Nevada* was launched for fitting out afloat on 11 July 1914 – and after completion she was commissioned on 11 March 1916. *Nevada* joined the Atlantic Fleet on 26 May 1916 at a time when the USA had not yet entered the First World War. She finally transferred to Europe just three months before the Armistice came into effect on 11 November 1918 and halted the fighting – but saw no action.

USS *NEVADA* (BB-36)

USS *Nevada* (BB-36) looking aft from bow towards lower No. 1 triple 14in/45-cal. turret, with twin-mount superfiring No. 2 turret above. (*NH 76577 courtesy of US Naval History & Heritage Command*)

The Nevada-class units were characterised by a single smokestack abaft the bridge superstructure that was flanked by two large cage masts, intended to be less vulnerable to damage by shells from enemy ships, which might pass right through the latticework. The US Navy was the only major navy to use lattice masts, and they would prove less sound than had been intended.

(a) Underwater Protection

The Nevadas had poor underwater protection as built of an 11ft 9in inboard void – and this would be addressed during a major reconstruction and modernisation from 1927–9, when torpedo blisters were fitted.

The torpedo blisters, or bulges, added to either beam, greatly increased the original poor underwater protection giving her a total depth of 22ft of torpedo protection, comprising voids and oil-filled bulkheads outboard of the final torpedo bulkhead that protected the innards of the ship. The addition of the two beam torpedo blisters increased her beam to 107ft 11in. The boiler rooms received torpedo bulkheads and a triple bottom was installed.

(b) Armament

(i) Main Battery

Nevada was constructed with ten 14in/45-cal. main-battery guns set in two pairs of superfiring turrets, one pair set forward of the superstructure and the other pair aft.

The 14in gun fired a 1,400lb AP projectile utilising as propellant four silk bags of smokeless powder that gave a maximum firing range of 23,000yd, about 13 miles. *Nevada* was the first US battleship to be fitted with triple 14in gun turrets in the No. 1 and No. 4 positions – the superfiring turret of each pair, Nos 2 and 3 being dual mount. This arrangement allowed *Nevada* to fire all ten guns in a broadside.

During her 1927–9 modernisation the elevation of her main-battery weapons was increased from 15° to 30° and this increased the range from 23,000yd to some 36,000yd, about 20 miles.

(ii) Secondary Battery

As constructed, twenty-one 5in/51-cal. weapons were installed in single casemates, mounted ten on either beam and one in the stern.

These single-purpose secondary guns could fire a 50lb shell for a distance of about 17,000yd, just over 9 miles, using a propellant charge of smokeless powder. The guns had a rate of fire of 8–9 rounds per minute and an elevation of +20°. In 1918, the secondary battery was reduced from 21 to 12 x 5in/51-cal. guns – and during the post-Pearl Harbor refit, the remaining 12 x 5in/51-cal. guns were removed, along with the 8 x 5in/25-cal. High Angle (HA) guns, and 16 more versatile 5in/38-cal. DP guns were installed in 8 twin mounts that offered an elevation from -15° to +85° and were controlled by 4 Mk 37 directors.

(iii) AA Battery
When *Nevada* was commissioned, it was thought that a heavily armoured capital ship had little to fear from attack by aircraft with the small aerial bombs of the day. But the threat of air attack increased and two 3in guns were added for AA protection. The number of 3in guns was increased to eight in 1925.

1927–9 Refit
During the 1927–9 reconstruction, the 3in guns were replaced by eight 5in/25-cal. HA guns. The manually trained lightweight 5in/25-cal. HA gun was the standard heavy AA weapon for US Navy cruisers commissioned in the 1920s and 1930s and offered a maximum elevation of +85°. The gun used fixed ammunition where the case and 54lb projectile were handled as a single assembled unit. The short barrel made it easier to train manually against fast-moving targets. Eight light AA 0.50-cal. machine guns were set on the fighting tops of the new tripod masts.
   AA Battery:
   1. 8 x 5-in/25-cal. HA guns.
   2. 8 x 0.50MG on fighting tops of replacement tripod masts.
   3. 8 x 1.1-in AA guns (added 1935).

1942 Refit
In 1942, during the refit after the Pearl Harbor raid, the existing AA battery was removed and replaced by 38 Oerlikon 20mm autocannons and 40 more powerful 40mm Bofors autocannons in 10 quad mounts.
   AA Battery:
   1. 40 x 40mm Bofors.
   2. 38 x 20 mm Oerlikon.

(iv) Torpedo Tubes
Nevada was originally fitted with two submerged 21in torpedo tubes, one on either beam towards the bow. An outdated legacy of the dreadnought era, these were removed during the 1927–9 reconstruction.

(c) Armour

Adopting the new 'all-or-nothing' armour concept, of the 575ft of the ship's waterline length, only 400ft was protected, and this allowed a greater focus on deck protection.

The main waterline armour belt rose vertically for 17.3ft, with almost half the belt below the waterline. The belt was 13.5in-thick from the top to below the waterline – from where the belt tapered, from just over the halfway point, to 8in-thick at its lowest edge.

The armoured athwartships bulkheads that connected either edge of the vertical armour belts to complete the citadel were 13in-thick.

The turret faces had 18in-thick armour, with the sides and back being 10 and 9in. The conning tower had 16in-thick armour.

The uppermost horizontal armour deck ran across the ship and connected both tops of the armour belt that ran along each side of the ship. The uppermost protected deck comprised three layers of STS and mild steel that totalled 3in-thick and covered the full length of the citadel. There were additional layers aft to increase protection.

Deeper in the ship, the horizontal watertight, or splinter, deck, was 1.5in-thick with 2in-thick sloping sides that angled downwards to meet the lower edge of the vertical armour belt along the side of the ship. Both decks combined gave 4.5–5in of deck armour along the whole length of the citadel.

During the 1927–9 reconstruction, the upper armour deck was increased to 5in and the lower armour deck increased to a maximum of 3in.

(d) Propulsion

Nevada was the first US battleship to receive direct-drive Curtis steam turbines fed by twelve oil-fired Yarrow water-tube boilers. A pair of reduction geared cruising turbines was clutched into the high-pressure turbines for fuel economy at low speeds. *Nevada* could make a design speed of 20.5 knots.

The ability to steam great distances in the vast expanses of the Pacific without refuelling was a major concern for the US Navy at the time – and battleships after 1908 were mostly designed with a standard endurance of 8,000nm at a cruising speed of 10 knots. This range was extrapolated from the distance of 6,550nm between San Pedro, on the West Coast of the USA where the fleet would be based, and Manila, where the fleet was expected to have to fight Japan under War Plan Orange in any Pacific conflict.

Nevada's oil-fired geared turbines increased fuel economy and range compared with earlier direct-drive turbines. Oil-fired boilers gave an ability to refuel at sea, and significantly reduced boiler-room crew numbers as no stokers were required. Refuelling with oil was much easier and quicker than recoaling – whilst oil also allowed more compact boiler rooms, producing a shorter space to protect.

Modernisation, 1927–9

Nevada was modernised at the Norfolk Naval Shipyard between August 1927 and January 1930. The ship's original steam turbines were changed out for newer geared turbines. Her speed remained the same at 20.5 knots – but the new more efficient turbines increased her operational range.

Amongst a number of other modifications made at this time, the elevation of her main-battery 14in/45-cal. guns was increased to 30°, increasing the range of the guns from about 13 miles to just over 19 miles. Anti-torpedo bulges were fitted to her submerged hull to improve her poor underwater protection. The twelve original Yarrow boilers were replaced with 6 more efficient Bureau Express boilers in a new arrangement to accommodate the new torpedo bulges and torpedo bulkheads, and a triple bottom was incorporated. Both her by now outdated cage masts

USS *Nevada* (BB-36) post-refit, 1930s. Both cage masts have been replaced by tripod masts. (*NH 64520 courtesy of US Naval History & Heritage Command*)

were replaced with tripod masts that were more stable for rangefinding. The bridge was enlarged, and two floatplane catapults added, one on the after twin 14in Turret 3 and the other on the quarter deck.

All twelve of her remaining secondary battery casemate 5in/51-cal. guns were moved one deck higher, above the hull in an arrangement similar to that of the newer New Mexico class. The eight 3in guns were replaced by eight of the US Navy's standard 5in/25 cal. heavy AA guns.

PEARL HARBOR, 7 DECEMBER 1941

As dawn broke over Pearl Harbor Naval Base on Sunday, 7 December 1941, the crisp early morning light revealed *Nevada* moored on her own in about 40ft of water to the interrupted quay F-8 at the northeasternmost end of Battleship Row, astern of *Arizona*. *Nevada*'s starboard side looked over towards Ford Island – and with all the ships' bows pointing southwest towards the southern entrance into the Naval Base, *Nevada* was essentially moored at the aft end of the row of battleships.

Just before 0800, as the *Nevada* ship's band began playing 'Morning Colors' for the ceremonial hoisting of the national ensign, the Japanese air raid began with the dive-bombing of the Air Station on Ford Island. This was followed immediately by the torpedo-plane attack on the battleships with the first enemy planes being observed at 0801.[1] General Quarters was sounded immediately.

Two machine guns forward and two aft were on continuous watch and they opened fire at 0802, quickly bringing down one plane that crashed about 100yd off the port quarter before it had dropped its torpedo. At about 0803 the 5in AA battery opened fire under local control as the guns were manned – without waiting for fire control to be manned. One 5in shell was a direct hit on another plane, 'the shell probably striking the torpedo, resulting in the disintegration of the plane in mid-air'.[2]

Moored on her own abaft *Arizona*, *Nevada* was free to cast off and begin to manoeuvre, unlike most of the other seven battleships present. Only *California* was moored singly and not rafted up to another unit. Fortuitously, earlier that morning, a second boiler had been lit on *Nevada* with the intention of switching the power load from one boiler to the other at about 0800. As the Japanese planes continued to attack, and as *Nevada*'s gunners returned fire, engineers scrambled to raise steam.

Just a few minutes after the attack began, at about 0810, a single Type 91 aerial torpedo struck *Nevada* on her port bow against Frame 41, about 15ft below the waterline and some 14–15ft above the keel.

The torpedo had hit 5–6ft below the bottom of the vertical armour belt between the second and first platform decks and roughly even with the forward edge of No. 2 barbette. The outer shell of the torpedo blister detonated the torpedo as intended, the steel plating of the bulge being ripped open and allowing water to rush into the exposed internal void spaces. The blast opened up the bulkheads to the first (or outer) oil-filled space of the underwater side-protection system – and the bulkheads to the inner ring of fuel tanks also gave way. Although the final bulkhead of the underwater protection system held, it was dished in by about 2ft in places over a large area of some 400sq ft. Gaps in the plating seams about 7in long had been sprung between joints, and leaking through these split joints caused flooding of port side compartments below the first platform deck between Frames 30 and 43. The flooding spread aft along the second deck down into practically all of the compartments forward of Frame 60 below the second deck. An ordnance storeroom on the second platform deck flooded immediately, whilst the 5in powder magazine aft began to flood slowly.

Above the storeroom on the first platform deck was a powder magazine for the main-battery 14in guns. Oil and water from the ruptured side-protection-system voids and tanks below began to enter the powder magazine.

The first platform deck voids and smaller triangular voids just above them were accessed by manholes on the third deck above. The watertight covers to the manholes had been sprung open by the explosion, or were loose, and oil and water began to spout up from them.

As the bow of the great ship flooded, she began to take on a list of 4–5° and her bow began to settle into the water. In the crew spaces between the turret barbettes (situated along the centre line of the ship), oil and water were spurting out from the sounding tubes that led to the fuel tanks. Counterflooding of compartments on the starboard side of the ship was able to correct the list – although her head was soon down by about 3ft.[3]

It took until 0840 to raise enough steam to allow *Nevada* to begin backing away from her berth, F-8. By this time, her forward machine guns had brought down within 200yd of the ship another three enemy torpedo planes that had been strafing. As the flooding from the torpedo damage became more pronounced, *Nevada* was ordered to proceed to the west side of Ford Island.

At 0845, just minutes after *Nevada* began to move out of Berth F-8, the second wave of 167 Japanese level bombers, dive bombers and fighter aircraft swept over Pearl Harbor.

Nevada began moving slowly southwest down Battleship Row towards the Navy Yard. As she passed by the shattered *Arizona*, *Nevada*'s after magazines were flooded in error by direct sea connection rather than by the sprinkler system – and as they rapidly filled with water, the added weight aft began to raise her bow. *Nevada* moved past *West Virginia*, which was now sunk – with *Tennessee* trapped inboard.

Nevada continued on, past the capsized *Oklahoma*, with the largely undamaged *Maryland* inboard. The ship had nearly reached the channel entrance and was about opposite the crippled *California* at Berth F-3 when signals were received not to leave the harbour – if she were to be sunk in the narrow entrance channel, she could block the entire Naval Base. At about 0900, the engines were stopped and her crew prepared to drop anchor.

Seeing the *Nevada* under way, *Nevada* became a prime target for the Aichi D3A Val dive bombers of the second wave – whose pilots no

USS *Nevada* (BB-36) headed down channel after being heavily attacked by Japanese dive bombers. (*NH 97396 courtesy of US Naval History & Heritage Command*)

USS *NEVADA* (BB-36)

doubt hoped to sink her in the navigation channel of the Naval Base. As *Nevada* approached Ten-Ten Dock and prepared to drop anchor opposite the southeasternmost end of Ford Island, Val dive bombers attacked her and within 2–3 minutes was struck by a total of some five 550lb delayed fuze bombs. But dreadnought battleships were designed to withstand punishment like this – and it was in fact unlikely that the Vals, carrying modest 550lb bombs, would be able to sink her. The Commanding Officer of the *Nevada* in his subsequent Report to CINCPAC (BB36/A9/A16) stated that there was reason to believe that one bomb that hit the fo'c'sle deck was a much larger bomb, such as destroyed *Arizona*. Both AA batteries opened continuous fire on enemy planes until 0908 when the attack slackened.[4]

Of the bomb hits, one 550lb bomb exploded over the crew's galley whilst a second struck the port director platform and exploded at the base of the smokestack on the upper deck. A third bomb hit near Turret 1, inboard from the port waterway and blew large holes in the upper and main decks.

Two bombs struck the forecastle – one passed out through the side of the second deck before exploding, causing near-miss damage. The other bomb however detonated inside the ship on the port side near the gasoline tank – and leaking fuel and vapours from this tank caused intense fires to ignite around the ship. Men standing by on the fo'c'sle deck to anchor handle were blown overboard.

The gasoline fires that flared up around Turret 1 had the potential to cause a catastrophic magazine explosion as had destroyed *Arizona* earlier. However, *Nevada*'s main-battery magazines were in fact empty – as over the last few days, all of the 14in-gun battleships had been replacing their standard-weight main-battery projectiles with a new heavier projectile that offered greater penetration and a larger explosive charge in exchange for a slight decrease in range. All of the older projectiles and their potentially volatile powder charges had been removed from *Nevada*'s magazines – the crew had been due to begin loading the new powder charges later on the day of the attack.

Nevada was by now on fire and flooding from the forward torpedo damage. In addition, she had been hit by some five 550lb bombs. At 0907 she was attacked heavily again and hit by a sixth 550lb bomb, which started further fires. Gasoline fires prevented damage-control parties from containing flooding forward of the main torpedo defence system. The flooding of the main 14in magazine and counterflooding to correct her trim had lowered the bow – allowing water to enter the ship at the second deck level through the exit hole made by one of the bombs. Lack of watertight subdivision between the second and main decks from

Frame 30 to Frame 115 allowed water entering through bomb holes in the forecastle to flow aft through the ship's ventilation system to flood the dynamo and boiler rooms. Her gunners however had managed to down three more planes.

At about 0910, as it was imperative to get clear of the channel as other ships were leaving the harbour, *Nevada* was beached with her bow on the shallows at Hospital Point, south of the southernmost end of Ford Island, on the east side of the entrance channel. The forward magazines were flooded at about 0920, when the magazine bulkheads were reported hot. The sprinkling system was turned on and supplemented by fire hoses. The destroyer *Shaw* was on blocks in a floating dry dock nearby. She was hit by three bombs and began to burn fiercely – and shortly after 0930, the magazines of *Shaw* exploded and showered the decks of *Nevada* with debris.

Water pressure on *Nevada*'s firemain however was not enough to fight the fires, particularly the intense fire in the foremast structure – and two tugs were summoned to assist with firefighting. The wind however was from the east, and the stern of *Nevada* began to swing around across the channel in the way of departing ships. As a result, it was decided to move *Nevada* to the other side of the channel.

A tug pushed *Nevada*'s stern further round until the bow floated off. The tugs then slowly moved the ship most of the way across the channel, with *Nevada*'s own engines only being used at the last moment, when they were backed until her stern was hard aground at Waipi'o Point at about 1030, about an hour and a half after the bomb hits.

Nevada came to a halt with a list of about 8° to starboard with only her stern resting on the coral shelf – her bow projected into deeper water, and remained afloat.

Nevada continued to take on water to her bow and middle section, slowly sinking deeper. By the evening, the water inside her extended aft to Frame 80 on the second deck. Flooding on the third deck was checked at bulkhead 60 during the afternoon and at bulkhead 76 at midnight.

Some of the fires started by the bomb hits were still burning on Monday, 8 December – and the minesweepers *Rail* and *Turkey* positioned themselves on either side of her bow and swept her with hoses to keep the flames in check. Meanwhile, the flooding continued – and that night, the stern was dragged off the coral ledge and the ship finally settled with a list of about 2° to starboard. The main deck was about 4ft underwater forward and only dry at high tide abaft frame 90 starboard and frame 75 port. *Nevada* would remain in this half-sunken position for the next two months.

During the attack, *Nevada* suffered a total of 50 killed and 109 wounded.

USS *NEVADA* (BB-36)

USS *Nevada* (BB-36) beached and burning after being hit forward by Japanese bombs and torpedoes. The harbour tug *Hoga* (YT-146) is alongside *Nevada*'s port bow helping fight fires on the battleship's forecastle. (*80-G-19940 courtesy of US Naval History & Heritage Command*)

USS *Nevada* (BB-36) from bow looking aft over bomb damage to forecastle deck, 12 December 1941. (*NH 50104 courtesy of US Naval History & Heritage Command*)

Salvage

Over the course of the coming weeks steps were taken to patch the holes in the underwater parts of the hull. Smaller wooden 'window-frame' patches were placed over three bomb holes in her hull, being the entry and near-miss holes at the forecastle – and the hole in the gasoline storage compartment. On New Year's Day divers placed a 10ft x 12ft window-frame patch over the bomb hole in her port bow at the turn of the bilge at about Frame 7.

A sketch of what became known as the 'big patch' was made up and taken to the workshops so that the outline of the torpedo hole in her port side could be painted on it. A large wooden patch, 55ft x 32ft, was then fabricated to cover the torpedo damage and A-frames and chain falls were set up aboard.

Pumping out of the ship with 6in and 10in pumps began on 7 January – in preparation for dewatering the ship. The 'big patch' arrived alongside *Nevada* at 0900 on 8 January 1942 – and as preparations were made to attach it, the water level inside the ship was lowered by 9in and work began to clear out the first compartments being exposed on the main deck. By 12 January, *Nevada* had been dewatered to just below the second deck. A steel patch was welded to the inside of the bomb hole through the hull at Frame 14 as the external patch was failing to keep the water out.

The big patch was fitted over the torpedo hole – with some initial difficulty as the bottom edge was found to be fouling the outer docking keel. The offending section of docking keel had to be removed by underwater cutting and small charges of dynamite.

It was then found that the forward edge of the patch could not be brought up against the hull – due to a bulge in the torpedo blister plating that had not been detected when the original measurements for the patch were taken. The muddy bottom, into which the ship had settled, covered a layer of hard coral, which was also preventing the mating of the patch. The coral and mud would have to be removed, by dredging and by divers using power hand tools. But after unsuccessful attempts to attach it and get a good seal, the patch was removed.

By 3 February 1942, *Nevada* had been dewatered down to the third deck. But a few days later, on 7 February, as the water level dropped inside the ship, a lieutenant in a trunk at first platform level unscrewed the air test cap at a doorway. As water squirted out, he suddenly collapsed.

A machinist rushed to his aid – and he also collapsed, falling into the water and dying. More men rushed over and another four collapsed almost immediately. Taken to hospital, the four recovered, but the lieutenant who had first unscrewed the air test cap later died at the Naval Hospital. The cause of the two deaths was hydrogen sulfide, a rotten-egg sewer smell caused by rotting and disintegrating organic material within the confines of the hull. It had been noticed as ever-present during the dewatering – dissipating quickly as it rose. But in these lower compartments, under pressure, the gas was odourless and lethal, able to kill in minutes. Blowers and ventilation pipes were immediately run deep into the *Nevada* to bring fresh air in and force contaminated air out. The dewatering of the ship continued.

Nevada Afloat, 12 February 1942

On 12 February 1942, *Nevada* was once again afloat – but still sitting low in the water. The dewatering of the ship continued as efforts were made to lighten the ship and reduce her draft. On 17 February 1942, tugs ran lines to her stern and towed her out to deeper water in the channel.

Watched by crowds of service personnel, USS *Nevada* is low in the water and listing to starboard as she enters Dry Dock No. 2 at Pearl Harbor Navy Yard on 18 February 1942 after being refloated on 12 February. (*NH 83056 courtesy of US Naval History & Heritage Command*)

Early on the morning of 18 February, the cables holding *Nevada* in position were slipped as tugs came alongside and began to push *Nevada* across the channel, the pumps still running to keep pace with leaks of buoyancy. The ship drew 31ft aft and almost 42ft forward – so after ballast tanks were flooded to bring the bow up. She slid across the sill of Dry Dock 2 just before 1000.

Once the water had been drained from the dry dock, men got to work making tight the burst seams and butts of the innermost torpedo bulkhead damaged by the torpedo blast, by welding half sections of pipe over them. The damaged inner bottom, shell and framing were cleared away. A new blister was fabricated and temporarily installed between frames 35 and 45. The damage caused at the bow by the near-miss bomb explosion was covered with a temporary all-welded patch – and no repairs to the inboard structure were made. The damaged gasoline tank and surrounding structure was completely repaired. All principal bulkheads in the damaged area were renewed and damaged deck plating renewed as needed. All six boilers were rebricked and re-insulated and boilers retubed as needed. The starboard shaft had been slightly bent and the rudder damaged when the ship was backed hard aground. These were temporarily repaired and made watertight.

Once the temporary repairs had been completed in the Navy Yard, *Nevada* was undocked and on 22 April 1942 she departed Pearl Harbor, northeast bound for Puget Sound Navy Yard on the West Coast of the USA for final repair and refit.

The subsequent refit had been completed by October 1942, with the old battleship's appearance being dramatically changed such that she now slightly resembled a South Dakota-class battleship from a distance. The dreadnought-era heavy armoured conning tower had been removed and a new superstructure fitted. A raked extension to her smokestack, immediately abaft the bridge, was fitted to keep smoke clear of the bridge. Her Secondary Battery 5in/51-cal. weapons were removed along with her 5in/25-cal. AA battery and a new battery of sixteen 5in/38-cal. DP guns in eight twin mounts was installed that were controlled by four Mark 37 directors. Ten quad-mount 40mm Bofors and thirty-eight single-mount 20mm Oerlikon weapons were also added. The mainmast tripod and fighting top was removed and replaced by a stump mainmast, improving fields of fire for the AA battery. The catapult on the aft turret was removed.

Nevada was ready to return to the war.

USS *NEVADA* (BB-36)

Torpedo hole in *Nevada*'s port side between Frames 38 and 46. The battleship's side armour is visible in the hole's upper section. (*NH 64306 courtesy of US Naval History & Heritage Command*)

BATTLESHIP REVENGE

Return to Service, 1943

(I) The Aleutian Islands Campaign, 11–30 May 1943

The chain of almost seventy Aleutian Islands stretches west across the North Pacific from Alaska towards the Kamchatka peninsula of Russia. The Aleutians are part of the US state of Alaska and have the Bering Sea to their north.

Japan had seized the two Aleutian Islands of Attu and Kiska on 7 June 1942, just six months after the Pearl Harbor raid, at roughly the same time as the failed Japanese invasion of Midway. The Japanese force now occupying both islands had control of the sea-lanes across the North Pacific Ocean – and it was feared that both islands could be turned into strategic Japanese airbases from where long-range bombing missions could be launched against mainland Alaskan and West-Coast cities of the USA such as Anchorage, Seattle and San Francisco. As the USA got ready to take the war back to Japan, the two Aleutian Islands in Japanese control would be taken back. Attu would be invaded between 11 and 18 May 1943, whilst Kiska would be seized a few months later in August 1943.

Nevada was assigned to the Fire Support TG 51.1 along with *Pennsylvania* and *Idaho* and despatched with a destroyer screen from San Pedro, California on 23 April 1943. The Fire Support Group arrived in Cold Bay, Alaska on 1 May and then sailed for Attu on 4 May.

On 11 May 1943, heavy naval bombardments of Japanese positions ashore preceded US amphibious landings by some 15,000 US troops that met determined opposition from 2,900 dug-in Japanese troops. On 13 May 1943, *Nevada*'s firepower was called into action to destroy a network of Japanese defensive hill positions.

Although fierce fighting continued ashore, by 18 May 1943 the position had improved such that *Nevada* was detached from Attu and sent to the Norfolk Navy Yard for further modernisation in June 1943.

(II) Atlantic Convoy Duty, Mid-1943

After completion of her refit, *Nevada* joined the Atlantic Fleet on convoy duty in mid-1943. The slower older battleships such as *Nevada* screened many convoys carrying troops and supplies across the Atlantic, where they were ideally suited to deal with any German capital ship that might break out into the Atlantic on a raiding sortie.

(III) Normandy Invasion, June 1944

After completing her convoy escort duties, in April 1944 *Nevada* sailed for Great Britain in anticipation of the forthcoming Normandy invasion, the largest seaborne invasion in history. *Nevada* became flagship for Rear Admiral Morton Deyo who commanded Operation NEPTUNE, the naval element of the D-Day landings, Operation OVERLORD. *Nevada* would lead the Western Task Force for the landings on UTAH and OMAHA beaches on D-Day, 6 June 1944. The Eastern Task Force would land on GOLD, JUNO and SWORD beaches. The combined force of almost 7,000 invasion vessels included 1,213 warships.

Minesweepers began clearing channels to the invasion beaches in darkness, shortly after midnight on 6 June 1944 – finishing just after dawn. Early on 6 June 1944, the Western Task Force bombardment ships, which included the US battleships *Nevada*, *Arkansas* and *Texas*, 8 cruisers, 28 destroyers and 1 monitor, assumed their bombardment positions 6 miles off UTAH and OMAHA beaches to commence a naval bombardment at first light at 0545 of the area behind the invasion beaches. As soon as it became light enough, the bombardment would switch to shore positions at 0550. The landings were slated to begin at 0630 and so the beaches would receive only 40 minutes of naval bombardment before troops began landing. It was feared that a longer pre-invasion bombardment would allow the Germans time to assemble their forces and counterattack.

Nevada stood off UTAH Beach. To her northwest, the heavy cruiser USS *Quincy* (CA-71), the cruiser USS *Tuscaloosa* (CA-37) and the British light cruiser HMS *Black Prince* (81) were strung out in their firing positions, along with a screen of eight destroyers.

At 0545, the naval bombardment began – the flashes of *Nevada*'s 14in battery shattering the early morning half-light as she targeted the inland German battery at Azeville. *Quincy*'s 8in guns fired at a German battery at Fontenay, whilst *Tuscaloosa*'s 8in main-battery guns targeted the Ozeville battery. The 5.25in guns of the light cruiser *Black Prince* fired at the Morsalines battery. Amphibious troops heading to shore in their small Higgins boats watched in awe as shells flew over their heads towards enemy positions.

Nevada's 14in main-battery and 5in secondary battery guns fired salvo after salvo at shore targets. On D-Day alone, *Nevada*'s gunners would go on to fire 337 main-battery 14in rounds and almost 2,700 5in secondary battery rounds against shore-defence targets on UTAH Beach.[5] Nearly 160,000 troops had crossed the English Channel by the end of D-Day.

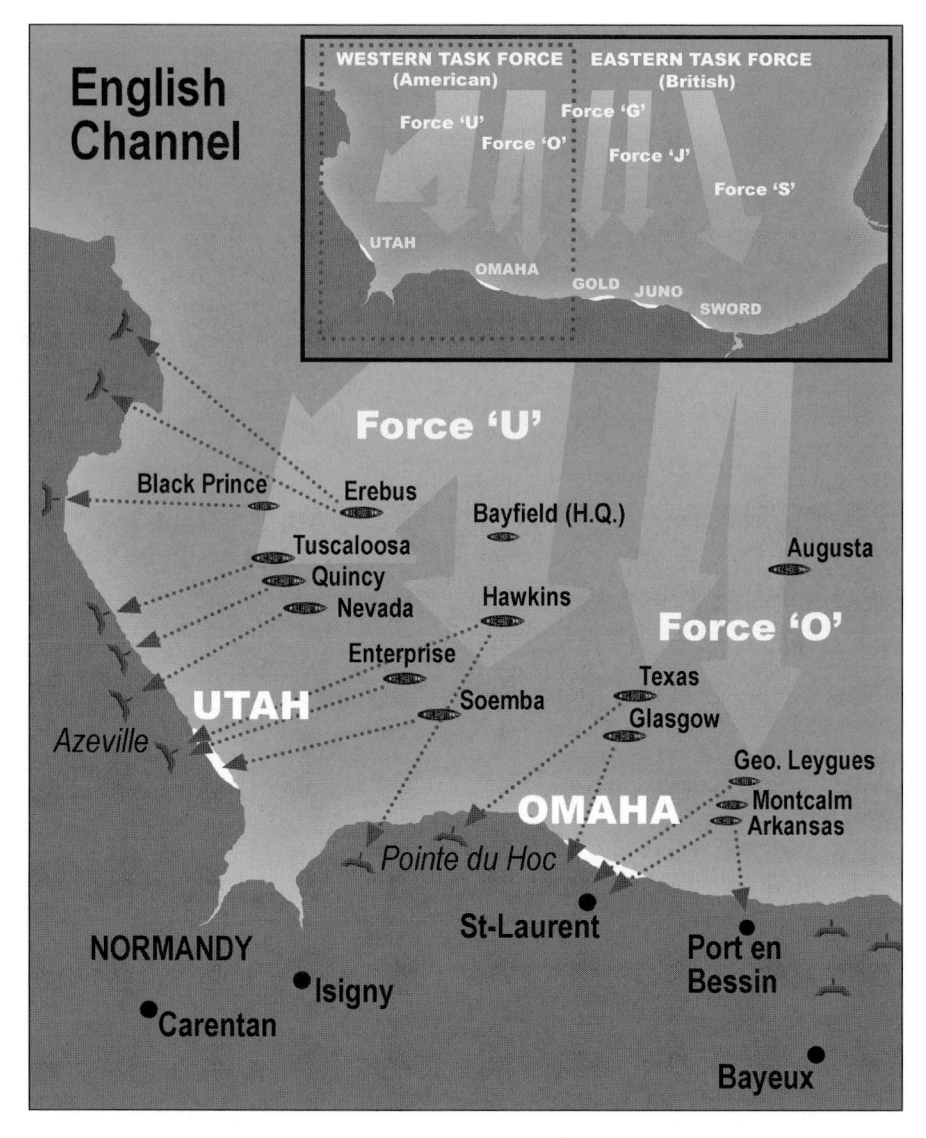

Nevada's bombardment position off UTAH Beach on D-Day Normandy, 6 June 1944. Her guns target enemy batteries ashore at Azeville.

As Allied troops began to fight their way inland, *Nevada* continued support until 17 June 1944, her main-battery guns providing accurate fire as far as 17 miles inland to break up German formations and counterattacks. On occasion, her guns would target enemy positions that were just 600yd in front of Allied troops.

USS *NEVADA* (BB-36)

Forward 14in/45-cal. guns of USS *Nevada* fire on positions ashore during the landings on UTAH Beach, 6 June 1944. (*80-G-252412 courtesy of US Naval History & Heritage Command*)

On 25 June 1944, along with the battleships *Texas* and *Arkansas* and four US and British cruisers, *Nevada* engaged in a duel with the German Shore Battery Hamburg on the Cherbourg peninsula, which was equipped with four 9.4in (24cm)/40 SK L/40 naval guns from decommissioned pre-dreadnoughts. During the 3.5-hour-long exchange, *Nevada* was straddled by German counter-battery fire twenty-seven times (though never hit).[6] The same German battery successfully hit the battleship *Texas* during the exchange with a 24cm shell – although the shell did not explode and was safely defuzed.

Mediterranean Sea, 15 August–25 September 1944
By the end of June 1944, 875,000 men had disembarked to the Allied Normandy beachhead and the Allies now mounted another amphibious

assault, this time landing on French Riviera beaches of the port of Toulon in the Mediterranean, codenamed Operation DRAGOON. The aim of the operation was to secure vital ports on the French Mediterranean coast and increase pressure on Germany by opening another front.

In support of this operation, *Nevada* and four other battleships, along with heavy cruisers, destroyers, landing craft and support ships, were sent south from the beaches of Normandy, to pass through the Strait of Gibraltar into the Mediterranean.

Operation DRAGOON began north of Toulon in the early hours of 15 August 1944 as ships of the Western Task Force approached under cover of darkness to be in position at dawn.

Allied bombers from Italy, Sardinia and Corsica began an aerial bombardment of enemy positions at 0600. Then, at 0730, a pre-invasion naval bombardment began, which ceased as landing craft approached the beaches at 0800.

The important port of Toulon was protected by a heavily reinforced fortress at Saint-Mandrier-sur-Mer that had four 340mm (13.4in) naval guns set in two twin turrets. These guns had been salvaged from the French battleship *Provence*, which had scuttled along with seventy-six other units of the French Fleet in Toulon on 27 November 1942 to prevent seizure by the Nazis. The guns from *Provence* had been set in reinforced concrete emplacements and with a range of nearly 22 miles, they commanded every approach to the port of Toulon. The German fortress had acquired the nickname 'Big Willie' – the Fire Support Group ships were tasked to level the fortress.

On Saturday, 19 August, *Nevada*, along with the cruisers *Augusta* (CA-31), *Quincy* (CA-71) and the French battleship *Lorraine* arrived offshore and began firing an estimated 200 shells that day at the Nazi fortress – in conjunction with low-level bomber strikes. Big Willie did not reply until the following day, Sunday, 20 August – when 340mm shells began to fall amongst the Allied ships, the shells creeping closer until there was a 30yd near miss that forced the Allied ships to open the range. On 23 August 1944, *Nevada* fired more than 354 rounds during a 6½-hour gunnery exchange with the fortress.

Toulon itself fell to the Allies a few days later on 27 August 1944 – and at dawn on 28 August, the 2,000 German sailors manning Big Willie capitulated. Allied warships had by then fired more than 1,000 shells at the fortress.

Having seen so much action, following the fall of Toulon, as Allied forces moved inland towards Berlin, the pressing need for battleships to support landing forces was diminished. *Nevada* was detached and

USS *NEVADA* (BB-36)

sent west across the Atlantic to New York, where she would have her worn gun barrels relined in preparation for being moved to the Pacific Fleet. The Philippine campaign had begun a few months after D-Day Normandy, with landings on Leyte in October 1944. *Nevada* however would still be far away in the Atlantic – and so would not take part in the Battle of Leyte.

After *Nevada* reached New York, the three 14in/45-cal. guns of Turret 1 were replaced with Mark 8 guns salved from Turret 3 of *Arizona*, which had been straightened and relined after the Pearl Harbor raid to Mark 12 specifications.

USS *Nevada* (BB-36) underway off the Atlantic coast, 17 September 1944. She has by now been fully refitted with a new superstructure, a raked extension of the single enlarged stack and a new battery of sixteen 5in/38-cal. secondary guns in eight twin mounts arranged four on either side of the superstructure. (*80-G-282709 courtesy of US Naval History & Heritage Command*)

(IV) Battle of Iwo Jima, 19 February–26 March 1945

At the end of the successful Battle of Leyte in the Philippines in December 1944, the Allies had a two-month lull in their offensive operations before the next major operation, the invasion of Okinawa. By now in early 1945, the Japanese surface fleet was largely destroyed – and with the corking of the Luzon bottleneck, Japan had been cut off from her major fuel supplies.

The volcanic island of Iwo Jima lies some 760 miles south of Tokyo and was a strategically important airbase for Japanese fighter planes – from where they could intercept US long-range B-29 Superfortress four-engine heavy bombers, which were now flying from the Mariana Islands far to the south, on direct raids against Japan. Japanese planes flying south from Iwo Jima's three airfields had made a number of air attacks on the Mariana Islands between November 1944 and January 1945.

The small island of Iwo Jima is only 8 square miles – and is dominated by Mount Suribachi at its southwest end. Mount Suribachi is a dormant volcanic vent some 160m high, which is a resurgent dome, or raised centre, of a larger submerged volcanic caldera that surrounds the island.

If seized by the Allies, Iwo Jima could be quickly utilised as an airbase for US long-range P-51 Mustang fighters, which would escort the Boeing B-29 Superfortress bombers on their raids over Japan. Iwo Jima could also serve as an emergency landing base for any damaged B-29s returning from those raids that were unable to reach their own Mariana Island bases on Guam and Saipan. It was therefore decided to eliminate these problems by seizing Iwo Jima on 19 February 1945 in Operation DETACHMENT.

After her refit was completed, *Nevada* sailed for the Pacific where she formed up in the Marianas as one of six TF 54 fire-support battleships for the Iwo Jima operation. The six TF 54 battleships *Tennessee, Idaho, Nevada, Texas, New York* and *Arkansas* began rehearsals off the Marianas on 12 February 1945 – before moving to soften up Iwo Jima with heavy cruisers, light cruisers and destroyers. TF 54 arrived off Iwo Jima four days later on 16 February 1945.

At Iwo Jima, TF 54 was joined three days later, on D-Day Iwo Jima, 19 February 1945, by that other casualty of the Pearl Harbor raid, *West Virginia*, fresh from providing fire support for the invasion of Lingayen Gulf, on northwest Luzon in the Philippines.

The naval bombardment of Iwo Jima by TF 54 began on 17 February 1945. The bombardment ships were met by accurate Japanese counter-battery fire from coastal batteries that damaged *Tennessee*, the cruiser

USS *NEVADA* (BB-36)

USS *Nevada* bombarding Iwo Jima, 19 February 1945. (*80-G-K-3510 courtesy of US Naval History & Heritage Command*)

Pensacola (CA-24) and the destroyer *Leutze* (DD-481), as they protected UDT teams of swimmers reconnoitring the landing beaches.

Nevada continued to pound Iwo Jima throughout D-Day 19 February as US Marines landed on the black volcanic beach. Troops and equipment piled up against 15ft-high slopes of soft, black volcanic ash that neither allowed a secure footing or the digging of foxholes. For the first hour, the landings met little response, leading the navy to believe that the bombardment had successfully destroyed Japanese defences. The Japanese however were holding their fire for the first hour, to allow the Marines to pile up men and machinery on the beach. Then, as the Marines started to move slowly forward, the Japanese opened fire with everything they had, from machine guns to mortars and heavy artillery.

The US Marines were subjected to withering Japanese fire from Mount Suribachi, in which the Japanese had emplaced heavy artillery in bunkers and gun pits that were protected by reinforced steel doors and connected by an elaborate tunnel system. The doors of the gun pits would open to fire, before closing again to prevent effective counter-battery fire from the Marines ashore and vessels offshore.

Despite vicious fighting ashore, the US flag was eventually raised atop Mount Suribachi on 23 February 1945 – and *Nevada* was subsequently able to withdraw on 7 March. During the invasion, she had moved to within 600yd of the shore to provide maximum accurate fire support for the troops ashore as they advanced.

(V) Battle of Okinawa – Operation ICEBERG, 1 April 1945–22 June 1945

After withdrawing from Iwo Jima, TF 54 under the command of Rear Admiral Morton L. Deyo in his flagship *Tennessee* began training east of Ulithi for the invasion of Okinawa – codename Operation ICEBERG. On 17 March, the Gunfire Support TG 54.1 was joined by that other veteran of the Pearl Harbor raid, the battleship *Maryland*, fresh from her recent repair and refit at Pearl Harbor. *Pennsylvania* and *California* meantime were undergoing refits on the West Coast of the USA.

Training off Ulithi ended on 21 March 1945 – when TF 54 deployed northwest towards Okinawa. TF 54 arrived off Okinawa and moved into position on the night of 25 March 1945, ready to begin the bombardment mission at dawn on 26 March 1945. D-Day Okinawa was slated for 1 April 1945.

Nevada was assigned to Fire Support Unit 3 of the Gunfire Support Group, tasked to cover the Hagushi Beaches Area along with *Tennessee*, the heavy cruiser *Wichita*, light cruisers and destroyers. The other Fire Support Units were tasked to different areas, initially covering minesweeping operations in fire-support sectors.

Beginning on 26 March 1945, *Nevada* used her main and secondary batteries to shell Japanese airfields, shore defences, supply dumps and troop concentrations before retiring well offshore for the night. Early the following morning, 27 March, several kamikazes attacked the Gunfire Support Group ships, damaging several. One kamikaze, though hit repeatedly by AA fire, penetrated the screen and dived into the main deck of *Nevada*, next to Turret 3, killing eleven and wounding forty-nine crew. The explosion disabled both Turret 3 14in guns along with three nearby 20mm Oerlikon AA weapons – but nevertheless, the daily shelling of Okinawa continued unabated until D-Day, 1 April 1945.

Kamikazes were now being used in numbers against Allied shipping and would inflict much damage. On D-Day, as troops landed and began to move inshore, *West Virginia* was hit by a kamikaze whilst *Tennessee* was damaged by shell fragments.

As the days progressed, the attacks by kamikazes, conventional level bombers, dive bombers and torpedo planes – and by suicide boats –

continued in force, as US troops ashore faced fierce opposition. Each day, destroyers, attack transports and cargo ships were hit, damaged or sunk. On 5 April, whilst providing gunfire support 3 miles northwest of the city of Naha for the troops ashore on the southern part of Okinawa, *Nevada* was hit by an artillery shell from a Japanese coastal battery – two more of her crew were killed. On 6 April, the kamikaze attacks intensified with more destroyers being damaged or sunk. *Maryland* was then damaged by a bomb on 7 April, 18 miles northwest of Okinawa, whilst the same day a kamikaze hit the carrier *Hancock* (CV-19), cartwheeling across the flight deck and crashing into a group of planes. The kamikaze's bomb hit the port catapult and caused a large explosion, killing sixty-two men and wounding seventy-one. *Tennessee* was hit by a kamikaze on the 12th.

The Battle of Okinawa ashore would last eighty-two days until 22 June 1945 and would turn into one of the bloodiest of the Pacific campaign. By the time the island was declared secure, the USA had suffered some 75,000–80,000 casualties, of whom some 12,500 were KIA whilst 7,700 died of wounds or non-combat deaths. Hundreds of Allied naval vessels had been damaged or sunk. Okinawan civilian deaths are estimated at almost 150,000, Japanese fatalities at more than 110,000.

Now that Okinawa was secure, the Allies had a fleet anchorage, troop staging areas and airfields close to Japan for Operation DOWNFALL, the eventual planned invasion of Japan that was slated to begin on 1 November 1945. The attacks by kamikazes had been ferocious – and it was thought that the defence of the Japanese homeland islands would see even more determined resistance – the most optimistic estimates of Allied deaths during DOWNFALL were 500,000.

On 30 June 1945, *Nevada* departed Okinawa to operate with the 3rd Fleet from 10 July 1945, close to the Japanese home islands. With the dropping of the two atomic bombs on Hiroshima and Nagasaki on 6 and 9 August 1945, Japan would finally be forced to surrender on 2 September 1945.

The Pacific War was over.

(VI) Post-War
Following the surrender of Japan, *Nevada* was initially stationed in Tokyo Bay as the occupation of Japan began. But with the war over, there was no need to keep battleships and their war weary crews operational any longer than was necessary – *Nevada* was sent back east to Pearl Harbor. Once there, she was surveyed – and now more than

thirty-two years old, she was deemed too old to be kept in the slimmed down post-war fleet.

The venerable *Nevada*, which had participated in both world wars – and fought in both European and Pacific theatres, was assigned as a target ship for the first of the atomic experiments to be held at Bikini Atoll – Operation CROSSROADS in July 1946.

After evacuating the local residents of the atoll islands, two atomic bombs would be detonated in Tests ABLE and BAKER to test the effectiveness of nuclear weapons against warships. The old tough battleship *Nevada* was chosen as the bombardier's target for the first Test ABLE, an air-dropped weapon. *Nevada* was painted a reddish-orange colour with her gun barrels and gunwales painted white to help the bombardier identify her from the many other vessels that were anchored around her in the atoll lagoon. However, even with

BAKER atomic-bomb test, Bikini Atoll, 25 July 1946. Identifiable ships are *Pennsylvania*, *New York*, *Salt Lake City*, *Nagato* and *Nevada*. The dark area on the right side of the water column marks the location of USS *Arkansas*. (NH 96241 courtesy of US Naval History & Heritage Command)

USS *NEVADA* (BB-36)

the hi-vis colour scheme, the bomb fell a few thousand feet off target, and exploded about 520ft above the 4,247-ton attack transport *Gilliam* (APA-57). Although *Gilliam* was destroyed and sunk quickly, the blast in fact caused less damage to the test ships than had been expected – and *Nevada* survived.

For Test BAKER, the atomic weapon was suspended beneath a landing craft anchored in the midst of the target fleet and detonated at a depth of 90ft, halfway to the bottom of the lagoon. The landing craft above was vaporised, and ten ships were sunk. *Nevada* also survived this second test – but was damaged and heavily contaminated with radioactive spray.

Nevada was towed the following month to Pearl Harbor, where after she had been closely examined, she was decommissioned on 29 August 1946. Two years later, on 31 July 1948, the modern fast battleship *Iowa* (BB-61) and two other vessels used the antique *Nevada* as a practice gunnery target, some 65 miles southwest of Pearl Harbor. The tough, old dreadnought refused to sink to shellfire – and had to be finally sent to the bottom by an aerial torpedo strike amidships. *Nevada* capsized on the surface before going down slowly by the stern and landing upside down on the seabed, more than 15,000ft below. The wreck of *Nevada* was located on 11 May 2020.

After being bombarded in ordnance tests off Pearl Harbor, the capsized USS *Nevada* is scuttled by torpedo on 31 July 1948. The track can be seen coming in from bottom right. (*80-G-498282 courtesy of US Naval History & Heritage Command*)

Chapter 8

USS *Pennsylvania* (BB-38)

USS *Pennsylvania* (BB-38) at sea prior to the Bikini atom-bomb tests, 15 June 1946. (80-G-627428 courtesy of US Naval History & Heritage Command)

USS *PENNSYLVANIA* (BB-38)

Specifications (as built): Pennsylvania class
Builder: Newport News Shipbuilding & Drydock Co.
Launched: 16 March 1915
Commissioned: 12 June 1916
Decommissioned: 29 August 1946
Displacement: 31,400 tons (S). 32,440 tons (F)
Length: 608ft (oa)
600ft (wl)
Beam: 97ft (wl)
Draft: 28.9ft
Speed: 21 knots
Endurance: 8,000nm at 10 knots

Armament:
  Main battery: 12 x 14in/45cal. in 4 triple turrets set in 2 superfiring pairs
  Secondary battery: 22 x single 5in/51-cal. guns
  AA battery: 4 x single 3in/50-cal. guns
  Torpedo tubes: 2 x 21in submerged

Armour:
  Belt: 13.5in tapering to 8in at bottom edge
  Barbettes: 13in max.
  Turrets: Face: 18in. Sides: 9in. Roof: 5in
  Decks: Upper armour deck: 3in in 3 layers. Aft over steering gear 6.25in in 2 layers
  Lower splinter deck: 1.5–2in in 2 layers
  Conning tower: 16in

Sister ships in class: *Arizona* (BB-39)
Fate: Scuttled off Kwajalein Atoll on 10 February 1948

USS *Pennsylvania* (BB-38) was the lead ship of the Pennsylvania class of two super-dreadnought battleships built as the second class of the Standard-Type BB series begun with the preceding Nevada class. The Nevadas had employed the first triple 14in turrets in positions 1 and 4. For the Pennsylvania class, each of the two superfiring twin turrets of the Nevadas was improved to a triple turret – producing twelve 14in guns in four triple superfiring turrets. The second ship in the class, *Arizona* (BB-39), would later be destroyed at Pearl Harbor on 7 December 1941.

Pennsylvania was laid down at the Newport News Shipbuilding & Drydock Company on 27 October 1913 – and was launched for fitting out some eighteen months later on 16 March 1915. She was commissioned the following year on 12 June 1916 and on 12 October 1916 became flagship of the Atlantic Fleet.

As constructed, *Pennsylvania* had a single smokestack flanked by two cage masts. (For a discussion of cage masts, see Chapter 7, USS *Nevada*.)

The two Pennsylvania-class BBs were significantly larger than the preceding Nevada-class units – with *Pennsylvania* and her sister *Arizona* having an overall length of 608ft and a beam of 97ft (wl) compared with the 583ft overall length and 95ft (wl) beam of *Nevada*. The Pennsylvania-class units were thus some 25ft longer and slightly wider in the beam than the Nevadas.

The two Pennsylvania-class battleships had a design displacement (as constructed) of 31,400 tons and a Full Load displacement of 32,440 tons, substantially greater than the 27,500-ton (S) and 28,400-ton (F) displacement of the Nevadas.

(a) Armament

i. Main Battery

Pennsylvania was fitted with twelve of the same 14in/45-cal. guns as on the preceding Nevada class, set in four triple superfiring turrets arranged one superfiring pair of turrets forward of the superstructure and one pair of superfiring turrets abaft. This arrangement allowed a broadside of all twelve guns. The 14in/45-cal. gun fired a 1,400lb AP projectile with four silk bags of smokeless powder as propellant.

The three 14in/45-cal. guns of each turret could not elevate independently – and were limited to a maximum elevation of +15°. This gave a maximum firing range of about 23,000yd, roughly 13 miles. During her 1929–30 modernisation the elevation of her main-battery weapons was increased from 15° to 30° – and this increased the range from 23,000yd to about 36,000yd, some 20 miles. There were 100 shells carried for each gun.

ii. Secondary Battery

Pennsylvania was constructed with twenty-two single 5in/51-cal. guns, most of which were set in casemates with ten guns mounted along either beam. The number of these guns would in common with other

USS *PENNSYLVANIA* (BB-38)

USS *Pennsylvania* (BB-38), 1930s. The forward three-gun 14in/45-cal. turrets and forward superstructure are seen here. (*NH 50758 courtesy of US Naval History & Heritage Command*)

battleships be reduced to fourteen after the First World War, with two guns on either fo'c'sle beam and two guns on either beam in the lower hull towards the stern being removed due to poor performance in moderate seas. The secondary battery would be further reduced to twelve 5in/51-cal. guns in 1921.

These single-purpose 5in/51-cal. guns had an effective range of about 15,850yd, some 9 miles, with a rate of fire of eight to nine rounds per minute.

iii. AA Protection

When she was constructed, the threat to heavily armoured capital ships from aircraft was minimal – but for the first time, AA protection was built into the design of a US battleship, with *Pennsylvania* and her sister *Arizona* being fitted with four single 3in/50-cal. DP guns. These AA guns used fixed ammunition where the shell and propellant were one assembled unit – with a rate of fire of fifteen to twenty rounds per minute. The 24lb shell could be fired effectively out to a range of 14,000yd, over 5 miles, at a 43° elevation – with a ceiling of about 30,000ft.

When flying off platforms for floatplanes were fitted in 1921 to the roofs of the two after superfiring 14in turrets, two of the original 3in/50-cal. guns were removed – but with two of the 5in/51-cal. secondary battery guns also removed, this allowed an increase to eight 3in/50-cal. guns.

Submerged Beam Torpedo Tubes
Pennsylvania was originally fitted with two submerged 21in torpedo tubes, one on either beam towards the bow. The torpedo tubes were removed during modernisation in 1929 when a new anti-torpedo blister was added outboard of the former torpedo bulkhead, over most of the ship's length.

Underwater Protection
Underwater protection was improved from the Nevada class with a 3in torpedo bulkhead being installed 9ft 6in inboard from the ship's side, with a width of almost 12ft, which with the new torpedo blister increased the depth of torpedo protection to 19ft. Testing in mid-1914 revealed that this underwater side-protection system could withstand 300lb (140kg) of TNT. A complete double bottom was installed.

With the rearrangement of the boilers in 1929, an additional torpedo bulkhead was worked through the refitted boiler rooms and an additional inner bottom under the boiler rooms was installed.

(b) Armour

The *Pennsylvania*-class design continued the 'all-or-nothing' armour principle, begun with the Nevada class.

Main Belt: The waterline belt of Krupp armour was 13.5in at its thickest and the protected length was 444ft, covering only the most important of ship's spaces such as machinery spaces and magazines within the citadel. The vertical belt was 17ft 6in high, of which 8ft 9¾in was below the waterline. Beginning 2ft 4in below the waterline, the belt tapered to its minimum thickness of 8in at its lower edge.

Transverse Bulkheads: The transverse bulkheads at each end of the citadel ranged from 13–8in thick.

Turrets: The faces of the four triple main-battery turrets were 18in thick whilst the sides were 9in thick and the roofs 5in thick.

Horizontal Armour Decks: The uppermost horizontal armour deck of the citadel was three plates thick with a total thickness of 3in. Above the steering gear aft, the armour increased to 6.25in on the upper deck in two plates.

The lower armoured splinter deck was 1.5–2in thick, with sides that sloped down to meet the bottom of the armour belt. The upper armour deck would detonate any plunging shell whilst the lower armour deck (above the magazines and propulsion systems) would catch any splinters caused by the explosion. The boiler uptakes were protected by 13in of armour.

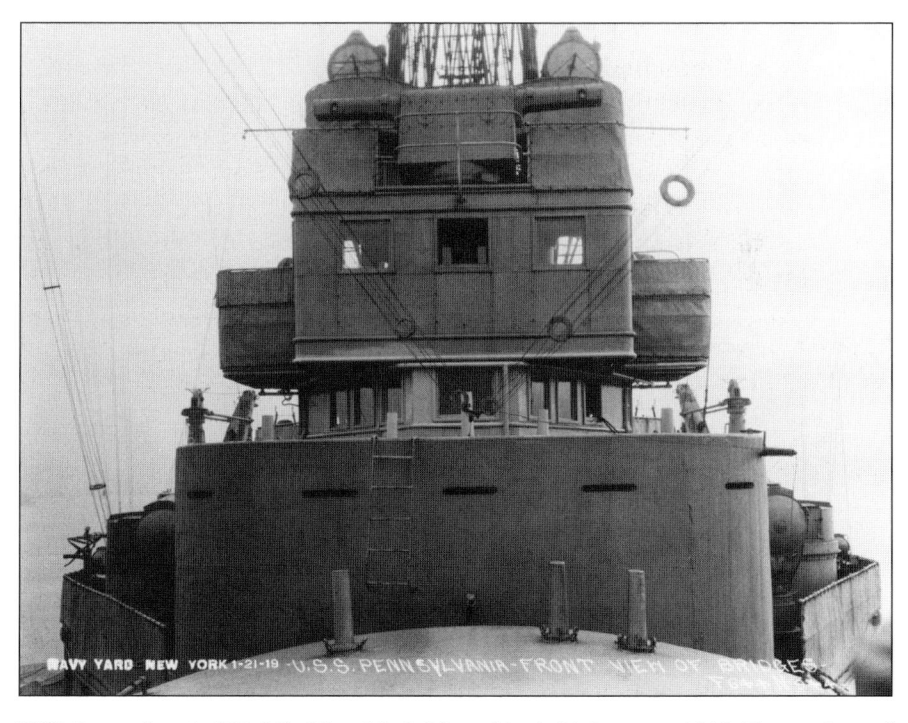

USS *Pennsylvania* (BB-38), New York Navy Yard, 21 January 1919. Front view of the armoured conning tower ringed by viewing slits, with navigating bridge and flag bridge above. (*NH76571 courtesy of US Naval History & Heritage Command*)

(c) Propulsion

Pennsylvania was fitted with four direct-drive Curtis steam turbines; steam being provided by twelve Babcock & Wilcox boilers. The four turbines drove four propeller shafts, producing 29,366 shaft horsepower to give a design speed of 21 knots and an endurance of 8,000nm at a cruising speed of 10 knots.

Service Modifications: 1929–31

Pennsylvania entered the Philadelphia Navy Yard on 1 June 1929 for a major refit and modernisation. Her propulsion system was upgraded and modernised with six new Bureau Express three-drum small-tube boilers, delivering steam at 300psi, replacing the twelve original Babcock &Wilcock boilers. New geared turbines and new turbo generators replaced her older system. The horizontal deck armour was increased with another layer on the upper armoured deck that brought its thickness to 4.75in. A torpedo blister was added on either beam, outboard of her original torpedo bulkhead and over most of her length and the outdated submerged beam torpedo tubes were removed.

The elevation of the twelve main-battery 14in/45-cal. guns was increased to +30°, significantly improving their effective range. The AA battery was beefed up with the addition of eight manually trained lightweight 5in/25-cal. HA guns. The mount offered a maximum elevation of +85° whilst the short barrel made it easier to train manually against fast-moving targets. Eight .50in machine guns were added.

The two outdated lattice cage masts were removed and replaced with tripod masts. The protected flag bridge was also enlarged to increase available space for an admiral's staff, when operating as flagship. Two new catapults for seaplanes were fitted, one on the quarter deck and one on top of Turret 3. All of this work added more than 3,000 tons to the ship and on completion of the work, as reconstructed in 1931, she now displaced 34,400 tons (S) and 39,224 (F). The reconstructed *Pennsylvania* returned to service on 1 March 1931.

On 12 September 1940, the battleship transferred to Puget Sound for an overhaul that lasted until 27 December 1940 – she returned to San Pedro on 31 December 1940.

On 7 January 1941, *Pennsylvania* steamed to Pearl Harbor.

USS *PENNSYLVANIA* (BB-38)

PEARL HARBOR, 7 DECEMBER 1941

Pennsylvania, now flagship of Admiral Husband E. Kimmel, the Commander-in-Chief of the US Fleet (CINCUS) was on blocks in Dry Dock No. 1 undergoing a refit, with three of her four screws already removed. The destroyers *Cassin* and *Downes* were on blocks side by side in the same dry dock, forward of, and dwarfed by, the large battleship. A new dry dock west of *Pennsylvania* was dry and unoccupied – whilst the destroyer *Shaw* (DD-373) occupied a Floating Dock adjacent, further to the west. Although the dry-docked *Pennsylvania* had been excused from AA drills, machine guns in her foremast were manned.

First Call to colours had been sounded, when at about 0757, those aboard heard explosions on Ford Island, opposite the dry dock across Battleship Row. When it was realised that an air raid had started, General Quarters was sounded and men began knocking off locks on ready use ammunition boxes and ready stowages, not waiting for the keys to arrive.

As an estimated twelve to fifteen Japanese torpedo planes came in from the west and south to strike the battleships lined up in Battleship Row, the Japanese expected *Pennsylvania* to be in her usual berth at Ten-Ten Dock. They were unaware that *Pennsylvania* had been moved to dry dock – and B5N Kate torpedo bombers mistakenly attacked the 10,000-ton light cruiser *Helena* (CL-50), which was tied up in *Pennsylvania*'s usual Ten-Ten Dock berth with the 4,779-ton minelayer *Oglala* alongside. An aerial torpedo passed under *Oglala* and detonated on *Helena*'s starboard side amidships.

Pennsylvania's AA gunners opened fire on the attacking planes from the dry dock. Spotting *Pennsylvania*, three torpedo planes came in low, releasing their torpedoes in an unsuccessful attempt to torpedo the side of the dry dock and flood it – whilst strafing *Pennsylvania*.

Between 0830 and 0900, ten to fifteen dive bombers began a series of attack runs from the port bow towards the dry-docked *Pennsylvania*. Just before they reached *Pennsylvania*, about two-thirds of them broke off to attack the *Nevada*, which was by now underway and about 600yd off the *Pennsylvania*'s starboard quarter. The bombs dropped over *Pennsylvania* fell harmlessly into the water beyond the caisson.

An estimated five high-level bombing attacks of four to six planes each, in a V formation, passed over *Pennsylvania* at about 10,000–12,000ft, one from the port bow, one from ahead, one from ahead passing to starboard and two from astern. At about 0906, one bomb landed in the dry dock between the dry-docked destroyers *Downes* and *Cassin*, in front of *Pennsylvania*. Fragments penetrated *Downes'* thin shell plating to the fuel bunkers – releasing fuel oil that caught fire. The two destroyers were soon heavily on fire from stem to stern.

One bomb hit the dry dock on *Pennsylvania's* starboard side abreast frame 20. Another bomb hit *Pennsylvania* a few feet abaft the No. 7 5in/25-cal. gun, passing through the boat deck and exploding in the casemate for the No. 9 5in/51-cal. gun. As fires took hold, sporadic attacks continued for the next 15 minutes.

In the course of the attack, eighteen men aboard *Pennsylvania* had been killed, including her executive officer – and thirty-eight wounded.

At about 0920, shore crew flooded the dry dock in an effort to help extinguish the fires aboard the two destroyers. As the water in the dock rose, *Cassin* became partially afloat, and slipping from her keel blocks, she rolled to starboard against *Downes*. Burning fuel lying on the rising surface of the water began to burn both destroyers out.

Ten minutes later, at about 0930, explosions began as the fires reached magazines and ammunition began to cook off. At 0941, *Downes* was rocked by a heavy explosion as one of her own torpedoes blew up, creating a large hole in her port side amidships and scattering parts of the ship around the area. One of her heavy torpedo tubes was thrown into the air and struck *Pennsylvania's* forecastle.

Despite the mayhem in the dry dock, *Pennsylvania* had however escaped serious damage. She had been hit by one bomb amidships, by flying debris from *Cassin* and suffered superficial damage to her bow by the fires on the two destroyers ahead of her, which set fire to the paint on her starboard bow. The bomb hit opened up the boat deck and casemate deck for about 20ft x 20ft – whilst the bulkhead abaft No. 9 5in/51-cal. gun was blown out and the gun was put out of action.

As soon as the attack was over, repair work began – and the next day, 8 December, a 5in/51-cal. gun and a 5in/25-cal. gun were removed from *West Virginia* and hoisted aboard *Pennsylvania* to replace those damaged.

On 12 December 1941, just five days after the attack, *Pennsylvania* was moved out of dry dock. She was ready to go to sea, with the exception of not yet having the replacement No. 9 5in/51-cal. gun serviceable.

On 20 December 1941, just two weeks after the attack, *Pennsylvania* departed Hawaii for final repairs at Hunter's Point Naval Shipyard in San Francisco, crossing with *Maryland*, *Tennessee* and an escort of four destroyers. En route there were many stands at General Quarters brought about by sightings, real or imagined, of Japanese submarines.

USS *PENNSYLVANIA* (BB-38)

As the flotilla neared the West Coast, *Maryland* and *Tennessee* detached and took a more northerly bearing for the Puget Sound Navy Yard at Bremerton, Washington.

Pennsylvania arrived at San Francisco after an eight-day passage and entered dry dock at Hunter's Point Naval Shipyard on 1 January 1942 for final repairs. With *Pennsylvania*, *Maryland* and *Tennessee* desperately needed back in action as quickly as possible, they would be speedily repaired and have their AA capabilities beefed up.

Repairs to *Pennsylvania* were completed by 12 January 1942. Sixteen 20mm Oerlikon autocannon were installed along with four quad-mount 1.1in/75-cal. rapid-fire Chicago Piano weapons, that had a rate of fire of 150 rounds per minute. The 1.1in/75-cal. AA guns would prove to be ineffective against modern, fast enemy planes and would be replaced by more 20mm Oerlikons and 40mm Bofors at the next scheduled overhaul.

USS *Pennsylvania* (BB-38), starboard side amidships at San Francisco, 3 February 1942. Note the 5in/51-cal. casemate guns at main deck level with 5in/25-cal. DP guns with splinter shields above. A quad 1.1in gun tub is at right of shot just abaft the triple 14in Turret No. 2. Abaft and above Turret No. 2 is the armoured conning tower, ringed by viewing slits, with the bridges abaft. (19-N-28413 courtesy of US Naval History & Heritage Command)

BATTLESHIP REVENGE

Pennsylvania joined TF 1, commanded by Vice Admiral William S. Pye, which was being kept at a 48-hour state of readiness on the West Coast due to continued fears of Japanese strikes. *Pennsylvania* briefly went to sea with TF 1 at the time of the Battle of Midway – but the ships did not see action.

1942 Refit
Following the convincing US victory at Midway in early June 1942, the strategic situation was deemed secure enough to allow *Pennsylvania* to be detached from TF 1 to undergo a major refit and modernisation at Mare Island Naval Yard in San Francisco from October 1942 to February 1943.

At Mare Island, the heavily armoured dreadnought-era conning tower was removed to reduce top weight – and the bridge was modernised. Whilst the tripod foremast remained, the tripod mainmast was removed and replaced by a small deckhouse above which the after main-battery director cupola was housed with one of the new CXAM-1 radars installed above the cupola. Mark 3 FC radar-equipped fire-control directors were installed along with two additional SG radar sets.

All the older 5in/51-cal. secondary battery weapons in casemates, along with all the 5in/25-cal. and 1.1in/75-cal. AA guns, were now removed. A new deckhouse was constructed to support sixteen new 5in/38-cal. DP secondary battery weapons, set in eight twin enclosed mounts. These manually loaded DP guns were fitted with powered projectile and powder-case hoists and powered training and elevating drives. The barrels could depress to -15° and elevate to +85° and could fire one round every 4 seconds operating under the Mark 37 Gun Fire Control System.

Pennsylvania's AA capability was further strengthened by the installation of ten powerful quad Bofors 40mm mounts and the Oerlikon 20mm weapons suite was increased to fifty-one.

With her refit completed, *Pennsylvania* returned to the fleet.

(I) The Aleutian Islands Campaign, 11–30 May 1943
The Aleutian Islands of Attu and Kiska had been seized by Japan on 7 June 1942, just six months after the Pearl Harbor raid, giving Japan control of the sea-lanes across the Northern Pacific Ocean and the potential to fly long-range bombing missions against mainland Alaska and the US West-Coast cities. US forces would retake the Aleutian Islands during the summer of 1943.

USS *PENNSYLVANIA* (BB-38)

Assigned as flagship, *Pennsylvania* joined *Idaho* and *Nevada* in the Fire Support TG 51.1 for Operation LANDCRAB, the Attu landings – where 2,500 Japanese troops were dug in. Kiska would be seized later, in August 1943.

On 23 April 1943, the TF 51 invasion ships departed San Pedro heading north for Cold Bay, Alaska and from there they deployed towards the westernmost Aleutian Island of Attu.

On 11 May 1943, heavy naval bombardments of Japanese positions ashore preceded landings by the army's 4th and 7th Infantry Divisions at Holtz Bay and Massacre Bay on Attu. The landings met determined enemy opposition and *Pennsylvania* and the other bombardment ships were called upon to shell several Japanese positions, with fire being directed by shore-control parties.

The large Japanese 1st class cruiser-submarine *I-31* had been engaged making regular return supply runs from Paramushiro, in the Kuril Island chain off northern Japan, to both Attu and Kiska. By coincidence, *I-31* had arrived at Attu on 9 May 1943, just two days before the US landings. She had unloaded her cargo for that island – before moving off towards Kiska, where she arrived the following day, 10 May 1943. After unloading stores and ammunition to the garrison stationed there, she departed Kiska the same day to return to Attu.

On the evening of 12 May 1943, having completed her fire mission on Attu for the day, *Pennsylvania* was proceeding northward away from Attu to rendezvous with *Idaho*. Unknowingly, *I-31* closed on the great battleship some 9 miles northeast of Holtz Bay – and manoeuvred to attain a firing position.

Suddenly, a PBY Catalina flying boat on anti-submarine patrol radioed *Pennsylvania* to report a torpedo headed straight for the battleship. Captain William A. Corn made an immediate crash turn at full speed to comb the track of the torpedo – and relieved lookouts aloft spotted the torpedo's wake passing safely astern. The PBY Catalina then flew back along the bubble trail of the torpedo – and dropped a smoke bomb at the point where the track first appeared.

The destroyer *Phelps* (DD-360) then closed the marked position and obtained a sound contact. At 1939, *Phelps* dropped two depth charges – but then contact was lost.

The two destroyers *Farragut* (DD-348) and *Edwards* (DD-619) were detached from the screen to hunt down the submarine with sonar. They searched and carried out depth-charge attacks for some 10 hours before eventually forcing a Japanese submarine, likely *I-31*, to the surface.

Edwards opened fire with her main battery, damaging the submarine and forcing it to dive again.

The destroyer *Frazier* (DD-607) subsequently spotted *I-31*'s periscopes breaking the surface and opened fire, scoring hits on the periscopes. *Frazier* then locked onto *I-31* on sonar and made a depth-charge attack that brought air bubbles, debris and oil to the surface. *Frazier* then made two more attacks – sending *I-31* to the bottom in abyssal depths of more than 2,000m. Diesel oil rose up from far below, slowly spreading out inexorably to cover an area of about 5 square miles.

US troops met fierce opposition ashore on Attu – and faced Artic weather that caused many casualties from exposure. *Pennsylvania*'s guns were called into action on 14 May in support of infantry on the west side of Holtz Bay, with her own Kingfisher floatplanes spotting the fall of shot.

On 19 May 1943, *Pennsylvania* steamed to Adak Island, near the western end of the Aleutian Islands, to support an amphibious assault. During the passage there, a gasoline stowage compartment exploded, causing some structural damage but no casualties. Her guns had not been affected, but with Japanese troops being pushed back ashore to a pocket around Chichagof Harbor, and the battleships *New Mexico* and *Mississippi* joining the Fire Support Group on 22 May, the situation was deemed secure enough to allow *Pennsylvania* to depart on 21 May 1943 for repair and overhaul at Pearl Harbor.

After she had departed, some 600 surviving Japanese troops made a final banzai charge on 29 May 1943, which broke through the US front line. Soon rear echelon US troops found themselves fighting hand-to-hand with determined Japanese troops – who fought until almost the last man. The banzai charge effectively ended the fighting on Attu.

In 19 days of fighting, more than 500 US soldiers had been killed with more than 1,200 injured. The Japanese lost an estimated 2,350 men with only 28 prisoners being taken.

Pennsylvania reached Pearl Harbor on 31 May 1943 – where her repair and overhaul took until 15 June 1943 to complete. On 1 August 1943, *Pennsylvania* departed Pearl Harbor bound once again for the Aleutians for the invasion of Kiska, where she would again operate as flagship. She arrived off Kiska on 7 August 1943 and US troops went ashore unopposed on 15 August 1943 – to find that the island had been evacuated by the Japanese after the earlier Attu landings.

After patrolling off Adak, *Pennsylvania* was detached and sent back to Pearl Harbor, where she arrived on 1 September 1943.

(II) The Gilbert and Marshall Islands Campaign
Battle of Makin – Operation GALVANIC, 20–24 November 1943
(For a full account of the Gilbert Island landings, see Chapter 6, USS *Maryland*.)

The bulk of the Pacific Fleet, the Central Pacific Force, was deployed for the invasion of the Gilbert Islands, under the command of Vice Admiral Raymond Spruance, the immediate subordinate of Admiral Nimitz, CINCPAC-CINCPOA. It was the largest invasion force yet assembled and comprised some 17 aircraft carriers, 12 battleships (including the Pearl Harbor veterans *Pennsylvania*, *Maryland* and *Tennessee*), 8 heavy cruisers, 4 light cruisers, almost 70 destroyers and 36 transport ships. The actual landings of about 35,000 troops would be conducted by V Amphibious Force under Rear Admiral Richmond Kelly Turner who flew his flag aboard *Pennsylvania*.

Kelly Turner's Assault Force was divided into two attack forces: The Northern Attack Force (TF 52), under Turner's command from *Pennsylvania*, would capture Makin Atoll, the northmost of the Gilberts, which has a deep central lagoon suitable for large ships and would be an important harbour for advancing US forces. The Fire Support TG 52.2 was split into 3 fire-support units – and comprised *Pennsylvania*, the 3 New Mexico-class battleships *New Mexico*, *Mississippi* and *Idaho*, 4 heavy cruisers and 6 destroyers. TG 52.2 sailed for the Gilberts from Pearl Harbor on 10 November 1943, refuelling at sea en route. A Southern Attack Force (TF 53) would seize Tarawa and Apamama, the Fire Support TG 53.4 included the battleships *Tennessee*, *Colorado* and the flagship, *Maryland*.

TF 52 arrived off Makin Atoll in the early hours of D-Day, 20 November 1943. As the Fire Support Group warships prepared to commence a 3-hour pre-invasion bombardment, in the Transport Area, troop transport ships launched their tracked landing vehicles (LVTs) and untracked Higgins boats to proceed to the Rendezvous Area.

The Fire Support Group began the pre-invasion bombardment at first light, *Pennsylvania* opening fire with her 14in/45-cal. main-battery guns on Japanese positions on atoll islets at a range of 14,200yd, about 8 miles.

Under cover of the pre-invasion bombardment, US troops in amphibious landing vehicles landed smoothly on the ocean side of the island – the troops moving rapidly inland. However, due to a miscalculation of the lagoon's depth, the untracked landing craft approaching Yellow Beach on the lagoon side of the island ran aground on the reef. US troops had to walk the last 250yd to the beach over the reef in waist-deep water. Despite this difficulty, after two days of determined fighting, Makin was declared secure on the morning of 23 November 1943.

The invasion of the Gilbert Islands had caught the Japanese by surprise – and Admiral Mineichi Koga tasked four submarines to converge on the Gilberts to attack US shipping. The Japanese cruiser-submarine *I-175* arrived off Makin on 23 November 1943 (the day US forces declared Makin secure) and located a US carrier task group, 20 miles southwest of Makin. The carrier task group was arranged in a circular formation – with the three escort carriers *Liscome Bay* (CVE-56), *Corregidor* (CVE-58) and *Coral Sea* (CVE-57) in the middle, ringed by the battleships *Pennsylvania*, *New Mexico* and *Mississippi*, seven destroyers and the cruiser *Baltimore* (CA-68).

At first light the next morning, 24 November 1943, *I-175* successfully torpedoed the *Liscome Bay*, the torpedo detonating the carrier's bomb magazine and producing a catastrophic secondary explosion that rocked the ships around it and sent a mushroom cloud thousands of feet into the air. *Pennsylvania* was hit by the blast on her starboard bow, although no damage was done.

With Makin now secure, *Pennsylvania* departed six days later on 30 November for Pearl Harbor to replenish and regroup in advance of the next operation in the campaign, the simultaneous seizure of the two strategically important Marshall Islands atolls of Majuro and Kwajalein.

Battle of Kwajalein – Operation FLINTLOCK, 31 January–3 February 1944
(For a full account of the landings, see Chapter 6, USS *Maryland*.)

In late January 1944, the US 5th Fleet Amphibious Force commanded by Rear Admiral Richmond Kelly Turner sortied from Pearl towards Kwajalein Atoll, the troop transports once again carrying V Amphibious Corps, under the command of Major General Holland M. Smith. This would be the last fleet sortie in force from Hawaii – as on completion of the Marshall Islands campaign, Hawaii would be left far to the rear. The new forward base would be Majuro, which lay at the southeast of the Marshall Islands and had a large lagoon of some 114 square miles.

Pennsylvania was assigned, as at Makin two months earlier, with the three Standard-Type battleships *New Mexico*, *Mississippi* and *Idaho* to Fire Support TG 52.8 of the Southern Attack Force. TG 52.8 would support the landings on Kwajalein Island, the southernmost and largest island in the atoll. The Northern Attack Force, with *Tennessee*, *Maryland* and *Colorado* in their Fire Support Group, was tasked to assault the linked northern Kwajalein Atoll islands of Roi-Namur.

After shelling the Marshall Islands atoll of Maloelap en route on 29 January, the Southern Attack Force arrived 60 miles southwest of Kwajalein Atoll on 30 January 1944. Early the next day, 31 January 1944, the Fire Support Group closed Kwajalein Island and commenced the preparatory softening up bombardment in advance of the main D-Day landings the following day.

Kwajalein Island is only 2.5 miles long and 880yd wide – so with no possibility of defence in depth, the Japanese had no alternative but to endure the coming bombardment and prepare to counterattack US forces on the landing beaches. But until the Battle of Tarawa two months earlier in November 1943, the Japanese had not appreciated that tracked US amphibious vehicles (LVTs) could cross coral reefs and land on the lagoon side of an atoll. They had thus concentrated their strongest defences on the other side of Kwajalein, facing the open ocean.

As the naval bombardment began on 31 January, US troops seized small islands and islets on the east and west of the atoll, on which artillery could be established to support the main landings. US troops meanwhile were landing on Majuro Atoll, which was found to be only lightly defended and was seized in one day without any casualties.

1 February 1944
The simultaneous amphibious assault on the twin islands of Roi-Namur (to the north of Kwajalein Atoll) and Kwajalein Island at the south began at 0930. The pre-invasion air attacks and the heavy naval bombardment had wreaked havoc with the enemy on the landing beaches – such that resistance would be much weaker than in the Gilberts. Of some 3,000 Japanese troops garrisoned on Kwajalein, only about 300 were left alive to oppose the landings and US troops had reached halfway across the airfield runway on Kwajalein Island by sunset. The concentrated pre-invasion bombardment so effectively reduced US infantry casualties that it established the template for future assaults in the Pacific.

Pennsylvania remained offshore providing artillery support for the troops ashore as they fought to secure the island. Although the Japanese counterattacked every night, by the evening of 3 February, they had been defeated and *Pennsylvania* was able to enter the lagoon and drop anchor. The atoll was declared secured by the end of the fourth day.

With all opposition ended, *Pennsylvania* departed Kwajalein Atoll on 12 February, for the Marshall Islands, where she would provide fire support for Operation CATCHPOLE, the invasion of the three main islands of Eniwetok Atoll.

Battle of Eniwetok – Operation CATCHPOLE, 17–23 February 1944
Enewetak Atoll is a large almost circular coral atoll of some forty islands surrounding a deep lagoon that is roughly 50 miles in circumference and some 23 miles in diameter. Enewetak lies about 360nm northwest of Kwajalein Atoll – and approximately 190nm west of Bikini Atoll. (During the Second World War, the atoll was called Eniwetok, its name being changed to Enewetak in 1974.) The invasion of Eniwetok Atoll would provide Allied forces with a well-placed airfield and a large lagoon harbour that could support the forthcoming campaign to take the Mariana Islands, which lie more than 1,000 nautical miles to the westnorthwest, towards the Philippines.

Enewetak's forty narrow strips of coral have a total land area of just over 2 square miles, and none rise more than 5m above sea level. At the south of the large central lagoon, to the west of one of the larger islands of the atoll, Enewetak itself, is a wide entrance passage that is suitable for large ships to navigate. At the northern top of the circle of islands is the large island of Engebi, which Japan had possessed since 1914. In late 1942, Japan had constructed an airfield on Engebi, which was used for refuelling aircraft travelling between Truk (almost 800 miles to its southwest) and other islands to the east. A seaplane base was also established at Parry Island, in the southeast of the atoll.

On 11 February 1944, TF 58 carrier planes from *Saratoga*, *Princeton* and *Langley* began working over the Eniwetok Atoll islets – destroying most of the atoll's defences.

The main elements of Fire Support TG 51.17, *Pennsylvania*, *Tennessee* and *Colorado*, with cruisers and destroyers, departed Kwajalein on 15 February, arriving off Eniwetok Atoll early on 17 February 1944. The Fire Support Groups moved to their assigned bombardment stations for the first operation, the invasion of Engebi Island, which held the Japanese air strip. As the naval bombardment began, US troops landed that afternoon without opposition on several smaller islands situated close to Engebi, where artillery could be established for fire support.

The same day that the naval bombardment of Eniwetok began, 17 February 1944, the nine fast carriers of TF 58 began Operation HAILSTONE, the famous two-day air attack on the powerful Japanese advanced base of Truk, some 800 miles southwest in the Caroline Islands. TF 58 planes would sink more than forty Japanese ships and destroy hundreds of Japanese planes based there – ensuring that no Japanese aircraft interfered with the Eniwetok landings.

At dawn the following day, 18 February 1944, the naval bombardment of the atoll islands recommenced with the battleship *Colorado* and the cruiser *Louisville* targeting the north and east ends of Engebi as *Pennsylvania* and *Tennessee* fired at beach defences. Cruisers and destroyers targeted Japanese positions on atoll islands whilst the artillery emplaced on the smaller islands captured the day before also opened up.

At 0843, LVTs carrying the 22nd Marine Regiment landed on Engebi, meeting resistance that cost 85 US dead and missing – and more than 160 wounded. The airfield was however quickly captured, and naval gunfire ceased at 0925. By the time the island was declared secure, the Japanese had lost almost 1,300 dead with only 16 taken prisoner. Meanwhile, troops were simultaneously landing on Eniwetok Island, where they faced counterattacks until the fighting ended on the morning of 20 February.

On 22 February, *Pennsylvania* and *Tennessee*, along with the heavy cruisers *Indianapolis* and *Louisville* and destroyers supported US Marines as they landed on the smaller Parry Island, the last of the three island targets in the atoll.

The US 110th Naval Construction Battalion arrived between 21 and 27 February and began constructing a bomber airfield and the first US aircraft landed on the new strip on 11 March 1944. The first operational bombing mission had taken place by 5 April 1944. Eniwetok lagoon would become a major forward anchorage and base for future operations – and during the first half of 1944, almost 500 ships thronged the lagoon waters daily.

Now that the Gilberts and Marshalls had been taken, the Allies had secured valuable safe fleet anchorages and were able to construct strategic naval bases and airfields for land-based air to target the Mariana Islands to the west. The new forward base at Majuro in the Marshalls, some 2,000 miles west of Pearl Harbor, was of the utmost importance – as well as the airfield on Kwajalein, which was suitable for long-range bombers.

With Eniwetok Atoll now secure, *Pennsylvania* departed southeast on 1 March, to replenish at Majuro. From Majuro, *Pennsylvania* headed south to the New Hebrides where she remained until 24 April, when she set off for a short passage to Sydney, Australia from 29 April–11 May 1944.

(III) The Mariana and Palau Islands Campaign – Operation FORAGER

After returning from Australia, and after participating in amphibious assault exercises in the Solomon Islands, *Pennsylvania* moved north to stage with the 5th Fleet at Kwajalein Atoll for Operation FORAGER, the Mariana and Palau Islands campaign. The Japanese still held the Philippines, the Caroline Islands, the Palau Islands and the Mariana Islands – but if the Allies could seize the Palaus and the Marianas, they would have airfields from which the new US ultra-long-range Boeing B-29 Superfortress heavy bomber could be deployed directly against the Japanese home islands. Operation FORAGER would begin in June 1944 when the large island of Saipan would be assaulted, followed by Guam and then smaller Tinian, just south of Saipan.

Pennsylvania was assigned to the Northern Attack Force for the Saipan assault – forming up again with *Idaho* and *New Mexico* as the core of Fire Support Group 2 of TG 52.10. The Pearl Harbor veterans *Tennessee, California* and *Maryland*, together with *Colorado*, formed the core of Fire Support Group 1.

The Fire Support Group ships departed Kwajalein for the Marianas on 8 June 1944, reaching Eniwetok the next day. As the fleet pressed on towards the Marianas, on the night of 10 June, one of the escort destroyers reported a sonar contact that could possibly be a Japanese submarine. As the ships took evasive manoeuvres in the darkness, *Pennsylvania* collided with the fast troop transport destroyer *Talbot* (DD-114). Although the large armoured battleship *Pennsylvania* incurred only minor damage and was able to continue with the fleet, several compartments on the much smaller *Talbot* were flooded and she had to return to Eniwetok for emergency repairs.

Vice Admiral Ching Lee's seven TG 58.7 fast battleships, which normally operated as a screen for the fast carrier TF 58, began the naval bombardment of Saipan and Tinian on 13 June 1944 – whilst the Northern Attack Force invasion force and Fire Support Groups were still en route. The 16in guns of the fast battleships opened up from 10,000yd (more than 5 miles), staying well offshore to avoid near shore minefields as they fired some 2,400 16in shells.

The two main landing Fire Support Groups, under the command of Rear Admiral Jesse B. Oldendorf, arrived the following day, 14 June. His 7 older Standard-Type battleships, along with 6 heavy cruisers, 5 light cruisers and 26 destroyers, then began their naval bombardment, which continued throughout the landings on 15 June with devastating accuracy. The OBB gunners had trained with Marine Corps fire-control experts at the shore bombardment range at Kahoolawe, southwest of Maui in Hawaii, and had more experience and expertise in shore bombardment than Lee's fast battleships, which were more suited to naval engagements. In all, over the course of the pre-invasion bombardment, the combined fourteen battleships, along with cruisers and destroyers fired some 165,000 shells as they destroyed land targets, conducted counter-battery missions, eliminated AA gun emplacements and burnt all cane fields that would offer the enemy cover.

Battle of Saipan, 15 June–9 July 1944
(For a full account of the Battle of Saipan, see Chapter 5, USS *California*.)

D-Day Saipan was 15 June 1944 – and as more than 300 assault LVTs landed some 8,000 Marines on the west coast of Saipan, *Pennsylvania* continued shelling shore positions as TG 52.10 cruised northeast of the smaller island of Tinian, south of Saipan.

With US Marines successfully ashore on Saipan, whilst TG 52.17 *Tennessee, California, Maryland* and *Colorado* continued to shell Saipan, TG 52.10 *Pennsylvania, Idaho* and *New Mexico* moved about 100 miles south towards the next objective – the large island of Guam.

The next day, 16 June 1944, *Pennsylvania* and the other units of TG 52.10 began shelling Japanese positions at Orote Point, Guam – before returning to Saipan and anchoring up at Garapan Harbor on 22 June. *Pennsylvania* was detached from TG 52.10 on 25 June to head for Eniwetok with the fast carriers of TF 58 where she would replenish as the Fire Support Groups were reorganised ahead of the next target for Operation FORAGER – Guam.

Battle of Guam – Operation STEVEDORE, 21 July–10 August 1944
(For a full account of the Battle of Guam, see Chapter 5, USS *California*.)

At Eniwetok, *Pennsylvania* was assigned to TG 53.5, the Fire Support Group commanded by Rear Admiral Jesse B. Oldendorf and comprising the battleships *Tennessee, California, Colorado, Idaho* and *New Mexico*, along with 6 heavy cruisers, 3 light cruisers and 21 destroyers.

With D-Day Guam slated for 21 July 1944, TG 53.5 departed Eniwetok on 8 July 1944, the same day that TG 53.18 heavy cruisers, light cruisers and destroyers arrived off Guam and began shelling enemy positions. The two escort carriers *Corregidor* (CVE-58) and *Coral Sea* (CVE-57) would arrive off Guam the following day to provide Combat Air Patrol and close support once troops began landing.

The Fire Support TG 53.5 arrived off Guam on 12 July and began shelling enemy positions ashore. After two days of the bombardment, *Pennsylvania* was detached on 14 July to Saipan to replenish her ammunition. She was back on station off Guam three days later – suppressing Japanese guns that were firing on UDT swimmers operating off the landing beaches as they cleared underwater obstacles and beach

USS *Pennsylvania* fires her 14in/45-cal. and 5in/38-cal. guns whilst bombarding Guam, south of the Orote peninsula, on the first day of the landings, 21 July 1944. (*NH 67584 courtesy of US Naval History & Heritage Command*)

approaches. On the morning of D-Day Guam, 21 July 1944, *Pennsylvania* took up her bombardment position off Orote Point for the assault to begin.

Pennsylvania would continue to operate off Guam for the next two weeks, providing fire support for troops ashore, before departing the Marianas on 3 August to replenish at Eniwetok –where she arrived on 19 August 1944.

Battle of Peleliu – Operation STALEMATE II, 15 September–27 November 1944
(For a full account of the Battle of Peleliu, see Chapter 6, USS *Maryland*.)

Pennsylvania departed Eniwetok on 6 September 1944 as part of TG 32.5, the Palau Bombardment & Fire Support Group of the Western Attack Force destined for the invasion of the islands of Peleliu and Angaur in the Palauan archipelago.

On 12 September, the three-day long pre-invasion naval bombardment of the tiny island of Peleliu began as the battleships *Pennsylvania, Maryland, Mississippi, Tennessee* and *Idaho* and the heavy cruisers *Columbus, Indianapolis, Louisville, Minneapolis* and *Portland*, along with light cruisers and destroyers, opened up on the 5 square mile island. As the bombardment began, minesweepers were clearing the approaches whilst underwater demolition teams reconnoitred and cleared the invasion beaches of submerged obstacles.

On D-Day Peleliu, 15 September 1944, the Fire Support Groups continued the shore bombardment as the landing craft approached the beaches. But the estimated 11,000 Japanese troops on Peleliu had adopted a new defence-in-depth tactic and would fight from heavily fortified cave defences in hills inland, from where they would offer stiff resistance for the next two months.

Rather than enduring close fighting in the cave systems with likely high casualties, US troops eventually used bulldozers and explosives to seal up the entrances to the caves, trapping the defenders inside. Today there are an estimated 2,900 Japanese troops still missing on Peleliu, most still sealed up in booby-trapped cave systems.

On D-Day Angaur, 17 September 1944, *Pennsylvania* shelled the small 3-mile-long island as US troops landed. *Pennsylvania* then remained offshore Angaur for three days as the Japanese defenders were driven back to defensive cave systems dug into a hill on the northwest coast called 'the Bowl' – where they intended to make a last stand.

Pennsylvania departed Palauan waters on 20 September 1944, steaming southeast for Seeadler Harbor, at Manus in the Admiralty Islands, which had been secured six months earlier in March 1944. Seeadler Harbor was now a floating base – with tenders, repair ships, concrete barges and floating dry docks large enough to accommodate a battleship.

After a week at sea, *Pennsylvania* arrived at Seeadler Harbor on 28 September – and entered a large floating dry dock on 1 October 1944 for repair and maintenance.

(IV) The Philippines Campaign
Battle of Leyte Gulf – Operation KING II, 23–26 October 1944
(For a full description of the build-up to the Battle of Leyte Gulf, see Chapter 5, USS *California*.)

Following completion of her repairs at Seeadler Harbor, *Pennsylvania* was undocked and formed up along with *Tennessee, California, West Virginia, Maryland, Mississippi* and attendant cruisers and destroyers, as the Fire Support TG 77.2 of the Central Philippines Attack Force for Operation KING II. Under the overall command of Vice Admiral Thomas C. Kinkaid, the Fire Support Group would support the amphibious landings slated for A-Day, 20 October 1944 at Leyte Gulf, at the south of Leyte, one of the larger islands in the Central Philippines.

The slow-moving invasion ships began departing Manus on 10 October, whilst the Fire Support Group, commanded by Rear Admiral Jesse B. Oldendorf, departed two days later on 12 October 1944, arriving off Dinagat Island on the south side of Leyte Gulf on D-Day Dinagat, 17 October 1944. When the 6th Ranger Battalion of the US 6th Army landed on Dinagat, the US flag flew again on Philippine soil for the first time since the Japanese invasion in 1941.

The next day, 18 October 1944, with Dinagat secure, the Fire Support Group warships entered Leyte Gulf and took up their bombardment

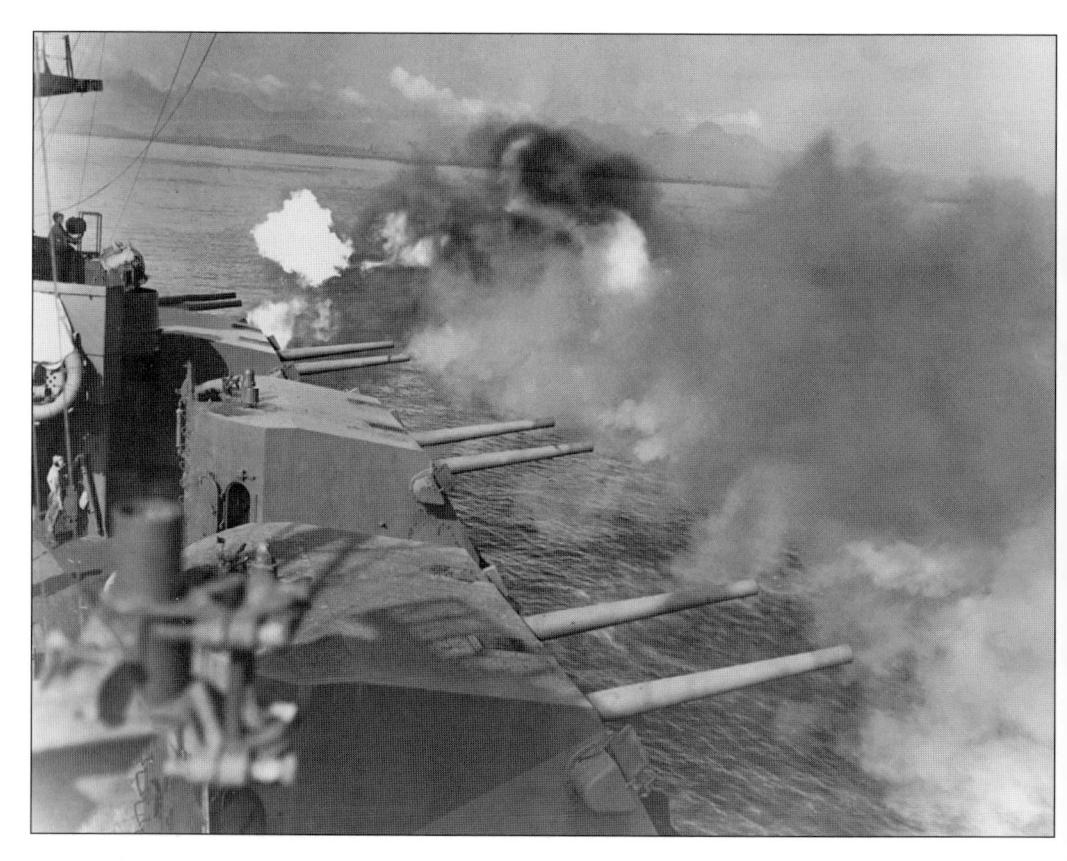

The 5in/38-cal. battery of USS *Pennsylvania* bombarding Leyte, 20 October 1944. (*80-G-288468 courtesy of US Naval History & Heritage Command*)

positions. Over the course of the next days, they covered Underwater Demolition Teams of swimmers, carrying out beach reconnaissance operations, and minesweepers clearing the approaches to the landing areas. At 0645 on 19 October, the bombardment ships shelled the area around the city of Tacloban, at the north end of Leyte Gulf, before withdrawing for the night.

On A-Day, 20 October 1944, the Fire Support Group ships resumed firing at 0600, targeting the landing beaches. After 3½ hours, as US 6th Army troops began their approaches to the beaches in their amphibious transports, the Fire Support Group ships fired at positions ahead of their advance. The landings triggered Japanese command to initiate their pre-planned response Operation *Shō-Gō* 1, which saw a number of Japanese naval forces converging to strike at Allied shipping and the troops ashore in Leyte Gulf.

The 14in/45-cal. main-battery guns of USS *Pennsylvania* firing on Leyte, 20 October 1944. (*80-G-288473 courtesy of US Naval History & Heritage Command*)

PEARL HARBOR'S REVENGE

Battle of Surigao Strait, 25 October 1944
On 24 October 1944, following reports of Japanese naval forces approaching Leyte Gulf, when Vice Admiral Kinkaid instructed Rear Admiral Oldendorf to prepare for a night action in the Surigao Strait, Oldendorf deployed his Battleship Force in a battle line across the easternmost exit of the Surigao Strait, the channel between the two islands of Leyte and Mindanao that could allow a Japanese naval force to approach the Allied landing areas in Leyte Gulf from the west.

Pennsylvania formed up in the battle line across the strait with the OBBS *California, Tennessee, Mississippi, Maryland* and *West Virginia*. Oldendorf split his cruisers into a Left Flank Force and a Right Flank Force and arranged the destroyers of DesRon 24, DesRon 54 and DesRon 56 in forward attacking positions. He sent the thirty-nine PT Boats of his Patrol Craft Force down the strait to seek out the enemy.

After crossing the Sulu and Mindanao Seas, the powerful Japanese Southern Force, comprising the two battleships *Fusō* and *Yamashiro*, the heavy cruiser *Mogami* and escort destroyers, was attempting to pass through the Surigao Strait and hit Leyte Gulf from the south. Up north, another Japanese battleship force was making for the San Bernardino Strait, intent on targeting the Allied forces at Leyte Gulf from the north.

As the Japanese Southern Force entered the strait during the night of 24/25 October, the Japanese ships ran into Oldendorf's carefully positioned Battle Line. In the last clash of battleship against battleship in naval history, the Japanese force was decimated, with both battleships being sunk.

During the clash, the older Mark 3 radar on *Pennsylvania* was not as effective as the state-of-the-art radar on the modernised battleships *Tennessee, California* and *West Virginia*. *Pennsylvania* was unable to locate a target and to the dismay of her crew, did not fire her main-battery 14in guns.

Pennsylvania remained on station off Leyte until 25 November 1944, when she headed back to Manus for replenishment in advance of the next operation in the Central Philippines campaign, Operation MIKE I, the invasion on 9 January 1945 of Lingayen Gulf on the northwestern side of Luzon Island, the largest and northmost island of the Philippine archipelago. On 15 December 1944, *Pennsylvania* headed northwest towards the Kossol Roads at the north of the Palauan archipelago, which had just been secured in November after many months of intense fighting.

USS *PENNSYLVANIA* (BB-38)

The Invasion of Lingayen Gulf – Operation MIKE I, 3–13 January 1945
(For a full description of the invasion of Lingayen Gulf, see Chapter 5, USS *California*.)

On 1 January 1945, *Pennsylvania* rejoined Vice Admiral Jesse B. Oldendorf's TG 77.2 Bombardment and Fire Support Group, which was deploying to western Luzon for the invasion of Lingayen Gulf. If the 34-mile-long and 22-mile-wide Lingayen Gulf could be secured, then landing troops would have a 100-mile overland route south to approach Luzon's capital city of Manila. En route to west Luzon through the Philippines, the Allied invasion ships faced repeated kamikaze attack.

On 6 January 1945, the Fire Support warships arrived before dawn off the wide entrance to Lingayen Gulf – the minesweepers entered the gulf first, followed by the bombardment ships. After sunrise, the naval bombardment began – with *Pennsylvania* shelling enemy positions on Santiago Island, at the northwest tip of the entrance to the gulf. The naval bombardment triggered strong kamikaze attacks throughout the day, which disabled *California* and damaged *New Mexico* and many other ships.

The next day, 7 January, the bombardment and fire-support ships re-entered the gulf and recommenced shelling positions ashore. By the afternoon, six UDT teams were in operation as *Pennsylvania* suppressed Japanese guns whilst minesweepers cleared the area. The bombardment of the landing beaches continued throughout 8 January under sustained kamikaze attack.

On 9 January 1945, S-Day Lingayen Gulf, the invasion of Luzon began as more than seventy Allied warships entered the gulf and began a sustained pre-invasion bombardment of Japanese shore positions at 0700, triggering yet more kamikaze attacks. But unknown to the Allies, following on from their bitter experiences in earlier pre-invasion beach bombardments, the Japanese would not defend at the beaches but instead would fight inland in hill positions. As a result, some 68,000 US troops were successfully landed, meeting little opposition. Over the next few days more than 200,000 troops were landed and had soon established a 20-mile-wide beachhead that was 5 miles deep.

Although the landings had been successful, US and Australian naval forces suffered heavy losses to kamikazes and attack by 30-knot *Shin'yō* suicide boats carrying 600lb of explosives. Japanese aircraft attacked the invasion fleet on 10 January, and although four bombs landed close to *Pennsylvania*, she was undamaged. Later that day, a fire-control party ashore directed *Pennsylvania* to shell a group of Japanese tanks that were massing to launch a counterattack on the beachhead.

After S-Day, *Pennsylvania* began patrolling the approaches to Lingayen Gulf, outside the gulf, from 10–17 January. Four weeks later, *Pennsylvania, Mississippi* and *West Virginia* were disjoined from the Fire Support Task Group and departed Lingayen on 10 February 1945 for replenishment at Manus – before setting out on 22 February, homeward bound to San Francisco, with stops in the Marshall Islands and at Pearl Harbor.

After arriving at San Francisco on 13 March 1945, *Pennsylvania* underwent a thorough overhaul that would last until July 1945. Her worn-out main-battery and secondary guns, which had seen much action, were replaced. Having had some of the oldest radar of the six old battleships at the Battle of Surigao Strait, and consequently being unable to find a target and open fire, *Pennsylvania* now received more modern radar with a Mark 34 main-battery director being installed on the aft superstructure, which was equipped with the modern Mark 8 fire-control radar. Faced with the continued threat of intense kamikaze attack, her AA suite was beefed up to 27 single and 22 twin 20mm Oerlikon guns to give a total of 71. An additional twin 40mm Bofors mount was installed on top of Turret 2 forward – to give a total of 42 Bofors 40mm.

When the work was completed, *Pennsylvania* departed San Francisco on 12 July 1945 – arriving at Pearl Harbor on 18 July 1945. She departed Pearl Harbor a week later on 24 July 1945 to join the invasion fleet off Okinawa, which had been secured the month before.

(V) Task Force 95 – the 2nd East China Sea Antishipping Sweep

As the refitted *Pennsylvania* headed west across the Pacific to join the fleet off Okinawa, she paused on 1 August 1945 to bombard the long by-passed Japanese garrison on Wake Island. Japanese coastal defence guns opened counter-battery fire and during the artillery exchange, a Japanese shell disabled one of *Pennsylvania*'s fire-control directors for her secondary battery 5in guns.

Pennsylvania stopped over at Saipan in the Marianas to load ammunition before continuing on to Okinawa, where she arrived on 12 August 1945 to become flagship of TF 95 for the 2nd East China Sea Antishipping Sweep. TF 95 comprised the battleships *Tennessee, California, Nevada, Arkansas* and *Texas* with cruisers, destroyers and destroyer escorts, under the command of Vice Admiral Jesse B. Oldendorf.

That night, whilst moored next to *Tennessee* in Buckner Bay on the south coast of Okinawa Island, a Japanese torpedo bomber

USS *PENNSYLVANIA* (BB-38)

managed to penetrate the Allied defensive screen undetected and hit *Pennsylvania* with an aerial torpedo. The torpedo hit near the stern, opening a 30ft hole in her hull and damaging three of her four shafts. The old battleship took on a considerable amount of water, which began to search its way through the ship. As compartments slowly flooded, *Pennsylvania* began to settle by the stern.

Although damage-control teams were able to contain the flooding, twenty men had been killed in the explosion and another ten injured, including Oldendorf himself, who suffered several broken ribs. The war was however, unknown to most, approaching its nuclear finale – and *Pennsylvania* would be the last major US warship to be damaged.

USS *Pennsylvania*, low in the water and under salvage, after being torpedoed in Buckner Bay, Okinawa on 12 August 1945. Hoses run through her 14in/45-cal. guns to help bring water from below decks. (*80-G-490327 courtesy of US Naval History & Heritage Command*)

The following day, 13 August 1945, temporary repairs began – but as these were being carried out, the surrender of Japan was announced by Emperor Hirohito on 15 August. On 18 August 1945, *Pennsylvania* was taken under tow by a pair of tugs for Guam, the tow arriving on 6 September 1945, four days after Japan's formal surrender on 2 September 1945.

At Guam, *Pennsylvania* entered a floating dry dock where a large steel patch was welded over the torpedo hole, which would allow the ship to make the long voyage back to the West Coast of the USA for repair.

Pennsylvania was undocked on 2 October 1945 and two days later, she departed Guam escorted by a light cruiser and destroyer, northeastbound for Puget Sound, where permanent repairs would be carried out.

En route to the West Coast of the USA, on 17 October, the number 3 propeller shaft slipped aft and divers had to be sent down to cut the shaft loose, leaving *Pennsylvania* now with just one operational propeller. The great battleship continued her voyage, arriving at Puget Sound on 24 October 1945.

(VI) The 1946 Bikini Atoll Atomic Tests – Operation CROSSROADS
On 16 January 1946, *Pennsylvania* was allocated to the target fleet for the Operation CROSSROADS nuclear tests at Bikini Atoll – the old battlewagon would thus only be repaired sufficient to allow her to make the voyage to Bikini.

Pennsylvania departed Puget Sound on 24 February 1946 – and after stopping at Pearl Harbor en route, she arrived at Bikini Atoll on 31 May 1946 where she was anchored in her test position, along with another eighty-three warships. *Nevada* was the target ship for the first Test ABLE air burst on 1 July 1946 — both tough old battleships survived.

The second Test BAKER took place on 25 July 1946 and was an underwater detonation. *Pennsylvania* was moored some 1,100yd from surface zero and although she was only lightly damaged by the actual blast, the huge surge of water thrown up by the blast caused heavy radioactive contamination.

On 21 August 1946, *Pennsylvania* was taken in tow for Kwajalein Atoll in the Marshall Islands. There she was decommissioned on 19 August 1946 and then carefully studied over the next eighteen months to understand the effects of a nuclear blast on a capital ship.

On 10 February 1948, the grand old battleship was scuttled in deep water off Kwajalein Atoll. Listing to starboard, she settled slowly by the stern, before finally disappearing beneath the waves.

Chapter 9

USS *Tennessee* (BB-43)

USS *Tennessee* (BB-43) in her early configuration. (*NH 2227 courtesy of US Naval History & Heritage Command*)

Specifications (as built): Tennessee class
Builder: New York Naval Shipyard
Launched: 30 April 1919
Commissioned: 3 June 1920
Decommissioned: 14 February 1947
Displacement: 32,300 tons (S). 33,190 tons (F)
Length: 624ft (oa)
 600ft (wl)
Beam: 97ft 5.75in
Draft: 30ft 2in
Speed: 21 knots
Endurance: 8,000nm at 10 knots

Armament:
  Main Battery: 12 x 14in/50-cal. (in 4 x 3-gun turrets)
  Secondary Battery: 14 x single 5in/51-cal. casemate guns
  AA Battery: 4 x single 3in/50-cal.
  Torpedo Tubes: 2 x 21in submerged torpedo tubes

Armour:
  Belt: 13.5in tapering to 8in at lower edge
  Barbettes: 13in max.
  Turrets: Face: 18in. Sides: 10in. Roof: 5in
  Decks: Main armoured deck: 3.5in in 2 layers. 6in aft over steering in 2 layers
 Lower splinter deck: 1.5–2in
  Conning tower: 16in

Sister ships in class: USS *California* (BB-44)
Fate: Broken up for scrap in 1959

(For a full discussion of the Tennessee-class units, their specifications, design, all-or-nothing armour, armament and turbo-electric propulsion systems see Chapter 5, USS *California*.)

USS *Tennessee* (BB-43) was the lead ship of the two Tennessee-class battleships authorised on 3 March 1915. Her sister was USS *California* (BB-44). The two Tennessee-class battleships were mostly design copies of the preceding New Mexico-class battleships.

The Tennessees carried twelve of the newer 14in/50-cal. guns, introduced with the New Mexico-class units, set in two pairs of superfiring three-gun turrets, one pair forward of the bridge superstructure and one pair abaft. The Tennessee class would be the last US battleships to use the 14in gun, the succeeding Colorado class would employ the 16in gun.

Equipped with all-or-nothing armour, the primary differences to the preceding New Mexico class were enlarged bridges, greater elevation for the main-battery weapons and relocation of the secondary battery to the upper deck. The Tennessees had a noticeably raked stem – in preference to the plumb stem of the early First World War-era dreadnoughts.

Tennessee was laid down on 14 May 1917 at the New York Naval Shipyard in Brooklyn, New York City but the First World War was already over by the time her hull was launched for fitting out on 30 April 1919. She was commissioned on 3 June 1920.

In 1922, the AA suite was increased to eight 3in/50-cal. guns and in 1928 a crane and an aircraft catapult was fitted to her fantail to take reconnaissance floatplanes.

During 1929–30, the eight 3in/50-cal. AA battery weapons were replaced by eight 5in/25-cal. heavy AA guns. In the 1930s eight .50-cal. M2 Browning machine guns were fitted, two on the forward foretop, with two more adjacent – and four on the aft foretop. The two outdated submerged beam torpedo tubes were removed in 1934.

In December 1940, four 3in/50-cal. guns were added in tubs, one either side of the forward superstructure and one either side abreast the cranes aft.

PEARL HARBOR, 7 DECEMBER 1941

As the first-wave Japanese planes swooped over Pearl Harbor just before 0800, *Tennessee* was moored in about 40ft of water with her starboard side to interrupted quay Fox 6 off Ford Island, alongside and inboard of *West Virginia*. *Arizona* was moored to quay Fox 7 immediately astern, with the repair ship *Vestal* outboard. In front of *Tennessee* was *Maryland*, with *Oklahoma* tied up outboard of her.

As the attack began, General Quarters was sounded, and the AA guns were manned within a few minutes, gunners opening up with the 5in/25-cal. and 3in/50-cal. weapons and .50 machine guns about 5 minutes after the first attack.

Tennessee received orders to get underway – but it would take until 0930 to get steam up in her boilers, by when she had been hemmed in and trapped as the other battleships around her received crippling damage. *West Virginia*, outboard of her, was torpedoed and began to list heavily – whilst forward of *Tennessee*, *Oklahoma*, in the outboard position to *Maryland*, had been hit by at least five torpedoes and listing rapidly, would capsize within 10–15 minutes.

Japanese dive and level bombers arrived overhead, and A6M Zero fighters strafed the *Tennessee*'s AA batteries to suppress fire – as astern of her the *Arizona* blew up catastrophically at 0806. The explosion on *Arizona* showered burning oil over *Tennessee*'s stern, and she was quickly surrounded by fire, which was augmented by oil leaking from *West Virginia*.

Japanese bombers hit the trapped *Tennessee* twice with the same large-calibre adapted naval AP shell with welded tail fins on it as had just destroyed the *Arizona*.

But neither of the two AP bombs that hit *Tennessee* detonated properly. One bomb hit the starboard yard of the mainmast, smashing the catapult atop the aft superfiring Turret 3 before partially penetrating the 5in-thick roof armour of the turret and breaking apart without detonating. The training gear and rammers of the left gun were knocked out of commission by the fragmenting bomb, the rangefinder was wrecked and a small fire was started.

A fragment of a second bomb penetrated the face of the three-gun forward superfiring Turret 2 – and split the hoop of the centre gun, disabling the gun. Lethal splinters were flung around by the bomb's impact on the turret roof and a shard of shrapnel struck and killed the captain of *West Virginia*, Mervyn S. Bennion, who had walked out to the open bridge of his own ship alongside. *Tennessee*'s AA gunners were credited with shooting down or assisting in the destruction of five Japanese aircraft.

Although a number of casualties were taken, neither bomb had inflicted serious damage to the ship itself – the worst damage was by fire. Burning debris from the devastated *Arizona* started fires on *Tennessee*'s wooden deck abaft Turret 4, whilst burning oil on the water cracked and warped hull plating on both port and starboard sides of *Tennessee*'s hull as far back as Turret 3. The red-hot hull prompted her crew to flood three magazines lest they ignite.[1]

By 1030 the crew had suppressed the fires aboard the ship, and it was decided to try and move the ship forward to escape the badly burning *Arizona*. Both engines went ahead at 5 knots, but the ship did not move. *Tennessee* was trapped in her berth, starboard side towards Ford Island, by *West Virginia*, which had listed to port after being torpedoed. *West*

Virginia's hull had risen up against the bottom edge of *Tennessee*'s armour belt – possibly stopping *West Virginia* from rolling further whilst counterflooding reduced her dramatic list. When counterflooding had settled *West Virginia* back down to starboard, she had pinned *Tennessee*, inboard of her, against the top of the forward concrete mooring quay.

In an effort to push the burning oil away from the ship, her screws were slowly turned at a speed of about 5–10 knots throughout the day and into the night – but oil would continue to burn in the water around the ship for another two days. *Tennessee* had reported three dead and twenty injured during the attack.

Other than the two bomb hits and fire damage, *Tennessee* came out of the attack largely undamaged. Once the fires had been extinguished, *Tennessee* was ready for action – except that she could not move. Forward of her, the lightly damaged *Maryland* – with the capsized *Oklahoma* outboard of her – initially blocked any means of extricating *Tennessee*. *Tennessee*'s high catapult and after airplane crane were out of commission – but she had no underwater damage. All bar one of the forward main battery of six 14in guns were still able to fire, whilst five of the six after turret 14in guns were also able to fire, if any Japanese ships appeared on the horizon. The AA battery was largely unaffected and ready for action. Officers aboard *Tennessee* were soon looking to her slowly sinking sister ship *California* for replacement parts for the two inoperable main-battery guns.

Maryland was pulled clear three days later at noon on 10 December and taken to the Navy Yard – opening the way to now get *Tennessee* out of her berth. But to move *Tennessee*, either the *West Virginia* on her port side would have to be pulled outboard – or the interrupted concrete mooring quay she was pinned against on her starboard side would have to be removed. *West Virginia* had however taken several torpedo hits and had flooded – settling on the bottom of the harbour with her decks awash. She could not be moved quickly – so removal of the concrete quay was the most practical way to get her out.

Removal of the quay was completed on 16 December, when *Tennessee* was pulled slowly forward past *West Virginia* and through *Maryland*'s now vacant berth – passing alongside inboard of the capsized *Oklahoma*. She then was moved across to the Navy Yard for repair.

The heat from the fierce fires had warped some of her hull plates, damaging seams and loosening rivets, all of which needed to be repaired before she could get underway for permanent repairs at Puget Sound on the West Coast. The hull would be made fully watertight again and the damaged roof of the after superfiring Turret 3 would receive a patch cover.

USS *Tennessee* at left, alongside the sunken USS *West Virginia*, photographed from the capsized hull of USS *Oklahoma* on 10 December 1941, three days after the raid. (*NH 50770 courtesy of US Naval History & Heritage Command*)

The US Battle Force may have been crippled by the *Kidō Butai* attack, but within a week, by 16 December 1941, the main-battery guns and AA weaponry of the lightly damaged *Tennessee*, *Pennsylvania* and *Maryland* were now all nearly ready for action.

(a) Repair and Modernisation of AA Suite, 29 December 1941–Late February 1942

On 20 December 1941, just two weeks after the surprise attack, and with temporary repairs made and Turret 3 patched, *Tennessee* departed Pearl Harbor Naval Base, along with *Maryland*, *Pennsylvania* and an escort of four destroyers. As the flotilla neared the West Coast, *Pennsylvania* detached for Mare Island, north of San Francisco whilst

Tennessee and *Maryland* headed for Puget Sound Naval Yard, arriving there on 29 December 1941. *Tennessee* would have minimum urgent repairs carried out to allow her to get her back into service as quickly as possible. Hull plates and wiring damaged by fire would be replaced and the cage mainmast was removed to increase the field of fire for her AA suite. In its place went a small tower, the top of which now carried her after fire controls.

Tennessee's AA suite was beefed up with sixteen 1.1in/75-cal. guns set in four quadruple mounts (the famous Chicago Piano) replacing the older less effective 3in/50-cal. mounts and the .50-cal. machine guns. Fourteen single Oerlikon 20mm autocannons were added.

New Mark 11 versions of her 14in/50-cal. guns replaced the original old Mark 4 14in/50-cal. barrels, correcting dispersion problems. SC and FC radars were fitted forward but nothing aft. Two Mk 33 directors controlled the main battery whilst Mark 37 directors controlled the secondary battery.

In late February 1942, with her repairs and modernisation of her AA battery completed, *Tennessee* rejoined the Pacific Fleet and began operating with TF 1, commanded by Rear Admiral William S. Pye, to shield the West Coast of the USA. In June 1942, two more quad 1.1in/75-cal. Chicago Piano mounts were added aft on the quarter deck.

In August 1942, *Tennessee* escorted the carrier *Hornet* (CV-8) to Pearl Harbor on her way to the Guadalcanal campaign. The oil-burning old battleships themselves were not deployed to the South Pacific due to losses of US fleet oilers, the remaining seven fleet oilers in the South Pacific were now too few to support the fast carriers *and* a fleet of old oil-burning dreadnoughts. As *Hornet* disappeared over the horizon towards distant Guadalcanal, with the situation in the Pacific now under control following Japan's crushing defeat at the Battle of Midway, *Tennessee* was detached for Puget Sound for reconstruction and modernisation.

(b) Reconstruction and Modernisation, September 1942–47 May 1943

The planned reconstruction and modernisation work to *Tennessee* would last until May 1943 and would mirror the work carried out on her sister *California*, which began her own reconstruction in October 1942. New anti-torpedo bulges were fitted to each beam, increasing the ship's beam from 97ft to 114ft, and making her too wide to transit the Panama Canal. Internal compartmentalisation was improved, increasing her survivability against underwater strikes by mine or torpedo. The old

PEARL HARBOR'S REVENGE

First World War-era heavily armoured conning tower was removed and a smaller tower from a recently rebuilt cruiser was installed in its place that would reduce obstruction to the fields of fire of the AA battery.

The cage foremast was removed and replaced with a tower that housed the bridge and main-battery director. One of her two smokestacks was removed with those boilers being trunked into an enlarged forward smokestack.

Horizontal protection was improved to give added protection against plunging fire and bombing with an additional 3in of STS armour being added over the magazines and 2in elsewhere.

USS *Tennessee* underway in Puget Sound after reconstruction, seen from astern, 12 May 1943. No. 4 14in main-battery turret is swung to starboard. Both cage masts have been removed and a new superstructure added with an enlarged single smokestack in place of the two previous stacks. The original secondary 5in battery has been removed and replaced by sixteen 5in/38-cal. DP guns in eight dual mounts, four on either beam abreast the superstructure. (*19-N-45072 courtesy of US Naval History & Heritage Command*)

The battleship's suite of weapons was also overhauled and modernised. The mixed secondary battery of 5in/51-cal. and 5in/25-cal. guns was replaced by a new battery of sixteen 5in/38-cal. DP guns in eight twin mounts controlled by four Mk 37 directors, equipped with the Mark 4 radar, which had a range out to 30,000yd (17 miles). The Mk 37 director gave the same gun orders as the earlier Mark 33, but with greater reliability and improved performance whether the 5in gun batteries were being used for surface or AA duties.

New air-search and fire-control radars for her main 14in battery and the secondary battery were fitted. *Tennessee* now carried the latest state-of-the-art visible horizon short wavelength Surface Search SG radar on her foremast that could detect ships out to 22 miles. It was the first radar to incorporate Plan Position Indicator, the display common with radar today with a number of range circles surrounding the ship in the centre. A longwave SC-2 radar installed on the mainmast searched for planes and surface vessels and had a visible horizon range out to 20nm.

The Mark 34 main-battery directors were fitted with new Mark 8 fire-control radars, which gave accurate range and bearing to targets out to 35,000–45,000yd (approximately 20–25 miles). The Mark 8 would have its combat debut at the Battle of the Surigao Strait in October 1944, where the three battleships equipped with it, *West Virginia*, *Tennessee* and *California*, would be the first to acquire targets.

The AA battery was improved with the addition of forty powerful 40mm Bofors autocannon in ten quad mounts and an increase to forty-three rapid-fire Oerlikons.

After sea trials, the reconstructed battleship *Tennessee* departed Puget Sound on 22 May 1943 to rejoin the Pacific Fleet at San Pedro.

BATTLESHIP REVENGE

(I) The Aleutian Islands Campaign, 11 May–15 August 1943

(For a full account of the Aleutian Islands campaign, see Chapter 7, USS *Nevada*.)

On 11 May 1943, as *Tennessee* was completing her modernisation works at Puget Sound, US forces began their operation to recapture the Aleutian Islands of Attu and Kiska, in Alaska, seized by Japan in June 1942. Attu had been retaken by 29 May 1943 – landings on Kiska were slated to begin on 15 August 1943.

On 31 May 1943, *Tennessee* and the heavy cruiser *Portland* (CA-33) departed San Pedro bound for Adak Island, some 1,200 miles southwest of Anchorage, Alaska. The squadron arrived in the Aleutians on 9 June and commenced patrol duties before closing Kiska Island on 29 July.

On 1 August 1943, two weeks before D-Day Kiska, *Tennessee* (flagship), *Idaho* and four destroyers approached Kiska from the north whilst another task group of five cruisers and five destroyers approached from the south.

That afternoon, after launching her spotter seaplanes, *Tennessee* closed Kiska to a distance of 7,000yd (about 4 miles), whilst streaming paravanes from her bow to cut the mooring cables of any lurking Japanese mines. Although a 1,000ft cloud ceiling hampered her floatplane spotters, in what was the ship's first blooding in action she opened fire with her 14in main battery and her 5in secondary battery, firing 30 14in shells at what had been a Japanese submarine base whilst her secondary battery fired more than 300 rounds.

The D-Day invasion landings on Kiska began two weeks later on 15 August 1943 and *Tennessee* was back off the invasion beaches in a fire-support group that included *Idaho*, *Pennsylvania*, two cruisers and several destroyers.

USS *Tennessee* at Adak, Aleutians, on 12 August 1943, just before the Kiska operation. (*SC 217808 courtesy of US Naval History & Heritage Command*)

The fire-support ships commenced their pre-invasion bombardment at about 0500, *Tennessee* targeting Japanese coastal batteries on Little Kiska Island before switching her 14in fire towards Japanese AA batteries on Kiska. Her 5in battery targeted a Japanese artillery observation post on Little Kiska – setting it on fire.

Some 34,400 Allied troops then went ashore just after 0600 – only to discover that the Japanese had withdrawn from the island two weeks earlier.

With her fire mission over, *Tennessee* withdrew towards San Francisco, arriving there on 31 August 1943. After replenishment, she set sail for the New Hebrides – where the Allies were staging for the invasion of the Gilbert Islands.

(II) The Gilbert and Marshall Islands Campaign
Battle of Tarawa – Operation GALVANIC, 20–23 November 1943
(For a full account of the Battle of Tarawa, see Chapter 6, USS *Maryland*.)

The invasion of Tarawa and Makin in the Gilbert Islands saw the largest gathering of ships to date by either side in the Pacific War – split into two forces. The Northern Attack Force would invade Makin Atoll whilst the Southern Attack Force would land on Tarawa Atoll, a string of islands encompassing a large lagoon. *Tennessee* was assigned to the Fire Support TG 53.4 of the Southern Attack Force, headed for Tarawa.

The Southern Attack Force approached Tarawa early on the morning of 20 November 1943 and began a 3-hour pre-invasion bombardment. As US Marines began their amphibious assault, they found that the untracked Higgins boats were unable to get over the reef – forcing Marines to wade ashore under withering fire.

Over the coming days, as the Marines worked inland, *Tennessee* provided AA cover for the invasion fleet and fired in support of troops ashore as they pushed the Japanese back – before withdrawing from the area each night to reduce the risk of a submarine attack. The Japanese were pushed back to a small defensive perimeter on the east end of the island, which *Tennessee* bombarded on the morning of 22 November with some seventy 14in shells and more than 300 5in secondary battery shells.

At about 1400 on 23 November 1943, west of Tarawa, the destroyer *Meade* (DD-602) on anti-submarine patrol detected the propeller sounds of the Japanese submarine *I-35*. TG 53.4 destroyer *Frazier* (DD-607) joined *Meade* in five attacks with depth charges that forced the submarine to the surface, where the two destroyers opened fire with 5in and 40mm weapons – *Tennessee* also opened fire with her secondary 5in battery. Several hits were scored before *Frazier* rammed the submarine's port quarter abaft the conning tower, badly damaging her own bow. The ramming attack and bombing by two Allied planes breached the submarine's pressure hull and as she flooded with water, she sank stern first with only four of her crew escaping. Whilst three were plucked from the water, one was killed after opening fire on his rescuers.

Tennessee remained off Tarawa until 3 December 1943, when she was detached for Hawaii. At Pearl, she formed up with *Colorado* and *Maryland* for passage to San Francisco where she would be dazzle-painted and begin shore bombardment training on 29 December 1943.

Tennessee departed San Francisco for the return passage to Hawaii on 13 January 1944, arriving off Maui on 21 January 1944, where the fleet was staging for the next large-scale operation of the Gilbert and Marshall Islands campaign, the invasion of strategic islands in the Marshalls.

Battle of Kwajalein – Operation FLINTLOCK, 31 January–3 February 1944
(For a full account of Operation FLINTLOCK, see Chapter 6, USS *Maryland* and Chapter 8, USS *Pennsylvania*.)

In late January 1944, the US 5th Fleet deployed towards Kwajalein, in the Marshall Islands. *Tennessee* was assigned to the Northern Attack Force tasked to assault the twin linked islands of Roi-Namur situated in the north part of Kwajalein Atoll, forming up with the battleships *Maryland* and *Colorado*, cruisers and destroyers as the Fire Support TG 53.5, under the command of Rear Admiral Jesse B. Oldendorf.

TG 53.5 departed Hawaii on 22 January 1944, and after shelling Japanese positions en route in the Marshall Islands on 30 January, the Fire Support Group arrived off Kwajalein on 31 January 1944.

That morning, in the pre-dawn hours of 31 January 1944, the Fire Support Group closed to about 3,000yd, just under 2 miles, of the twin islands of Roi-Namur. At 0625, *Tennessee* launched her Kingfisher float planes to spot the fall of shot and once they had gained altitude and were in position, fire commenced just after 0700, the battlewagon's main-battery 14in guns targeting pillboxes and other defensive positions. *Tennessee* paused fire to allow a strike by fast-carrier aircraft, which were engaged by Japanese AA guns, revealing their whereabouts. Once the carrier planes had completed their strike, *Tennessee* was able to target the enemy AA guns and suppress their fire.

Tennessee, *Maryland* and *Colorado* continued to shoot for 3 hours, silencing Japanese counter-battery fire and AA fire as they gradually closed to just 1,000yd offshore, when small-arms fire began ricocheting off the ships. At 12 noon, the battleships withdrew from the fire-support area to recover and refuel their spotter floatplanes. Once refuelled, the battleships then resumed firing – until withdrawing for the night at about 1700.

As the naval bombardment was under way, US troops landed on a number of smaller islands to secure the entrance into the lagoon and establish artillery positions for the next day's assault. Minesweepers meanwhile cleared the entrance channel.

The Fire Support Group closed Roi-Namur to their bombardment positions early the next day, D-Day Roi-Namur, 1 February 1943, and resumed their naval bombardment just after 0700. After 5 hours shooting, US Marines landed at about noon – and the Fire Support Group ships continued to shoot for 45 minutes in support as the Marines advanced.

The Marines quickly captured Roi – whilst the Japanese troops on Namur held out until the following day, 2 February, when *Tennessee* was able to enter the lagoon. Vice Admiral Raymond Spruance boarded *Tennessee* later in the day for a conference of commanders.

Kwajalein Atoll had been secured by 7 February 1944 and TG 53.5 was able to depart for Majuro, seized simultaneously with the Kwajalein landings – and which was rapidly being developed into the US Fleet's main anchorage and staging area for the Marshall Islands campaign. *Tennessee* would replenish at Majuro from the Service Squadron before returning to Kwajalein, where the fleet was assembling for the next operation, the seizure of Eniwetok Atoll.

Battle of Eniwetok – Operation CATCHPOLE, 17–23 February 1944
(For a full account of the Battle of Eniwetok, see Chapter 8, USS *Pennsylvania*.)

Further west in the Marshalls than Kwajalein, the almost circular atoll of Eniwetok is some 50 nautical miles in circumference, its forty islands surrounding a deep lagoon, which is 23 miles in diameter and has a wide entrance passage at the south. The invasion of the three Eniwetok Atoll islands of Engebi, Eniwetok and Parry on D-Day 17 February 1944 would provide US forces with an airfield and a large lagoon harbour that could be used to support the forthcoming campaign to take the Mariana Islands, more than 1,000nm to the west towards the Philippines.

In advance of the operation, on 11 February 1944, aircraft from the TF 58 fast carriers began working over Eniwetok – destroying most of the atoll's defences. On 15 February as TF 58 air strikes continued, the invasion transports deployed west from Kwajalein towards Eniwetok, screened by the TF 58 fast carriers and three Fire Support TG 53.5

battleships, *Tennessee*, *Colorado* and *Pennsylvania*, with escort cruisers and destroyers.

The naval bombardment of Eniwetok Atoll began early on the morning of 17 February as minesweepers cleared the entrance channel into the lagoon. At 0915, *Tennessee* led the invasion-troop transport ships into the wide lagoon and approached the first target, Engebi Island – as simultaneously landings were made on smaller islets that could be used to establish artillery fire bases. *Tennessee* fired in support of marines that were setting up marker buoys to guide the D-Day landing craft the following day.

After remaining in the lagoon overnight, the pre-invasion bombardment of Engebi Island commenced at 0700 on 18 February, with the first wave of marines landing at 0845 and quickly securing the island. *Tennessee* remained at anchor some 5,500yd offshore using her main and secondary batteries to support the marines as they moved across Eniwetok. At night she fired illumination star shells to aid marines ashore spot any night counterattack or infiltration by Japanese troops.

The next morning, 19 February 1944, *Tennessee* moved close to the beach on Parry Island and anchored. From there she would support the landings, delivering devastating fire with her main and secondary batteries as well as her 40mm Bofors. Firing continued until the morning of 22 February – by which time, everything above ground level on Parry Island had been demolished – including all the trees.

The landing craft then approached the beach, and with the island having had a much heavier bombardment than Tarawa, most of the defenders were already dead and US casualties were light. Parry Island was declared secure that afternoon and *Tennessee* was able to leave Eniwetok Atoll for Majuro the following day to replenish.

Eniwetok Atoll would quickly become a major forward anchorage and base for future Allied operations, with almost 500 ships thronging the lagoon waters daily during the first half of 1944.

Now that the Gilberts and Marshalls had been taken, the Allies had secured valuable safe fleet anchorages and were able to construct strategic naval bases, fortifications and airfields for land-based air to prepare for an assault on the Mariana Islands.

(III) The New Guinea Campaign – Operation CARTWHEEL
Emirau Island Landing, Bismarck Archipelago, 20 March 1944
At Majuro, *Tennessee* was assigned to TF 36 for the landing by 4,000 troops on Emirau Island, in the Bismarck archipelago of Papua New Guinea. The landing was the last in a series of operations for Operation

CARTWHEEL, General Douglas MacArthur's plan to surround, isolate and bypass the powerful Japanese base at Rabaul in New Britain.

Forming up as TG 36.2, *Tennessee, New Mexico, Idaho* and *Mississippi* and seven destroyers departed Majuro on 15 March 1944 bound for Kavieng at the northwesternmost tip of the Papua New Guinean province of New Ireland in the Bismarck archipelago.

Emirau Island lies some 75nm northwest of Kavieng, in northern New Ireland – and the plan was that TG 36.2 would attack Kavieng as a diversion, to confuse the Japanese as to the Allies' true intentions, whilst US Marines landed on the real objective – Emirau – where an airfield would be built to complete the encirclement of Rabaul. Rabaul would then be neutralised by land-based bombers.

Hidden by rain squalls and poor visibility, the four-battleship-strong force arrived off Kavieng early on D-Day Emirau, 20 March 1944, and at 0700, *Tennessee* launched her Kingfisher float planes to spot the fall of shot and identify enemy positions. The bombardment ships then closed to about 15,000yd, some 8–9 miles offshore, the limit of the range of Japanese coastal batteries, before opening fire whilst still under way.

As *Tennessee* closed the range to about 7,500yd, a Japanese coastal counter-bombardment gun engaged her, and *Tennessee*'s secondary battery returned fire. Accurate Japanese rangefinding managed to straddle *Tennessee* several times. As shells splashed close to her starboard side, *Tennessee* was forced to divert and open the range. Once safely out of range, she was able to shoot at the Japanese battery for some 10 minutes until the Japanese guns fell silent. The bombardment warships then patrolled off Kavieng for 3 more hours bombarding Japanese positions ashore – although their gunners were hampered by poor visibility.

Meanwhile, US Marines landed without opposition on the true target of Emirau, to find out from locals that the main Japanese force had evacuated Emirau some two months previously. At 1235, with the US Marines now safely ashore on Emirau, TG 36.2 withdrew from Kavieng waters.

Following the conclusion of Operation CARTWHEEL with the Emirau landings, *Tennessee* was detached for Pearl Harbor for routine maintenance – entering her old base on 16 April 1944.

In May 1944, preparations were under way at Hawaii for the next major operation, the Mariana and Palau Islands campaign – Operation FORAGER. Amphibious landing exercises were carried out and *Tennessee* and the other old battleships took part in shore-bombardment training off the volcanic island of Kahoolawe, 7 miles southwest of Maui, honing their skills to support landing forces with deadly accuracy.

(IV) The Mariana and Palau Islands Campaign – Operation FORAGER

Battle of Saipan, 15 June–9 July 1944
(For a full account of the Battle of Saipan, see Chapter 5, USS *California* and Chapter 6, USS *Maryland*.)

By May 1944, the Japanese still held the Philippines, the Caroline Islands, the Palau Islands and the Mariana Islands. If the Allies could take the Marianas, airbases could be established from which the new US ultra-long-range Boeing B-29 Superfortress heavy bomber could hit the Japanese home islands. The large northern Mariana island of Saipan would be assaulted first, followed by Guam and then the smaller island of Tinian, just to the south of Saipan.

At Hawaii, in anticipation of her new fire-support duties with TF 52, the Northern Attack Force, *Tennessee* was assigned to Fire Support Group 1 (TG 52.17) under the command of Rear Admiral Jesse B. Oldendorf. Fire Support Group 1 now consisted of the four old Standard-Type battleships *Tennessee*, *California*, *Maryland* and *Colorado*, along with heavy and light cruisers and a screen of destroyers. Fire Support Group 2, under the command of Rear Admiral Walden L. Ainsworth, comprised the three old battleships *Pennsylvania*, *Idaho* and *New Mexico*, along with cruisers and their screen. In all, the Fire Support Group now comprised seven old battleships, of which *Tennessee*, *California*, *Maryland* and *Pennsylvania* were all survivors of the Pearl Harbor raid.

Before any landings in the Marianas took place, a heavy naval and air bombardment by 8 escort carriers, 7 Standard-Type battleships, 6 heavy cruisers, 5 light cruisers and a screen of destroyers would soften up the enemy.

Elements of the Northern Attack Force departed Hawaii on 31 May 1944, heading 2,500 miles west for Kwajalein Atoll in the Marshalls, seized five months earlier in January 1944. The two Fire Support Groups arrived at Kwajalein Atoll on 8 June 1944, from where the 5th Fleet deployed towards the Mariana Islands to begin Operation FORAGER.

As the Fire Support Groups closed Saipan, the planes of the fast-carrier TF 58 began hitting the Marianas on 11 June, carrying out a successful initial fighter sweep on the afternoon of 11 June before pounding the islands for the next three days. Hellcats cratered and strafed the Saipan airfields, destroying hundreds of Japanese planes on the tarmac and in the air. On Saipan, clouds of smoke billowed from fires deliberately lit by the Japanese to obscure ground installations.

With D-Day Saipan slated for 15 June 1944, the Fire Support Groups arrived off Saipan, late on 13 June and in the pre-dawn darkness of

14 June moved into their bombardment positions to begin their treatment of Saipan at first light. If the enemy threatened a surface engagement, the seven Fire Support Group battleships and three cruisers would form their own battle line 25 miles west of Saipan.

Tennessee's main-battery guns commenced fire at about 0545 on 14 June, targeting coastal batteries that were engaging minesweepers clearing lanes for the LVTs and landing craft to approach the beaches. When *California* was damaged by Japanese coastal batteries on nearby Tinian Island later that morning, *Tennessee* turned her guns on those Japanese positions – before switching fire back to the landing beaches. Most of the other battleships had taken near misses by the time *Tennessee* ceased fire and withdrew for the night.

The next morning, D-Day Saipan, 15 June 1944, *Tennessee* closed the landing beaches and opened fire with her main and secondary batteries, and her 40mm Bofors, from a range of 3,000yd, under 2 miles.

Just after 0800, as US Marines began their amphibious assault in LVTs and Higgins boats, *Tennessee* held station at the south of the landing zone, providing covering fire as necessary as the Marines closed the landing beaches.

A battery of Japanese 120mm artillery weapons hidden in a cave on Tinian opened fire on *Tennessee*, scoring three hits on the battlewagon, one of which disabled one of her secondary weapons. Although eight of her crew were killed and more than twenty wounded, little other damage was done, and the fighting capability of the ship was unaffected. That afternoon, *Tennessee* withdrew to protect the vulnerable troop transports offshore against an expected Japanese counterattack.

USS *Tennessee* bombards Japanese positions on Guam, 19 July 1944. (*80-G-K-14224 courtesy of US Naval History & Heritage Command*)

Throughout the following day, 16 June and into 17 June, *Tennessee* continued to provide close support for troops ashore – until intelligence was received of the deployment in force of the IJN for what would develop into the 1st Battle of the Philippine Sea. Although the old battleships moved into their battle line to protect the fleet transports, the Japanese naval forces were routed by the planes of the TF 58 fast carriers at what became known as the Great Marianas Turkey Shoot and the old battleships were not called upon to participate.

With the Japanese fleet having withdrawn from the area in disarray, *Tennessee* was able to depart the Marianas on 22 June and steam to Eniwetok for replenishment and repair of the light damage sustained.

Battle of Guam – Operation STEVEDORE, 21 July–10 August 1944
The next strategic target for the Allies after Saipan was Guam, at the south of the Mariana Island chain. At some 32 miles long and 4–12 miles wide, Guam is the largest island in the Marianas. D-Day Guam was slated for 21 July 1944.

After replenishment at Eniwetok, *Tennessee* and *California* were assigned to the Fire Support Group of the Southern Attack Force, commanded by Rear Admiral Jesse B. Oldendorf, the main element of which had departed Eniwetok for Guam on 8 July and had been shelling the island's defences since. *California* and *Tennessee* and their screen of four destroyers departed Eniwetok on 16 July, arriving off Guam on 19 July, to join the bombardment force.

With the arrival of *Tennessee* and *California*, the naval bombardment intensified in the days before the landings began on D-Day, 21 July, in a determined attempt to neutralise Japanese defences around the landing beaches. From their assigned position offshore, on 20 July, *Tennessee* and *California* brought their main-battery 14in guns to bear on Japanese defensive positions around the possible landing beaches of Tumon Bay (on the northwest coast of Guam) and the capital city of Agana further south on the west coast. In all, the naval bombardment by some 274 Allied ships would deliver almost 45,000 rounds to Guam's defences. Every building that could be spotted – and all the palm trees near the landing beaches that could offer cover to the enemy – were destroyed.

At 0830 on D-Day, 21 July 1944, the 3rd Marine Division landed near Agana to the north of the Orote peninsula whilst the 1st Provisional Marine Brigade landed near Agat to the south. *Tennessee* and *California*'s guns fired in initial support for the amphibious assault, but with the Marines quickly ashore at both beaches and establishing a beachhead

6,600ft deep, *Tennessee* and *California* were detached later that day at 1500 and sent back up north to Saipan, now under Allied control, to replenish ammunition.

Early the next morning as part of a diversion to hide the true focus of the next landings, *Tennessee* appeared off the southwest coast of the small island of Tinian, just south of Saipan, and shelled positions ashore throughout the day before withdrawing for the night.

On 24 July, *Tennessee* and *California*, with the cruiser *Louisville* (CA-28) and several destroyers, acted as the Fire Support Group for D-Day Tinian on 24 July, shelling the island in advance of the 4th Marines going ashore. Tinian Town was virtually flattened, being hit by almost 500 14in shells and some 800 5in secondary battery shells.

Tennessee and *California* remained off Tinian in support of the 4th Marines until 26 July, when *Tennessee* was detached to return to Saipan to quickly replenish before returning the following day. It took until the morning of 31 July before Tinian was declared secure and *Tennessee*'s guns could fall silent.

Tennessee was sent back again to Saipan to replenish – before heading south back down the Marianas to Guam, where she would provide fire support until 8 August 1944 as fierce fighting continued. *Tennessee* then headed to Espiritu Santo in the New Hebrides, arriving there on 24 August 1944.

Battles of Peleliu and Angaur – Operation STALEMATE II, 17 September– 22 October 1944
(For a full account of the Battles of Peleliu and Angaur, see Chapter 6, USS *Maryland*.)

On 12 September 1944, a three-day-long naval bombardment of the small Palauan islands of Peleliu and Angaur began as the battleships *Pennsylvania*, *Maryland*, *Mississippi*, *Tennessee* and *Idaho*, with cruisers and destroyers, opened up. Peleliu was a tiny island of only 5 square miles but held an important Japanese airfield, the capture of which would secure the eastern flank for US forces preparing to attack Japanese forces in the Philippines. Peleliu alone was occupied by about 11,000 Japanese troops whilst some 14,000 IJA troops were stationed on the southernmost island of Angaur.

Tennessee closed Peleliu to 14,000yd (about 8 miles), before opening fire with her main and secondary batteries at 0630. As Japanese defences were progressively destroyed, she was able to close the range to under 4,000yd, just over 2 miles, when her 40mm Bofors guns could be fired.

On 15 September 1944, US Marines, and later the US Army's 81st Infantry Division, landed on Peleliu and Angaur. But unknown to the Allies, as a result of the devastating losses to earlier pre-invasion bombardments, rather than attempting to stop the US amphibious landings on the beaches, the majority of the Japanese troops on Peleliu were held inshore in tunnelled defensive cave systems in limestone hills and ridges. They would survive the pre-invasion bombardments – the new Japanese concept of defence in depth would see a long and brutal struggle on Peleliu of more than two months before it was secured.

On 28 September, as US troops ashore fought to clear the Japanese from their intricate cave systems, with little need now for bombardment ships, *Tennessee* departed for Seeadler Harbor, Manus in the Admiralty Islands where she would prepare for the Philippines campaign.

(V) The Philippines Campaign
Battle of Leyte Gulf, 23–26 October 1944
(For a full description of the build-up to the Battle of Leyte Gulf, see Chapter 5, USS *California*.)

At Manus, *Tennessee* formed up with the Standard-Type battleships *Pennsylvania*, *California*, *West Virginia*, *Maryland* and *Mississippi*, and their escorts, as the Fire Support TG 77.2, commanded by Rear Admiral Jesse B. Oldendorf, to support the amphibious landings at Leyte Gulf.

The slow-moving invasion ships began departing Manus on 10 October, whilst the Fire Support Group warships departed two days later on 12 October 1944, arriving off the Dinagat Islands on the south side of Leyte Gulf on D-Day Dinagat, 17 October 1944, when the 6th Ranger Battalion of the US 6th Army landed and flew the US flag on Philippine soil for the first time since the Japanese invasion in 1941.

The next day, 18 October, with Dinagat secure, the Fire Support Group warships entered Leyte Gulf and took up their bombardment positions. Over the course of the next days, they covered minesweepers clearing the approaches to the landing areas and Underwater Demolition Teams of swimmers reconnoitring the beaches. At 0645 on 19 October, the ships began shelling the area around the city of Tacloban, at the north end of Leyte Gulf, before withdrawing for the night.

A-Day for the Leyte landings was 20 October 1944 – and the Fire Support Group ships resumed firing at 0600, targeting the landing beaches. After 3½ hours, US 6th Army troops began their approaches to the beaches in their landing craft. As they began disembarking at 1000, *Tennessee* and the other Fire Support Group ships were able to fire at positions ahead of their advance.

The landings triggered Japanese command to initiate their pre-planned response Operation *Shō-Gō* 1, which saw a number of Japanese naval forces converging to strike at vulnerable Allied shipping in Leyte Gulf and the troops ashore.

Battle of Surigao Strait, 25 October 1944
On 24 October 1944, following reports of Japanese naval forces approaching from the west, Rear Admiral Jesse B. Oldendorf arranged his Battleships Force (BattFor) to guard the easternmost end of the Surigao Strait, the channel between the two southern islands of Leyte and Mindanao that could allow a Japanese naval force to approach the Allied landing areas in Leyte Gulf. BattFor included the 6 Standard-Type battleships *Pennsylvania, Tennessee, California, West Virginia, Maryland* and *Mississippi*, along with 8 cruisers, 28 destroyers and 39 small fast Patrol Boats (PT Boats) that mounted torpedoes. Oldendorf positioned his battle line of battleships across the northern exit from the Surigao Strait, flanked on either side by heavy and light cruisers with nimble destroyers in a more advanced position to the south. The PT Boats were deployed as pickets far south down the strait towards the enemy line of approach.

A powerful Japanese Southern Force consisting of the two battleships *Fusō* and *Yamashiro*, the heavy cruiser *Mogami* and escort destroyers had crossed the Sulu and Mindanao Seas from west to east. During the night of 24/25 October 1944, the Southern Force attempted to pass through the Surigao Strait to hit Leyte Gulf at first light from the south. Up north of Samar, another Japanese battleship force was making for the San Bernardino Strait, intending to strike the Allied forces at Leyte Gulf from the north on 25 October.

Just after 0230, once it became known that the Japanese force had penetrated the Surigao Strait, Rear Admiral Oldendorf brought BattFor to General Quarters and sent divisions of destroyers south down the strait in attack formation.

The US PT Boats, stationed at the south end of the strait, were first to attack the Japanese force, but they were beaten off without scoring any direct hits.

The Southern Force ships in line astern were then picked up on radar aboard the destroyers at a range of almost 23 miles, the destroyers increased speed to 30 knots, closing the enemy before launching their Mark 15 torpedoes. At least one torpedo hit the battleship *Fūso*, which began to slow down and shear out of line. Another torpedo hit the destroyer *Yamagumo*, which exploded spectacularly, broke in two and sank immediately. The two destroyers *Michishio* and *Asagumo* were also hit as was the flagship, the battleship *Yamashiro*. But still the Southern Force continued north towards Leyte.

At about 0300, the advanced SG search radar on *Tennessee*, in Oldendorf's battle line of OBBS at the north end of the strait, picked up the lead Japanese ships at 44,000yd. The main-battery Mark 8 fire-control radars also picked up the Japanese ships in the darkness, and at 0351, Oldendorf was able to give the order to fire. Shortly thereafter, a salvo from *Tennessee*'s main-battery guns shattered the darkness as each side opened up on the other. The brutal exchange of fire developed into the Battle of the Surigao Strait, which would be the last battleship v. battleship clash in history. The Southern Force would be decimated – with both battleships *Fusō* and *Yamashiro* being sunk.

After the battle, *Tennessee* left the Philippines on 29 October 1944 with *West Virginia, Maryland* and four cruisers, bound for overhaul at Puget Sound Navy Yard. When after the long passage east, she arrived at the West-Coast yard on 26 November 1944, she entered dry dock. The ship's dazzle camouflage was painted over in dark grey and she received new versions of the Mark 8 radar for her main battery and Mark 12 and Mark 22 systems for her secondary battery. A new SP radar for her AA suite was added that was able to determine the height of enemy planes.

The refit work took a couple of months to complete – but on 2 February 1945, *Tennessee* was able to get underway for Saipan via Pearl Harbor to rejoin the fleet for the next major operation – Iwo Jima.

(VI) Battle of Iwo Jima – Operation DETACHMENT, 19 February– 26 March 1945

(For a full account of the Battle of Iwo Jima, see Chapter 7, USS *Nevada*.)

The volcanic island of Iwo Jima lies some 750 miles south of Tokyo and almost halfway between the Mariana Islands and Japan. Iwo Jima is only 8 square miles and is dominated by Mount Suribachi at its southwest end, a dormant volcanic vent some 160m high, which is a resurgent dome or raised centre of a larger submerged volcanic caldera that surrounds the island.

The Japanese had established three airfields on Iwo Jima that enabled Japanese fighters to intercept the US long-range B-29 Superfortress heavy bombers flying from the Mariana Islands on raids against Japan. Japanese planes flying from Iwo Jima had already made direct air attacks on the Marianas between November 1944 and January 1945.

If the Allies could however take Iwo Jima, then as well as stopping these Japanese air raids, it could be used as an airbase for long-range

P-51 Mustang fighters, which could escort the Boeing B-29 Superfortress bombers on their raids over Japan. Iwo could also serve as an emergency landing base for damaged B-29s returning from Japan that were unable to reach their main bases at Guam and Saipan. It was therefore decided to eliminate these problems in the lull before the next major operation, the invasion of Okinawa. D-Day Iwo Jima would be 19 February 1945, the operation being given the code name DETACHMENT.

At Saipan, *Tennessee* was assigned to the bombardment group of TF 54, the main hitting power of which were the six battleships *Tennessee*, *Idaho*, *Nevada*, *Texas*, *New York* and *Arkansas*, with *West Virginia* joining a few days later on D-Day, 19 February. After rehearsals for the Iwo Jima assault off the Marianas, TF 54 began departing the Marianas for Iwo Jima on 14 February 1945.

Arriving off Iwo Jima on 16 February 1945, the bombardment ships moved to their designated firing positions and early on 17 February, spotter float planes were launched before the naval bombardment commenced at about 0700 – although rain squalls and poor visibility hampered the accuracy of fire.

Tennessee, *Nevada* and *Idaho* opened fire at a range of about 10,000yd (just under 6 miles) before closing to 3,000yd – under 2 miles – as they protected UDT teams of swimmers that were reconnoitring the landing beaches. As they closed, Japanese counter-battery fire commenced from coastal batteries, scoring hits that damaged *Tennessee*, the heavy cruiser *Pensacola* and the destroyer *Leutze* (DD-481).

The bombardment group continued shelling Iwo Jima on 18 February, *Tennessee*'s guns destroying a number of pillboxes and an ammunition dump. On D-Day, 19 February, the invasion-troop transports arrived off Iwo Jima and *West Virginia* also arrived to join the bombardment force. The two fast battleships *North Carolina* and *Washington* and three cruisers from the TF 58 fast-carrier screen also temporarily joined the bombardment group.

The guns of TF 54 pounded Iwo Jima throughout D-Day, 19 February, as US Marines landed on the black volcanic beach and were subjected to withering Japanese heavy artillery from Mount Suribachi. The Japanese opened the reinforced doors of their gun pits hewn into Mount Suribachi to fire, before immediately closing them to prevent effective counter-battery fire from the Marines and naval vessels offshore. After vicious fighting ashore, the US flag was raised on Mount Suribachi on 23 February 1945, although fighting would continue on until 26 March 1945.

On 7 March 1945, two weeks after the flag was raised, *Tennessee*, *Nevada*, *Arkansas* and *Idaho* with their escorts departed Iwo Jima to replenish at Ulithi, where the US Fleet was staging for Operation ICEBERG – the invasion of Okinawa, slated to begin on 1 April 1945.

On arrival at Ulithi, *Tennessee* anchored up in the great lagoon and her crew got to work restocking shell rooms and powder magazines and replenishing with fuel, stores and supplies. She had fired some 1,370 main-battery shells and more than 6,000 secondary battery 5in rounds at Iwo Jima – and more than 11,000 Bofors 40mm rounds.

(VII) Battle of Okinawa – Operation ICEBERG, 1 April–22 June 1945
(For a full account of the Battle of Okinawa, see Chapter 6, USS *Maryland* and Chapter 7, USS *Nevada*.)

Okinawa is the smallest and least populated of the five main islands of Japan and lies towards the end of a long chain of outer islands that stretch 400 miles back to Japan. *Tennessee* had been assigned as flagship to TG 54.1, the Gunfire Support Group for Operation ICEBERG, and would operate with *Nevada* in Fire Support Unit 3.

On 5 March 1945, TF 54, under the command of Rear Admiral Morton L. Deyo, began training for the invasion of Okinawa, east of Ulithi – being joined on 17 March 1945 by the battleship *Maryland*, fresh from her recent repair and refit at Pearl Harbor. She would operate in Fire Support Unit 1 with *Texas*, whilst that other veteran of the Pearl Harbor raid, *West Virginia*, was assigned to FSU 4 along with *Idaho*. In all, there would be 6 TG 54.1 Fire Support Units for the Okinawa invasion – comprising a total of 10 battleships, 10 cruisers and 32 destroyers.

TF 54 got underway from Ulithi on 21 March 1945, bound for the small group of Kerama Retto islands, which lie off southwest Okinawa. They would be seized first to provide an advanced staging area for the assault on Okinawa.

TF 54.1 arrived in the Okinawa area on 25 March 1945 and initially covered pre-invasion minesweeping and the largest UDT swimmer operation of the Second World War, with nearly 1,000 men carrying out reconnaissance, removing pointed poles set into the coral and blasting channels to the beaches through the reef.

The next day, 26 March, Fire Support Units began shelling enemy positions on the Kerama Retto islands and on Okinawa itself from long range. As the pre-invasion softening up strikes and naval bombardment took place, Allied Combat Air Patrols continually fought off Japanese planes approaching the invasion force.

The Japanese had discovered that US shipboard radar could not detect their aircraft coming in low singly – or in small groups at very high altitude. On 26 March, a wave of kamikazes broke through the CAP

USS *TENNESSEE* (BB-43)

fighter cover and attacked the Task Group. One Val kamikaze crashed near *Tennessee*, whilst another Val kamikaze crashed into *Nevada*. Another Val kamikaze was engaged by AA gunners and burning after being hit, it crashed into the light cruiser *Biloxi* (CL-80) amidships.

The attacks by kamikazes would continue remorselessly as the Allied naval bombardment pounded Okinawa from 28–31 March, in advance of D-Day Okinawa, 1 April 1945.

As US Marines landed on D-Day, they at first faced little opposition, the Japanese having once again adopted the defence-in-depth tactic, withdrawing the main bulk of an estimated 100,000 troops to hilly terrain in the southern two-thirds of the island which offered better defensive positions. On D-Day, as troops ashore fought to secure Okinawa and the Fire Support Units remained offshore in support, *West Virginia* was damaged by a kamikaze whilst *Tennessee* was hit by shell fragments.

Later, on 11 April, *Tennessee* was again damaged – and then the following afternoon, 12 April 1945, when Japanese planes attacked

USS *Tennessee* bombards Purple and Orange beaches just prior to H-hour for the invasion of Okinawa, 1 April 1945. Troop-filled LVT-4 amphibious tractors are churning by in the foreground. (*NH 42390 courtesy of US Naval History & Heritage Command*)

USS *Tennessee* trains her guns on Okinawa during the initial landings, 1 April 1945. (*80-G-314670 courtesy of US Naval History & Heritage Command*)

Allied shipping 15nm southeast of Nakagusuku Bay, *Tennessee* was targeted by five Val dive bombers, who swept down from high altitude. AA gunners shot down all five – but with their focus up high, the battlewagon's crew initially missed a single Val that approached at low altitude. When the Val was spotted, the AA gunners turned their fire on it – and although the Val was damaged, it was still able to crash into the signal bridge, destroying a Bofors 40mm mount and fire directors for the Oerlikon 20mm weapons. The Val's aviation fuel started fires whilst the 250lb bomb it was carrying penetrated the upper deck before exploding and killing more than 20 crew and wounding about 100. Later that night, 12 April, *Tennessee* and *Idaho* were targeted by a Japanese submarine, and narrowly evaded the torpedoes in the darkness.

After some five weeks operating off Okinawa, *Tennessee* was detached on 1 May 1945 to head for Ulithi for repair and replenishment. At Ulithi, damaged plating in the superstructure was cut away and replaced and new AA guns installed in place of those that had been destroyed.

On 3 June 1945, *Tennessee* was able to depart Ulithi once again for Okinawa, where she arrived six days later. By this time, the ground offensive was nearing its conclusion and the Japanese had been pushed back to the southern part of the island. *Tennessee*'s guns fired in support of ground troops until the island was finally declared secure on 21 June 1945.

After the Battle of Leyte, where he had distinguished himself at the Battle of the Surigao Strait, Rear Admiral Jesse B. Oldendorf had been promoted to Vice Admiral on 15 December 1945. Now in command of all naval forces in the area, Oldendorf made *Tennessee* his flagship and on 23 June 1945, *Tennessee* embarked on a series of patrols in the East China Sea.

From 26–28 July 1945, warships under Oldendorf's command took part in a raid into the Yangtze estuary off Shanghai, China. *Tennessee* would remain in the East China Sea until the Pacific War ended in August 1945 following the nuclear strikes against Hiroshima and Nagasaki.

Tennessee subsequently covered the landing of occupation troops at Wakayama, Japan, arriving there on 23 September 1945. She then moved to Yokosuka, Japan.

(VIII) Post-War

On 16 October 1945, *Tennessee* left Japanese home waters and headed south to Singapore. The anti-torpedo blisters added to *Tennessee* in the 1943 reconstruction had increased her beam such that she was unable to transit eastwards through the Panama Canal. As a result, *Tennessee* headed southwest from Singapore across the Indian Ocean, before rounding the Cape of Good Hope at the southern tip of Africa and crossing the Atlantic.

Finally arriving in home waters, *Tennessee* headed up north to the Philadelphia Navy Yard, where she arrived on 7 December 1945. On 8 December, *Tennessee* was assigned to the Philadelphia Group of the 16th Fleet, an inactive reserve fleet, pending the shrinking of the fleet for peacetime.

Tennessee remained in reserve for twelve years until 1959, by which time the First World War-era dreadnought was some forty years old. She was stricken from the Naval Vessel Register and sold on 10 July 1959 to Bethlehem Steel Corporation to be broken up for scrap in Pennsylvania. She was towed to their yard at the Patapsco River, Baltimore, just to the north of Washington, where she was broken up alongside her sister battlewagon *California*.

Chapter 10

USS *West Virginia* (BB-48)

USS *West Virginia* (BB-48) off the Puget Sound Navy Yard, Washington following reconstruction, 2 July 1944. (*19-N-68376 courtesy of US Naval History & Heritage Command*)

USS *WEST VIRGINIA* (BB-48)

Specifications (as built): Colorado class BB
Builder: Newport News Shipbuilding & Drydock Co., Virginia
Launched: 19 November 1921
Commissioned: 1 December 1923
Decommissioned: 9 January 1947
Displacement: 32,693 tons (S). 33,590 tons (F)
Length: 624ft (oa)
600ft (wl)
Beam: 97.5ft
Draft: 30.5ft
Speed: 21 knots
Endurance: 8,000nm at 10 knots

Armour:
  Belt: 13.5in tapering to 8in on lower edge
  Barbettes: 13in
  Turrets: Face: 18in. Sides: 10in. Roof: 5in
  Conning tower: 16in
  Decks: Armour Deck: 3.5in in 2 layers. Aft over steering, 6in
  Splinter Deck: 1.5in

Armament:
  Main Battery: 8 x 16in/45cal. in four 2-gun superfiring turrets
  Secondary Battery: 12 x single 5in/51-cal.
  AA Battery: 8 x single 3in/50-cal.
  Torpedo tubes: 2 x 21in submerged

Ships in class: *Colorado, Maryland, Washington* (cancelled), *West Virginia*
Fate: Sold to shipbreakers in 1959 and dismantled

(For full details of the design and all-or-nothing armour, see Chapter 7, USS *Nevada*. For details of the armament and propulsion systems of the Colorado-class units see Chapter 6, USS *Maryland*.)

USS *West Virginia* (BB-48) was the fourth Colorado-class battleship ordered, the final class of the Standard-Type series built for the US Navy during and immediately after the First World War that had begun with the Nevada-class units. The Colorado class originally was to comprise the four BBs, *Colorado, Maryland, Washington* (BB-47) and *West Virginia* but the well-advanced construction of *Washington* was cancelled two days after signing the Washington Naval Treaty. This left *West Virginia* as the third and final unit of the Colorado class – and the last of the Standard-Type battleships. The *Washington* was subsequently sunk in 1924 as a gunnery target by the battleships *New York* and *Texas*.

West Virginia's keel was laid down at the Newport News Shipbuilding & Drydock Co. yard in Virginia on 12 April 1920 and the ship was launched for fitting out afloat on 19 November 1921. The completed ship was commissioned on 1 December 1923.

The Colorado-class units were essentially a development of the preceding Tennessee class and broadly had the same dimensions, propulsion systems and protection. But largely as a result of the Japanese Nagato-class battleships, which mounted eight 16in guns, the Colorado-class units were up-gunned with a more powerful main battery of eight 16in/45-cal. Mark 1 guns in four two-gun turrets in place of the twelve 14in guns carried by the Tennessee-class units. The eight 16in/45-cal. guns were placed as a superfiring pair forward of the superstructure and a superfiring pair aft.

The secondary battery was the same as on the previous Tennessee-class units with twelve 5in/51-cal. single guns and an AA battery of eight 3in/50-cal. guns.

The ship had a noticeably raked bow and sported two cage masts, between which were two slender smokestacks.

Propulsion was delivered by four General Electric turbo-electric drives, with steam from eight oil-fired Babcock & Wilcox boilers at 285psi giving a top speed of 21 knots. The eight boilers were set in individual compartments surrounding the two turbines, which were set in tandem. The turbo-electric drives were not directly connected to the propeller shafts –increasing underwater protection and compartmentalisation.* *West Virginia* had a design endurance of 8,000nm at 10 knots and carried 64 officers and 1,241 crew.

In the early 1930s the ship was modified with the original AA Battery of eight single 3in/50-cal AA guns being replaced by the more versatile manually trained 5in/25-cal. heavy AA gun. The 5in/25-cal. HA gun used fixed ammunition and offered a maximum elevation of +85°. There were 0.50-cal. machine guns installed on her foremast and mainmast – and aircraft catapults were fitted on her quarterdeck and atop the after superfiring turret.

---

* For detail on turbo-electric propulsion systems, see Chapter 5, USS *California*.

Plans for more extensive modernisation of *West Virginia* and the other two Tennessee-class battleships with new boilers, modern fire-control equipment and anti-torpedo blisters were proposed but rejected in 1938 on cost grounds. For even as modernised, these older Standard-Type BBs would still be inferior to the new South Dakota-class and North Carolina-class 28-knot, fast battleships then under construction.

PEARL HARBOR, 7 DECEMBER 1941

West Virginia was rafted up in Berth F-6 in 40ft of water on Battleship Row in the outboard position to *Tennessee*, which lay alongside to starboard and was secured to the interrupted quays of Ford Island. Both ships pointed towards the southern entrance channel to Pearl Harbor.

West Virginia and *Tennessee* lay astern of *Oklahoma* and *Maryland*. Abaft *West Virginia*, the *Arizona* was moored with her starboard beam towards Ford Island. The repair ship *Vestal* was secured alongside *Arizona*'s port beam in the outboard position.

Immediately the attack began, Japanese torpedo bombers hit the exposed port beam of *West Virginia* with at least five Type 91 torpedoes. Her rudder was blown off by another torpedo, damaging the steering engine. One of the torpedo hits may have been from one of the midget submarines that had penetrated Pearl's defences. In all, she would be hit by as many as eight or nine torpedoes.

After the *Arizona* had been hit by an adapted naval shell aerial bomb and had blown up in a catastrophic magazine explosion, Kate torpedo bombers from the carrier *Hiryū* hit *West Virginia* from above with a pair of similar large-calibre naval shells, adapted to be AP aerial bombs.

The first adapted AP bomb hit *West Virginia* forward on the port side of the deck between the fo'c'sle and Turret 1, penetrating the superstructure deck before exploding and causing extensive damage to four of the port secondary battery casemates below. Secondary explosions of ready-use ammunition stored in the casemates caused serious fires there and in the galley deck below. Most of the ship between the fo'c'sle and Turret 1 would be burned out.

The second AP bomb hit the 5in-thick armoured roof of the after superfiring Turret 3. The bomb penetrated but failed to explode – although the devastation caused by shards and splinters nevertheless put one of the 16in guns out of action. The OS2U Kingfisher floatplane on the catapult atop the turret was destroyed whilst a second Kingfisher was knocked down to the main deck. That Kingfisher spilled aviation gasoline onto the deck that then caught fire. Fuel oil leaking from the destroyed *Arizona* astern, caught fire and engulfed *West Virginia* in a wall of flames, which were also fed by her own leaking fuel oil.

At least one torpedo had hit the vertical main armour belt, damaging seven armour plates. At least three other torpedoes hit amidships below the vertical armour belt, opening up two holes in the shell plating into the outboard void of the underwater side-protection system of the hull from frames 43 to 52 and from 62 to 97. It appeared that at least one torpedo passed through one of the two holes and exploded inside the ship, completely breaking through the inner oil-filled tanks of the ship's multi-layered anti-torpedo side-protection system.

The torpedo hits caused extensive internal damage and as the ship began to flood with water, she took on a list to port of 20–25°. As the ship listed, more torpedoes struck above the armour belt, seriously damaging the hull structure. A capsize was only prevented by prompt counterflooding of starboard compartments to correct the trim.

The after-port beam of the sunken battleship USS *West Virginia* after her fires were put out, possibly on 8 December 1941. An OS2U floatplane is upside down on the main deck abreast Turret No. 4 turret whilst a second OS2U is partially burned out atop Turret No. 3. USS *Tennessee* lies inboard. (*80-G-19945 courtesy of US Naval History & Heritage Command*)

USS *WEST VIRGINIA* (BB-48)

Captain Mervyn S. Bennion was mortally wounded on his bridge wing by fragments from a bomb hit on one of *Tennessee*'s turrets alongside.

As *West Virginia*'s list was corrected, this allowed her to slowly settle to the bottom on an even keel, with a slight list to port. All spaces of the ship were flooded up to 2–3ft below the main deck.

The crew were evacuated, though a group returned to fight the fires that had broken out on their ship and were met with a new phenomenon not seen before. For as the flames were controlled in one area, fire broke out in adjacent spaces causing considerable damage to the inside of the ship. It was later determined that the heat from burning oil-based paint on one side of a bulkhead was igniting oil-based paint on the opposite side. As a result, warships would subsequently be stripped of all oil-based paint and repainted with fire-retardant paint.[1]

By the afternoon of the following day, 8 December 1941, the fires had been extinguished. A total of 106 men had been killed.

USS *Tern* (AM-31) alongside the sunken *West Virginia*'s port beam, fighting fires aboard the battleship on 7 December 1941, immediately after the Japanese raid. (*NH 64477 courtesy of US Naval History & Heritage Command*)

Salvage

West Virginia had been hit by two AP bombs, at least seven torpedoes and set ablaze. For about three-quarters of the length of the ship, all of the deck plating above the second deck and some of the bulkheading was seriously damaged from the heat of fires. She was clearly too badly damaged for immediate salvage – and was obviously out of the war for some considerable time, if not permanently.

West Virginia had settled on the bottom upright, with a slight list of about 3° to port and a draft of 50ft 6in forward and 40ft 10in aft. Her sunken hull was pinning *Tennessee*'s starboard foreship against the forward interrupted mooring quay on Ford Island.

Her remaining crew began work to lighten the ship as far as possible to assist with refloating and a subsequent transfer to dry dock. Secondary and AA battery guns would be removed to replace those damaged on other ships and provide guns ashore for island defence.

On 9 December 1941, two days after the attack, a 5in/25-cal. gun was removed from *West Virginia*'s undamaged starboard side and lifted aboard *Pennsylvania* to replace one of hers with a damaged barrel. The other seven of *West Virginia*'s battery of eight 5in/25-cal. guns were subsequently removed. Four were set up as a shore battery at West Loch in Pearl Harbor, one went to the heavy cruiser *Chicago* (CA-29) and two went to the heavy cruiser *Salt Lake City* (CA-25). A 5in/51-cal. secondary battery gun went to the *Pennsylvania* whilst six more were turned over to the army for use ashore in defence of Oahu. A pair of machine guns went to *Tennessee*. Other crew cleared up the ship, reducing the fire hazard by removing oily trash from the ship, along with parts of damaged superstructure. Soon, some 50 tons of debris and damaged equipment had been piled up for removal ashore.

As the trio of temporarily repaired but serviceable battleships, *Pennsylvania*, *Tennessee* and *Maryland*, left Pearl Harbor for navy yards at Puget Sound and San Francisco on Saturday 20 December 1941, no one knew yet how badly *West Virginia* had been damaged below the waterline.

Now that the ship had been cleared up, work could begin to lighten her – and orders went out on 20 December from the Navy Yard to the Salvage Organization that once *California*'s main battery had been removed, the eight main-battery 16in guns on *West Virginia* were to be removed – along with both cage masts, both smokestacks, cranes and catapults.

The tops of all four turrets were removed and hundreds of shells and powder charges for each of her eight 16in main guns were hoisted off the ship in the case of upper stowages in the turrets, by a barge crane through the turret tops. The 16in shells from the handling rooms below were hoisted through the ammunition handling hatches. The 5in shells were brought up by the regular ammunition hoists operated by divers using air drills, before being passed by hand.

Some 800,000 gallons of fuel oil were pumped out of her oil tanks into fuel-oil barges. Stanchions and lifelines were removed from the quarter deck and fo'c'sle, whilst lifeboat cradles, davits and skids were removed. Doors and hatches were removed where possible along with the anchors and 150 fathoms of heavy anchor chain.

On 30 December, from a float tied up near Frame 46 abreast Turret 2, divers began the underwater exploration of the port beam of *West Virginia* to determine how best to salvage her. Another float was moored 220ft aft, at Frame 102 just forward of Turret 3. These two fixed datum floats would allow investigation of the 220ft span between them, the site of the likely foremost and aftmost torpedo damage.

Five dives were made directly under the forward float near Frame 46 on the first day, which had been placed in the middle of the forward damage. As they descended, divers began initially to explore forward from the datum line at the Frame 46 float. Finding no additional damage, they moved aft and between Frames 43 and 52 they found a split in the hull, just above the bilge keel, below the lower edge of the vertical armour belt. A torpedo had exploded here at the bottom of the armour belt, pushing in the lower edge of the belt by 6–8in. The pressure wave from the hit blew in the unarmoured hull below the belt, creating the split that was about 2ft wide and 10ft high. There were also more small ruptures, the edges bent outwards as though from an internal explosion – the third deck was buckled and ruptured. From Frame 52 aft to Frame 60 there was no damage.[2]

Working further aft from Frame 60, during four to five dives a day, the divers found a torpedo hit at Frame 70 on the armour belt. This strike, roughly between the two smokestacks topsides, had pushed in the belt at this point by about 2ft and blown in the shell plating below the belt, creating a large hole 25ft in length and 17ft high.

After measuring the second hole, the divers continued aft – locating another torpedo or near-miss bomb hit at Frame 80, which had likely impacted high up on the armour belt and caused damage to the shell plating above the belt. Another torpedo or near-miss bomb had opened an 8ft x 4ft hole at Frame 92, roughly under the mainmast. Plumb lines were rigged at each of the holes to allow for easy return to make more detailed measurements.

As a result of the survey dives, the destruction on the port side, though bad, was less than had been assumed after the attack. The battleship could be 'floated in a reasonable length of time by patching and dewatering'.[3] It was decided to install one large cofferdam-type patch in the midship area, from Frame 61.5 to Frame 97.5 that would completely cover the damage from torpedoes and bombs here both below and above the armour belt. A similar patch would also be installed over the forward torpedo hit at Frame 43 to Frame 52. The damage from the torpedo hit at the rudder and steering gear room would be isolated by watertight doors and air pressure.[4]

Divers spent weeks inside *West Virginia*, opening closed doors and hatches that would allow water to drain to lower spaces as the ship rose – and then be removed by deep-well pumps.

In April 1942, the two cofferdam patches were fitted in sections over the two main torpedo holes on *West Virginia*'s port beam. Skimmers then began to remove oil on the water inside the ship. A power cable from Ford Island was hooked up on 16 April 1942 and a deep-well pump installed. The eleventh and last section of patch was fitted on 1 May 1942.

Once the ship had been cleared up, lightened and her hull made watertight, dewatering began, and she was successfully refloated on 17 May 1942. On 9 June 1942, *West Virginia* was manoeuvred by tugs into Dry Dock No. 1, where once the dock gates were closed and the dock drained, her hull could be fully inspected.

At the time of the attack, it had been thought that she had been hit by five aerial torpedoes, whilst a sixth impact had been discovered during the temporary patching. The inspection of her hull in dry dock revealed damage from a seventh torpedo hit. Six of them had run quite shallow, the deepest only 11ft beneath the surface, the seventh was 19ft down and struck aft nearly destroying her steering gear. The shallow runners struck on or above the belt armour and so were relatively ineffective. Whilst belt damage itself was limited, the pressure wave from the explosion had pushed in the shell plating below the belt so far that it split. The inner torpedo bulkhead had been dished in and torn loose at its lower edge – and it was this that had allowed water to flood the fire rooms and cause the ship to list. The list subsequently allowed two more torpedoes to strike the upper part of the armour belt, damaging the structure of the ship above the belt and causing extensive flooding across and down through the second and third decks – and sinking the ship.

The ship's crew got to work with the immense task of cleaning the rest of her oily and filthy interior to make her fit for sea – and in the

USS *West Virginia* in Dry Dock No. 1 – port side amidships looking aft from Frame 64. The armour belt is heavily distorted and the hull plating below and above has been badly damaged by several Japanese Type 91 torpedoes. (*NH 64488 courtesy of US Naval History & Heritage Command*)

process two adapted Japanese AP bombs that had penetrated but not exploded were discovered.

The shipyard workers began temporary repairs to make the ship seaworthy, discovering the remains of sixty-six to seventy men who had been trapped below decks when she sank. Some of these had survived for several days in air bubbles with emergency rations and fresh water,

USS *West Virginia* is moved to a pier after being undocked from Dry Dock No. 1 at the Pearl Harbor Navy Yard, 9 September 1942. A large area of her midships upper hull still requires to be replaced. (*84005 courtesy of US Naval History & Heritage Command*)

but their air and supplies ran out long before the ship was refloated. Three of them had survived for sixteen days, as a calendar was found with an 'X' marked on each date from 7 December 1941 to 23 December 1941 inclusive.[5]

The turbo-electric drive powerplant had to be dried out as the water was removed – it was painstakingly disassembled, cleaned and then reassembled.

After completing three months of temporary repairs, *West Virginia* was undocked from Dry Dock No. 1 on 9 September 1942 and got underway for the Puget Sound Navy Yard in Bremerton, Washington for a thorough reconstruction.

Reconstruction and Modernisation, September 1942–September 1944

Being one of the most heavily damaged of the battleships at Pearl Harbor, *West Virginia* would undergo one of the most extensive reconstruction and modernisations of the Pearl Harbor battleships. Although the main

USS WEST VIRGINIA (BB-48)

battery of eight 16in/45-cal. guns would remain, the appearance of the ship would be radically altered from her pre-war configuration.

With the threat to capital ships from aerial torpedoes having been brutally reinforced at Pearl, 8ft 3in-wide torpedo bulges were fitted along each side of the ship, increasing her beam to 114ft and making her too wide to transit the Panama Canal.

The two First World War-era cage masts had been removed at Pearl during lightening of the ship for refloating. Now the heavy First World War-era armoured conning tower was also removed and a new lighter and smaller tower superstructure housing the bridge was installed, which had been removed from one of the recently rebuilt Brooklyn-class cruisers. The smaller tower was similar to the new tower fitted on *Tennessee* and reduced interference with fields of fire of the AA guns.

Near the top of the new tower was a new Mark 34 main-battery director with Mark 8 radar mounted atop – used to detect battleship-sized targets. A foremast rose from the top of the tower superstructure that accommodated an SK air-search radar and an SG surface-search radar. Abaft the new tower superstructure, the after smokestack was removed and those boiler uptakes trunked to a single enlarged forward smokestack.

A short mainmast abaft the smokestack held another SG surface-search radar at its top, whilst the low after superstructure held the after Mark 34 main-battery director and Mark 8 radar.

To increase internal compartmentalisation and improve her ability to withstand mine or torpedo strikes, the number of internal longitudinal torpedo bulkheads was increased from six to eight. To improve the ship's ability to withstand plunging fire by AP shells and bombs, an extra 3in of horizontal deck armour was added over the magazines and 2in added over the machinery spaces. The additional deck armour added some 1,400 tons to the ship – but this would be offset by the added buoyancy gained by the air spaces within the new torpedo bulges.

All the old 5in/51-cal. and 5in/25-cal. secondary and AA battery weapons were removed and replaced by sixteen more versatile 5in/38-cal. DP guns set in in eight twin mounts. These DP guns had an elevation from -15° to +85° and were controlled by four new Mark 37 analogue fire-control directors with Mark 4 radars that tracked the bearing, elevation and range of aircraft.

The light AA battery was also improved with the installation of forty Bofors 40mm autocannon in ten quad mounts and forty-three Oerlikon 20mm autocannon.

The limited number of available dry docks on the West Coast slowed the pace of reconstruction, and the badly damaged *West Virginia* had to wait until *Tennessee* and *California* were rebuilt. With less damage, they could be reconstructed and returned to the war more quickly.

Being one of the most heavily damaged of the battleships on 7 December 1941, it took two-and-a-half years before the reconstructed *West Virginia* was ready to get back into the war. When she emerged from reconstruction, she was a very different ship to the ship that had been sunk at Pearl Harbor.

BATTLESHIP REVENGE

Return to Service – September 1944

West Virginia loaded ammunition on 2 July 1944 and departed for her sea trials off Port Townsend, Washington. On 14 September 1944, escorted by two destroyers, she set off from the West Coast of the USA, west bound for her old home at Pearl Harbor.

On arrival at Pearl Harbor on 23 September 1944, *West Virginia* was assigned to Battleship Division 4 (BatDiv4) and then sailed for Seeadler Harbor at Manus with the new Essex-class fast-carrier *Hancock* (CV-19), which was en route to join the fast carriers of TF 58, assembling west of the Marianas for operations in the Ryukyus, Formosa and the Philippines.

The flotilla arrived at Seeadler Harbor on 5 October 1944, where the following day *West Virginia* became flagship of Rear Admiral Theodore D. Ruddock, commander of BatDiv4 and was assigned to Fire Support Group TG 77.2, which included *Pennsylvania, California, Tennessee, Maryland* and *Mississippi*.

(I) The Philippines Campaign
Battle of Leyte Gulf, 23–26 October 1944
(For a full description of the build-up to the Battle of Leyte Gulf, see Chapter 5, USS *California*.)

West Virginia departed Manus with the Fire Support Group on 12 October 1944 under the command of Rear Admiral Jesse B. Oldendorf, to support the amphibious landings at Leyte Gulf, at the south of Leyte, one of the larger islands in the Philippines.

The Fire Support Group ships arrived off Leyte on D-Day Dinagat, 17 October 1944, entering Leyte Gulf the following day to take up their bombardment positions. Over the course of the next days, they covered UDT swimmers as they carried out beach reconnaissance and clearance operations and minesweepers as they cleared the approaches to the landing areas.

At 0645 on 19 October, the Fire Support ships began a naval bombardment of the Tacloban area at the north of the gulf. By the time they withdrew for the night, *West Virginia* had fired almost 300 16in main-battery rounds and more than 1,500 5in secondary battery rounds.

A-Day for the Leyte landings was 20 October 1944 – and the Fire Support Group ships resumed firing at 0600, targeting the landing beaches. After 3½ hours, the Marines began their approaches to the beaches in their LVTs and Higgins boats. As they began disembarking at 1000, the Fire Support warships fired at positions ahead of their advance.

Whilst operating close inshore in her bombardment position in Leyte Gulf in support of the landing forces, *West Virginia* lightly touched the bottom, damaging three of her four propellers and causing a shaft vibration that limited her speed to 16 knots. Her fighting ability had not been affected – and she remained on station in the Fire Support Group.

The landings triggered Japanese command to initiate their pre-planned response Operation *Shō-Gō* 1, which would in turn lead to the series of actions which together are known as the Battle of Leyte Gulf. *West Virginia* would feature heavily in one of those actions, the Battle of the Surigao Strait, the last clash between battleships.

Battle of Surigao Strait, 25 October 1944
On 24 October 1944, following reports of Japanese naval forces approaching the Leyte Gulf area, Oldendorf poisoned his battle line of six battleships, *Pennsylvania*, *Tennessee*, *California*, *West Virginia*, *Maryland* and *Mississippi*, across the northern exit from the Surigao Strait. The battleships were flanked by eight cruisers whilst twenty-eight nimble destroyers took up position further down the strait in the line of enemy advance. Fast Patrol Boats (PT Boats) carrying torpedoes took up the most advanced position towards the southern end of the Surigao Strait, the channel between the two southern islands of Leyte and Mindanao that allowed an approach to the Allied landing areas in Leyte Gulf.

The Japanese Southern Force of two battleships, *Yamashiro* and *Fusō*, the heavy cruiser *Mogami* and four destroyers attempted to transit east and north through the Surigao Strait on the night of 24/25 October 1944 – they were running straight into Oldendorf's carefully positioned battle line.

Oldendorf's PT Boats attacked the oncoming Southern Force first of all – but the Japanese ships beat them off and kept moving in line ahead, pressing on to break through to Leyte Gulf. US destroyers then attacked, scoring one to two torpedo hits on the battleship *Fusō* on her starboard side amidships at 0309 that disabled her. Nevertheless, the remainder of the Southern Force continued on through the Surigao Strait.

But 10 minutes later, the battleship *Yamashiro* and three destroyers were also hit, although *Yamashiro* was able to continue on towards Leyte Gulf with the heavy cruiser *Mogami* and escort destroyers. At about 0330, *Yamashiro* was hit by another torpedo – but even so, she was still able to make speed for battle. Meanwhile, far astern of the flotilla, the crippled battleship *Fusō* exploded catastrophically at about 0345 – and broke in two.

In Oldendorf's battle line, *West Virginia*'s new radar picked up the oncoming Japanese squadron in darkness at a range of 42,000yd, over 20 miles. Oldendorf gave the order to open fire at 0351, and *West Virginia*, fresh from refit and equipped with the latest state-of-the-art radar fire-control systems, was the first of the battleships to open fire. The main-battery guns of *Tennessee* and *California* opened up shortly after – concentrating their fire on the remaining battleship *Yamashiro*. The other US battleships with their older, less-effective radars had trouble locating a target in the darkness and held their fire. *Yamashiro* was hit several times by the Allied warships and was forced to turn to withdraw. But she was then hit by a third torpedo – and then a fourth.

Shortly thereafter, Oldendorf ordered his battleships to make a 150-degree turn, and *West Virginia* began her turn at 0402, leading the other battleships onto the new course, which ran parallel to *Yamashiro*'s line of retreat. *California* however fell out of position, and in so doing, masked the rest of the battleships.

At 0409, Oldendorf ordered his ships to cease firing following reports that he was hitting his own ships. Shortly thereafter, reports of Japanese torpedoes in the water prompted the US battleships to make an evasive turn to the north at 0418. By this time, *Yamashiro* was rolling over and sinking.

With both Japanese battleships now sunk, the badly damaged heavy cruiser *Mogami* and surviving destroyers withdrew, exiting westwards from the Surigao Strait at about 0600. *Mogami* would be sunk later in the day by US fast-carrier planes.

The Battle of the Surigao Strait was over – it would, in time, prove to be the last clash of battleships in history. *West Virginia* had fired sixteen salvos of her 16in main-battery guns.

Post-Leyte Operations
Four days after the Battle of the Surigao Strait, with the landings on Leyte secure and the IJN now comprehensively defeated and having withdrawn west, *West Virginia*, *Tennessee* and *Maryland* departed Leyte on 29 October 1944 and headed almost 1,000nm east to replenish at the forward base at Ulithi Atoll, almost midway between Guam and Palau.

USS *WEST VIRGINIA* (BB-48)

From Ulithi, *West Virginia* was despatched more than 2,000nm southeast to the naval base at Espiritu Santo, where she entered the large ten-section auxiliary floating dry dock USS *Artisan* (ABSD-1), which had been towed in sections from San Francisco the previous summer and assembled there.

Once repairs to her shafts and maintenance had been completed, she was undocked and headed more than 3,000nm back to the Philippines – where intense opposition was still being offered by more than 400,000 Japanese troops stationed throughout its thousands of islands. After calling at Manus, *West Virginia* re-entered Leyte Gulf on 25 November 1944 and began patrolling the area to defend Allied forces ashore and afloat.

During repeated attacks on US shipping by enemy aircraft, *West Virginia*'s AA gunners shot down a kamikaze on 27 November 1944,

USS *West Virginia* in floating dry dock USS *Artisan* (ABSD-1) at Espiritu Santo, New Hebrides, 13 November 1944. She is undergoing repairs after touching ground off Leyte with her propellers on 21 October 1944. (*80-G-314220 courtesy of US Naval History & Heritage Command*)

and then the next day her guns were in action again as several more kamikazes were destroyed.

West Virginia remained off Leyte until 2 December 1944, when she departed for the Palau Islands for replenishment. On arrival at Palau, she was selected as the flagship of TG 77.12, the Heavy Cover and Carrier Group, for the next landing in the central Philippines on the island of Mindoro. Once seized, airfields would be established that could allow fighter cover for the next major operation in the Philippines, the invasion of Lingayen Gulf in northern Luzon Island.

The invasion fleet departed from Palau west bound, passing through Leyte Gulf on 12 December 1944 and pushing on southwest through the Surigao Strait and into the wide expanses of the central Sulu Sea. As amphibious troops landed on Mindoro, they encountered little Japanese opposition and the island was secured in three days. The transports withdrew on 15 December, screened by *West Virginia* and the other units of the Heavy Cover Group.

West Virginia replenished in Leyte Gulf before heading southwest to the Kossol Roads anchorage at the north of the Palauan archipelago, where the fleet was staging for the invasion of Lingayen Gulf on the northwest coast of Luzon Island, the largest and northernmost island of the Philippine archipelago. *West Virginia* arrived in the Palaus on 19 December 1944.

The Invasion of Lingayen Gulf, 3–13 January 1945
(For a full description of the invasion of Lingayen Gulf, see Chapter 5, USS *California*.)

On 1 January 1945, *West Virginia* sortied from the Palaus for the invasion of Lingayen Gulf with the Bombardment and Fire Support Group TG 77.2, which held the battleships *Mississippi*, *California*, *Pennsylvania*, *Colorado* and *New Mexico* along with heavy cruisers, light cruisers and destroyers. Vice Admiral Jesse B. Oldendorf was once again in command.

After entering Leyte Gulf on 3 January, the invasion armada steamed into the Sulu Sea, where they came under heavy Japanese air attack the next day. The escort carrier *Ommaney Bay* (CVE-79) was hit and badly damaged by kamikazes, fires took hold and explosions rocked the carrier after the crew had abandoned ship, *West Virginia* receiving some of the crew. The carrier was eventually scuttled by torpedoes from the destroyer *Burns* (DD-588).

The invasion armada turned north toward Lingayen Gulf on 5 January under continual Japanese attack. AA gunners aboard *West*

USS *WEST VIRGINIA* (BB-48)

Virginia had a busy day as she approached her bombardment position off San Fernando Point.

Early on 6 January 1945, protected by the heavily armoured battleships, Allied minesweepers swept two channels into Lingayen Gulf, from its entrance to the landing beaches. UDT swimmers inspected the beaches but found no submerged beach obstacles.

At about noon, Vice Admiral Jesse B. Oldendorf, aboard *California*, led the bombardment group into Lingayen Gulf to begin the pre-invasion naval bombardment. The Fire Support Group was heavily attacked by kamikazes, with *California* being disabled and *New Mexico* and several other warships being damaged.

West Virginia and other fire-support ships bombarded enemy positions near the town of San Fabian on 8 and 9 January, virtually flattening the town. As ground troops went ashore later on S-Day,

USS *Pennsylvania* fires her 14in/45-cal. guns during the pre-invasion bombardment of Lingayen Gulf, c. 7–9 January 1945. (*80-G-59523 courtesy of US Naval History & Heritage Command*)

9 January 1945, *West Virginia* continued firing in support through to the following day, 10 January S-Day+1.

Following the successful landings, *West Virginia* spent the next week patrolling in the South China Sea off Lingayen Gulf, screening the beachhead against enemy approach by air or sea – and being called on to neutralise enemy defensive positions and destroy ammunition dumps ashore. Her guns fired to destroy rail and road infrastructure and disrupt the Japanese from bringing in reinforcements.

Over the course of the bombardment, *West Virginia* had fired almost 400 main-battery shells and nearly 3,000 rounds from her secondary 5in battery. She was detached on 17 January to replenish – before returning once again to resume fire-support duties.

West Virginia remained off Luzon until 10 February 1945 – firing as required to support ground troops fighting ashore who were pressing north across Luzon and covering transport ships carrying supplies for the army as they arrived to unload at the Lingayen Gulf beachhead.

On 10 February 1945, *Pennsylvania*, *Mississippi* and *West Virginia* were disjoined for Manus, via Ulithi, for replenishment. *West Virginia* reached Ulithi on 16 February where she was attached to the 5th Fleet for the next operation, the invasion of Iwo Jima.

(II) Battle of Iwo Jima – Operation DETACHMENT, 19 February–26 March 1945

(For a full account of the Battle of Iwo Jima, see Chapter 7, USS *Nevada*.)

The volcanic island of Iwo Jima held three Japanese airfields from which enemy planes could strike at Allied shipping and positions in the northern Marianas. Lying 750 miles south of Tokyo, once taken, Iwo Jima could be used as an airbase for long-range P-51 Mustang fighters to escort the Boeing B-29 Superfortress four-engine heavy bomber on raids over Japan. Iwo Jima could also serve as an emergency landing base for damaged B-29s returning from those raids that were unable to reach their main bases at Guam and Saipan.

As *West Virginia* was inbound to Ulithi from Lingayen Gulf, the TF 54 Fire Support Group battleships, cruisers and destroyers arrived off Iwo Jima on 16 February 1945 to begin the pre-invasion naval bombardment on 17 February. As they closed, the TF 54 bombardment group ships were met by accurate Japanese counter-battery fire from coastal batteries that damaged the battleship *Tennessee*, the cruiser *Pensacola* (CA-24) and the destroyer *Leutze* (DD-481), as they protected UDT swimmers reconnoitring the landing beaches.

USS *WEST VIRGINIA* (BB-48)

As the TF 54 bombardment of Iwo Jima was beginning on 17 February 1945, *West Virginia* departed Ulithi at first light with a destroyer screen, arriving on the third day of the naval bombardment on D-Day Iwo Jima, 19 February 1945.

West Virginia received her orders almost immediately via despatch boat – her guns quickly opening up on enemy gun positions, blockhouses, revetments, tanks, vehicles, caves and supply dumps as US Marines landed on the black volcanic beach and were subjected to withering Japanese heavy artillery from Mount Suribachi.

Despite vicious fighting ashore, the US flag was raised on Mount Suribachi on 23 February 1945 and *West Virginia* was able to withdraw for Ulithi on 4 March to replenish.

(III) Battle of Okinawa – Operation ICEBERG, 1 April–22 June 1945

(For a full account of the Battle of Okinawa, see Chapter 5, USS *California*.)

TF 54, under the command of Rear Admiral Morton L. Deyo, began training east of Ulithi for the invasion of Okinawa, codenamed Operation ICEBERG, slated for 1 April 1945. *West Virginia* was assigned to Fire Support Unit 4 of the Gunfire Support TG 54.1, along with the battleship *Idaho*, the heavy cruisers *Pensacola* and *Portland*, the light cruiser *Biloxi* and six destroyers – with FSU4 being tasked to target the Hagushi Beaches Area of Okinawa and cover minesweeping activities. Training ended on 21 March 1945 – when TF 54 deployed northwest towards Okinawa.

TG 54.1 arrived off Okinawa on 25 March and moved into position that night, ready to begin their bombardment missions at dawn on 26 March 1945. As their guns opened up, attacks by kamikazes on FSU4 damaged the light cruiser *Biloxi* and the destroyer *Porterfield*. At 1029, lookouts on *West Virginia* reported a gun flash from shore, and when a Japanese shell fell some 5,000yd off *West Virginia*'s port bow, she opened counter-battery fire in response, her main-battery guns firing twenty-eight 16in shells.

The TG 54.1 Gunfire Support Group continued to pound enemy positions ashore during the following days in the lead-up to D-Day Okinawa, 1 April 1945. The bombardment ships attracted intense Japanese aerial counterattacks – and *West Virginia*'s AA gunners shot down a Yokosuka P1Y bomber on 27 March. In advance of D-Day, *West Virginia* retired to refuel and rearm at Kerama Retto, seized at the outset of the campaign to provide an advance base.

West Virginia closed Okinawa once again in the early hours of D-Day 1 April to take up her allocated fire support station, her AA gunners

PEARL HARBOR'S REVENGE

Crewmen on watch on a Bofors 40mm quad gun mount aboard USS *West Virginia* during the invasion of Okinawa, 1 April 1945. (*80-G-K-4707 courtesy of US Naval History & Heritage Command*)

shooting down an enemy aircraft that was closing the Allied vessels. Shortly thereafter, a group of four more Japanese aircraft appeared, one of which was shot down by *West Virginia*'s AA battery.

By 0630, *West Virginia* had reached her assigned position just 900yd (half a mile) from shore and began shelling the Hagushi landing beach as landing craft filled with Marines slowly made their runs ashore, encountering little resistance on the beaches. *West Virginia* remained offshore on D-Day – although her guns were not immediately needed.

A wave of kamikazes attacked Allied shipping that evening just after dusk, with one kamikaze getting through the AA fire and crashing at 1903 into *West Virginia*'s superstructure, just forward of the No. 2 director for the secondary battery. The resulting explosion killed four crew and wounded seven more in one of the 20mm Oerlikon gun galleries. The kamikaze plane was carrying a bomb that penetrated to the second deck, though it failed to detonate and was subsequently defuzed by the ship's bomb disposal officer.

Despite the kamikaze hit, *West Virginia*'s fighting ability was unaffected, and the ship remained off Okinawa through the night, firing star shells to illuminate US troop positions ashore and help thwart any infiltration by Japanese troops. On 6 April, her AA gunners shot down a Val dive bomber.

On 7 April, whilst *West Virginia* was tasked to patrol to the west of Okinawa, six Fire Support Unit battleships, cruisers and destroyers were sent north to intercept a powerful southbound Japanese force of the 64,000-ton superbattleship *Yamato*, the cruiser *Yahagi* and eight destroyers, spotted departing the Bungo Strait between the Japanese home islands of Kyushu and Shikoku. The IJN was committing much of its remaining surface strength in an operation to relieve Okinawa, where operating with kamikaze and Okinawa-based army units the Japanese warships would sail directly into the Allied ships and troop transports and inflict as much damage as possible. *Yamato* would then be beached to act as a devastating, heavily armoured and unsinkable gun battery – to fight until she was destroyed.

As the Fire Support Group battleships headed north to intercept, the Japanese warships headed for Okinawa came under constant air attack from the fast carriers of TF 58, which successfully sunk six of the ten enemy ships in the force, including *Yamato*.

On 8 April, word reached *West Virginia* that most of the Japanese warships had been sunk or fled – and *West Virginia* was able to resume her bombardment position off Okinawa.

Some two weeks later, *West Virginia* was detached on 20 April to head to Ulithi for replenishment – however en route, when her sister *Colorado* was damaged by an accidental ammunition explosion at Kerama Retto, *West Virginia* was recalled to Okinawa where she once again operated off the Hagushi Beaches Area in support of ground troops, firing night harassment and interdiction fire through to June 1945. Her guns were repeatedly called into action to hit enemy blockhouses, break up enemy troop concentrations and destroy enemy caves.

(IV) Occupation of Japan

At the end of June 1945, *West Virginia* left Okinawan waters to begin training in the Philippines for the expected invasion of the Japanese home island of Kyushu. She arrived back in Okinawa on 6 August 1945, the day the first atomic bomb was dropped on Hiroshima. On 15 August

1945, Emperor Hirohito announced Japan's surrender following the second atomic bomb on Nagasaki on 9 August 1945.

West Virginia departed Okinawa on 24 August for Tokyo Bay, assigned to TG 35, the Support Force of the 3rd Fleet for the occupation of the Japanese homeland. The Support Force entered Tokyo Bay on 31 August 1945 and *West Virginia* was present during the formal surrender ceremonies aboard the battleship *Missouri* on 2 September 1945.

West Virginia remained in Tokyo for the next two weeks to assist with the initial occupation of Japan, before getting underway on 20 September 1945, with a group of 270 passengers for repatriation to the USA, heading initially southbound with TG 30.4 for Okinawa. After pausing at Okinawa for a few days, *West Virginia* then set off east bound for the passage of more than 4,000nm to Pearl Harbor, where she arrived on 4 October 1945.

West Virginia departed Pearl Harbor on 9 October 1945 for San Diego in California, reaching home waters for the first time in two years on 22 October 1945. Just over one week later, on 30 October 1945, *West Virginia* departed San Diego, westbound for Pearl Harbor for Operation MAGIC CARPET, the repatriation of US servicemen from the Pacific theatre. She would make several repatriation runs from Hawaii to San Diego towards the end of 1945.

On 4 January 1946, *West Virginia* departed San Diego for Puget Sound Navy Yard, Bremerton. On arrival at Bremerton on 12 January, she was deactivated and subsequently moved to Seattle, Washington four days later – where she was laid up alongside her sister *Colorado*. The great battleship was formally decommissioned on 9 January 1947 and assigned to the Pacific Reserve Fleet.

On 1 March 1959, *West Virginia* was struck from the Naval Vessel Register. Later than year, she was sold on 24 August 1959 to the Union Minerals & Alloys Corporation to be broken up for scrap.

West Virginia was towed to the Todd-Pacific Shipyard in Seattle on 3 January 1961 to be dismantled. When the ship was sold for scrap, students at West Virginia University helped raise funds to preserve the ship's mast, which arrived on the West Virginia University campus on 17 March 1961 and was installed at Memorial Plaza there. The ship's bell is on display at the West Virginia State Museum in Charleston.

Notes

Chapter 1

1. Captain Mitsuo Fuchida, 'I led the Air Attack on Pearl Harbor', ed. Roger Pineau, *US Naval Institute Proceedings*, Vol. 78/9/595, September 1952.
2. Okumiya Masatake and Jiro Horikoshi, *Zero! The Story of the Japanese Navy Air Force 1937–1945* (Cassell & Co. Ltd, 1957), p. 42.
3. H.P. Willmott, *Pearl Harbor* (Cassell & Co., 2001), p. 74.
4. Masatake and Horikoshi, *Zero!*, p. 42.
5. Peter Wetzler, *Hirohito and War: Imperial Tradition and Military Decision Making in Pre-war Japan* (University of Hawaii Press, 1998), pp. 28–30, 39.
6. William Koenig, *Epic Sea Battles* (Octopus Books Ltd, 1975), p. 141.

Chapter 2

1. Masatake and Horikoshi, *Zero!*, p. 50.
2. Ibid., p. 43.
3. Ibid.
4. Ibid., p. 44.
5. Ibid.
6. Ibid., pp. 44–5.
7. Edward C. Raymer, *Descent into Darkness: Pearl Harbor, 1941 – A Navy Diver's Memoir* (Naval Institute Press, 2006), p. 76.
8. Daniel Madsen, *Resurrection: Salvaging the Battle Fleet at Pearl Harbor* (Naval Institute Press, 2003), p. 17.
9. Masatake and Horikoshi, *Zero!*, p. 45.
10. Fuchida, 'I Led the Air Attack on Pearl Harbor', ed. Pineau, *US Naval Institute Proceedings*, Vol. 78/9/595, September 1952.

11. Raymer, *Descent into Darkness*, pp. 26–7.
12. Ibid., pp. 124–5.
13. *Report of the Repair & Salvage of Naval Vessels Damaged at Pearl Harbor, T.H. on December 7, 1941, by the Salvage Officer,* 13 July 1942, NA, RG 181.
14. D.H. Clark, 'Battleship Condition as Reported by Commander Kranzfelter and Lieutenant Mandelkorn at 1000', 7 December 1941, NHC, Wallin Papers.
15. Captain H.N. Wallin, memorandum No. 7, 'Check-up of the Situation on the Battleships as of 1600 This Date. December 9 1941', NHC, Wallin Papers.

Chapter 3

1. Base Force salvage memorandum, 17 December 1941, From NA, RG 181.
2. Planning officer, memorandum for the manager, 8 December 1941, commanding officer, USS *Maryland*, 'Damage Sustained in Action December 7, 1941', December 19, 1941, NHC, Wallin Papers.
3. Madsen, *Resurrection*, p. 49.
4. H.N. Wallin, 'Memorandum Covering Apparent Damage to Vessels in Pearl as of 1600 This Date', 7 December 1941, NHC, Wallin Papers.
5. 'USS *Nevada* – Summary of Action Taken', NA, RG 181.
6. Log of the CALIFORNIA, NA, RG 24.
7. Ibid.
8. USS TENNESSEE: ACTION REPORT-JAPANESE ATTACK ON PEARL HARBOR, 7 DECEMBER 1941, Department of the Navy, Naval History & Heritage Command.
9. USS TENNESSEE: BOMB DAMAGE, DECEMBER 7, 1941, PEARL HARBOR, War Damage Report No. 22, Submitted November 15, 1942, Department of the Navy, Naval History & Heritage Command.
10. Madsen, *Resurrection*, p. 85.
11. USS WEST VIRGINIA: REPORT OF SALVAGE OF, Submitted June 15, 1942, Department of the Navy, Naval History & Heritage Command.
12. Base Force Salvage Memorandum (BFSM), 3 January 1942.

Chapter 4

1. Norman Friedman, *U.S. Battleships – An illustrated Design History* (Naval Institute Press, 1985), pp. 101–2.
2. Norman Friedman, *The British Battleship, 1906–1946* (Seaforth Publishing, 2015), p. 207.

NOTES

3. www.navsource.org.
4. G. von Hase, *Kiel and Jutland* (Leonaur Ltd, 2011, 1st edn 1923), p. 51.
5. Friedman, *U.S. Battleships*, p. 438.

Chapter 5

1. Madsen, *Resurrection*, p. 23.
2. USS CALIFORNIA: TORPEDO AND BOMB DAMAGE. DECEMBER 7, 1941. PEARL HARBOR, War Damage Report No. 21, Bureau of Ships, Department of the Navy, Naval History & Heritage Command, p. 16.
3. Ibid., p. 14.
4. Ibid., pp. 22–3.
5. Medal of Honor citation.
6. Madsen, *Resurrection*, p. 86.
7. USS CALIFORNIA: TORPEDO AND BOMB DAMAGE. DECEMBER 7, 1941. PEARL HARBOR, War Damage Report No. 21, Bureau of Ships, Department of the Navy, Naval History & Heritage Command, p. 19.
8. Base Force Salvage Memorandum (BFSM), 27 December 19421.
9. Madsen, *Resurrection*, pp. 106–8.
10. Ibid., p. 157.
11. USS CALIFORNIA: TORPEDO AND BOMB DAMAGE. DECEMBER 7, 1941. PEARL HARBOR, War Damage Report No. 21, Bureau of Ships, Department of the Navy, Naval History & Heritage Command, p. 19.
12. Madsen, *Resurrection*, p. 166.
13. Samuel E. Morison, *History of U.S. Naval Operations in World War II*: Vol. XII, *Leyte* (Little, Brown and Co., 1958), p. 58.
14. Masatake and Horikoshi, *Zero!*, p. 260.
15. Masanori Ito, *The End of the Imperial Japanese Navy* (1956), p. 209; Morison, *History of U.S. Naval Operations in World War II*: Vol. XII, *Leyte*, p. 91; James A. Field, *The Japanese at Leyte Gulf* (Princeton University Press, 1947), p. 27.
16. Morison, *History of U.S. Naval Operations in World War II*: Vol. XII, *Leyte*, pp. 165–9.
17. William F. Halsey and Joseph Bryan, *Admiral Halsey's Story* (Whittlesey House, 1947), p. 169.
18. Ibid.
19. Clark G. Reynolds, *The Fast Carriers – The Forging of an Air Navy* (Naval Institute Press, 1968), p. 266. Halsey and Bryan, *Admiral Halsey's Story*, p. 170.

20. Sherman Action Report, 0090, 2 December 1944.
21. Halsey and Bryan, *Admiral Halsey's Story*, p. 170.
22. Ibid., p. 171.
23. CINCPAC Nimitz, Communique No. 16G, 2.
24. Sherman Action Report, 0090, 2 December 1944.
25. Morison, *History of U.S. Naval Operations in World War II*: Vol. XII, *Leyte*, p. 194; Theodore Taylor, *The Magnificent Mitscher* (Naval Institute Press, 1954), p. 262.
26. Harold E. Stassen, Halsey's flag secretary to Clark G. Reynolds, 25 June 1964.
27. Halsey Action Report, 0088, 13 November 1944.
28. Halsey and Bryan, *Admiral Halsey's Story*, p. 171.
29. Ibid., p. 172.
30. Ibid.
31. Ibid.
32. Ibid.; Hanson Baldwin, *The Battle of Leyte Gulf* (1955), p. 327.
33. Comer Vann Woodward, *The Battle for Leyte Gulf* (Macmillan, 1947).
34. *US Naval Institute Proceedings*, April 1959.
35. Kinkaid's notes to Baldwin's *Battle of Leyte Gulf*, p. 354.
36. Halsey and Bryan, *Admiral Halsey's Story*, p. 174.
37. Ibid.
38. Ibid., p. 179.
39. Kurita interviewed by Masanori Ito and quoted in *End of the Imperial Japanese Navy*, p. 166.
40. Ibid., pp. 166–7; Field, *Japanese at Leyte Gulf*, pp. 125–8.
41. Halsey and Bryan, *Admiral Halsey's Story*, p. 179.
42. Ibid., p. 173.
43. Ibid., p. 174.
44. Ibid.
45. Ibid.
46. Ibid.
47. Ibid.
48. Ibid., p. 173.
49. Ibid., p. 175.
50. Ibid.
51. Captain Andrew Hamilton, USNR, 'Where is Task Force Thirty-Four?', *US Naval Institute Proceedings*, 86 (October 1960), pp. 76–80.
52. Sherman Action Report, 2 December 1944.
53. Halsey and Bryan, *Admiral Halsey's Story*, p. 176.
54. Halsey to Nimitz, 250215, from Messages, Halsey Action Report, 13 November 1944.

NOTES

55. Halsey and Bryan, *Admiral Halsey's Story*, p. 177.
56. Ibid., p. 179.
57. Woodward, *Battle for Leyte Gulf*, p. 185.
58. Halsey Action Report, 13 November 1944.
59. Halsey and Bryan, *Admiral Halsey's Story*, p. 181.
60. Ernest J. King and Walter King, *Fleet Admiral King: A Naval Record* (Eyre & Spottiswoode, 1953), pp. 598, 621.
61. Fleet Admiral William D. Leahy, USN, *I Was There* (1950), pp. 383–5.
62. King and King, *Fleet Admiral King*, p. 611.

Chapter 6

1. Friedman, *U.S. Battleships*, p. 207.
2. USS MARYLAND: REPORT OF PEARL HARBOR ATTACK, DECEMBER 7, 1941, Submitted December 15, 1941, BB48/A16/Of10(0229), Department of the Navy, Naval History & Heritage Command.
3. Planning officer, memorandum for the manager, 8 December 1941; commanding officer, USS *Maryland*, 'Damage Sustained in Action December 7, 1941', December 19, 1941, NHC, Wallin Papers (p. 223, No. 13 resurrection).
4. Friedman, *U.S. Battleships*, p. 364.
5. US Marine Corps Historical Branch, G-3 Division, *History of U.S. Marine Corps Operations in WWII. Central Pacific Drive* (US Government Printing Office, 1966), pp. 53–71.
6. Friedman, *U.S. Battleships*, p. 364.
7. Ibid., p. 368.

Chapter 7

1. USS NEVADA: REPORT OF PEARL HARBOR ATTACK, DECEMBER 7, 1941, BB36/A9/A16, Submitted December 15, 1941, Department of the Navy, Naval History & Heritage Command, Commanding Officer – Offensive Measures Taken.
2. Ibid.
3. Madsen, *Resurrection*, p. 17.
4. USS NEVADA: REPORT OF PEARL HARBOR ATTACK, DECEMBER 7, 1941, BB36/A9/A16, Submitted December 15, 1941, Department of the Navy, Naval History & Heritage Command, Commanding Officer – Offensive Measures Taken, 1.5.

5. US Naval History and Heritage Command, *Operation Neptune. The U.S. Navy on D-Day, 6 June 1944*, www.history.navy.mil.
6. *Nevada, Dictionary of American Naval Fighting Ships* (Navy Department, Government Printing Office, Washington DC, 1963–81).

Chapter 8

1. USS TENNESSEE: BOMB DAMAGE, DECEMBER 7, 1941, PEARL HARBOR, War Damage Report No. 22, Submitted November 15, 1942, Department of the Navy, Naval History & Heritage Command.

Chapter 10

1. Raymer, *Descent into Darkness*, p. 113.
2. Madsen, *Resurrection*, pp. 84–5.
3. Base Force Salvage Memorandum, 3 January 1942.
4. USS WEST VIRGINIA: REPORT OF SALVAGE OF, Submitted June 15, 1942, Department of the Navy, Naval History & Heritage Command.
5. Ibid., para 31.

Select Bibliography

Admiralty, SW1, Gunnery Branch. *The Gunnery Pocket Book*, BR 224/45, 1945

Alden, Carroll Storrs, and Allan Westcott, *The United States Navy*, 2nd edn, rev., Lippincott, 1945

Alden, John D., *U.S. Submarine Attacks during WWII*, Naval Institute Press, 1989

Baldwin, Hanson, *The Battle of Leyte Gulf*, 1955

Bartholomew, C.A., *Mud, Muscle and Miracles: Marine Salvage in the United States Navy*, Naval Historical Center and Naval Sea Systems Command, 1990

Blair, Clay, Jr, *Silent Victory – the U.S. Submarine War against Japan*, J.B. Lippincott Company, 1975

Boyd, Carl and Yoshida, Akihiko, *The Japanese Submarine Force and World War II*, Naval Institute Press, 1995

Congress of the United States, *Report of the Joint Committee on the Investigation of the Pearl Harbor Attack*, US Government Printing Office, 1946

Costello, John, *The Pacific War: 1941–1945*, William Morrow, 1982

Cressman, Robert J., *Official Chronology of the U.S. Navy in World War II*, US Naval Institute Press, 1999

Crowl, Phillip A. and Edmond F. Love, *The United States Army in World War II – The War in the Pacific – Seizure of the Gilberts and Marshalls*, US Government Printing Office, 1955

Cutler, Thomas J., *The Battle of Leyte Gulf, 23–26 October 1944*, HarperCollins, 1994

Dictionary of American Naval Fighting Ships, Navy Department, Government Printing Office, Washington DC, 1963–81

Doyle, David, *USS Tennessee (BB-43): From Pearl Harbor to Okinawa in World War II*, Schiffer Publishing Ltd, 2019

Falk, Stanley, *Bloodiest Victory – Palaus*, Ballantine Books, 1974
Field, James A., *The Japanese at Leyte Gulf*, Princeton University Press, 1947
Forrestal, Vice Admiral Emmet. P., USN, *Admiral Raymond A. Spruance, USN: A Study in Command*, US Government Printing Office, 1966
Friedman, Kenneth I., *Afternoon of the Rising Sun: The Battle of Leyte Gulf*, Presidio Press, 2001
Friedman, Norman, *U.S. Battleships – An Illustrated Design History*, Naval Institute Press, 1985
——, *The British Battleship, 1906–1946*, Seaforth Publishing, 2015
Halsey, William F. and Joseph Bryan, *Admiral Halsey's Story*, Whittlesey House, 1947
Harmsen, Peter, *Storm Clouds over the Pacific, 1931–1941*, Casemate Publishers, 2019
Hase, G. von. *Kiel and Jutland*, Leonaur Ltd, 2011, 1st edn 1923
Hough, Major Frank O., USMCR, *The Assault on Peleliu*, Historical Division HQ US Marine Corps, 1950
Ito, Masanori, *The End of the Imperial Japanese Navy*, Macfadden-Bartell, 1965
Jane, Fred T., *Jane's Fighting Ships 1944–45*, David & Charles Ltd, 1971
Jentschura, Hansgeorg, *Warships of the Imperial Japanese Navy 1869–1945*, Naval Institute Press, 1977
Kimmel, Husband E., *Admiral Kimmel's Story*, Henry Regnery Co., 1955
King, Fleet Admiral Ernest J., *U.S. Navy at War, 1941–1945*, US Navy Department, 1946
King, Ernest J. and Walter King, *Fleet Admiral King: A Naval Record*, Eyre & Spottiswoode, 1953
Koenig, William, *Epic Sea Battles*, Octopus Books Ltd, 1975
Layton, Edwin T., *And I was There: Pearl Harbor and Midway – Breaking the Secrets*, Naval Institute Press, 1985
Leahy, Fleet Admiral William D., USN, 'I Was There', *The American Historical Review*, Vol. 55, Issue 4, 1950
Lloyd, Keith Warren, *Avenging Pearl Harbour*, Lyons Press, 2022
Lord, Walter, *Day of Infamy: The Bombing of Pearl Harbor*, Henry Holt & Co., 1957
Macdonald, Rod, *Task Force 58: The US Navy's Fast Carrier Strike Force That Won the War in The Pacific*, Frontline Books and Naval Institute Press, 2021
Madsen, Daniel, *Resurrection: Salvaging the Battle Fleet at Pearl Harbor*, Naval Institute Press, 2003
Masatake, Okumiya and Jiro Horikoshi, *Zero! The Story of the Japanese Navy Air Force, 1937–1945*, Cassell & Co. Ltd, 1957

SELECT BIBLIOGRAPHY

Mitchell, Robert J., Sewell Tappan Tyng, Nelson L. Drummond Jr and Gregory J.W. Urwin, *The Capture of Attu: A World War II Battle as Told by the Men Who Fought There*, University of Nebraska Press, 2000

Morison, Samuel E., *History of U.S. Naval Operations in World War II*, Little, Brown and Co., 1949–60:
  Vol. IV, *Coral Sea, Midway and Submarine Actions*, 1949
  Vol. V, *The Struggle for Guadalcanal*, 1949
  Vol. VI, *Breaking the Bismarcks Barrier*, 1950
  Vol. VII, *Aleutians, Gilberts and Marshalls*, 1957
  Vol. VIII, *New Guinea and the Marianas*, 1957
  Vol. XII: *Leyte*, 1958
  Vol. XIII, *The Liberation of the Philippines*, 1959
  Vol. XIV, *Victory in the Pacific*, 1960
——, *The Two Ocean War*, 1963

Peattie, Mark R., *Nanyo – The Rise and Fall of the Japanese in Micronesia 1885–1945*, University of Hawaii Press, 1988

Prados, John, *Combined Fleet Decoded*, Random House, 1995

Raymer, Edward C., *Descent into Darkness: Pearl Harbor, 1941 – A Navy Diver's Memoir*, Naval Institute Press, 2006

Reynolds, Clark G., *The Fast Carriers – The Forging of an Air Navy*, Naval Institute Press, 1968

Rottman, Gordon L., *The Marshall Islands 1944: Operation Flintlock, the Capture of Kwajalein and Eniwetok*, Osprey Publishing, 2004

Russ, Martin, *Line of Departure: Tarawa*, Doubleday & Co., 1975

Sledge, Eugene B., *With the Old Breed at Peleliu and Okinawa*, Presidion Press, 1981

Sloan, B., *Brotherhood of Heroes: The Marines at Peleliu, 1944 – The Bloodiest Battle of the Pacific War*, Simon & Schuster, 2005

Smith, Myron J., Jr, *Mountaineer Battlewagon: USS West Virginia (BB-48)*, Pictorial Histories Publishing Co., 1982

Spector, Ronald H., *Eagle Against the Sun: The American War with Japan*, Random House, 1992

Stille, Mark, *US Standard-Type Battleships 1941–45 (1)*, Osprey Publishing, 2015

——, *US Standard-Type Battleships 1941–45 (2)* Osprey Publishing, 2015

Taylor, Theodore, *The Magnificent Mitscher*, Naval Institute Press, 1954

Toland, John, *But Not in Shame: The Six Months After Pearl Harbor*, Random House, 1961

Toll, Ian W., *Pacific Crucible: War at Sea in the Pacific, 1941–1943*, W.W. Norton & Co., 2012
——, *The Conquering Tide: War in the Pacific Islands, 1942–1944*, W.W. Norton & Co., 2020
US Marine Corps Historical Branch, G-3 Division, *History of U.S. Marine Corps Operations in WWII. Central Pacific Drive*, US Government Printing Office, 1966
U.S. Navy Action and Operational Reports from World War II. Pacific Theater. Part 3. Fifth Fleet and Fifth Fleet Carrier Task Forces, University Publications of America, 1990
Utley, Jonathan G., *An American Battleship at Peace and War: The USS Tennessee*, University Press of Kansas, 1991
Vreeken, Fred R., *USS Maryland (BB-46)*, Turner Publishing Company, 1997
Wallin, Homer N., *Pearl Harbor: Why, How, Fleet Salvage and Final Appraisal*, US Government Printing Office Naval History Division, 1968
Watts, A.J., *Japanese Warships of World War II*, Doubleday & Co. Inc., 1966
Willmott, H.P., *Pearl Harbor*, Cassell & Co., 2001
Woodward, C. Vann, *The Battle for Leyte Gulf*, Macmillan, 1947

Additional Resources

CINC PACFLT to CINC/CNO, Report of Japanese Raid on Pearl Harbor, 7 December 1941, CINCPAC File A16-3/02088
USS CALIFORNIA: REPORT OF RAID, 7 DECEMBER 1941, Submitted 13 December 1941, Department of the Navy, Naval History & Heritage Command
USS CALIFORNIA: TORPEDO AND BOMB DAMAGE. DECEMBER 7, 1941. PEARL HARBOR, War Damage Report No. 21, Bureau of Ships, Department of the Navy, Naval History & Heritage Command
USS MARYLAND: REPORT OF PEARL HARBOR ATTACK, DECEMBER 7, 1941, Submitted December 15, 1941, BB48/A16/Of10(0229), Department of the Navy, Naval History & Heritage Command
USS MARYLAND: REPORT OF DAMAGE SUSTAINED IN ACTION, DECEMBER 7, 1941, Submitted December 19, 1941, Department of the Navy, Naval History & Heritage Command
USS NEVADA: REPORT OF PEARL HARBOR ATTACK, DECEMBER 7, 1941, BB36/A9/A16, Submitted December 15, 1941, Department of the Navy, Naval History & Heritage Command

SELECT BIBLIOGRAPHY

USS NEVADA: TORPEDO AND BOMB DAMAGE, DECEMBER 7, 1941, PEARL HARBOR, War Damage Report Number 17, Bureau of Ships, Submitted September 18, 1942, Department of the Navy, Naval History & Heritage Command

USS OKLAHOMA: REPORT OF DAMAGE SUSTAINED DURING ACTION AT PEARL HARBOR, DECEMBER 7, 1941, Submitted December 20, 1941, Department of the Navy, Naval History & Heritage Command

USS PENNSYLVANIA: REPORT OF ACTION DURING ENEMY AIR ATTACK, MORNING OF SUNDAY 7 DECEMEBR 1941, Submitted December 16, 1941, Department of the Navy, Naval History & Heritage Command

USS TENNESSEE: ACTION REPORT-JAPANESE ATTACK ON PEARL HARBOR, 7 DECEMBER 1941, Department of the Navy, Naval History & Heritage Command

USS TENNESSEE: BOMB DAMAGE, DECEMBER 7, 1941, PEARL HARBOR, War Damage Report No. 22, Submitted November 15, 1942, Department of the Navy, Naval History & Heritage Command

USS WEST VIRGINIA: ACTION of DECEMBER 7, 1941, Report of Department of the Navy, Naval History & Heritage Command

USS WEST VIRGINIA: REPORT OF SALVAGE OF, Submitted June 15, 1942, Department of the Navy, Naval History & Heritage Command

Websites

Nihon Kaigun, www.combinedfleet.com
Pearl Harbor: National Memorial Hawaii, www.nps.gov

Index

Abukuma, IJN 7, 131, 140, 152
Adak Island, Aleutians 254, 279, 280
Agana, Guam 121–2, 288
Aichi D3A dive bomber, Allied reporting name VAL xii; Pearl Harbor attack first wave 17–36, 101, 104; second wave and attack on *Nevada* 36–9, 53, 222–3; Wake attack 49; attack on *Tennessee* 295–6; attack on *West Virginia* 319
Ainsworth, Rear Admiral Walden L., USN 117, 286
Akagi, IJN, Pearl Harbor attack 3, 9, 11, 17, 20–2, 26, 40, 50, 184
Alabama (BB-60), USS 118, 158, 198
Alalakeiki Channel, Hawaii 6
Aleutian Islands campaign viii, ix, 67, 184, 230, 252–4, 279–80
'All-or-nothing' armour **70–1**, 73; *California* 98; *Maryland* 175; *Nevada* 214, 218; *Pennsylvania* 246; *Tennessee* 272–3; *West Virginia* 299
angle on the bow 79
Antares (AG-10), USS 18–19
Apamama, Gilbert Islands 188, 192, 195, 255

Arizona ((BB-38), USS 13, 17, 24–5, 28–9, 31–5, 37–9, 45–9, 56, 65, 68, 72, 220, 223, 235, 243–4, 246, 273–4, 301–2
Arkansas (BB-33), USS 231, 233, 236, 240, 268, 293
Artisan (ABSD-1), USS, floating dry dock 124, 313
Asagumo, IJN 150, 152–3, 291
Ashigara, IJN 131, 140
Atago, IJN 137, 142
Attu, Aleutians 67, 90, 230 (*Nevada*); 252–4 (*Pennsylvania*); 279 (*Tennessee*)
Augusta (CA-31), USS 234

B-24 Consolidated Liberator heavy bomber xi, 121, 195
B-29 Boeing Superfortress long-range bomber xi, 260, 286, 292–3, 316
Baltimore (CA-68), USS 256
battles
    Cape Engaño (off) (1944) vii, 132, 134, 144–5, **158–66**, 204
    Coral Sea (1942) 43, 89, 106, 183–4

INDEX

Eniwetok (1944) **258–9** (*Pennsylvania*), 283 (*Tennessee*)
Guam (1944) **121–2** (*California*), 261 (*Pennsylvania*), 287–9 (*Tennessee*)
Iwo Jima (1945) 90; 117, 121 (*California*); 203 (*Maryland*); 236–8 (*Nevada*); 292–4 (*Tennessee*); 316–17 (*West Virginia*)
Kwajalein (1944) 192–7 (*Maryland*); 256–9 (*Pennsylvania*); 282–3 (*Tennessee*)
Leyte (1944) 67, 124 et sequens, 203 et sequens, 297
Leyte Gulf (1944) **134–66**, 203–8, 263–6, 290–2, 310–12
Makin (1942) 185–9, 255
Midway (1942) 42, 64, 89, 126, 183–4, 252, 277
Okinawa (1945) 169 (*California*); 208 (*Maryland*); 238–9 (*Nevada*); 294 (*Tennessee*); 317 (*West Virginia*)
Peleliu (1944) 124, **200–3** (*Maryland*); 262–3 (*Pennsylvania*); 289–90 (*Tennessee*)
Saipan (1944) **115–24** (*California*); 197–200 (*Maryland*); 261 (*Pennsylvania*); 285–8 (*Tennessee*)
Samar (off) (1944) 132, 134, **154–8**, 160, 204, 207
Sibuyan Sea (1944) 132, 134, **138–48**, 204
Surigao Strait (1944) 132, 134–5, **148–58**, 166, 204, 205–8, 279, 292, 312

Tarawa (1943) **187–92**, 195, 257, 281
Tinian (1944) **122–4**
Tsushima (1905) 11
Belleau Wood (CVL-24), USS 138, 158
Bellows Field, Oahu 14, 22, 43
Bennion (DD-662), USS 152
Bethlehem Shipbuilding Corporation 173, 297
Betio, Tarawa Atoll 186–7, 190–2
Bikini Atoll 186, 240, 242, 258, 270
Biloxi (CL-80), USS 295, 317
Black Prince, HMS 231
Bockscar, Boeing B-29 Superfortress bomber, 172
Bogan, Rear Admiral Gerry F., USN 138–40, 162–3, 165
Boise (CL-47), USS 148, 166, 168, 205
Bremerton Navy Yard, Washington 14, 197, 210–11, 251, 308, 320
Bunker Hill (CV-17), USS 138
Burns (DD-588), USS 167, 314

Cabot (CVL-28), USS 138, 141, 158
California (BB-44), USS **95–173**: Pearl Harbor 101–6; salvage 106–15; **Battleship Revenge**: Mariana and Palau Islands Campaign: Saipan 115–21: Guam 121–2: Tinian 122–4: The Philippines Campaign: Leyte Gulf 134 onwards: Battle of Sibuyan Sea 138–48: Battle of the Surigao Strait 148–58: Battle off Cape Engaño 158–66: The Philippines Campaign: Invasion of Lingayen Gulf 166–9: Battle of Okinawa

333

169–70: End of war, occupation of Japan and return home
Invasion of Japan 170–3: 197–8, 203, 205–7, 210, 220, 222, 238, 260–1, 263, 266–8, 272, 275, 277, 279, 286–9, 290–1, 297, 304, 310–12, 315
Cape Engaño, Battle of vii, 132, 134, 144–5, **158–66**, 204
Cassin (DD-372), USS 18, 33, 35–6, 47, 52–3, 250
Chikuma, IJN 7, 156–7
Chitose, IJN 130, 158, 160, 163, 165
Chiyoda, IJN 130, 158, 162–3, 164–5
Colorado (BB-45), USS 13, 50, 61, 67, 69, 73, 85, 117, 121, 166, 175–6, 182, 184–5, 189, 190, 194–5, 197, 255–6, 258, 260–1, 282, 284, 286, 299, 300, 314, 319, 320
Columbia (CL-56), USS 148, 205
Condor (AMc–14), USS 16
Connecticut (BB-18), USS 214
Coral Sea (CVE-57), USS 256, 261
cordite propellant 85
Corregidor (CVE-58) 256, 261
Crosshill (AMS-45), USS 16
Curtiss (AV-4), USS 36, 39

Dace (SS-247), USS/M 137, 142
Darter (SS-227), USS/M 137, 142
Davison, Rear Admiral R.E., USN 138–40, 147, 162
Delaware (BB-28), USS 214
Denver (CL-58), USS 148, 200, 205
Dinagat Island, Philippines 130, 264, 290, 310
Downes (DD-372), USS 18, 33, 35, 36, 47, 52–3, 249, 250
Dry Dock No. 1, Pearl Harbor Navy Yard 306–8, 23, 33, 56, 62, 249

Dry Dock No. 2, Pearl Harbor Navy Yard 112, 227

Edwards (DD-619), USS 253–4
Emirau Island landing, Bismarck archipelago 284–5
Eniwetok, Battle of, **258–9** (*Pennsylvania*); 283 (*Tennessee*)
Enola Gay, Boeing B-29 Superfortress bomber, 171
Enterprise (CV-6), USS 14, 45, 89, 138, 141, 158, 183
Espiritu Santo (Naval Base) 64, 124, 185, 289, 313
Essex (CV-9), USS 138, 141, 158, 160
Ewa, Marine Corps Air Station, Oahu 14, 37

Farragut (DD-348), USS 253
Ford Island Naval Air Station, Oahu 14
Fore River Shipbuilding Co., Massachusetts 213–14
Franklin (CV-13), USS 138, 141, 158
Frazier (DD-607), USS 254, 281–2
Fuchida, Commander Mitsuo, IJN 17, 20–3, 40
Fusō, IJN 131, 140, 148, 150, 152, 165, 204–6, 266, 291–2, 311–12

Gambier Bay (CVE-73), USS 157, 165, 207
Gansevoort (DD-608), USS 112
Garapan, Saipan 119–21, 198, 261
Genda, Commander Minoru, IJN 40
Gilliam (APA-57), USS 241
Guam, Battle of, **121–2** (*California*); 261 (*Pennsylvania*); 287–9 (*Tennessee*)

INDEX

Ha-15, IJN 15
Ha-16, IJN 15
Ha-17, IJN 15
Ha-18, IJN 15
Ha-19, IJN 15, 43
Haguro, IJN 156
Haleiwa Fighter Strip, Oahu 14, 44
Halsey, Admiral William F., USN Battle of Leyte Gulf, 125 et sequens, 204
Hammann (DD-412), USS 184
Hancock (CV-19), USS 239, 310
Haruna, IJN 131, 133, 136, 153, 156, 204, 206
Hayate, IJN 49
Heermann (DD-532), USS 155, 156
Helena (CL-50), USS 18, 39, 53–4, 249
Hickam Air Base, Oahu 14, 21–3, 37, 101
Hiei, IJN 7
Hirohito, Emperor of Japan 172, 270, 320
Hiroshima 5, 7, 171, 188, 239, 297, 319
Hiryū, IJN 3, 17, 19, 21, 31, 49, 50, 184, 301
Hitokappu Bay 5, 7, 8
Hoel (DD-533), USS 155–6, 165
Honolulu (CL-48), USS 39
Hornet (CV-8), USS 14, 89, 139, 183, 277
Hospital Point, Pearl Harbor 38, 47, 224
Hovey (DMS-11), USS 168
Hyūga, IJN 128, 130, 144, 146–7, 158–9, 162–4

I-16, IJN 15
I-18, IJN 15
I-20, IJN 15
I-22, IJN 15
I-24, IJN 15
I-31, IJN 253
I-35, IJN 281
I-68, IJN 6, 16
I-69, IJN 6, 16
I-70, IJN 6
I-71, IJN 6
I-72, IJN 6
I-73, IJN 6
I-175, IJN 256
Idaho (BB-42), USS 61, 117, 121, 182, 188, 194–5, 197, 200, 230, 236, 253, 255–6, 260–1, 263, 280, 285–6, 289, 293–4, 296, 317
Independence (CVL-22), USS 138, 147, 158–9, 164
Indiana (BB-58), USS 118, 198
Indianapolis (CA-35), USS 13, 188, 200, 259, 263
Intrepid (CV-11), USS 138, 140–1, 158
Iowa (BB-61), USS 118, 158, 163, 198, 241
Ise, IJN 128, 130
Iwo Jima, Battle of 90; 117, 121 (*California*); 203 (*Maryland*); 236–8 (*Nevada*); 292–4 (*Tennessee*); 316–17 (*West Virginia*)

Jallao (SS-358), USS/M 164
Johnston (DD-557), USS 155, 165

Kaga, IJN 3, 17, 21, 26, 31, 50, 184
Kahoolawe, Hawaii 6, 117, 119, 198, 260, 285
Kahuku Point, Oahu 21
Kalohi Channel, Hawaii 6
Kamchatka Peninsula 5, 230
Kaneohe NAS 14, 22, 37

Kerama Retto Islands, SW Okinawa 170, 294, 317, 319
Kidō Butai creation and insertion to Hawaii 3–12: the strike against Pearl 13–45; aftermath and extraction 46–50; 69, 101
Kiefer, Lieutenant Dixie, USN 101
Kimmel, Admiral Husband E., CINCUS, USN 20, 23, 33, 52, 56, 249,
King, Admiral Ernest, CNO, USN 64, 142
Kinkaid, Vice Admiral Thomas C., USN 125–6, 132, 135–6, 140, 143, 145–8, 153–6, 159–66, 202, 205, 264, 266
Kirishima, IJN 7
Kisaragi, IJN 49
Kishinami, IJN 137, 140
Kiska, Aleutians 230, 252–5, 279–81
Kitkun Bay (CVE-71), USS 168
Kongō, IJN 131, 133, 136, 153, 155–6, 204, 206
Kumano, IJN 155
Kuril Islands 5–7, 9, 129, 253
Kurita, Vice Admiral Takeo, IJN 126, 131, 133, 136–8, 141–7, 153–8, 160, 163–5
Kwajalein, Battle of 192–7 (*Maryland*); 256–9 (*Pennsylvania*); 282–3 (*Tennessee*)
Kwajalein Atoll, 5–7, 10, 49, 90, 117–18, 186, 198, 243, 259, 260, 270, 286, 329
Kyushu, Japan 126, 169–71, 208–9, 319

Lahaina Roads anchorage, Hawaii 6, 11, 14, 194
Langley (CV-1), USS 14, 138, 158, 258
Lee, Vice Admiral Willis Augustus 'Ching', USN 118–19, 145, 198, 260
Leutze (DD-481), USS 237, 293, 316
Leyte, Battle of 67, 124 et sequens, 203 et sequens, 297
Leyte Gulf, Battle of **134–66**, 203–8, 263–6, 290–2, 310–12
Lexington (CV-2), USS 14, 89, 111–12, 138, 141, 144, 158, 183
Lingayen Gulf, invasion of 128, **166–9**, 236, 266–8, 313, 314–16
Lingga Roads, Singapore 131, 133
Liscome Bay (CVE-56), USS 256
London Naval Treaty (1930) 100
Louisville (CA-28), USS 13, 119, 124, 148, 194, 197, 200, 205, 259, 263, 289
Luzon 125–8, 130–1, 135–9, 144–5, 147–8, 157–8, 164, 166–7, 204, 208, 236, 266–7, 316

MacArthur, General Douglas, US Army 125–6, 128, 134–5, 166–8, 172, 186–7, 203, 285
Makin 187, 192, 281
Makin, Battle of, 185–9, 255–6
Majuro 186, 256–7, 159, 283–5
Majuro, invasion of 192–6
Manus Island, Papua New Guinea 124, 129, 166, 202–3, 263, 264, 266, 268, 290, 310, 313, 316
Mare Island Naval Shipyard, Vallejo, California 57, 96, 182, 252, 276
Mariana and Palau Islands Campaign 115, 197, 259, 260, 285, 286
Maryland (BB-46), USS **174–211**: Pearl Harbor 13, 23–46; salvage

INDEX

52–7; 61, 64–5, 67–8, 73, 85, 117–18, 120–1, 136, 148, 151, 174–82; **Battleship Revenge**: Gilbert and Marshall Islands Campaign 185–7; Tarawa 187–92; Kwajalein and Majuro 192–7: Mariana and Palau Islands Campaign 197–203: The Philippines Campaign 203 et sequens; Surigao Strait 205–8: Okinawa 208–10; 222, 238–9, 250–1, 256, 260–3, 266, 273–7, 281–2, 286, 289– 92, 294, 299, 300, 301, 304, 310–12
Massachusetts (BB-59), USS 158
Maui 6, 117, 119, 194, 260, 282, 285
Maury (DD-401), USS 111
Maya, IJN 137, 142
Meade (DD-602), USS 281
Melvin (DD-680), USS 150, 206
Michishio, IJN 150, 291
Midway Atoll, Battle of 42, 64, 89, 126, 183–4, 252, 277
Mikuma, IJN 184
Mindanao Island 125, 130–1, 143, 266, 291, 311
Mindoro Island 128, 138, 166, 314
Minneapolis (CA-36), USS 13, 111, 118, 148, 198, 200, 205, 209, 263
Mississippi (BB-41), USS 61, 126, 136, 148, 151, 166, 182, 188, 194–5, 200–1, 203, 205–6, 255–6, 263, 266, 268, 185, 289, 290–1, 310–11, 314, 316
Missouri (BB-63), USS 172, 320
Mitsubishi A6M Zero fighter, Allied reporting name ZEKE 17, 18, 20, 30, 36–7, 49, 102, 134, 157, 167, 274
Mobile (CL-63), USS 194

Mogami, IJN 131, 140, 148, 150, 152, 153, 205, 266, 291, 311–12
Monaghan (DD-354), USS 36, 43, 44
Musashi, IJN 131, 133, 136; sinking **139–42**, 153, 165, 204
Myōkō, IJN 140

Nachi, IJN 131, 140, 152
Nagato, IJN 22, 131, 133, 136, 140, 153, 172, 204, 206, 240
Nagumo, Vice Admiral Chūichi, IJN 4–6, 8–10, 21, 22, 40–2
Nakajima B5N torpedo bomber, Allied reporting name KATE 5, 16, 20, 36, 102
Neosho (AO-23), USS 23, 101, 106, 180, 183
Nevada (BB-36), USS **212–41**; Pearl Harbor 13, 24, 25 29, 33–9, 44–5, 47–8, **220–5**: salvage 51, 53, 59, **226–8**; fatalities 60; general: 67–8, 70–1, 73–4, 86–8, 90: **Battleship Revenge**: Aleutian Islands Campaign 230; Atlantic convoy duty 230; Normandy invasion 231–3; Mediterranean Sea 233–5; Iwo Jima 236–8; Okinawa 238–9; post-war and Bikini Atoll tests 239–41
Newport News Shipbuilding & Drydock Co., Virginia 175, 176, 243–4, 299, 300
New Guinea 10, 64, 115–17, 125, 185–6: campaign 284
New Jersey (BB-62), USS 118, 142, 153, 158, 160–5, 198
New Mexico (BB-40), USS 61, 73, 88, 117, 121, 166–7, 182, 188, 194, 195, 197, 254–6, 260–1, 267, 285–6, 314–15

337

New Orleans (CA-32), USS 118, 164, 169, 198
New York Naval Shipyard 272–3
'*Niitakayama nobore* (Climb Mount Niitaka) *1208*' 9
Nimitz, Admiral Chester, CINCPAC-CINCPOA, USN 4, 65, 118, 125–6, 142–3, 145–6, 162, 165, 171, 186, 188, 255, 324
Nippon Maru 11
Nishimura, Vice Admiral Shoji, IJN 131, 133, 136, 139, 140, 147–8, 150–3
Normandy 67, 90, 231–5
North Carolina (BB-55), USS xiv, 70, 118, 198, 293

Oglala (CM-4), USS 18, 39, 249
Okinawa, Battle of 90, 126, 129, 169–70 (*California*); 203, 208–11 (*Maryland*); 238–9 (*Nevada*); 268–9 (*Pennsylvania*); 294–7 (*Tennessee*); 317–20 (*West Virginia*)
Oklahoma (BB-37), USS 13, 23; Pearl Harbor raid 24–48, 102, 105, 180–2, 222, 273–6, 301; salvage 52–6, 59, 65, 67–8; 70–1, 87
Oldendorf, Rear (Vice) Admiral Jesse B., USN 70, 117, 119, 120–1, 126, 129, 133–4, 136, 140, 143, 146–7: Surigao Strait 148–65; Lingayen Gulf 166–8, 267–8, 314–5; Battle of Kwajalein Atoll 192–5, 282; Saipan 197–9, 260; Peleliu 200–3: Battle of Leyte Gulf/Surigao Strait 203–6, 263–6, 290–2, 310–12: Guam 261, 288; East China Sweep 268–9, Saipan 286

Ommaney Bay (CVE-79), USS 167, 314
Ōnishi, Takijirō, Vice Admiral, IJN 126, 133, 139, 157
Opana Radar Site, Oahu 15, 19
Operation CARTWHEEL – Rabaul 284–5
Operation CATCHPOLE – Eniwetok Atoll, 257–8, 283
Operation CORONET – second part of planned invasion of Japan 171
Operation CROSSROADS – Bikini Atoll nuclear experiments 240, 270
Operation DETACHMENT – Iwo Jima 136, 292–3, 316
Operation DOWNFALL – invasion of Japan 170–1, 208, 239
Operation DRAGOON – Toulon 234
Operation FLINTLOCK – Kwajalein 192–4, 256, 282
Operation FORAGER – Mariana and Palau Islands 115, 118, 197, 259, 260–1, 285–6
Operation GALVANIC – Gilberts 187–8, 255, 281
Operation HAILSTONE – Truk 258
Operation ICEBERG – Okinawa 169, 208, 238, 294, 317
Operation KING II – Leyte Gulf 263–4
Operation LANDCRAB – Aleutian Islands invasion 67, 253
Operation MAGIC CARPET – repatriation 211, 320
Operation MAJESTIC – first part of planned invasion of Japan 171

INDEX

Operation MIKE I – Lingayen Gulf 266–7
Operation OLYMPIC – invasion of Japan 171
Operation OVERLORD – Normandy 231
Operation NEPTUNE – Normandy 231, 326
Operation STALEMATE II – Peleliu 200, 262, 289
Operation STEVEDORE – Guam 261, 288
Operation Z, the IJN Hawaiian operation 5
Ōyodo, IJN 163
Ozawa, Vice Admiral Jisaburō, IJN 126, 130–1, 133, 135, 144–7, 153–4, 158–60, 163, 165, 204

Palau Islands 10, 115, 117, 128, 166, 186, 197, 200, 259, 260, 262–3, 266, 285–6, 289, 312, 314
Palawan Passage, submarine action, Battle of Leyte Gulf 134, 136–8, 142, 204
Palmer (DD-161), USS 168
Peleliu, Battle of 124, **200–3** (*Maryland*); 262–3 (*Pennsylvania*); 289–90 (*Tennessee*)
Pennsylvania (BB-38), USS **242–70**; Pearl Harbor 13, 18, 23, 33–45, 47, **249–52**; salvage 51–3, 56–7, 60–1, 64–8, 304; general 72–3, 86, 177, 182, 187–8, **242–70, 276**: Battleship Revenge; Aleutian Islands 230 **252–4, 280**; Gilbert and Marshall Islands, Makin 255–6, Kwajalein 194–5, **256–7**; Eniwetok 258–9; Mariana and Palau Islands 197–200, 259–61, 262–3, 289; Saipan 117–18, 121, 261, 286; Guam 121, 261–2; Philippines – Leyte 126, 136, 203, 263–5, 290; Surigao Strait 148, 151, 205–6, 266, 291, 311; Lingayen Gulf 166, 267–8, 314–16; Okinawa 238, East China Sea Sweep 268–70; postwar and Bikini tests 240, 270
Pensacola (CA-24), USS 13, 237, 293, 316–17
Phelps (DD-360), USS 111, 253
Philippine Sea 125, 130, 134, 138–9, 144, 153, 288
Philippines Campaign 67, 124, 130, 166, 203, 263, 266, 290, 310
Phoenix (CL-46), USS 148, 205
Polillo Islands, Luzon 138
Portland (CA-33), USS 148, 200, 205, 263, 279, 317
Prince of Wales, HMS xvi, 63, 66
Princeton (CVL-23), USS 138–9, 143–5, 165, 258
Puget Sound Navy Yard 50, 57, 60–3, 65, 69, 112, 114–15, 169, 179, 180, 182, 196–7, 210–11, 228, 248, 251, 270, 275, 277–9, 292, 298, 304, 308, 320
Pursuit (AM-108), USS 190
Pye, Vice Admiral William S., USN 61, 64–5, 104, 182, 252, 277

Quincy (CA-71), USS 214, 231, 234

Raleigh (CL-7), USS 24, 39
rangefinding, gun range, true range 78–9
Ranger (CV-4), USS 14, 50
Repulse, HMS xvi, 66
Requisite (AM-109), USS 190

339

Roosevelt, President Franklin D. 13
Royal Oak, HMS xvi, 63, 65
Ryukyu Islands 129, 169, 310

Saida Maru 192
St Lo (CVE-63), USS 157, 165, 207
St Louis (CL-49), USS 43
Saipan, Battle of **115–24** (*California*); 197–200 (*Maryland*); 261 (*Pennsylvania*); 285–8 (*Tennessee*)
Samar, Battle of 132, 134, **154–8**, 160, 204, 207
Samuel B. Roberts (DD-413), USS 155–6, 165
San Bernardino Strait 131, 133, 136–47, 153–4, 158–9, 162–5, 204, 206, 291
San Jacinto (CVL-30), USS 138, 158
Santa Fe (CL-60), USS 164, 194
Saratoga (CV-3), USS 14, 89, 258
Seeadler Harbor, Manus 166, 202, 203, 263, 290, 310
Shaw (DD-373), USS 39, 224, 249
Sherman, Rear Admiral F.C. (Ted), USN 138, 139, 144, 147, 162, 324
Shigure, IJN 150, 152–3, 206
Shima, Vice Admiral Kiyohide, IJN 131, 136, 140, 148, 150, 152
Shō-Gō 1, IJN – Philippines 128, 130, 134, 265, 291, 311
Shō-Gō 2, IJN – Formosa 129
Shō-Gō 3, IJN – Ryuku Islands 129
Shō-Gō 4, IJN – Kuril Islands 129
Shōhō, IJN 183
Shōkaku, IJN 3, 17, 50
Shropshire, HMAS 148, 205
Sibuyan Sea, Philippines, Battle of 132, 134, **138–48**, 204
Sims (DD-409), USS 183

Solomon Islands 10, 64, 115, 124, 185–6, 200, 259
Sōryū, IJN 3, 17, 21, 49, 50, 184
South Dakota (BB-57), USS 118, 158, 198, 228, 301
Special Treatment Steel (STS) 66, 74, 114
Sprague, Rear Admiral Thomas L., USN 135
Spruance, Vice Admiral Raymond, USN 188, 195, 209, 255, 283, 328
Standard Type BB xiv, 40, 50, **69–91**
Sulu Sea, Philippines 131, 136–40, 148, 166–7, 266, 291, 314
Surigao Strait, Battle of 132, 134–5, **148–58**, 166, 204, 205–8, 279, 292, 312

Taiyo Maru 5
Talbot (DD-114), USS 260
Tama, IJN 164
Tarawa Atoll, Battle of **187–92**, 195, 257, 281
Task Force 1 – West Coast USA defence 61
Task Force 36 – Emirau landing 284
Task Force 38 – US Navy's fast-carrier strike force 128–30, 133, 135–6, 138–48, 153–4, 158–65, 204
Task Force 51 – Aleutian Islands 253
Task Force 52 – Makin, Kwajalein, Eniwetok, Saipan 188–9, 255, 286
Task Force 53 – Tarawa, Kwajalein, Eniwetok, Saipan 188–9, 193, 255
Task Force 54 – Iwo Jima 209, 236, 238, 293–4, 316–17
Task Force 54 – Okinawa 209, 236, 238, 293–4, 316–17

INDEX

Task Force 58 – the US Navy's fast-carrier strike force 90, 117–18, 121, 209, 258, 260–1, 283, 286, 288, 293, 310, 319
Task Force 77 – Philippines 166
Task Force 95 – East China Sea 170, 268
Ten-Ten Dock, Pearl Harbor Navy Yard 23, 37, 39, 54, 223, 249
Tennessee (BB-43), USS **271–97**; Pearl Harbor 180, 182, 222, **273–6;** salvage, repair and modernisation 173, 250–1, 276–9: Battleship Revenge: Aleutian Islands 279–81; Gilbert and Marshall Islands – Tarawa 187–9, 281–2, Makin 255, Kwajalein 194–5, 256, 282–3; Eniwetok 258–9, 283–4; New Guinea – Emirau landings 284–5; Mariana and Palau Islands – Saipan 197–8, 260–1, 286–8; Guam 288–9; Peleliu 200, 263, 289–90: Philippines – Leyte Gulf 203, 290–1; Surigao Strait 205–6, 266, 291–2; Iwo Jima 236, 292–4; Okinawa 238–9, 294–7; East China Sea Sweep 268, 298; post-war 172, 297
Texas (BB-35), USS 79, 98, 208, 231, 233, 236, 268, 293–4, 300
Tinian, Marianas, Battle of 122–4
Toei Maru 11
Tōgō Heihachirō, Fleet Admiral IJN 11
Toho Maru 11
Tōjō, Army Minister General Hideki, IJA, Prime Minister of Japan 7, 9
Tone, IJN 140, 156

Toyoda, Admiral Soemu, Commander-in-Chief, IJN 128–9, 135, 144
Truk 10, 117, 128, 186, 193, 258
Truman, USA President Harry S. 171
Tsushima, Battle of (1905) 11
turbo-electric power plant 73, 88, 99, 100, 178, 179, 248, 300, 308
Turner, Rear Admiral Richmond Kelly, USN 188, 194, 255–6
Tuscaloosa (CA-37), USS 170, 231
Type 6A *Kaidai* first-class submarine, IJN 5, 6, 7, 11
Type 91 aerial torpedo 5, 16, 20, 25–7, 30, 33–4, 39, 102–3, 220, 301, 307
Type 99 #80 Mk 5 1,760lb armour-piercing bomb 16, 20, 25–6, 31
Type A midget submarine, IJN 7, 43–4
Type C-1 submarine, IJN 7

Ulithi 129, 136, 138–9, 164, 169, 203, 208, 238, 294, 296–7, 312–13, 316–17, 319,
Underwater Demolition Teams (UDT), USN 168, 200, 203–4, 237, 261, 267, 293–4, 310, 315–16
Underwater Side Protection Systems 27–8, 30, 33, 72, 76–7, 102, 221, 246, 302
Utah (BB-31/AG-16)), USS 24–5, 39, 40

Vacant Sea 5
Vestal (AR-4), USS 24, 39, 273, 301
Visayas Islands, Philippines 125–6

Wake Atoll 8, 10, 12–14, 46, 49, 50, 117, 268
Ward (DD-139), USS 16, 19
Wasatch (AGC-9), USS 146
Washington (BB-47), USS 300
Washington (BB-56), USS xiv
Washington Naval Treaty (1922) xiv, 76, 88, 100, 176, 300
Wasp (CV-7), USS 14
West Virginia (BB-48), USS 85, 175, **299–320**: Pearl Harbor 13, 21–34, 37, 45–7, 102, 180, 203, 205–6, 222, 273–6, **301–3**; salvage 54–9, 62–3, 250, **303–8**; reconstruction 63–5, 67–8, 308–10: **Battleship Revenge**: Philippines campaign 310 et sequens; Leyte Gulf 126, 136, 148, 263, 290–2, 310 et sequens; Surigao Strait 266, 311–12; Lingayen Gulf 166, 314–16; Iwo Jima 236, 293, 316–17; Okinawa 294–5, 317–19; occupation of Japan 319–20
Wheeler Army Airfield, Oahu 14, 20, 22–3, 37

Wichita (CA-45), USS 118, 164, 198, 238
Wotje Atoll 195

Yahagi, IJN 206, 209, 319
Yamagumo, IJN 150, 291
Yamamoto, Admiral Isoroku, Commander-in-Chief, IJN 3, 4, 9, 22, 40, 183
Yamashiro, IJN 131, 140, 148, 150–2, 165, 204–6, 266, 291–2, 311–12
Yamato, IJN 131, 133, 136–7, 140, 153, 155–7, 164, 170, 204, 206, 209, 319
Yayoi, IJN 49
Yokosuka D4Y3, IJN dive bomber, Allied reporting name JUDY 139
Yorktown (CV-5), USS 14, 89, 183–4

Zuihō, IJN – light carrier 130, 158, 160, 162–3, 165
Zuikaku, IJN 3, 17, 19, 50, 130, 158, 161–3, 165